UNDER WESTERN EYES

**VULNERABLE
MINORITIES
AND THE RUSSIAN STATE
IN NEW COLD WAR
CULTURES**

Other Titles in this Series

For more information on this series, please visit:
https://www.academicstudiespress.com/myths-and-taboos-in-russian-culture/

UNDER WESTERN EYES

VULNERABLE MINORITIES AND THE RUSSIAN STATE IN NEW COLD WAR CULTURES

Katharina Wiedlack

ACADEMIC STUDIES PRESS
BOSTON
2025

LCCN 2025005917

Copyright © 2025, Academic Studies Press
ISBN 9798887197487 (hardback)
ISBN 9798887197494 (paperback)
ISBN 9798887197500 (Adobe PDF)
ISBN 9798887197517 (ePub)

Book design by PHi Business Solutions.
Cover design by Ivan Grave
On the cover: photograph by Bela Talovski, reproduced by permission.

Published by Academic Studies Press
1007 Chestnut Street
Newton, MA 02464, USA
www.academicstudiespress.com

Contents

Acknowledgments

It has taken me over ten years to write this book. I could not have done it without the constant support of my partner, my friends and family, and the many colleagues and students who challenged me to rethink my analyses, theses, and findings, over and over again. Sylvia Mieszkowski and Alexandra Ganser-Blumenau from the Department of English and American Studies at the University of Vienna, in particular, have been trusted mentors for me throughout the years, offering constructive criticism and constant encouragement. It is evident that financial support was instrumental in the completion of this project. I extend my gratitude to the Austrian Academy of Science and the Young Academy for their generous funding of this publication. The Young Academy represents an invaluable peer group and a staunch supporter of cutting-edge research. I am deeply honored to be part of this esteemed body of academics.

Some of the research for this book was made possible by the Austrian Science Fund (FWF). I started to gather the material for this project while working on the project "Looking Eastward" (T767-G28). Since then, the project "The Magic Closet and the Dream Machine: Post-Soviet Queerness, Archiving, and the Art of Resistance" (AR 567) has allowed me to meet people from across post-Soviet spaces, Eurasia, and Central Asia, broadening my knowledge of post-Soviet experiences and the legacies of Russian imperialism. Last, but not least, my thinking about the legacies of Russian colonialism and imperialism, and its intersections with American imperialism, was developed within my project "Rivals of the Past, Children of the Future: Localizing Russia within US National Identity Formations from a Historical Perspective" (V 741). Funding by the FWF allowed me to work with my wonderful colleagues on different aspects of my critical approach, which I could later on draw on for this book. I thank Anna T., Tegiye Birey, and Lesia Pahulich for supporting me with their labor, and particularly Iain Zabolotny, for their continuous critical advice, for thinking through much of this work with me, and for their important input and reflections on issues of race and racialization in Russia, anti-feminist post-Soviet discourses, and Manizha. A very special thanks goes to my friend, mentor, role model, and collaborator Polly Gannon for helping me put this manuscript into the best shape possible. I could not have done it without your loving support, Polly! You are such a knowledgeable scholar, and it means the world to me that you contributed so much to this work.

Many of the ideas in this book were conceived and developed while I was working as writer-in-residence at the Jordan Center for the Advanced Study of Russia at New York University. I thank all of the professors, lecturers, fellows, and students, especially Eliot Borenstein and Rossen Djagalov, for the many discussions and the good advice you had to offer. The chapter on masculinity, Putin, and queer visual critique owes much to Bernadette Wegenstein, a wonderful mentor and colleague, who hosted me as visiting professor at the Center for Advanced Media Studies at Johns Hopkins University, Baltimore. I am forever grateful for the kind support and exchange, and of course for your warm hospitality. I want to express my gratitude to Birgit Däwes, colleagues from the American Seminar at Europa-Universität Flensburg, Elahe Haschemi Yekani from the Department of English and American Studies at Humboldt University, Berlin, as well as the Humboldt Foundation, for supporting my work through a research fellowship. I thank Lisa Diedrich, Victoria Hesford, and Ann Kaplan for hosting me as guest researcher at the Women's, Gender, and Sexuality Studies Department at Stony Brook University, where I had the luxury to do more research on the topic of this book. Last, but not least, I thank my friend, occasional boss, colleague, and co-conspirator, John Bailyn, and everyone at the NYI Global Institute of Cultural, Cognitive, and Linguistic Studies. Working with NYI is a continuous inspiration, and the years with all of you has shaped me and my thinking so much.

Some ideas in the subchapters "The New Othering of Russia; or, Public Masculinities: Putin, Trump, Obama, and (New) Cold War Nationalism" and "From Putin to Icarus—the Killing Machine (2010): Imagining Russian Strong Men" have been previously discussed in my article "Enemy Number One or Gay Clown? The Russian President, Masculinity, and Populism in US Media" (*Norma* 15, no. 1 (2020): 59–75). An earlier version of the chapter "Vulnerable Russian Gays, the White Male-Centric Gaze, and the Reaffirmation of the East/West Divide" was published as "Gays vs. Russia: Media Representations, Vulnerable Bodies, and the Construction of a (Post)Modern West" (*European Journal of English Studies* 21, no. 3 (September 2017): 241–57). Some of the core theses about the group Pussy Riot were previously developed in the article "Pussy Riot and the Western Gaze: Punk Music, Solidarity and the Production of Similarity and Difference" (*Popular Music and Society* 39, no. 4 (2015): 410–22), and the anthology chapters "The Spectacle of Russian Feminism: Questioning Visibility and the Western Gaze" (Samantha Holland, ed., *Subcultures, Bodies and Spaces: Essays on Alternativity and Marginalization* (Bingley: Emerald Publishing, 2018): 131–49) and "'Both Married, Both Moms, Both Determined to Keep Getting their Message Out'—The Russian Pussy Riot and US Popular

Culture" (Astrid M. Fellner, Marta Fernández, and Martina Martausová, eds., *Marlboro Men and California Gurls: Rethinking Gender in Popular Culture in the 21st Century* (Newcastle upon Tyne: Cambridge Scholars Publishing, 2017): 131–159). Finally, the analysis of *Manizha, or the Missed Chance to Challenge Russian Whiteness*, was developed and previously published in the co-authored article "Race, Whiteness, Russianness, and the Discourses on the 'Black Lives Matter' Movement and Manizha" (Rikke Andreassen, Catrin Lundström, Suvi Keskinen, and Shirley Anne Tate, eds., *The Routledge International Handbook of New Critical Race and Whiteness Studies* (London: Routledge, 2023): 251–264). I thank my co-author Iain Zabolotny for granting me permission to revise and build on our findings in this book.

CHAPTER 1

A Study of New Cold War Cultures from a Queer, Feminist, Anti-Imperialist Stance

The "Russia-West divide boils down to the gay issue,"[1] lamented the Anglophone pro-Kremlin media site *Russia Insider* in early January 2015, belittling and mocking gay identities and pro-gay stances within American politics, and implicitly defending Russian anti-gay policies as a legitimate attempt to protect children from "in vogue" postmodernism. Most of the text, published by the self-proclaimed "crowdfunded" news website run by American expatriates living in Russia was, not coincidentally, concerned with the attempt to defame and delegitimize the prominent Russian American journalist Masha Gessen, who had attracted significant attention in the US and international media since 2013 as a queer critic of Vladimir Putin. Clearly, the site, which is not only anti-semitic, but has also been accused of receiving significant support from a right-wing Russian oligarch,[2] tried to garner sympathy for contemporary Russia and Russian cultural politics by rallying American and other Anglophone homophobes against Gessen. Despite their thinly veiled transnational homophobia, and despite my own criticism of Gessen's media politics, the headline caught my eye. I was infuriated not only by their obviously anti-queer stance, but also because they directly and unabashedly used LGBTIQ+[3]—or, on this

---

1   Boyd D. Cathey (The Unz Review), "Russia-West Divide Boils Down to the Gay Issue: Conservative Russia, Post-Modern West," *Russia Insider*, January 5, 2015, https://russia-insider.com/en/2015/01/05/2226.
2   Anton Shekhovtsov, "Is Russia Insider Sponsored by a Russian Oligarch with Ties to the European Far Right?" *Interpreter*, November 23, 2015, http://www.interpretermag.com/is-russia-insider-sponsored-by-a-russian-oligarch-with-ties-to-the-european-far-right/.
3   LGBTIQ+ stands for lesbian, gay, bisexual, transgender, intersex, queer, as well as sexually and gender-fluid. The reason for choosing the abbreviations instead of the umbrella term

occasion, only gay—issues as the lynchpin for value negotiations between the West and Russia. Since that time, such journalistic attitudes and practices have become not only common, but pivotal, in the emergence and production of the New Cold War.

This New Cold War between the Anglophone (particularly American) and Russian media, and its circling of LGBTIQ+ issues, as well as its gendered, racist, and ableist politics, is the subject of this book. I discuss the underlying rationale, cultural significance, and goals behind the invocation of LGBTIQ+ issues—part of a larger spectrum of Russian minorities' vulnerabilities—in Anglophone and Russian political and cultural discourses. I examine their relationship, and the construction of images of Russian femininity, masculinity, physical and mental impairment, racial and gender difference, and disability. My central argument, which the various chapters support from different angles, and through a wide range of media analyses, is that the Anglophone media constructs images of vulnerable bodies and groups vis-à-vis the Russian state, and particularly Vladimir Putin, in order to delineate and unify liberal values as American or, more broadly, Western values in contradistinction to Russian values. In this way, the media creates notions of American national belonging that stress American superiority and its responsibility for influencing international affairs.

I analyze these American discourses from the perspective of a queer, feminist, antiracist, and anti-imperialist internationalism, which thereby critiques both American and Russian imperialisms. Such an account acknowledges that Anglophone imperial discourses intersect with, correspond to, shape, and are shaped by Russian media narratives and cultural discourses, and vice versa. Building on Russian media and discourse analyses by scholars such as Valerie Sperling,[4]

---

queer is that in Russia the term queer is used only by a small and elitist minority, whereas the terms gay, lesbian and transgender as well as other local terms are used quite frequently (see: Katharina Wiedlack and Masha Neufeld, "Lynchpin for Value Negotiations: Lesbians, Gays and Transgender between Russia and 'the West,'" in *Queering Paradigms VI* (London: Peter Lang, 2016), 189n1.

4   Valerie Sperling, "A Case of Putin Envy: Behind the Obsession with Russia's Leader," *Foreign Affairs*, November 5, 2015, https://www.foreignaffairs.com/articles/russian-federation/2015-11-05/case-putin-envy. Valerie Sperling, *Sex, Politics, and Putin: Political Legitimacy in Russia* (Oxford: Oxford University Press, 2014).

Emil Edenborg,[5] Darja Davydova,[6] and Helena Goscilo,[7] I argue that the Western media, often unintentionally or unknowingly, supports and produces ideas of a strong, potent Russia, with a virile president, as the defender of conservative values internationally—ideas that the official Russian mainstream media is only too happy to embrace. In short, the conservative, liberal, and leftist media converge in their co-construction of New Cold War bipolarity. They visualize such ideas, using masculinist images—of muscular American and Russian men arm wrestling, for example, or engaging in other forms of man-on-man sports.[8]

The growing, highly gendered, and sexualized division between Russian and Western values, and the ways in which this division is being produced, is the subject of this book. I explore Anglophone, predominantly but not exclusively American, media reports, tabloids, TV shows, and popular culture, as well as countercultural discourses. I identify how these discourses focus on and construct vulnerable Russian bodies, and in so doing, produce knowledge about both the Russian and the American nations, amplifying their seemingly divergent/unified values and reaffirming concepts of "Russia" and "the West."

Following Benedict Anderson, I understand the "nation" to be not only an imagined community, but also a very recent cultural construct.[9] In contrast to Anderson, however, I understand empire not solely as a pre-modern "dynastic realm."[10] According to Anderson's conceptualization, neither contemporary Russia nor the US would qualify as empires. I would argue that although both nations are modern capitalist nations, both of them embrace nationalist and imperialist logics as a basis for what it means to be American and Russian. Moreover, both nations actively construct national belonging using the idea of the West as their point of reference. This West is, of course, "a project, not

---

5   Emil Edenborg, "Homophobia as Geopolitics: 'Traditional Values' and the Negotiation of Russia's Place in the World," in *Gendering Nationalism: Intersections of Nation, Gender and Sexuality,* ed. Jon Mulholland, Erin Sanders-McDonagh, and Nicola Montagna (Cham: Palgrave Macmillan, 2018), 1–388, https://doi.org/10.1007/978-3-319-76699-7. Emil Edenborg, "Putin's Anti-Gay War on Ukraine," Boston Review, March 14, 2022, https://www.bostonreview.net/articles/putins-anti-gay-war-on-ukraine/.

6   Darja Davydova, "Between Heteropatriarchy and Homonationalism: Codes of Gender, Sexuality, and Race/Ethnicity in Putin's Russia" (PhD diss., York University, 2019).

7   Helena Goscilo, "Russia's Ultimate Celebrity: VVP as VIP Objet d'Art," in *Putin as Celebrity and Cultural Icon,* ed. Helena Goscilo (London: Routledge, 2013), 6–36.

8   Adrià Fruitós created for example a graphic of a very muscular arm with an American eagle wrestling a very muscular other arm with a growling Russian bear for issue 4, no. 11 of the *Nation,* in August/September 2023.

9   Anderson, *Imagined Communities.*

10 Stefan Berger and Alexei Miller, *Nationalizing Empires* (Budapest: Central European University Press, 2015), 574.

a place,"[11] as the anti-imperialist decolonial poet and philosopher Édouard Glissant has so aptly pointed out.

Reading the construction of Russian LGBTIQ+ and other groups as vulnerable, assessing their victimization critically, and drawing on the notion of Western "queer imperialism"[12] developed by Jin Haritaworn, Tamsila Tauqir, and Esra Erdem, I point to the abuse of these imaginary groups, as well as of actual people, in-between imperial spaces. Such a queer imperialism supports white privilege and projects onto Russian people and contexts LGBTIQ+ ideas and practices of identity, neoliberal models of sexual citizenship, visibility, and LGBT-rights advocacy, all of them bound to white hegemonic US-American and other Western metropolitan centers. In doing so, American queer imperialism creates ideas of Russian LGBTIQ+ martyrs, which allows those queer subjects to self-identify and be identified by others as champions of progress, modernity, and development. By focusing exclusively on these white, enlightened Russians, who are themselves mostly members of the educated Russian intelligentsia—an elite social strata that is not necessarily wealthy but holds significant social capital—queer imperialism supports, in complex and problematic ways, Russian imperialism, and the superiority of white Russianness over racialized and culturalized post-Soviet Otherness, which also includes Ukrainians.

Inspired by Olga Plakhotnik and Maria Mayerchyk, who show how the territory of Ukraine and Ukrainian Pride politics are located as a kind of contested "buffer"[13] zone between Western and Russian imperialism, I focus on how Russian LGBTIQ+s and feminists, such as the infamous group Pussy Riot, in and through their support of Anglophone queer imperialism deny the white privilege they embody, and support Russian imperialist discourses through their media productions and beyond. Throughout the book, I delineate how debates on LGBTIQ+ rights and feminism have become the locus of shared US-American and Russian value negotiations, but have also become a pivotal factor in the current Russian war against Ukraine. I thus demonstrate how these cultural politics became an organizing feature of the New Cold War.

---

11 Édouard Glissant, *Caribbean Discourse: Selected Essays* (Charlottesville: University Press of Virginia, 1989).

12 Jin Haritaworn, Tamsila Tauqir, and Esra Erdem, "Queer-Imperialismus: Eine Intervention in die Debatte über 'muslimische Homophobie'," in *Re/Visionen: postkoloniale Perspektiven von People of Color auf Rassismus, Kulturpolitik und Widerstand in Deutschland*, ed. Kien Nghi Ha, Nicola Lauré al-Samarai, and Sheila Mysorekar (Münster: Unrast, 2007), 409–454.

13 Olga Plakhotnik and Maria Mayerchyk, "Pride Contested: Geopolitics of Liberation at the Buffer Periphery of Europe," *Lambda Nordica* 28 (2023): 25–53, https://doi:10.34041/ln.v.874.

"Ukraine fell victim to the relentless spread of the empire of capital where Russian and Western capitalist geopolitical imperialisms collided,"[14] as Yuliya Yurchenko noted already in 2020, unknowingly anticipating what would become clear beyond doubt not two years later with Russia's full-scale invasion of Ukraine. Interestingly, Russian LGBTIQ+ individuals, feminist activists, and artists became enmeshed in this collision. Rather than idealizing the figures who acquired visibility amid these colliding imperialisms, *Under Western Eyes: Vulnerable Minorities and the Russian State in New Cold War Cultures* investigates why and how they came to prominence. Concomitantly, it also inquires after the issues, groups, and individuals made invisible by what Tatsiana Shchurko has recently called "Entangled Imperialisms."[15] It focuses, then, on the racism—one locus of such erasure or "invisibilizing"—of both American and Russian imperialisms.

Ignorance about Russian racial imperialism and its linkages with Western imperialism was revealed in the context of the invasion of Ukraine in relation to two tragic events. At first glance, these events seem unrelated; but one can argue that they were both points at which the discursive entanglement of Western and Russian imperialism became indisputable. The first event was what became known as the Bucha massacre, in which several hundred civilians were tortured and killed by Russian forces during the occupation of the city. The first reports about the massacre appeared in April 2022. These reports fabricated and disseminated the "myth"[16] that ethnic Buryats had committed the atrocities. The reports were co-produced by Russian and Ukrainian sources, and were almost immediately and unremittingly challenged by analysts, journalists, and members of the Free Buryatia Foundation.[17] Yet the myth was stubbornly repeated by many others, including the pope, who called "Chechens and Buryats 'the cruelest' Russian troops fighting in Ukraine"[18] in an interview with the Roman

---

14 Yuliya Yurchenko, "Ukraine and the (Dis)Integrating Empire of Capital," *Lefteast*, January 9, 2020, http://www.criticatac.ro/lefteast/ukraine-disintegratingempire-of-capital/.

15 Tatsiana Shchurko in a private conversation with the author.

16 "Buryats in Bucha: The Biggest Myth of the War," Buryats against War, April 28, 2022, https://freeburyatia.org/en/buryats-against-war/.

17 Dina Newman, "The 'Savage Warriors' of Siberia: How an Ethnic Minority in Russia Came to Be Unfairly Blamed for the Worst War Crimes in Ukraine," Media Diversity Institute, August 12, 2022, https://www.media-diversity.org/the-savage-warriors-of-siberia-how-an-ethnic-minority-in-russia-came-to-be-unfairly-blamed-for-the-worst-war-crimes-in-ukraine/.

18 Seb Shukla and Jack Guy, "Pope Francis Calls Chechens and Buryats 'the cruelest' Russian troops fighting in Ukraine," CNN, November 29, 2022, https://edition.cnn.com/2022/11/29/europe/pope-francis-chechens-buryats-intl/index.html.

Catholic magazine *America*.[19] This perpetuation of racialized Othering in the context of the war plays into Russian imperialist racism and white nationalism, which seeks to displace, exploit, and ultimately extinguish ethnic minorities as part of the war against Ukraine.

In their recent publication on the ethnic composition of Russian casualties to date since the Russian invasion of Ukraine in 2022, Mariya Vyushkova and Evgeny Sherkhonov demonstrate that Asian minorities, such as Tuvans, Buryats, and Kazakhs, were far more likely to be recruited, and even more likely to die, in the war than their ethnic Russian counterparts. Their analysis relies on data collected by volunteers, in collaboration with the Russian news outlet Mediazona, and by ethnic anti-war groups, such as the Free Buryatia Foundation, New Tuva, Kalmyks against the War, and the Free Yakutia Foundation. They further found that "the ethnic inequalities [. . .] stem from a number of reasons, including economic inequality, both among Russia's regions and within the regions where ethnic minorities live, discrimination, and Russian military leadership's policies."[20] While some Western media have started reporting on the oppression of ethnic minorities in the war, primarily after being prompted to do so by the Free Buryatia Foundation and other ethnic activist groups,[21] not many have connected this to the broader context of Russian imperialism and its sexual and gender discourses. Yet the extinction of Russian ethnic minorities is intrinsically linked to propaganda advocating heterosexuality, procreation, and the family. This is a Russian imperial nation-building project, which uses homophobia as expedient[22] and understands the nation as an

---

19 "Exclusive: Pope Francis discusses Ukraine, U.S. bishops and more," *America: The Jesuit Review*, November 28, 2022, https://www.americamagazine.org/faith/2022/11/28/pope-francis-interview-america-244225; Buryat Democratic Movement Erkheten, "The Pope Blames Our People for Russia's Crimes," *Wall Street Journal*, December 10, 2022, https://www.wsj.com/articles/pope-francis-russia-putin-ukraine-war-crimes-buryat-11670535297.

20 Mariya Vyushkova and Evgeny Sherkhonov, "Russia's Ethnic Minority Casualties of the 2022 Invasion of Ukraine," *Inner Asia* 25, no. 1 (2023): 126–136, https://doi:10.1163/22105018-02501011.

21 Mariya Petkova, "'Putin is using ethnic minorities to fight in Ukraine': Activist," *Aljazeera*, October 25, 2022, https://www.aljazeera.com/features/2022/10/25/russia-putin-is-using-ethnic-minorities-to-fight-in-ukraine; Amy Mackinnon, "Russia Is Sending Its Ethnic Minorities to the Meat Grinder," *Foreign Policy*, September 23, 2022, https://foreignpolicy.com/2022/09/23/russia-partial-military-mobilization-ethnic-minorities/; Ania Bessonov, "Russian ethnic minorities bearing brunt of Russia's war mobilization in Ukraine," *CBC News*, October 5, 2022, https://www.cbc.ca/news/world/russia-mobilization-ethnic-minorities-buryat-1.6605501.

22 Brian James Baer, "Now You See It: Gay (In)Visibility and the Performance of Post-Soviet Identity," in *Queer Visibility in Post-Socialist Cultures*, ed. Narcisz Fejes and Andrea P. Balogh (Bristol: Intellect, 2013), 35–55, 51.

empire requiring protection and expansion through white heteronormativity and the genocide in Ukraine.

The reporting on Bucha is just one consequence, albeit a very crucial one, of these entangled imperialisms. *Under Western Eyes* addresses a whole range of such entanglements, examining how gendered, racialized, and sexually vulnerable figures emerge at these discursive points. Importantly, my book draws upon political analysts who highlight how ideas central to Russian imperialism inadvertently, but crucially, influence Western discourses.[23]

Focusing on the case of Brittney Griner, the American professional basketball player who was detained and arrested on smuggling charges by Russian customs officials in February 2022 (she was carrying medically prescribed hash oil in her luggage), I contrast the celebration of white vulnerability with reluctant empathy for racialized individuals and groups who are victims of Russian oppression. Griner was arrested for possessing a minimal amount of marijuana oil, which is illegal in Russia, when she entered Russia to play for the Russian Premier League during the Women's National Basketball Association (WNBA) off-season. She was sentenced to nine years in prison in early August 2022 and served two months in a Russian penal colony before being returned to the US in early December 2022 in a highly controversial prisoner exchange. What interests me most about Griner's case is the lack of public outcry and support for the American publicly out lesbian WNBA player. This lack of solidarity is glaring, particularly in comparison with the immense solidarity with Pussy Riot[24] and Russian gays[25] not just by celebrities and politicians, but also by Anglophone civil society. In the conclusion of *Under Western Eyes*, I speculate on the reasons for the lack of both support

---

23   Marc-Olivier Bherer, "The West is much more influenced by Russian imperialism than it is willing to admit," *Le Monde*, May 15, 2022, https://www.lemonde.fr/en/opinion/article/2022/05/15/the-west-is-much-more-influenced-by-russian-imperialism-than-it-is-willing-to-admit_5983588_23.html.

24   Katharina Wiedlack, "Pussy Riot and the Western Gaze: Punk Music, Solidarity and the Production of Similarity and Difference," *Popular Music and Society* 23 (2015): https://doi:10.1080/03007766.2015.1088281; James Nichols, "Front Runners New York Launches 'To Russia with Love,'" *Huffington Post*, January 28, 2014, https://www.huffpost.com/entry/front-runners-new-york_n_4680750; Laura Mills, "Jailed Pussy Riot member ends hunger strike," *Associated Press* and *USA Today*, October 1, 2013, http://www.usatoday.com/story/news/world/2013/10/01/pussy-riot-russia-hunger/2902631/. Harvey Morris, "We're All Pussy Riot Now," *New York Times*, August 17, 2012, http://rendezvous.blogs.nytimes.com/2012/08/17/were-all-pussy-riot-now/.

25   Andy Greene, "Elton John Blasts Russia: 'Vicious Homophobia Has Been Legitimized,'" *Rolling Stone*, January 22, 2014, http://www.rollingstone.com/music/news/elton-john-blasts-russia-vicious-homophobia-has-been-legitimized-20140122.

for and media attention to Griner's predicament. I argue that while support for Pussy Riot and young white gay Russian men allowed the US to appear to be at the forefront of liberal progress, Griner challenged this self-image. Furthermore, I suggest that Griner's image, unlike that of her Russian gay and feminist counterparts, did not lend itself easily to the image of the damsel in distress, as the African American's 6' 9" stature and tomboyish style do not conform to (white) beauty standards.

Focusing in particular on contributions to the myth around Vladimir Putin, which cast him as a hyper-masculine monster and a formidable adversary to the US, the book further examines how the Anglophone media have systematically downplayed or overlooked Russian imperialism. This is the crux of my argument in Chapter One "A Study of New Cold War Cultures from a Queer, Feminist, Anti-Imperialist Stance."[26] In evaluating the reasons for and motives behind the full-scale war against Ukraine begun in February 2022,[27] the Anglophone media almost unanimously ignored Russian imperialism as a structural and cultural ideology, and declared the war to be a "mad idea" for which the Russian president was solely responsible. Many political[28] and academic analysts continue to proliferate this idea.[29] The media quickly turned this preoccupation with Putin into speculations about his mental health. This ableist line of thought is built on the aforementioned tendency—which can be observed in media discourses well beyond the Anglophone context—to understand the war in Ukraine as the evil project of a single madman.[30]

---

26 This title is borrowed from Claire Potter, "Is Putin a Mad King?" *Substack newsletter, Political Junkie* (blog), February 28, 2022, https://clairepotter.substack.com/p/is-putin-a-mad-king.

27 Volodymyr Vakhitov and Natalia Zaika, "Beyond Putin: Russian imperialism is the no. 1 threat to global security," *Atlantic Council,* April 27, 2022, https://www.atlanticcouncil.org/blogs/ukrainealert/beyond-putin-russian-imperialism-is-the-no-1-threat-to-global-security/.

28 Eugene Rumer, "Putin's War against Ukraine: The End of the Beginning," *Carnegie,* February 17, 2023, https://carnegieendowment.org/2023/02/17/putin-s-war-against-ukraine-end-of-beginning-pub-89071.

29 Kathryn Stoner, "The War in Ukraine: How Putin's War in Ukraine Has Ruined Russia," *Journal of Democracy* 33, no. 3 (2022): 38–44, https://doi:10.1353/jod.2022.0038; Samuel Ramani, *Putin's War on Ukraine: Russia's Campaign for Global Counter-Revolution* (London: Hurst, 2023).

30 Laura King, "Ill? 'Unhinged'? Or calculating? Russia's Putin keeps everyone guessing," *Los Angeles Times,* February 28, 2022, https://www.latimes.com/world-nation/story/2022-02-28/russia-putin-behavior-mental-health; Ben Kesslen, "Does Putin have 'roid rage'? Sources believe health could explain despot's behavior: report," *New York Post,* March 13, 2022, https://nypost.com/2022/03/13/does-putin-have-roid-rage-sources-believe-health-could-explain-despots-behavior-report/; Sam Tabahriti, "Financier Bill Browder: Vladimir Putin has been a 'psychopath' since childhood and lacks normal

I do not wish to argue that Putin is not responsible for the war. Putin is, however, supported by a system that backs and legitimizes his decisions and executes his orders. More importantly, this war has emerged out of an imperialist logic that is part of Russian self-knowledge, its understanding of its history and present. By late 2023, "the available data indicate[d] that many Russians do indeed back the invasion. Russia's only internationally respected independent pollster, the Levada Center, has identified overwhelming support in its monthly surveys, with more than 70% of respondents consistently voicing their approval of the so-called 'Special Military Operation.'"[31] Struggling to find answers to why so many Russians support the violence against Ukraine, most analysts agree that "the country's imperial past and the imperial intimacy of the Russian relationship with Ukraine [. . .] serve to justify the current war."[32]

Analysts from the New Approaches to Research and Security in Eurasia (PONARS Eurasia) network, which consists of 140 academics from North America and post-Soviet Eurasia, and which aims at advancing new approaches to research on security, politics, economics, and society in the post-Soviet region, identify a strong link between Russian national identity and support for the war. Maria Snegovaya argues in her policy memo from June 2024, for example, that by applying "the Soviet themes of exceptionalism, great power status, and the West as an existential threat to Russia, the Kremlin's territorial conquests have allowed Russians to regain a sense of collective belonging behind a comfortable psychological shield against reality that deflected unpleasant questions about Russia's past and future."[33] Moreover, "a majority of Russians" view Ukraine "as a rightful part of their former empire."[34]

Since an imperialist logic is part of Russian national cultural identity, it permeates Russian knowledge across all fields and spheres, and is thus shared by the

---

'human emotions,'" *Business Insider*, June 26, 2022, https://www.businessinsider.com/bill-browder-vladimir-putin-psychopath-since-childhood-2022-6.

31   Neringa Klumbytė, "Russian imperialism shapes public support for the war against Ukraine," *Atlantic Council*, October 9, 2023, https://www.atlanticcouncil.org/blogs/ukrainealert/russian-imperialism-shapes-public-support-for-the-war-against-ukraine/; Artem Shaipov and Yuliia Shaipova, "It's High Time to Decolonize Western Russia Studies," *Foreign Policy*, February 11, 2023, https://foreignpolicy.com/2023/02/11/russia-studies-war-ukraine-decolonize-imperialism-Western-academics-soviet-empire-eurasia-eastern-europe-university/.

32   Klumbytė, "Russian imperialism."

33   Maria Snegovaya, "Russian Identity and War Support," *PONARS Eurasia*, June 14, 2024, https://www.ponarseurasia.org/russian-identity-and-war-support/.

34   Ibid.

majority of Russian people, whether they are for or against the war, and whether they believe the Russian propaganda or not. It is a logic that makes claims to Ukrainian land based on imperial and Soviet history, and grounds itself in a paternalistic view of Ukrainians as an inferior people that needs to be enlightened by the Russians.[35] This imperialist ideology is deeply ingrained in Russian systems of knowledge and culture; it is present, for instance, throughout the Russian literary canon. It underlay Fyodor Dostoevsky's belief that Russians were superior to all other peoples, and were thus obliged to fulfill a messianic role in the world. The same ideology is also present in Lev Tolstoy's rather blunt words on the inferiority of Ukrainians, and in Joseph Brodsky's chauvinist mocking of Ukrainian independence.[36] To focus on Putin as the sole origin and originator of this war, and to endorse the ableist idea that his actions were the result of a mental condition, overlooks the structures that inform his thinking, that brought him to power, and that continue to enable him.

Rather than facilitating an understanding and critique of Russian imperialism, the importance of the idea of imperial superiority within Russian nationalism, or Western New Cold War logics, most of the US-American and Anglophone media feed into both the idea of imperial superiority undergirding Russian nationalism, and a Western New Cold War logic. My point is not simply to shift blame; however, I believe that the current demonization of Putin, which relies heavily on the abovementioned ableist discourses, among others, obscures important factors that should be part of every analysis attempting to understand the situation. One of these factors is that the war in Ukraine intersects with, and is supported by, a protracted, ongoing, New Cold War, on the terrain of culture in the media.

Since debates around Russia are overdetermined by discussions and representations of its president and focus heavily on aspects of his and his rivals' masculinity, the first chapter of *Under Western Eyes* analyzes the representations of Russian men in the Anglophone media, and examines how they correspond to

---

35 For more information on Russian imperialist views on Ukraine see: Ostap Kushnir, *Russian Neo-Imperialism: The Divergent Break* (London: Rowman & Littlefield, 2018); Alekseev Veniamin, "The Russian Idea: From Messianism to Pragmatism," *Russian Social Science Review* 56, no. 3 (2015); Pal Kolstø and Helge Blakkisrud, eds., *The New Russian Nationalism: Imperialism, Ethnicity and Authoritarianism 2000–2015* (Edinburgh: Edinburgh University Press, 2016).

36 Kasia Krzyżanowska and Ewa Thompson, "Imperialism in Russian Literature," *Review of Democracy*, June 7, 2022, https://revdem.ceu.edu/2022/06/07/imperialism-in-russian-literature/.

New Cold War discourses. I will focus on notions of Western superiority, particularly American nationalism, as important components in these discourses. Looking closely at Western queer criticism, I further point to the perpetuation of transphobia and misogyny in the image of Putin as "queer clown."

Under Western Eyes takes its title from Joseph Conrad's famous novel, published in 1911. The novel, which fictionalizes and reflects on the events of the failed first Russian Revolution in 1905, has frequently been read as a critical answer to Fyodor Dostoevsky's *Crime and Punishment*—an author and a work that Conrad detested, albeit strongly influencing his writing.[37] Conrad had a complicated and fraught relationship to imperial Russia, being the son of a Polish independence activist from Russian occupied territory. He was also an immigrant to England, where he mastered the English language and became one of the most important Anglophone authors of the colonial period, significantly shaping discourses of African Otherness, among other things. It seems only appropriate to borrow the title from such an ambivalent figure, who himself emerged at the intersection of Anglophone (British) and Russian imperialism. Additionally, *Under Western Eyes* is also a self-critical positionality that attempts to make visible my self-positioning as a queer, feminist, white-passing author of mixed East Asian, Slavic, and white European descent.

Finally, I would like to acknowledge the seminal work of Chandra Mohanty, which introduced a feminist decolonial perspective to contemporary gender studies. Mohanty's 1988 article "*Under Western Eyes*: Feminist Scholarship and Colonial Discourses,"[38] and its revised version titled "'*Under Western Eyes*' Revisited: Feminist Solidarity through Anticapitalist Struggles"[39] from 2003 were foundational texts in this field. Mohanty's work has taught me to examine Western liberal feminism and solidarity with a critical eye. I hope that my research will honor her title and legacy.

---

37 Gary Adelman, *Retelling Dostoyevsky* (Lewisburg, PA: Bucknell University Press, 2001).
38 Chandra Mohanty, "Under Western Eyes: Feminist Scholarship and Colonial Discourses," *Feminist Review* 30, no. 1 (1988): 61–88.
39 Chandra Mohanty, "'Under Western Eyes' Revisited: Feminist Solidarity through Anticapitalist Struggles," *Signs: Journal of Women in Culture and Society* 28, no. 2 (2003): 499–535.

Imperialisms and Enlightenment Legacies in New Cold War Cultures

Under Western Eyes: Vulnerable Minorities and the Russian State in New Cold War Cultures is an intervention into scholarly and activist debates on LGBTIQ+ solidarity across the Russia/West divide, as well as a contribution to Anglophone cultural studies. Over the last decade, writing has emerged, in the fields of political science and international relations and beyond, which draws attention to "Cold War patterns of thinking [that] have once again surfaced in discussion about Russia and its role in the world."[40] Many analysts have conducted research on the political implications of these "patterns." The dimension of culture, however, has received far less attention. This book takes up cultural debates around what Stephen Whitfield has aptly termed "Cold War Culture,"[41] which signified a cultural map that emerged during the time of the Cold War, structuring knowledge along an East-West continuum.

According to Whitfield, "American Cold War Culture" was not so much a specific historical period as it was a unique culture. At the heart of this culture were anti-Communist and anti-liberal sentiments, originating in the 1950s as a "phobic overreaction"[42] against the Stalinist regime. Today, the terminology of "Cold War Culture"[43] has become a commonly accepted technical term within cultural studies, referring to the specific cultural and political values that reigned during that period. The idea that cultural myths, stereotypes, and prejudice drive national and transnational identity formations, as well as the complex processes of Othering, are undisputed, as their content is negotiated.

While this East-West continuum never fully disappeared, it was revived with increasing speed and intensity from 2006[44] onwards, when notions of Russia as authoritarian, unfree, and undemocratic yet again entered mainstream media, as well as state discourses that favorably positioned the US and other "progressive" Western nations as a counter-model. After the demise of the Soviet Union, such

---

40 Richard Sakwa, "'New Cold War' or Twenty Years' Crisis? Russia and International Politics," *International Affairs* 84, no. 2 (2008): 241–267, 241. See also: Thomas Graham, "Was the Collapse of US-Russia Relations Inevitable?" *Nation*, August 22, 2023, https://www.thenation.com/article/archive/us-russia-putin-relations-nato/.

41 Stephen Whitfield, *The Culture of the Cold War*, 2nd ed. (Baltimore, MD: Johns Hopkins University Press, 1996).

42 Ibid.

43 Annette Vowinckel, Marcus Payk, and Thomas Lindenberger, *Cold War cultures: perspectives on Eastern and Western European societies* (New York: Berghahn Books, 2012).

44 Sakwa, "New Cold War," 241–267.

discourses abated. Russia no longer served as a common enemy and no longer allowed for a demarcation and unification of US national values in opposition to it. Although the "mental maps" of the binary antagonism between Russia/ East and the West were long valid after 1991, as Susan Buck-Morss[45] and David Caute[46] have shown, US state policies of the new millennium, as well as media discourses, turned their attention to different "enemies," in opposition to which they were able to construct national unity and identity, especially after 9/11. Russian support of the US in its fight against the so-called "axis of evil," in the aftermath of the attacks, and Putin's "sympathies to President [George W.] Bush,"[47] inspired the US media to propose that Russian-American relations were warming.

With Vladimir Putin's second term in office, and as a reaction to the emergence of an increasingly anti-NATO and anti-Western Russia,[48] however, discourses on Russian Otherness reemerged. Russia's "highly complex and undoubtedly contradictory process of re-establishing the authority of the state and some rudimentary notion of order was reduced to a single narrative of authoritarian restoration, and [. . .] a reprise of Cold War confrontation."[49] Within Russia, the discourses on the conflict increasingly led to critiques that were even more over-simplified than they had been during the Cold War. Russian political analysts close to the Kremlin, such as Sergei Karaganov, further fueled the New Cold War, publicly claiming that "[a]ny critic or opponent of the Russian president and the Kremlin automatically becomes a democrat and friend of the West."[50] And although his statement was purposely intended to exacerbate binary think-ing, it did contain a kernel of truth.

In March 2006, President George W. Bush took a further step towards escalat-ing the New Cold War, calling out Russia's questionable "morals" in the *National Security Strategy*,[51] and warning against Russian influence throughout the post-

---

45 Susan Buck-Morss, "Aesthetics and Anaesthetics: Walter Benjamin's Artwork Essay Reconsidered," *October* 62 (1992): 3–41.

46 David Caute, *The Dancer Defects: The Struggle for Cultural Supremacy during the Cold War* (Oxford: Oxford University Press, 2003).

47 Brian Whitmore, "Russia: Nemtsov urges opposition to back single candidate," *RFE/RL, Russia Report*, June 11, 2007, https://www.rferl.org/a/1077074.html.

48 Sakwa, "New Cold War," 241.

49 Ibid., 249.

50 Sergei Karaganov, "A new epoch of confrontation," *Russia in Global Affairs* 5, no. 4 (2007): 23–36, 23.

51 "The National Security Strategy of the United States of America," history.defense. gov, March 2006, https://history.defense.gov/Portals/70/Documents/nss/nss2006.

Soviet region.[52] Since then, the connection between US security interests, development efforts, and democratic ideals has often been emphasized, and the continuation of Cold War thinking has repeatedly been asserted.[53] At the same time, transnational political discourses seem to generalize the socialist past, radicalizing the tensions of oppositionality between the North/West and Russia even further. In its condemnation of totalitarian ideologies, mass crimes, and human rights violations,[54] a resolution passed by the Parliamentary Assembly of the Council of Europe (PACE) on January 25, 2006, for example, equated Communism with Nazism. By approaching twentieth-century history through "the totalitarian paradigm,"[55] PACE rendered the Soviet experience—its ideology, origin, development, and so on, hence the underpinning of Russia's claims to global power today—illegitimate.[56] The Russian response to this narrative of its history was to support an official version of the Soviet past that once again obfuscated some of its darker chapters, overemphasized Soviet achievements, and prompted it to add some anti-American rhetoric to high school textbooks.[57]

A briefing by Russia expert Eduard Lucas to the Commission for the 110th Congress in 2011 titled "The New Cold War: Putin's Russia and the Threat to the West" further added to the proliferation of New Cold War discourses. The discourses at play recall the Cold War oppositionality and tensions of the past, and share many or most of their ideological roots. Nevertheless, the ideological focus, and with it the subjects and figures in which ethical differences become marked, changed significantly. Mark von Hagen, the late director of the Harriman Institute at Columbia University, argued for an understanding of the current frictions between the US and Russia as a "civilizational conflict."[58]

---

pdf?ver=Hfo1-Y5B6CMl8yHpX4x6IA%3d%3d; quotations from President George W. Bush's prefatory comments, p. 2., see also Sakwa, "New Cold War," 262.

52 Ibid.

53 Ibid., 260; Graham, "Was the Collapse of US-Russia Relations Inevitable?"

54 Vladimir Socor, "Council of Europe condemns communism over Moscow's opposition," *Eurasia Daily Monitor* 3, no. 19, January 27, 2006, https://jamestown.org/program/council-of-europe-condemns-communism-over-moscows-opposition/.

55 Stéphane Courtois et al., *The Black Book of Communism: Crimes, Terror, Repression* (Cambridge, MA: Harvard University Press, 1999).

56 Sakwa, "New Cold War," 261.

57 Andrew Osborn, "A do-over for Russian history? Putin-backed manual spurs concern nation is whitewashing its past," *Wall Street Journal*, July 6, 2007, https://www.wsj.com/articles/SB118367568881058545.

58 Mark von Hagen, "Area Studies from Cold War to Civilizational Conflict: On Learning, Relearning, and Unlearning," *Harriman at 70* (Spring 2017): 29–41, http://www.columbia.edu/cu/creative/epub/harriman/2017/spring/from_cold_war_to_civilizational_conflict.pdf.

He proposed that within this "civilizational conflict," identity and cultural narratives become weaponized to create "a belief system that can be maintained within a much larger, chaotic information system by adroit manipulation of culture, psychology, beliefs, ideology, perceptions and opinions, and religions of subgroups using appropriate levers such as comment boards, blogs, websites, and, [. . .] traditional print and broadcast media [. . .]."[59] Von Hagen focused on Ukraine and Russia when arguing that "facts" are being "weaponized" "by framing contemporary politics in historical narratives of often-spurious ancestry and veracity, [. . .] social media and the multifaceted information or propaganda wars that accompany more traditional forms of armed conflict, diplomacy, and economic competition."[60] However, it is equally appropriate, and even necessary, to open up the discussion of media "objectivity" and the "weaponizing" of facts for the US and Anglophone media.

Both the US and Russian media weaponize identities, particularly around questions of gender equality and feminism, homosexuality, nonnormative gender representations, gender-based violence, and disability. Identities need to be constantly reconstructed and recognized in order to be intelligible. Like the nation or civilization, identities need to be constructed in differentiation from others. Edward Said insists that civilizations, cultures, and societies are not monolithic, fixed, or stable. Rather, they are mutable, reformed and reformulated through mixing, migrations, and boundary crossings characterized by complexity, hybridity, and contestation. The notion of the "West" is, by the same token, always in negotiation. The recent emergence of a language of condemnation of Russia for its legal and social ableist, sexist, homophobic, and transphobic climate, and the rhetoric of Russian authoritarianism, can be read as renewed attempts to re-stabilize the ideological apparatus of East/West oppositionality in favor of Western, especially American, superiority. Moreover, Western queer imperialism, paired with US "homonationalism,"[61] must be understood as supporting the construction of the North/Western world, led by the US, as a new progressive, tolerant, and free utopia, and a perpetuation of North/Western hegemony.

The negotiation of cultural values and global cultural hegemony, however, is not played out within the legal or theoretical sphere. In the midst of the

---

59 Ibid., 37.
60 Ibid.
61 Jasbir Puar, "Rethinking Homonationalism," *Middle East Studies* 45, no. 2 (2013): 336–339. Jasbir Puar, *Terrorist Assemblages: Homonationalism in Queer Times* (Durham, NC: Duke University Press, 2007).

cultural war, real as well as fictional figures emerge, marked by their vulnerability to ill-treatment by the Russian authorities. One of the most prominent figures is Nadezhda Tolokonnikova, a formerly incarcerated Russian member of the feminist activist group Pussy Riot. I will discuss Tolokonnikova and her role within Western queer imperialism in detail in Chapter Three: "Vulnerable Russian Gays, the White Male-Centric Gaze, and the Reaffirmation of the East/West Divide." Others are the aforementioned nonbinary gay activist and writer, Masha Gessen; gay activist Kirill Fedorov; and the refugee Dmitry Chizhevsky. These figures will be examined in detail in Chapter Two: "'Is Putin a Mad King?'" Russian Masculinities at the Height of the New Cold War." In analyzing the knowledge construction of the New Cold War, *Under Western Eyes* asks: How can a queer feminist critique examine and deconstruct both Western and Russian imperialisms and their entanglement with American (homo)nationalism and Russian nationalism? What role do LGBTIQ+ issues, feminism, and bodily and mental impairment play in the entanglement of Western and Russian imperialisms? With these questions, my book addresses the media through concepts and issues such as solidarity, public visibility, vulnerability, and war. While reflecting in large part on the news media and its representations, it also considers how popular culture influences and informs public knowledge on Russianness and Russian people through TV series (e.g., *Shameless*) and film characters (e.g., *Eastern Promises*).

To fully understand the New Cold War cultures, Russia, and the US as intrinsically interrelated clusters of signification, however, *Under Western Eyes* aligns itself with historical, economic, political, and cultural studies of the Cold War and the postsocialist period, which read the ideological conflict between Russia, the East, and the West beyond the competition between communism and capitalism as a legacy of the European Enlightenment.[62]

Larry Wolff argues that the foundation of the cultural signification of Russia today was established with the Enlightenment's invention of Eastern Europe as a cultural and intellectual construction.[63] In times of increasing political and social

---

62   Marina Gržinić, Tjaša Kancler, and Piro Rexhepi, "Decolonial Encounters and the Geopolitics of Racial Capitalism," *Feminist Critique: East European Journal of Feminist and Queer Studies* 3 (2020): 13–38. Manuela Boatcă, *Global Inequalities Beyond Occidentalism* (London: Routledge, 2016). Tjaša Kancler, "Speaking against the Void: Decolonial Transfeminist Relations and Radical Potentialities," in *Postcolonial and Postsocialist Dialogues: Intersections, Opacities, Challenges in Feminist Theorizing and Practice*, ed. Redi Koobak, Madina Tlostanova, and Suruchi Thapar-Björkert (New York: Routledge, 2021), 155–170.
63   Larry Wolff, *Inventing Eastern Europe: the map of civilization on the mind of the Enlightenment* (Stanford, CA: Stanford University Press, 1994).

turmoil, amid the French Revolution and the American Revolutionary War, philosophers in Western Europe agonized over the question whether Russia was
part of civilized Europe. Although "Western Europe perceived both Russia and
the United States as culturally inferior latecomers to the table of world power,"[64]
there is no doubt that American travelers, journalists, statesmen, and diplomats
echoed the European evaluation of Russia. Eager to create a stable concept of
Western superiority and development, they constructed Russia as a paradox—
both difference and similarity, in-between European civilization and the barbarian Orient. Edward Said proposes that the Orient was designed by the Occident
as "contrasting image, idea, personality, experience,"[65] as the representation
of otherness. Russia and Eastern Europe were designed within the project of
Orientalism as a buffer between the West and the Far East. The contradictory
evaluation of Russia as both European equal and Asian barbarian during the
seventeenth and eighteenth centuries located it (though not without frequently
leaning in one or the other direction) in a permanent process of becoming a
civilization. Indeed, the concept of development itself was invented in close relation to the concept of Russia, in reference to a territory and people that was
"always just having been tamed, civil, civilized; just having begun to participate
in European politics."[66]

Tightly allied with the notion of Russia as a "yet to become civilized" territory
and a world power "yet to be recognized" was the emergence of "the Russian
threat," as well as the racialized biopolitical design of the "Slav." Philosophers
such as Herder,[67] Ledyard, Lois Buffon, and David Hume,[68] along with many
Victorian writers like Lewis Caroll, contributed to the construction of Russia as
racially different/other. However, at "this early stage of racialist thinking, [. . .]
the place of Russians in the biological hierarchy was not fixed."[69] During the late
nineteenth century, an eclectic, yet quite familiar, picture of Russia was presented
to the American population "through translations of Fyodor Dostoevsky's and
Lev Tolstoy's great novels, [. . .] newspaper coverage and popular fiction that

---

64 Choi Chatterjee and Beth Holmgren, eds., *Americans Experience Russia: Encountering the
    Enigma, 1917 to the Present* (New York: Routledge, 2013), 2.
65 Edward Said, *Orientalism* (New York: Vintage Books, 1979).
66 Iver B. Neumann, *Uses of the Other: "The East" in European Identity Formation* (Manchester:
    Manchester University Press, 1999), 110.
67 Wolff, *Inventing Eastern Europe*, 365.
68 Ibid., 367.
69 Neumann, *Uses of the Other*, 86. One North-American contributor to the concept of 'the
    Slavic' was William Sloane, professor at Columbia in New York, with his book *The Balkans: A
    Laboratory of History* in 1914.

rendered Russia through clichés recycled to this day—fabulously wealthy aristo-crats, wild Cossacks, noble nihilists, beautiful prima ballerinas, bomb-throwing revolutionaries, and picturesque downtrodden folks."[70] Early twentieth-cen-tury Hollywood took up the theme of the proximity of Russian to European imperialism, glamorizing Russian imperial style in films like the *Scarlet Empress* (1934) or *Anna Karenina* (1935).[71] *We Live Again* (1934), *Once in a Blue Moon* (1936), and *Tovarich* (1927) "portrayed the Russian nobility [...] as tragic vic-tims of both the tsarist and the Bolshevik regimes,"[72] implicitly drawing parallels between Russia's (privileged) minorities and the ideal subjects of the European Enlightenment.

The first half of the twentieth century saw the emergence of the so-called *Ostforschung*, which designated Eastern Europe as a barely civilized "coher-ent racial domain."[73] Although Nazi race theories had some followers in the US, the Enlightenment's discourses on Russia were of far greater significance. They survived through World War II into the Cold War period. The general and surreptitious transfer of frameworks and connotations from the European Enlightenment into Cold War America was underpinned by Wolff's discovery of the history of the *Journal for Our Time*, by the Marquise de Custine. Wolff argues that the *Journal*, first published in 1839, transported "every basic ele-ment of the eighteenth century's invention of Eastern Europe" into "nineteenth-century phantasmagoria."[74] Custine already prefigured the geographical "iron curtain," which Winston Churchill famously traced "[from] Stettin in the Baltic to Trieste in the Adriatic,"[75] in Fulton, Missouri in 1946. In 1946, the *Journal* suddenly appeared in a new edition in France, and a couple of years later it was introduced to the American public accompanied by the words of Walter Bedell Smith, the postwar US ambassador to the Soviet Union. Smith praised Custine's description of Russia as "political observation so penetrating and timeless that it could be called the best work so far produced about the Soviet Union."[76] Furthermore, he argued that "Custine's letters were the greatest single contribution in helping us to unravel, in part, the mysteries that seem to envelop

---

70 Chatterjee and Holmgren, *Americans Experience Russia*, 3.
71 Choi Chatterjee, "The Russian Romance in American Popular Culture, 1890–1939," in *Americans Experience Russia: Encountering the Enigma, 1917 to the Present*, ed. Choi Chatterjee and Beth Holmgren (London: Routledge, 2013), 87–104, 90.
72 Chatterjee, "The Russian Romance," 90.
73 Wolff, *Inventing Eastern Europe*, 370.
74 Ibid., 365.
75 Churchill qtd. in Wolff, *Inventing Eastern Europe*, 1.
76 Smith quoted in ibid., 365.

Russia and the Russians."[77] In 1987 the *Journal* was published yet again, at the very end of the Cold War, with a comment by Zbigniew Brzezinski on the back cover. Brzezinski emphasized that "[n]o Sovietologist has yet improved on de Custine's insights into the Russian character and the Byzantine nature of the Russian political system."[78]

During the Cold War, Western Europe and the US detached themselves ideologically and explicitly from Eastern Europe. According to Iver B. Neumann, Russia came to be represented as an "Asiatic/barbarian political power that had availed itself of the opportunity offered by the Second World War to intrude into Europe by military means."[79] The dominant forces semantically equated the Communist politico-economic model with the "vanquished Nazi enemy," labeling it "totalitarian."[80] The epithet "totalitarian" was used interchangeably with "authoritarian," a word that comes up frequently with reference to Russia under Putin. "This dichotomy between democratic and totalitarian or authoritarian replaces the master dichotomy civilized/barbarian and European/Asian and had affinities to a number of others such as free/unfree, market/plan, West/East, defensive/offensive."[81] The replacements, however, are not disconnected from their predecessors. American popular fiction, film, and mass media further transferred the emerging ideological dichotomy into individualized, heartbreaking "romances spiked by political struggles"[82] between American and Russian lovers.

Discourses of civilization, however, never vanished. They came up in 1950s and 1960s textbooks like *A History of the Modern World*[83] and in James Bond films,[84] and were happily invoked again beginning with Perestroika, in August 1991, after the Soviet coup d'état had failed. "[T]he front page of the *New York Times* declared the Russians ready 'for the mammoth task of civilizing their country.' This presumably unconscious quotation by Voltaire's Peter the Great strongly suggests the power of old formulas, according to which Russia remains always just on the verge of becoming civilized, whether in the eighteenth or the

---

77 Ibid.
78 Zbigniew Brzezinski, *Strategic Vision: America and the Crisis of Global Power* (New York: Basic Books, 2012).
79 Neumann, *Uses of the Other*, 102.
80 Ibid., 103.
81 Ibid.
82 Chatterjee and Holmgren, *Americans Experience Russia*, 2.
83 Robert Roswell Palmer, *A History of the Modern World* (New York: Knopf, 1950).
84 Ian Fleming, *From Russia with Love* (London: Jonathan Cape, 1957); *From Russia with* Love, directed by Terence Young (London: Eon Productions, 1963).

twentieth century."[85] Later, in March 1992, the *New York Times* wrote about the "Chaos in Eastern Europe," reactivating the old "formula favored by Voltaire."[86]

Queer Feminist Anti-Imperialism as Methodology

Under Western Eyes combines a "critical discourse analysis"[87] with semiotic analysis of literature, film, TV series, music videos, and images in the tradition of cultural studies.[88] It looks at the intersectionality of gender, sexuality, race, class, and age in their full complexity, making contradictions transparent and necessarily implying self-reflection and self-questioning on the part of the researcher. According to Ruth Wodak, discourses are intertextual and must be thought historically; they are connected synchronically and diachronically with other communicative events, past and present.[89] Furthermore, discourses are fields of "recontextualization,"[90] which means that they incorporate references, topoi, and reformulations from other contexts. These different contexts, as well as the movements implied, need to be taken into consideration in the process of the analysis. Critical discourse analysis is problem-oriented, which necessarily includes an interdisciplinary approach and framework.

Under Western Eyes follows the recently emerging corpus of work within American studies that investigates the production of notions of modernity against the backdrop of the racialized 'other,' using postcolonial, gender, and queer theory, particularly the work of Chandan Reddy,[91] Roderick A. Ferguson, and Grace Hong.[92] Building on the seminal research of international scholars Jin Haritaworn, Tamsila Tauqir, and Esra Erdem,[93] I interrogate the media focus

---

85 Wolff, *Inventing Eastern Europe*, 372.

86 Ibid.

87 Ruth Wodak, "Critical Discourse Analysis at the End of the 20th Century," *Research on Language and Social Interaction* 32, no. 1–2 (1999): 185–193. Stuart Hall, "The West and the Rest: Discourse and Power," in *The Formations of Modernity*, ed. Stuart Hall and Bram Gieben (Cambridge: Polity, 1993), 275–331.

88 Stuart Hall, *Representation: Cultural Representations and Signifying Practices* (Thousand Oaks, CA: Sage Publications and Open University, 1997).

89 Wodak, "Discourse Analysis," 186.

90 Basil Bernstein, *The structure of pedagogic discourse. Class, codes and control* (London: Routledge, 1990).

91 Chandan Reddy, *Freedom with Violence: Race, Sexuality, and the US State* (Durham, NC: Duke University Press, 2011).

92 Roderick Ferguson and Grace Hong, *Strange Affinities: The Gender and Sexual Politics of Comparative Racialization* (Durham, NC: Duke University Press, 2011).

93 Haritaworn and Erdem, "Queer-Imperialismus."

and invocation of a positive legal and sociocultural attitude towards LGBTIQ+ and other vulnerable minorities, establishing moral hegemony as "queer imperialism," as already noted. Moreover, and no less importantly, I analyze queer imperialism at the juncture of what Jasbir Puar has called US "homonationalism." Puar developed the conceptual framework of "homonationalism" to discuss how "'acceptance' and 'tolerance' for gay and lesbian subjects have become a barometer by which the right to and capacity for national sovereignty is evaluated"[94] in the new millennium. It is "a facet of modernity and a historical shift marked by the entrance of (some) homosexual bodies as worthy of protection by nation-states."[95] Puar argues that the relationship between sexuality, the US state, and capitalism has changed, insofar as the narrative of progress, which is still culturally predominant, now includes an aspiration to gay rights. This change of narrative, however, "is thus built on the back of racialized others, for whom such progress was once achieved, but is now backsliding or has yet to arrive."[96] Although Puar developed her concept to understand the national and international consequences of the production of racialized Muslims as terrorists to delegitimize their cultural and territorial environment, her writing can be useful for understanding the current binary production of LGBTIQ+ victims and the 'Russian Other.' To fully understand the production of Russia as authoritarian and backward, Puar's concept of this new kind of nationalism, however, needs to be expanded. A single-issue focus on the support of gay rights through the US in reference to Russia is not sufficient, as the measurement of 'progress' is equally concerned with gender equality, gender-based violence, and disability.

Scholars working on Central and Eastern European studies, Eurasian studies, and queer studies, such as the aforementioned Olga Plakhotnik and Maria Mayerchyk,[97] but also John Binnie,[98] Robert Kulpa, Joanna Mizielińska and Agata Stasinska,[99] challenge the geo-temporal paradigm of Central Europe, Eastern Europe, and Eurasia within Western public discourses, demonstrating that the invocation of queerness more often than not produces a problematic concept of time and progress in which the North/Western model can only

---

94   Puar, *Terrorist*, 4.
95   Puar, "Rethinking," 337.
96   Ibid.
97   Plakhotnik and Mayerchyk, "Pride Contested."
98   John Binnie, *The Globalization of Sexuality* (London: Sage, 2004).
99   Robert Kulpa, Joanna Mizielińska, and Agatha Stasinska, "(Un)translatable Queer?, or What Is Lost and Can Be Found in Translation," in *Import—Export—Transport: Queer Theory, Queer Critique and Activism in Motion*, ed. Sushila Mesquita, Katharina Wiedlack, and Katrin Lasthofer (Vienna: Zaglossus, 2012), 115–146.

ever be seen as advanced, while the Eastern counterpart can only ever appear as backward and needing to catch up. Framing it as "'poor cousin' to the 'West,'" the East "is now, supposedly, catching up with normality (a.k.a. the 'West'), after coming out of history's closet in 1989" and after "being kept in history's freezer (a.k.a. 'communism')."[100] Like Wolff, Kulpa and Mizielińska emphasize the ambivalence of the "'Western' structural enclosing of [Eastern Europe and Eurasia] in toxically imbalanced relations of passivity and (expectations of) activity."[101] Moreover, they highlight the "'Western' (non-)recognition of the [Eastern] geo-temporality in hegemonic Occidentalist discourses (e.g., through the rejection of state communism as Modernity, one of many projects of it, and alternative to the 'Western' one, which is mounted as the one)."[102] I read the juxtaposition of the US and Russia within a media that focuses on LGBTIQ+, framed through a geo-temporal lens, as "Modernity vs. Forces of Yesteryear,"[103] with and against Kulpa's and Mizielińska's theories. And I argue that what Kulpa and Mizielińska discovered through their analysis of the implications of queerness and queers is equally true for women exposed to gender-based violence and people with disabilities.

While these authors investigate the configuration of concepts of Eastern non-normative sexualities, Anca Parvulescu[104] offers an account of the discursive construction of Eastern, and particularly Slavic, female bodies. She focuses on bodily difference within the spectrum of whiteness, addressing the exoticization and sexualization of white Eastern European migrant women. Following and challenging Parvulescu's work, and building on Claudia Sadowski-Smith's analysis of the racialization of post-Soviet immigrants in the US,[105] I question the hegemonic construction of Russian bodies within American discourses. Building on

---

100 Robert Kulpa and Joanna Mizielińska, "'Guest editors' Introduction: Central and Eastern European Sexualities 'in transition,'" *Lambda Nordica: Journal of LGBTQ Studies* (2012): 19–29, 23.

101 Ibid.

102 Kulpa and Mizielińska, "Guest," 23.

103 András Simonyi, "LGBT Rights–Modernity vs. Forces of Yesteryear," *World Post*, May 11, 2015, http://www.huffingtonpost.com/andras-simonyi/lgbt-rights-modernity-vs-forces-of-yesteryear_b_7256178.html.

104 Ana Parvulescu, *The Traffic in Women's Work: East European Migration and the Making of Europe* (Chicago, IL: University of Chicago Press, 2014).

105 Claudia Sadowski-Smith, *The New Immigrant Whiteness: Race, Neoliberalism, and Post-Soviet Migration to the United States* (New York: New York University Press, 2018).

concepts of (bodily) vulnerability in the work of Judith Butler,[106] Kate Kaul,[107] Martha Fineman,[108] Sherene Razack,[109] and others, *Under Western Eyes* traces the instrumentality of vulnerable human bodies in the invention of geographical, social, and cultural East/West difference/similarity, and reflect upon the roles of race, gender, disability, sexuality, and nation in such constructions.

Vulnerability, Martyrdom, and Suffering in the New Cold War

In *Precarious Life: The Powers of Mourning and Violence*, Judith Butler argues that the human body and mutual embodiment are the primal link between individuals and society. "[A]s bodies," we are "outside ourselves and for one another."[110] To be embodied, is also to be vulnerable. Thus, vulnerability is a universal human experience and point of interconnectedness, that renders the idea of the autonomous subject obsolete.

Butler formulates her political project of vulnerability around the questions of who counts as a human being, whose life counts as alive, and what it is that makes a life grievable.[111] They strongly advocate reimagining relationality through this universalized notion of vulnerability, arguing that vulnerability and the shared exposure to loss are what define humans as human. "Butler reads the post-9/11 United States as a melancholic subject, one that is unable to properly mourn its notion of itself as invulnerable on home soil. They point out that as states and as individuals, we mourn familiar lives more readily than unfamiliar lives. In refusing to fully recognize, to grieve, the casualties of US and US-supported military action abroad, we render those lives—and deaths—unreal. This 'derealization,' they argue, perpetuates violence."[112] Furthermore, Butler argues that the subject becomes vulnerable at the moment of recognition because recognition

---

106 Judith Butler, *Precarious Life: The Powers of Mourning and Violence* (London: Verso, 2006).

107 Kate Kaul, "Vulnerability, for Example: Disability Theory as Extraordinary Demand," *Canadian Journal of Women and the Law/Revue Femmes et Droit* 25, no. 1 (2013): 81–110.

108 Martha Albertson Fineman, "The vulnerable subject: Anchoring equality in the human condition," *Yale Journal of Law and Feminism* 1, no. 20 (2008): 1–23.

109 Sherene H. Razack, *Looking White People in the Eye: Gender, Race, and Culture in Courtrooms and Classrooms* (Toronto: University of Toronto Press, 1998).

110 Butler, *Precarious*, 27.

111 Ibid., 20.

112 Kaul, "Vulnerability," 102.

entails an opening up of the self to the other. The opposite of recognition is derealization.

Kate Kaul notes that Butler is not so much interested in "individual deaths but, rather, the state that is refusing to recognize and to grieve them—namely the United States."[113] Kaul turns to Martha Fineman's theory of vulnerability, which addresses the state and its subjects equally. "Fineman does not follow Butler's analogy between states and subjects, with the state operating like a subject [and] separates her 'vulnerable subject' from the notion of 'vulnerable populations current in feminist legal theory.'"[114] Fineman emphasizes that although vulnerability is a universal human condition, the particularity of individual vulnerability is what differentiates subjects from each other.[115] Speaking from a legal perspective, she further draws attention to the place of vulnerability as a central category for the need of state protection. She argues that establishing vulnerability as a universal facet of the human condition and putting it at the heart of the state's assessment of measures to ensure protection and care would guarantee a more equitable system.

Less concerned with the interdependence of humans and the psychic illusion of autonomy, the proposed project endorses Fineman's focus on vulnerability as the basis for state protection towards its citizens, and asks what this assertion means if the vulnerable person "gazed at" is a noncitizen. Within our current symbolic order, dependency, for the liberal subject, inevitably refers to the status of children.[116] People with disabilities, as Kaul rightly points out, have always been identified as vulnerable and incapable, hence subjects of institutional care.[117] "[T]he assumption that talking about bodies and vulnerability means talking about disability is itself an inescapable object of disability theory."[118] Another aspect of vulnerability and dependency, especially at the intersection of disability, is "pity." Sherene Razack emphasizes "the ableist gaze that sees the disabled as 'icons of pity.'"[119] She argues that "a politics of rescue prevails when women with disabilities are seen as doubly or triply vulnerable, as 'icons of pity.'"[120] It is, indeed, pity that is the emotional response to vulnerability, and saving is the activity that follows. Moreover, pity is oppositional to respect, an

---

113 Ibid., 102.
114 Ibid., 103.
115 Fineman, "The vulnerable subject."
116 Ibid., 2.
117 Kaul, "Vulnerability," 104.
118 Ibid., 101.
119 Razack, *Looking White People in the Eye*, 130.
120 Ibid., 132.

emotional state in which the person who feels pity complies in oppressing others. "But, as Razack's analysis of case law shows, pity is not the only response to vulnerability. Violence is another response to vulnerability."[121] Kaul and Razack both note that women with disabilities, in particular, have historically been constructed as vulnerable, and have faced social and sexual violence.[122] Both warn against an affirmation of vulnerability in terms of a moment for relationality or legal protection, without an equal focus on institutionalized and systematic oppression and violence. "At its core," Razack argues, "the argument of greater vulnerability invites a tautology: women from historically disadvantaged groups are more vulnerable because they are more vulnerable."[123] Her suggestion to avoid such tautology is to tell "the stories of women with disabilities [...] not as stories of vulnerability, but as stories of injustice."[124]

This narration of injustice towards people with disabilities, queers, women, and minorities in general, however, is produced and reproduced by mainstream media at the present moment, without ever reducing the vulnerability and object status of the human lives they talk about. Along with the reframing of vulnerability by philosophers like Butler as a chance to rethink and reimagine human connectedness, media discourses insist on vulnerability as problem to be solved through protection by the state or supranational powers. They produce vulnerable bodies through photos, writing, and film to point out the injustice of oppressive forces endangering these bodies. Yet homosexuality and disability are no longer presented as reasons for the bodies' vulnerability. The reason these subjects are vulnerable is, rather, the backwardness of the Russian state and people, which includes the chance to become free from vulnerability within a different system, ideological apparatus, or state.

Under Western Eyes analyzes the co-construction of individualized vulnerable bodies and its adversary body, the Russian state. After Iver Neumann,[125] the book focuses on biopolitical features within the discursive delineations of US identity/self from the cultural "other." Neumann shows that the cultural representations of Russia that appear at the turn of the millennium originated in the eighteenth and nineteenth centuries. These representations constructed a Western identity in opposition to a powerful military nation of morally

---

121 Kaul, "Vulnerability," 106.
122 Razack, *Looking White People in the Eye*, 136; Kaul, "Vulnerability," 107.
123 Razack, *Looking White People in the Eye*, 138.
124 Ibid., 156.
125 Neumann, *Uses of the other*.

questionable people—drunken, slothful, and lazy.[126] These ambivalently constructed Russian bodies/citizens—potent, yet morally suspect—allowed the
Western formation of identity through the identification of difference and similarity. Neumann draws attention to the fact that military action, body politics,
and the semantics of the everyday are interconnected, stating that the common
view of his time was that Russia's market was already established "and the rest
will therefore quickly follow [. . .]. [A]n alternative version has it that the learning process may quickly be discontinued. Aggressive nationalists may take over,
and a military threat to Europe may follow. [. . .] Russia's being a bad learner
in one particular but crucial area, namely, that of human rights in general and
minority policy in particular [. . .]."[127] The historical Western view of Russia
as unstable, ambivalent, and unreliable is still in place. Neumann summarizes
his analysis of the function of Russia towards European (and, I would add,
US-American identity formation) with the metaphor of the "pangolin." "The
pangolin is seen to have properties that do not go together and so it threatens
the very principles of [. . .] taxonomization and, by extension, taxonomization as
such. [It] is constructed as a monster but also by some as totem animal of a fer-
tility cult."[128] When Russia was deemed not-quite-ready for NATO participation
in the early 2000s, for example, "this representation may be offered in terms of
specific contemporary practices in the area of human rights."[129] The effect of this
representation, however, is "reinforced by the rich baggage of the 'not yet' and
'justs' of half a millennium."[130] *Under Western Eyes* follows Neumann's approach,
applying a gender-sensitive, queer, and anti-imperialist lens to the analysis of
representations of Russia and its most vulnerable subjects.

The critical perspective on the hegemonic production of national identity and
its Other needs to take the production of similarity and concomitant erasure of
differences in the Other into account. Feminist and gender studies have a long
history of having been challenged by Black feminists, disability theorists, trans
and queer activists, and so on, for promulgating a universal notion of "women,"
arguing for the recognition of difference and privilege.[131] The discussions among

---

126 Ibid., 104.
127 Ibid., 108.
128 Ibid., 109.
129 Ibid., 111.
130 Ibid.
131 Seyla Benhabib and Judith Butler, eds., *Der Streit um Differenz. Feminismus und Postmoderne
  in der Gegenwart* (Frankfurt: Fischer, 1993); Kimberlé Crenshaw, "Demarginalizing the
  Intersection of Race and Sex: A Black Feminist Critique of Antidiscrimination Doctrine,
  Feminist Theory and Antiracist Politics," *University of Chicago Legal Forum* (1989): 138–167;

gender studies scholars have had an impact on most fields within the humanities and social sciences, and unreflecting usage of the categories of gender and sexuality, without examining their interdependencies with race and class, no longer predominate. With regard to more traditional topics in feminist and gender studies, a similar awareness of the specific cultural and social circumstances of Eastern European and Russian "women" emerged already at the end of the 1990s.[132] Awareness of the fluidity of identities and identifications is less evident within contemporary discourses around the topic of homosexuality, despite the fact that homosexuality and LGBTIQ+ issues more broadly emerged as the quintessential sphere of the production of self/other and similarity/difference in the media, as well as in academic accounts in the West and East. Anglophone academics such as Dan Healey,[133] Katja Sarajeva,[134] Emil Edenborg,[135] Francesca Stella, and Nadya Nartova[136] have examined the negotiation of 'sexual values' within the Russian context, arguing that the topic has become "a critical battleground for national regeneration."[137] Healey concludes that "[c]onservatives and nationalists turned their attention to Russia's demographic implosion and prescribed the re-regulation of sexuality. Putin put the rapidly shrinking Russian population on the national agenda, and marshaled support in Russia's parliament, the Duma, to promote family values and to boost marriage and the birthrate, and to stigmatize divorce."[138] All of the aforementioned scholars agree that

Nira Yuval-Davis and Floya Anthias, *Racialized Boundaries. Race, Nation, Colour, Class and the Anti-Racist Struggle* (London: Routledge, 1997); Kathryn Woodward, *Identity and Difference. Culture, Media and Identities* (London: Sage, 2007).

132 Elena Zdravomyslova, "Die Konstruktion der 'arbeitenden Mutter' und die Krise der Männlichkeit," *Feministische Studien* 1 (1999): 23–34; Martina Ritter, "Kulturelle Modernisierung und Identitätskonzeptionen im sowjetischen und postsowjetischen Rußland," *Feministische Studien* 1 (1999): 8–22.

133 Dan Healey, "Active, passive, and Russian: The national idea in gay men's pornography," *Russian Review* 6, no. 2 (2010): 210–230.

134 Katja Sarajeva, "Lesbian Lives: Sexuality, Space and Subculture in Moscow" (PhD diss., University of Stockholm, 2011), 26.

135 Emil Edenborg, "Homophobia as Geopolitics: 'Traditional Values' and the Negotiation of Russia's Place in the World," in *Gendering Nationalism: Intersections of Nation, Gender and Sexuality*, ed. Jon Mulholland, Erin Sanders-McDonagh, and Nicola Montagna (Cham: Palgrave Macmillan, 2018), 1–388, accessed December 12, 2024, https://doi.org/10.1007/978-3-319-76699-7.

136 Francesca Stella, and Nadya Nartova, "Sexual Nationalisms and the Boundaries of Sexual Citizenship," in *Sexuality, Citizenship and Belonging: Trans-National and Intersectional Perspectives*, ed. Francesca Stella (London: Routledge, 2016), 17–36.

137 Healey, "Active," 211.

138 Ibid.

homosexuality in Russian state discourses and medical discourses needs to be understood in reference to its positioning towards the global North/West.

The Russian perspective has shifted over time: from the introduction of homophobic laws during the nineteenth century, to embracing Westernness, to a rejection of homosexuality as a Western phenomenon, while appropriating an anti-imperialist rhetoric to create the notion of an independent Russianness, which began in the twentieth century. With the increasing normalization of same-sex partnerships in the last twenty years, the North/Western gaze turned to the situation and treatment of Russian homosexuals or queers in order to criticize and stigmatize Russia. Supranational institutions, such as the European Court of Human Rights, ruled in 2010 that "Russia's bans on gay pride marches are against the right to freedom of assembly and ordered compensation to be paid to the organizers."[139] When the United States Supreme Court ruled in *Obergefell v. Hodges* that all states must license and recognize same-sex marriages, the US seemed to assume a position opposite to Russia's and further legitimized queer imperialism in Anglophone media discourses. Russian officials such as Valery Zorkin, "head of the Russian Constitutional Court," rejected Western interventions into Russian social politics, arguing that they "ignored Russian tradition and the reality on the ground."[140]

Within all the debates, homosexuality began to be produced as a genuinely North/Western concept on both sides: for the North/West, as evidence of its own (post)modern aspiration for bringing the world tolerance and freedom; for Russia, as a demarcation line, guarding against this ideological imperialism. None of these discourses ever questioned who the subject of their rejection or solidarity was, quickly assuming homosexuality, and LGBTIQ+ identification more broadly, to be universal concepts. This led to a paradoxical situation, by which the victims of the so-called 'anti-homosexual propaganda law,' 'foreign-agents law,' and the increasingly homophobic social climate, were systematically overlooked, while the media constructed rather phantasmic, male, and white model victims, or modern martyrs, as I will discuss in detail in Chapter Two.

Within Slavic, gender, and sexualities studies, scholars have questioned self-designations and self-identifications in the 1990s and 2000s Russian context. Laurie Essig has described the negotiations of nonnormative sexual identities in Moscow during the 1990s as "the story of Western imports clashing with the

---

139 John Anderson, "Rocks, Art, and Sex: The 'Culture Wars' Come to Russia?" *Journal of Church and State* 55, no. 2 (2013): 307–334, 331.
140 Ibid., 331.

economic, cultural and discursive realms of post-Soviet Russia."[141] She analyzes the way the American faith in identity politics, as well as other Western ideas of queer politics, have influenced the geographies of sexuality and queerness forming in the newly emerging state of Russia; concluding that in the 1990s, Moscow's "[s]exual otherness was a verb, a performance, a dance, rarely an identity."[142] Essig's evaluation has been challenged by scholars such as Stella, who rightfully argues that her enthusiasm about the queer fluidity of Russian sexuality needs to be viewed with caution, as it is framed through the Eastern othering of Orientalist and exoticizing thinking.[143] Yet Essig's study attests to the fact that during the 1990s, until approximately 2006, neither a political gay identity nor a lesbian identity existed in the mainstream. The attitude and view of the general public towards female same-sex desire, although derogatory, was relatively lenient, because lesbianism was understood as a mere phase, not something to be taken seriously. Discourses on gay identity politics emerged around the Moscow Pride March on May 27, 2006, following a very visible campaign led by Nikolai Alekseev, supported by ILGA Europe, and as a reaction to the government's harsh sanctions against that event.[144]

North/Western solidarity efforts did not focus much on women and trans-identified people; nor did the Russian LGBT movement, until recently, when trans* healthcare, as well as legal gender changes, were officially banned throughout the country.[145] The problem of lesbian (in)visibility and male hegemony is in part due to the misogynist social climate of contemporary Russia. The focus on male homosexuality, however, was promoted, if not introduced, by North/Western human rights discourses and activities sponsored by the aforementioned Alekseev and ILGA Europe. The preoccupation with discriminatory

---

141 Laurie Essig, *Queer in Russia: A Story of Sex, Self, and the Other* (Durham, NC: Duke University Press, 1999), 56.

142 Ibid., 87.

143 Francesca Stella, *Lesbian Lives in Soviet and Post-Soviet Russia: Post/Socialism and Gendered Sexualities* (London: Palgrave Macmillan, 2015).

144 Francesca Stella, "Queer Space, Pride, and Shame in Moscow," *Slavic Review* 72, no. 3 (2013): 458–480.

145 In Summer 2023, legislation was signed into law that bans Russian people from legally or medically changing their gender. Associated Press, "Vladimir Putin signs law banning gender changes in Russia," *Guardian*, July 24, 2023, https://www.theguardian.com/world/2023/jul/24/vladimir-putin-signs-law-banning-gender-changes-in-russia. Matt Murphy, "Russian parliament bans gender reassignment surgery for trans people," *BBC*, July 14, 2023, https://www.bbc.com/news/world-europe-66200194. Neil MacFarquhar and Georgy Birger, "Putin's Crackdown Leaves Transgender Russians Bracing for Worse," *New York Times*, August 1, 2023, https://www.nytimes.com/2023/08/01/world/europe/russia-transgender-ban.html.

practices against gay men only was furthered by the Anglophone media, which dubbed the 2013 Russian federal law forbidding the "propaganda of nontraditional sexual relationships" towards minors,[146] and its recent expansion to anyone of any age, as the "Russian anti-gay law." (In Russian, unlike in English, "gay" refers to homosexual men only.) The law propagates homophobic ideas, reiterating or confirming the discursive connection between pedophilia and homosexuality, stigmatizing LGBTIQ+ people, and implicitly sanctioning violence against them. Women, in particular those expressing same-sex desires and relationships, along with nonnormatively gendered and trans*gender people, have been the targets of an increasingly homophobic and transphobic social climate in Russia. They are not necessarily the beneficiaries of North/Western solidarity, however, unless their vulnerability can be utilized to garner support of American homonationalism and queer imperialism. Following Deborah Gould,[147] *Under Western Eyes* analyzes how vulnerable Russian LGBTIQ+ people, women, and people with disabilities emerge within Anglophone media discourses as "political imaginaries and their conditions of possibility."[148] I examine the affective construction of Russian figures in the media, literature, and film, as well as the affective relations of these figures towards materiality and the world. In looking at Anglophone queer imperialism, American homonationalism and Russian imperialism, and white nationalism, I hope to facilitate an understanding of East/West value negotiations and support efforts to create solidarity across the East/West divide. In each chapter, I address the construction of whiteness with reference to figures and tropes responsible for the othering of Russia. Chapter Four: "*Shameless*: The Racialized Whiteness of Russian Women in American TV" however, will examine most exhaustively the visual, bodily, and cultural representations of whiteness, by reading Russian female characters on North American TV.

---

146 The Law No. 135-FZ was initially "aimed at protecting children from information promoting the denial of traditional family values [. . .] spreading information aimed at instilling in minors nontraditional sexual arrangements, the attractiveness of nontraditional sexual relations and/or a distorted view that society places an equal value on traditional and nontraditional sexual relations or propagating information on nontraditional sexual relations making them appear interesting" ("License to Harm—Violence and Harassment against LGBT People and Activists in Russia, Report, December 15, 2014," Human Rights Watch, https://www.hrw.org/report/2014/12/15/license-harm/violence-and-harassment-against-lgbt-people-and-activists-russia).

147 Deborah B. Gould, *Moving Politics: Emotion and ACT UP's Fight against AIDS* (Chicago, IL: University of Chicago Press, 2009).

148 Ibid., 3.

CHAPTER 2

"Is Putin a Mad King?" Russian Masculinities at the Height of the New Cold War[1]

———————

In this chapter, I analyze the current trends of imagining Russian men, Russian male bodies, and Russian masculinity in the Anglophone, and particularly American, media. I argue that the ideas and images that we currently witness in the Anglophone media, which depict the Russian president as a paranoid megalomaniac[2] and an all-powerful dictator, are grounded in a long tradition of Russian male bodies in cinema and on TV, but also within other spheres of popular culture and various news media. This image is simultaneously a sign, and the discursive product of, a new (old) signifier of Russia as male aggressor and opponent to the West, most often represented by the US.[3] They are part of a new (old) politics of elderly white men, speaking to and revitalizing a new (old) cultural narrative of Russia as a masculine (New) Cold Warrior. Importantly, the idea of Russia as a masculine danger to the world collides with what historian Ellen Schrecker has coined "cold war triumphalism":[4] the idea that the US defeated Russia, which lost

---

1   This title is borrowed from Claire Potter, "Is Putin a Mad King?" Substack newsletter, *Political Junkie* (blog), February 28, 2022, https://clairepotter.substack.com/p/is-putin-a-mad-king.

2   Paul Taylor, "Inside Vladimir Putin's Head," *POLITICO*, February 27, 2022, https://www.politico.eu/article/vladimir-putin-russia-ukraine-nato-nuclear-inside-putins-head/; Ian McEwan, "We are haunted by ghosts—and Vladimir Putin's sickly dreams," *Guardian*, March 5, 2022, https://www.theguardian.com/commentisfree/2022/mar/05/vladimir-putin-ukraine; Michael Day, "As Putin mulls a Ukraine attack, experts paint scary psychological picture of what makes Russia's tyrant tick," *i-News*, January 26, 2022, https://inews.co.uk/news/world/russia-ukraine-vladimir-putin-attack-psychological-picture-what-make-tick-1424732.

3   Although I do not want to suggest that there are no differences between US and other Anglophone discourses at all, I propose that US views need to be seen as hegemonic within Anglophone media discourses in general and popular culture in particular.

4   Ellen Schrecker, "Introduction," in *Cold War Triumphalism: The Misuse of History after the Fall of Communism*, ed. Ellen Schrecker (New York: The New Press, 2004) 1–24, 1.

all global power whatsoever after the dissolution of the USSR. It proves those feelings of victory to be premature, picking up Cold War anxieties where they left off. This new view or image of Russia is bolstered by representations of the Russian president Vladimir Putin in the US media, and Anglophone media in general, marked by an intense interest in his virile masculinity, both political and personal, beginning with his second term as president in 2004, and continuing until now.

To clarify the importance of representations of embodied masculinity within imperialistic and nationalistic discourses on both sides, and particularly in discourses on US and Western superiority, I will first explain the gendered aspects of nationalism. Arguably, both American and Russian nationalism have imperialist tendencies that gauge and measure their own value by the influence they command globally. Russian imperialism is further marked by the idea of a humiliating loss of territory and influence, which need to be restored. While it acknowledges multiculturalism to a certain degree, it is national Russian pride that is at stake here. Both US and Russian nationalism use rhetorics of security concerns that need a strong masculine hand to further their imperialist agendas.

While the imperialist aspects of nationalism will be addressed, I will focus on the relationship between hegemonic masculinity and US nationalism, since it is most prevalent within Anglophone media discourses, and the US-centric gaze on Russia. Hegemonic masculinities are masculinities that are not only dominant, but understood to be superior to other forms of masculinity and femininity.[5] As such, they legitimize inequality. By briefly referencing literature on the Cold War culture between World War II and 1991, and the period that followed, I will show how current discourses on Russian masculinity continue old Cold War discourses prior to the 1990s, and transfer them to the here and now. In picking up historical discourses, they recycle the Cold War triumphalism prevalent during the 1990s and early 2000s, arguably amplifying the threat posed by Russia while simultaneously promoting a concept of time-space that signifies Russian backwardness. After elaborating on the connections between masculinity, nationalisms, and how ideas of Western superiority clash with Russian ideas of superiority, I will demonstrate how the strategy of "cultural othering" of Russia in the US media over the course of the last fifteen or twenty years has served to re-establish a sense of national unity and moral superiority within the US itself, and a larger Western unity beyond its borders, especially during times of crisis. I will show how representations and discourses of Russian masculinity circulate within all spheres of the media. In addition

---

5   James Messerschmidt, *Masculinities in the Making: From the Local to the Global* (Lanham, MD: Rowman & Littlefield, 2016), 34.

to the representations of Russian masculinity in the daily news sector, I support my arguments by drawing upon images from popular culture, political satire, and fictional TV dramas, science fiction, and Hollywood cinema.

Gendered Aspects of US Nationalism and the Role of Russia

Ann McClintock has pointed out very succinctly that "[a]ll nationalisms are gendered, all are invented, and all are dangerous—dangerous [. . .] in the sense of representing relations to political power and to the technologies of violence."[6] Her assertion that nationalisms "invent[. . .] nations where they do not exist"[7] has never been truer than in the most recent Russian rhetoric, nationalistic and unfounded, which lays claim to the lands of Donbas and other regions inside Ukraine in the name of ethnic Russians who are allegedly under threat of genocide.[8] As if having read McClintock, Russia appeals "to an august and immemorial past" to legitimize military interference, war, and the annexation of territories in Ukraine, Georgia, and other regions. As Liah Greenfield notes, nationalism invents the nation, based on an imaginary homogeneous or unitary people "which is seen as the bearer of sovereignty, the central object of loyalty, and the basis of collective solidarity."[9] Significantly, although the nation is the basis for individual identities, loyalty and solidarity should be paid first and foremost to the nation itself.[10]

Although Russia's nationalism, sometimes paradoxically paired with imperialism, is strikingly obvious, there is hardly any modern nation that is not deeply invested in similar structures following ideas of nationalistic superiority. Every nation is "an imagined political community,"[11] to quote Benedict Anderson. And "[i]f ever a nation was an imagined community, surely [it] is the United States of America"[12] which has reemerged as, or maybe always was, Russia's main adversary—certainly in the eyes of the Anglophone media.

---

6   Anne McClintock, "Family Feuds: Gender, Nationalism and the Family." *Feminist Review*, no. 44 (1993): 61.

7   Ibid.

8   Jon Greenberg, "Fact Check: Putin says Russians face 'genocide' in Ukraine," *WRAL*, February 28, 2022, https://www.wral.com/fact-check-putin-says-russians-face-genocide-in-ukraine/20163715/.

9   Liah Greenfield, *Nationalism: Five Roads to Modernity* (Cambridge, MA: Harvard University Press, 1992), 3.

10 John Fousek, *To Lead the Free World: American Nationalism and the Cultural Roots of the Cold War* (Chapel Hill: University of North Carolina Press, 2000), 5.

11 Anderson, *Imagined Communities*, 6.

12 Fousek, *To Lead the Free World*, 4.

While American nationalism shares many of the primary structural features of other nationalisms, it also differs from other nationalisms in certain ways. As I will show in what follows, these particularities are the reason why American nationalism is so invested in New Cold War discourses. One of the defining ideas of American nationalism is that of exceptionalism. Jewish American philosopher and historian Hans Kohn was one of the first to identify this idea, which lies at the heart of American nationalism. He argued that the idea, as it was laid out in the US Constitution, was an actualization of "the English tradition of liberty," which was transformed not only into the idea of American chosenness, mission, and destiny, but also into a kind of "a universal message" and model for the world.[13] Worldwide attention to the American Revolution and its integration into the philosophy of Enlightenment further disseminated this proclamation of "the rights of humankind,"[14] as the American studies scholar John Fousek calls it. It popularized the myth that "the 'discovery' and the subsequent settlement and colonization of the 'new world' [were] an inevitable step forward in the course of human progress,"[15] and planted it deeply within American national identity discourses. These discourses live on today, as Heike Paul, yet another American studies scholar, has pointed out.

The belief that "the United States has a unique and universal message of benefit to all the world"[16] would become a central theme in the Cold War. In his seminal study *To Lead the Free World: American Nationalism and the Cultural Roots of the Cold War*, the aforementioned Fousek shows that between the end of World War II and 1950, an increasingly cohesive nationalist ideology manifested itself. It was based on ideas of American exceptionalism, in competition with, and threatened by, Soviet Russia. This version of nationalism expanded the traditional nationalist ideas of destiny, chosenness, and mission into the "notion that the entire world was now the proper sphere of concern for US foreign policy."[17] Within this new scope of American nationalism, American values became a central cultural preoccupation. They were viewed as universal, and they legitimized the exercise of "extraordinary power globally."[18]

The US-American national narrative of exceptionalism is fundamentally entangled with discourses of (white) male superiority, masculinity and

---

13 Hans Kohn, *American Nationalism: An Interpretive Essay* (New York: The Macmillan Company, 1957), 8.
14 Fousek, *To Lead the Free World*, 5.
15 Heike Paul, *The Myths That Made America: An Introduction to American Studies* (Bielefeld: Transcript, 2014), 43.
16 Fousek, *To Lead the Free World*, 5.
17 Ibid., 7.
18 Ibid.

entitlement, capitalist competition, and the logic of male protectionism. Each of these separately, and in combination, were used to legitimize American expansionism and imperialism throughout its history. The ideas of exceptionalism and male protectionism, in particular, allow the American state to appear reluctant to intervene in the affairs of seemingly inferior foreign nations, as if their superiority forced them to become involved against their wishes or interests.

During the more than fifty years of political and ideological warfare with the Soviet Union, the propaganda that portrayed American values as universal and American capitalistic culture as universally desirable, as well as the cultural "othering" of the enemy, provided a legitimation for its continuation and its continued involvement in many proxy conflicts. Robert Dean,[19] Alan Nadel,[20] Kathleen Starck,[21] and many others have shown how tightly entangled ideas around American masculinity and discourses of American values became in politics and popular culture during the decades-long Cold War. Establishing the Soviet Union and communism as "Other" to the US nation and state reaffirmed and newly legitimized the male authority of the state as a father figure who must protect the nation from foreign threats and control it for its own good. The propagation of the myth of the "nuclear family as the universal container of democratic values, [...] made personal behavior part of a global strategy, at the same time as it personalized the international struggle with communism,"[22] with the breadwinner and father-protector as substitute for the American president, or America itself, within the smallest cell of the nation.

The "ideology of masculinity," as Dean calls it, structured political decisions domestically and abroad.[23] On a global level, new imperial alliances were formed to oppose the main opponent, the Soviet Union. Domestically, a "national security state" was established to contain the communist threat and guarantee "the expansion of a corporate capitalist world economic order."[24] The state, and an eagerly collaborating media apparatus, accomplished this task by deploying an "alarmist rhetoric to persuade the American public that the Soviets posed an immediate and direct threat to US interests and to world peace."[25] Misogyny, homophobia, and anti-intellectualism were important tools in the ideology of masculinity and its

---

19 Robert D. Dean, *Imperial Brotherhood: Gender and the Making of Cold War Foreign Policy* (Amherst, MA: University of Massachusetts Press, 2001).
20 Alan Nadel, *Containment Culture: American Narratives, Postmodernism, and the Atomic Age* (Durham, NC: Duke University Press, 1995).
21 Kathleen Starck, *Of Treason, God and Testicles: Political Masculinities in British and American Films of the Early Cold War* (Newcastle upon Tyne: Cambridge Scholars, 2016).
22 Nadel, *Containment Culture*, 11.
23 Dean, *Imperial Brotherhood*, 5.
24 Ibid.
25 Ibid., 63.

nationalistic propaganda, and furthered the goal of creating national unity against communism in favor of capitalist and military expansion. To emphasize the enemy status of the Soviet Union, US Cold War-era policy elites created the image of the "enemy within" as subversive cells of "effete 'cookie-pushing' Ivy league internationalist homosexuals and 'pinks.'"[26] Dean shows convincingly how within public discourses, "fears of domestic political subversion and foreign aggression" merged "with anxieties about the maintenance of domestic social and sexual order."[27] Looking back on these discursive strategies some decades later, it is almost ironic to see how contemporary Russian political discourses mirror these homo- and xenophobic nationalistic strategies.[28]

American Cold War homophobia during the second half of the twentieth century was fueled by a deliberate misinterpretation of Alfred Kinsey's findings—that homosexuality was more common than previously thought and that homosexual men did not commonly show feminine attributes (whatever those might be)—thereby creating the "national homosexual panic."[29] During the 1940s and 1950s, discourses on homosexuality became linked to countersubversive "Red Scare" rhetoric. Within these discourses, the notion of the subversion of society through communism became attached to the subversion of what were thought to be natural sexual relations. Like homosexuality, communism came to be represented as a relentless, expansionist, power hungry, evil foreign ideology, and was portrayed domestically as "an 'infection;' a conspiratorial, protean invasion of the boundaries of state and society, undermining national strength from within."[30] One of the most fatal of such cultural narratives, that of a homosexual communist menace threatening US sovereignty and superiority,

---

26 Ibid., 65.

27 Ibid.

28 For scholarly analyses, see Oleg Riabov and Tatiana Riabova, "The Decline of Gayropa?" *Eurozine*, February 5, 2014, 1–9, http://www.eurozine.com/the-decline-of-gayropa/; Emil Edenborg, "Homophobia as Geopolitics: 'Traditional Values' and the Negotiation of Russia's Place in the World," in *Gendering Nationalism: Intersections of Nation, Gender and Sexuality*, ed. Jon Mulholland, Erin Sanders-McDonagh, and Nicola Montagna (Cham: Palgrave Macmillan, 2018), 1–388; Masha Neufeld, and Katharina Wiedlack, "Visibility, Violence, and Vulnerability: Lesbians Stuck between the Post-Soviet Closet and the Western Media Space," in *LGBTQ+ Activism in Central and Eastern Europe*, ed. Radzhana Buyantueva and Maryna Shevtsova (Basingstoke: Palgrave Macmillan, 2019), 51–76.

29 Douglas Field, "Passing as a Cold War Novel: Anxiety and Assimilation in James Baldwin's *Giovanni's Room*," in *American Cold War Culture*, ed. Douglas Field (Edinburgh: Edinburgh University Press, 2005), 88–108, 89.

30 Dean, *Imperial Brotherhood*, 67.

was deployed during McCarthyism[31] and beyond. It was used to warrant the support of a unified nation, as well as to build and maintain control of this very same nation through a patriarchal security state.

The similarities to today's Russia, with its homophobic and anti-Western discourses, its legal restrictions on press and media freedoms, all of which go hand in hand with stark militarization, are eerie. Putin publicly announced that "Russia should undergo a 'self-cleansing of society' to get rid of the 'bastards and traitors,'" blaming "the collective West"[32] for inciting divisions within the country, when masses of people left Russia in reaction to the war in Ukraine. Only a few months after this announcement, lawmakers in the Russian Duma proposed legislation "extending a ban on the promotion of 'non-traditional' sexual relationships to minors to include adults as well."[33] After years of using homosexuality as a sign of Western corruption and moral decay, it was clearly understood that homosexuals and all other nonnormative people are part of the group of "bastards and traitors" that need to be eliminated. Unsurprisingly, in July 2023 the anti-LGBTIQ+ laws were further extended, barring access to transition for nonnormatively gendered people. "Aside from banning surgery and hormone therapy, the law also prohibits altering gender on official documents like passports, annuls any marriage when a spouse changes gender, and bans adoptions by such couples."[34]

During the 1950s in the US, the same people were targeted as dangerous traitors that needed to be exposed and eliminated. The House Un-American Activities Committee (HUAC) opened investigations into thousands of suspected gays and lesbians in the public service sector and beyond, alleging that they were "susceptible to blackmail by Soviet agents because they were

---

31 Joseph McCarthy was a US Senator, who agitated strongly against homosexuals and communists. McCarthyism usually refers to the late 1940s and the 1950s and the intensified political repression and persecution of left-wing individuals under the paranoid suspicion that they were Soviet agents.

32 Rebecca Cohen and Natalie Musumeci, "Putin says Russia must undergo a 'self-cleansing of society' to purge 'bastards and traitors' as thousands flee the country," *Business Insider*, March 16, 2022, https://www.businessinsider.com/putin-says-russia-must-undergo-self-cleansing-society-2022-3.

33 "Russian lawmakers propose extending 'gay propaganda' law to all adults," *Reuters*, https://www.reuters.com/world/europe/russian-lawmakers-propose-extending-gay-propaganda-law-all-adults-2022-07-11/.

34 Neil MacFarquhar, "Putin signs a harsh new law targeting transgender people in Russia," *New York Times*, July 24, 2023, https://www.nytimes.com/2023/07/24/world/europe/putin-transgender-transition-surgery-russia.html.

emotionally unstable."[35] These investigations often led to the loss of jobs in the government (including Hollywood blacklisting), social stigma, and oppression.

Numerous scholars have pointed out that throughout history, discourses on America's masculinity have proliferated whenever nationalism has been in jeopardy. Susan Jeffords has shown that the declining support of US nationalism during the late 1960s, and especially during the late Vietnam War years and after, was answered by a great effort to "remasculinize" America through a set of nationalistic discourses that attempted to establish the state as the male protector of a feminized nation.[36] Recent comments by right-wing hardliners offer evidence of how conservative politicians and political commentators continue to use patriarchal ideas of masculinity and femininity as a lens for evaluating US-military might within nationalistic discourses. In spring 2023, Senator Ted Cruz "circulated Russian propaganda" showing "shirtless men doing pushups or glowering paratroopers dropping from the skies"; he mocked "U.S. military recruiting efforts; and Fox News host Tucker Carlson is on the record complaining that the US military is 'more feminine' in comparison to the Chinese military's 'more masculine' nature."[37] These efforts attempt to alarm the public, the military, and the state about the danger of threats from outside, and push them to embrace and perpetuate militarized masculinity to protect a feminized US nation. As will be shown in the following chapters, in deploying this gendered logic, US conservatives reveal their alliance with what Kristina Stoeckl and Dmitry Uzlaner call the "moralist international."[38] They participate in a global cultural war that casts gender and sexual minorities as scapegoats and agitates for white patriarchal supremacy.

American Exceptionalism as Colonialism in Post-Soviet Russia

Nationalistic American Cold War discourses constructed Russia as a feminine nation under siege by a masculine Soviet enemy. The dissolution of the Soviet Union slightly changed this view, removing, as it were, the male Soviet aggressor, and thereby the threat. This did not mean, however, that the paranoid rhetoric of

---

35   Field, "Passing as a Cold War Novel," 89.

36   Susan Jeffords, *The Remasculinization of America: Gender and the Vietnam War* (Bloomington, IN: Indiana University Press, 1989), 12.

37   Blake Herzinger, "U.S. Right-Wingers Keep Confusing Culture War with Actual War," *Foreign Policy*, April 19, 2023, https://foreignpolicy.com/2023/04/19/us-military-culture-war-right-wing-russia-china-propaganda/.

38   Kristina Stoeckl and Dmitry Uzlaner, *The Moralist International: Russia in the Global Culture Wars* (Bronx, NY: Fordham University Press, 2022).

feminized American national vulnerability to gendered and sexualized (male, foreign) threats disappeared after the end of the Cold War. Since maintaining the idea of American exceptionalism and superiority requires a paranoid state of readiness to defend the nation at any moment from external and internal threats, American nationalism simply shifted the signification of the threat to other nations. This national concern continues to legitimize American imperialist (soft) politics that aim to shape the world according to the American model, often backed by military power. By means of this shift, the US could reaffirm its masculinity through a new relationship to Russia via Cold War triumphalism, deploying the narrative that the US had won the Cold War due to its seeming economic, military, and political superiority. Moreover, it found in post-Soviet Russia a helpless, feminized nation to be patronized through military, economic, and political interventions.

In her study of the gendered US cultural and political discourses on Russia from the 1990s to the early 2000s, Kimberly Williams[39] argues that US exceptionalism implies a strong desire to expand, if not territorially, then economically, in the form of capitalist globalization, as well as on the level of values. She suggests that in the post-Soviet sphere, and particularly in Russia, the US found the ideal territory to satisfy this desire. The rhetoric of a racialized, heteronormative, and gendered "language of colonial (masculinized) conquest justified by perceived (feminized) threats"[40] facilitates this nationalism based on exceptionalism and superiority. Reading *The Shock Doctrine: The Rise of Disaster Capitalism*,[41] Naomi Klein's analysis of the US-led economic reforms in Russia during the 1990s, Williams identified an astonishing resemblance between the American pastoral narratives of Western expansionism of the eighteenth and nineteenth centuries and the expansionist policies of the neoliberalism Klein describes.[42] Moreover, Klein's views about the facilitation of the "transition" from communism to capitalism as a form of American colonialism[43] allows Williams to identify US involvement in the hurried and intentional dismantling of communism as a continuation of the gendered logic of American nationalism.[44] With American support, a small group of what Klein calls "corporate conquistadors"[45] was able

---

39 Kimberly A. Williams, *Imagining Russia: Making Feminist Sense of American Nationalism in U.S.-Russian Relations* (Albany: State University of New York Press, 2012), 12.
40 Ibid., 182.
41 Naomi Klein, *The Shock Doctrine: The Rise of Disaster Capitalism* (New York: Metropolitan Books, 2007).
42 Williams, *Imagining Russia*, 183.
43 Klein, *The Shock Doctrine*, 220.
44 Williams, *Imagining Russia*, 182.
45 Klein, *The Shock Doctrine*, 241.

to collect (more precisely, steal) a large number of state assets and gain great wealth, while the rest of the Russian population was subjected to increasing poverty. In just eight years, "72 million people"[46] were impoverished by the Russian economic reforms, rampant alcohol and drug consumption, the rapid spread of HIV/AIDS, and the skyrocketing violent crime that ensued.

Significantly for the subject of this study, Williams,[47] Anatol Lieven,[48] and others demonstrate how US-American popular and political culture continued to construct and disseminate notions of Russia as an enemy nation striving to regain its superpower status in the world, despite the obvious fact that in the 1990s the Russian military and economic structures were on the brink of collapse, and in parallel to American triumphalism that declared the Russian enemy to be dead. The paranoid notion that the US was still in danger of falling prey to the possibly still dangerous enemy of Russia also legitimized US self-involvement in Russia's nation-building process, as well as the mission-like dissemination of American values within this sovereign country. By the mid- to late nineties, when it became clear that America's Russia policies had failed in their goals, the US media and US politicians launched a narrative about "communist hardliners" who had prevented a successful "transition to [capitalist] democracy" due to their "Soviet mentality" and corruption.[49]

Ironically, the rhetorical strategies that justified the continuation of what came to be known as "shock" or "disaster capitalism" not only brought the former KGB officer Vladimir Putin to power, but enabled him "to circumnavigate democratic processes by cracking down on political dissent that threatened to undermine economic reform."[50] Additionally, and most obviously, the paranoid expansionism and self-aggrandizement of these political strategies nurtured the American cultural myth that "Russia [continued to be] an obstructive and backward"[51] woman, and that the militarized masculine American state must therefore protect Russia from itself. US discourses thereby anticipated the Russian expansionism that started with the formal Russian annexation of the Georgian territories of South Ossetia and Abkhazia in 2008, fifteen years later.

---

46   Ibid., 238.
47   Williams, *Imagining Russia*, 183.
48   Anatol Lieven, *America Right or Wrong: An Anatomy of American Nationalism* (New York: Oxford University Press, 2004), 158.
49   Klein, *The Shock Doctrine*, 240, 226.
50   Williams, *Imagining Russia*, 183.
51   Ibid.

Both narratives—Russia as 1) the evil enemy that threatens US sovereignty and 2) Russia as an expansionist or colonial power purporting to bring aid and peace to the world—have never ceased to circulate within American mainstream media and culture. The idea of a feminized Russian nation and people is still in circulation within US popular culture, usually connected to female or queer figures, often migrants, who embody the perfect victims in need of saving (colonizing) and offer a kind of mirror for showing US-American cultural superiority, as I show in subsequent chapters. The young Russian state of the 1990s and early 2000s, however, previously feminized, impotent, broken, needy, and only mildly threatening, is now increasingly seen as masculine and very dangerous. Indeed, in today's US media, the Russian state is embodied in its president, who is shown to be a superhuman, Terminator-like mega-villain. The purpose of this new (old) narrative is to remasculinize the state, stabilizing the notion of a potent, safe, and superior male US state and solidifying its citizens' loyalty to their nation and state in times of domestic crisis. This strategy is not new, and the Russian state, under the leadership of President Putin, is surely not the only enemy the US media and officials are currently constructing. Jasbir Puar, Joseph Massad, Chandan Reddy, and many others have analyzed the gendered, sexualized, and racialized logic of the nationalism that "others" nations with predominantly Muslim populations.[52] Less attention, however, has been given to the "othering" of Russia.

In what follows, I will show how US national identity, purportedly morally superior and united, is shaped through the "othering" of Russia, citing various examples, for example, Russian hacking activity during the 2016 US presidential elections. Many of these discourses of Russian "othering" seem to refer in one way or another to the image of Putin. To put it differently, the figure of Vladimir Putin serves as the embodiment of Russian "badness." Such processes are reflected within political discourses and popular culture, prompting a sense of the moral superiority of the US and loyalty to the idea of the US as a bastion of progressive values.

---

52 Jasbir Puar, *Terrorist Assemblages: Homonationalism in Queer Times* (Durham, NC.: Duke University Press, 2007); Jasbir Puar, "Rethinking Homonationalism," *Middle East Studies* 45, no. 2 (2013): 336–339; Joseph A. Massad, *Desiring Arabs* (Chicago, IL: The University of Chicago Press, 2007); Chandan Reddy, *Freedom with Violence: Race, Sexuality, and the US State* (Durham, NC: Duke University Press, 2011).

The New Othering of Russia, or, Public Masculinities: Putin, Trump, Obama, and (New) Cold War Nationalism[53]

The rhetorical signification of a (morally) "bad" Russia and its threat to the US is made clear in the image below.

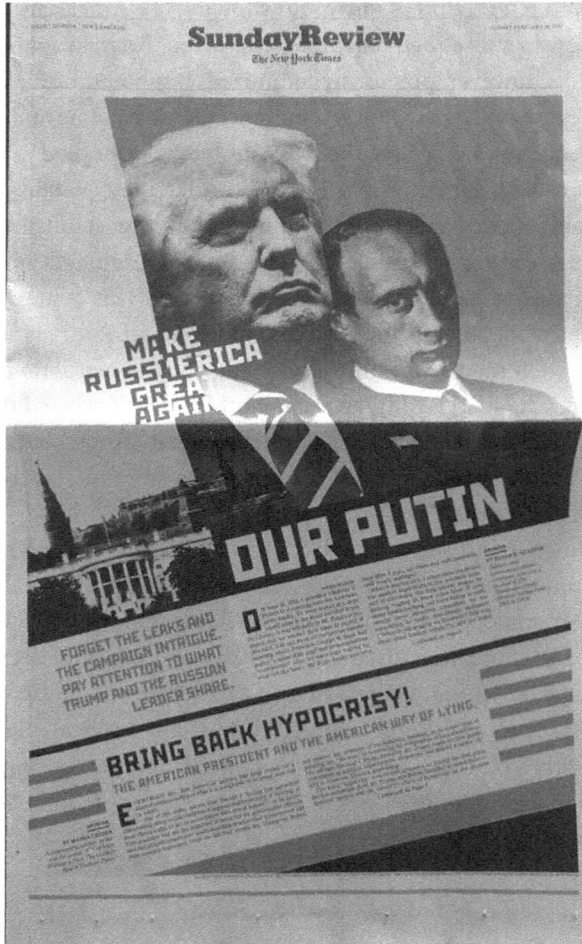

Figure 1. Screenshot of a photo in the *New York Times*, February 21, 2017. See "New Mexico Burns," Coffee Spoons, accessed December 12, 2024, http://coffeespoons.me/tag/print/.

---

53   Many ideas of this chapter have been previously discussed in the article: Katharina Wiedlack, "Enemy number one or gay clown? The Russian president, masculinity and populism in US media," *Norma* 15, no. 1 (2020): 59–75, https://doi:10.1080/18902138.2019.1707459.

Trump's proximity to Putin signifies unequivocally that the former is "bad by association." The signal word "Russia" and the red-and-black coloring, support this meaning; but readers, no matter what the coloring, and even without words, would have identified Putin as the Russian enemy and male aggressor.

The persistence of this gendered logic inherited from the Cold War becomes very visible in the liberal media, particularly political comedy. As I will show, with examples from *The Simpsons* to *Saturday Night Live*, political comedy draws on notions of a feminized US-nation under threat by Russia. Interestingly enough, these shows ridicule the Russian threat by satirizing Putin and depicting him as gay. Like nationalistic forces at the height of the Cold War, such liberal media conceptualizes the US as feminized and hence as "vulnerable to threats, which are also feminized—making them, by their very nature, both dangerous and easy to defeat,"[54] thus legitimizing US aggression towards Russia. Ironically, the patriarchal exercise of masculine economic and military power becomes sanctioned or legitimized through a rhetoric of equality and progressive liberal values (in comedy that is extremely homophobic!). This was most obvious in the sanctions against Russia by the Obama administration in the wake of the 'Anti-Homosexual Propaganda' laws and annexation of Crimea; but it also becomes visible in TV shows and films. The strategy of feminizing Russia, however, is not the same as assigning it femininity as such. Although there is an attempt to feminize Russian state power, the symbol of this power, President Putin, the Russian state apparatus, and, at times, the whole Russian nation are perceived as masculine. This menacing masculinity needs to be neutered or castrated through suggestions of homoerotic desire, or, more explicitly, homosexuality. One example of such a usage of homosexual acts as a spoof was an extremely popular sketch on *The Late Show with Stephen Colbert* called "Cartoon Trump and Cartoon Putin Make First Joint Public Appearance."[55] In the clip, released in the fall of 2016, Colbert talks to the cartoon version of the president-elect Donald Trump about his ties to Russia. All the answers are whispered into Trump's ear by the cartoon version of Russian president Putin. In the end, Putin rips off his shirt and hypnotizes Trump with his "d-cup man-bosom," before they start passionately making out.

I wish to re-emphasize my argument that the visualizations of Vladimir Putin and the references to his masculinity within political discourses in Russia and beyond—although at times comical and mocking—serve to "other" Russia as a

---

54 Williams, *Imagining Russia*, 31.
55 "Cartoon Trump and Cartoon Putin Make First Joint Public Appearance," *The Late Show with Stephen Colbert*, November 17, 2016, CBS, https://www.youtube.com/watch?v=0aU3kX5V634.

sphere of foreign and incompatible values and a source of political, moral, and military danger to the US. Through such othering, US-American national identity becomes constructed, although not exclusively by the liberal media, which seems generally more careful in the dissemination of nationalistic and patriotic rhetoric than the conservative media does.

Arguably, no naked male torso, its "real" as well as its diverse cartoon versions, has ever been exhibited as widely in the US news media, academic books, or popular culture as Russian president Vladimir Putin's—at least, not that of any other politician. Many political commentators and scholars have suggested that the media's intense focus on Putin's "man-bosom" is not simply an example of how public bodies become commoditized through the sensationalistic, visually oriented global media. They suggest, rather, that it is part of a deftly organized and extremely successful rebranding of President Putin and, by association, Russia as manly and potent, which caught on in Russia and quickly traveled across the Atlantic and to the rest of the world. Commentators agree that the frequent displays of images of strong masculinity in the Russian media—for example, the "pictures of a horse riding, bare-chested Putin"—are an integral "part of a political discourse, [and] play an important role in contemporary Russian politics and history, and are key to understanding Vladimir Putin's Russia."[56] In her exhaustive study on gender norms in Russian political discourse, Valery Sperling argues that during the first two decades of the new millennium, state discourses focused successfully on "Putin's machismo" as "a legitimation strategy"[57] for policies. These discourses succeeded in connecting "the country's increased standard of living and Russia's resurgent assertion of power in the former Soviet states"[58] to the image of Putin, who in turn was increasingly signified as masculine, potent, and virile. This celebration of Putin's machismo created a huge wave of support, not only for the Russian president, but also for "family values, military might, and national-patriotic pride."[59]

President Putin managed to deploy the cultural gender norms and discourses of signification in quite a blunt, but clearly effective, way. During the mid-2010s, his embodiment of masculinity was so popular that Sperling, or perhaps her publisher, could not resist depicting it on the cover of her study, addressing an Anglophone market that was willing to 'buy' Putin's masculinity. It is no secret that

---

56 Erik Vlaeminc, "Masculinity Politics in Putin's Russia," *New Eastern Europe*, October 12, 2016, http://neweasterneurope.eu/articles-and-commentary/2152-masculinity-politics-in-putin-s-russia.

57 Valerie Sperling, *Sex, Politics, and Putin: Political Legitimacy in Russia* (Oxford: Oxford University Press, 2014), 3.

58 Ibid.

59 Ibid.

normative masculinity signifies power in patriarchal societies and that the display of "traditional masculinity," to use Sperling's terminology, "enables male political leaders (and some female ones, as well) to assert their power over others."[60] Many past presidents used the display of bodily masculinity before Putin did, not least former US-American president George W. Bush. With his self-fashioning as a "hegemonic masculine heroic protector,"[61] Bush preceded the current Russian president by a couple of years. Both he and Putin performed a strong, hegemonic masculinity in order to render their nation and people, as well as their enemies, "as traditionally feminine,"[62] hence weaker and/or more submissive. Within such a political environment, "actors in contests over power [. . .] can readily adopt the use of gender norms—including machismo, homophobia, [...] gay-baiting,"[63] and misogyny, as a successful legitimation tool. Many American presidents, from Ronald Reagan to George W. Bush, focused on the embodiment of hegemonic masculinity,[64] in contrast to others, who drew attention to their superior male intellect—President Barack Obama, for example. So why is the US media so obsessed with the display of masculinity of a Russian president? What does it say about the Western, and specifically the liberal US, gaze on Russia that the image of a shirtless Putin comes up in popular media again and again?

In the following chapter, I analyze the current trends of visualizing Russian men and their masculinity within the US-American media, starting with Russian president Vladimir Putin. I show how depictions of his male body, through references to his deployment of masculinity within political discourses, serve to "other" Russia as a sphere of alien values and source of political, moral, and military danger to the US. This strategy of othering by liberals, legitimizes the US-American national identity, while managing to avoid accusations of nationalism.

Russia and the End of the WASP

"Do Not Be Fooled by Recent Struggles. Russia Poses a Direct Threat to America and Her Interests," warned journalist Benjamin Weingarten in *TheBlaze*.[65] In his article, which accompanied "The Root: Red Storm," a three-part series aired on

---

60 Ibid., 4.
61 James Messerschmidt, *Hegemonic Masculinities and Camouflaged Politics: Unmasking the Bush Dynasty and Its War against Iraq* (Boulder, CO: Paradigm Publishers, 2010), 112.
62 Ibid.
63 Sperling, *Sex, Politics, and Putin*, 4.
64 Messerschmidt, *Hegemonic Masculinities and Camouflaged Politics*, 1.
65 Benjamin Weingarten, "Do Not Be Fooled by Recent Struggles. Russia Poses a Direct Threat to America and Her Interests," *TheBlaze*, January 13, 2015, http://www.theblaze.com/

TheBlaze TV, he appealed to his fellow Americans, and the government, that "[i]n order to effectively deal with Russia, as with the Islamic world, America must understand the country's goals, strategies, and tactics. Only then can we devise a coherent plan to deter the threat, and with it, preserve Western civilization." The emotional cast of his writing overtly reactivates Cold War rhetoric, even resorting to past symbols and metaphors, and his stance is clearly populist, even by the currently very low standards of mainstream media. Interestingly, however, and indeed indicative of most current political analysis of Russian politics, the piece is accompanied by, among other things, a photo of Vladimir Putin, presenting him in a very masculine pose: namely, arm wrestling.

The stoking of fear towards Russia in the US news media featured many pictures that were meant to illustrate the threat posed by Putin in action. These pictures did not just give the threat a face; they also provided a hegemonically masculine body, performing very masculine tasks. Yes, the Russian media provided these pictures, and the US media had only to access them from the Internet. The interesting fact, however, is that the pictures were not targeted at the foreign media; rather, one might argue, they had a very Russian internal focus. Andrew Foxall analyses how the holiday photographs of Vladimir Putin released by the Kremlin in 2007, 2009, and 2010 successfully popularized a new male body-politics in Russia.[66] They militarized and sexualized masculinity, and linked it to Russian nationalism in a previously unseen way, helping to construct "a dominant Russian identity and political narrative that is highly masculinized and is at once both individual (Putin) and universal (Putin 'as' Russia)."[67] Foxall insists that the photographs of Putin are not simply a result or reflection of Russian politics, but that "they are also political, both manifesting and enabling power relations that are not so much about Russia's role and place in the world as they are about linking Putin's virility to a masculinized and militarized image of Russia."[68] Gaining currency through their circulation, these photographs, Foxall argues, need to be understood in connection with Putin's performances of masculinity, including during the Second Chechen War; his language, which frequently includes profanity and "street" talk; and his threats

---

contributions/do-not-be-fooled-by-recent-struggles-russia-poses-a-direct-threat-to-amer-ica-and-her-interests/.

66   Andrew Foxall, "Photographing Vladimir Putin: Masculinity, Nationalism and Visuality in Russian Political Culture," *Geopolitics* 18, no. 1 (2013): 132–156.

67   Ibid., 151.

68   Ibid.

of violence towards his opponents (including the press), as well as their 'de-masculinization,' in his speeches.

The availability of the pictures, and their usage within Russia, does not, however, entirely or sufficiently explain why various US media outlets chose to illustrate their political pieces with pictures of Putin carrying out his manly leisure activities, and not the usual men in suits. In order to answer the question why Putin's masculinity is so interesting for the US media, we need to reflect on the US political and social context, and the national state of hegemonic masculinity. The media attention given to Putin and his masculine body emerges at the intersection of social frictions and political differences concerning current changes within the socioeconomic strata of the US. Despite the fact that so-called culture war discourses have circulated in the US media since at least the 1950s,[69] they arguably gained new traction from 2010 onwards.

Identity politics connected to gender, sexuality, and race are now at the center of American culture wars, which appear to divide the US public, tearing it into two different political and philosophical camps. One side of the conflict is populated by those who advocate for more openness toward minorities and deeper engagement with global issues. Many of them define themselves as liberals or Democrats. Opposed to them are those who wish to preserve traditional hierarchies that have come under threat within large segments of society by closing off the nation state, economically and socially, shutting its borders, and strictly controlling the movement of people and goods. Many of these traditionalists define themselves as conservatives, others as working class; but it would be too simplistic to subsume the totality of the group in either or both of those labels. Many individuals within this group feel represented by, or are attracted to, Donald Trump; but by no means all of them. The common denominator for these conservatives, or preservationists, including both Trump supporters and those of his current Republican rivals, such as Florida governor Ron DeSantis, who strongly agitate against liberal values and openness,[70] is their fear of the deconstruction of white supremacist patriarchal capitalism and with it the loss of white male privilege. While DeSantis might be slightly more coy about his white supremacism (and perhaps more outspoken about his disdain for liberal ideas concerning gender and sexuality), Trump's notorious presidential

---

69 Kiara Alfonseca, "Culture wars: How identity became the center of politics in America," *BBC News,* July 7, 2023, https://abcnews.go.com/US/culture-wars-identity-center-politics-america/story?id=100768380.

70 Scott Detrow, "DeSantis and the culture wars," *NPR,* March 26, 2023, https://www.npr.org/2023/03/26/1166141385/desantis-and-the-culture-wars.

campaign slogan, "Make America Great Again," is easy to identify as in favor of defending white male hegemony.[71] What seems to be at stake is not only white male hegemony, but, indeed, what it means to be, to have, and to (be in) control as a white man in contemporary America.

Hegemonic masculinity is a myth; it is a symbolic, though consistently legitimatized, ideal type of masculinity. This symbolic ideal of masculinity has little to do with the variety of individually lived, enacted, and embodied masculinities of real, existing people. Yet this symbolic masculinity structures and determines the coherence and meanings of all other masculinities (and femininities), with their corresponding identities and positioning within the gender order—the "historically constructed pattern of power relations between men and women."[72] Raewyn W. Connell rejects the conceptual singularity of masculinity, understanding it, rather, as a socially constructed multiplicity. However, within the multiplicity of types, hegemonic masculinity persists as a symbolic ideal and reference point. Moreover, despite the fact that this ideal is a cultural construct, "it becomes essentialized and, ultimately, reified as the benchmark against which all men must gauge their success in the gender order."[73]

Masculinity studies scholars[74] agree that hegemonic masculinity always includes a strategy for the subordination of females. It is a culturally idealized form, simultaneously personal and collective. It is "the common sense about breadwinning and manhood."[75] It is necessarily exclusive, competitive, "tough," "internally and hierarchically differentiated, brutal and violent."[76] Moreover,

---

71   Sam Levine, "Bill Clinton Says 'Make America Great Again' Is Just a Racist Dog Whistle," *Huffington Post*, September 8, 2016, http://www.huffingtonpost.com/entry/bill-clinton-make-america-great-again_us_57d06ccfe4b0a48094a749fc. Marlow Stern, "Ethan Hawke on Violence, Masculinity, and Donald Trump's 'Fascist Behavior,'" *Daily Beast*, October 24, 2016, http://www.thedailybeast.com/articles/2016/10/24/ethan-hawke-on-violence-masculinity-and-donald-trump-s-fascist-behavior.html.

72   Raewyn W. Connell, *Gender and Power: Society, the Person and Sexual Politics* (Cambridge: Polity Press, 1987), 98.

73   Richard Howson, *Challenging Hegemonic Masculinity* (London: Routledge, 2006), 3.

74   Connell, *Gender and Power*; Raewyn W. Connell, *Masculinities* (St. Leonards, MD: Allen and Unwin, 1995); Raewyn W. Connell, *The Men and the Boys* (St. Leonards, MD: Allen and Unwin, 2000); Tim Carrigan, Bob Connell, and John Lee, "Toward a new sociology of masculinity," in *The Making of Masculinities: the New Men's Studies*, ed. Harry Brod (Winchester, VA: Allen and Unwin, 1987); Mike Donaldson, "What is hegemonic masculinity?" *Theory and Society* 22 (1993): 643–657; Michael Messner, *Politics of Masculinities: Men in Movements* (Thousand Oaks, CA: Sage Publications, 1997); Messerschmidt, *Masculinities in the Making*; Messerschmidt, *Hegemonic Masculinities and Camouflaged Politics*.

75   Donaldson, "What is hegemonic masculinity?" 645.

76   Ibid.

hegemonic masculinity is pseudo-objective, "crisis-prone and socially sustained," despite its contradictions.[77] Hegemonic masculinity is hierarchically structured along the lines of class, sexuality, and racialization. It is based on structures of male dominance, and although not all men perform it, most men benefit from it in one way or the other. Furthermore, hegemonic masculinity has economic and cultural dimensions, and a certain social structure. "Fragile, [but r]esilient, it incorporates its own critiques, but it is, nonetheless, 'unraveling.'"[78]

In postindustrial, US-America, the politics of gender, and, accordingly, the way in which actual men (and other genders) relate to hegemonic masculinity, has altered significantly. Through the impact of second-wave feminism, the LGBTIQ+ movement, and Black and People of Color (BIPOC) movements, among others, alternative models and ideals of male gender identities have gained significant ground within large segments of society. In his study of men and masculinities in popular culture, Kenneth MacKinnon summarizes the multiple alterations of more acceptable and appealing version of masculinity since the 1970s as the phenomenon of "the new man."[79] Although alternative models and ideals of male gender identities have become more popular, a hegemonic masculinity that emphasizes white, male, able-bodied superiority persists as biologically based gender delineations have not yet been abandoned, despite the celebration of, or outcry against, their alleged decline.

The reaction to the changes in perceptions of gender within public culture, and the normalization of "the new man" model, created, however, what David Savran terms "white male paranoia."[80] He argues that the loss of the Vietnam War, the emergence of the second wave of the women's movement, the considerable successes of the civil rights movement and the gay and lesbian rights movements, and the end of the post-World War II economic boom of the mid-1970s resulted in great anxieties on the part of white US-American men. He traces this paranoia to 1993, the year of its public acknowledgement in the United States. This was a turning point, he argues, after which events such as the Oklahoma City bombing were framed by "the popular concept of white male as victim and the paramilitary Right"[81] in discussions in the media. McKinnon identifies this

---

77 Ibid.
78 Ibid., 646.
79 Kenneth MacKinnon, *Representing Men: Maleness and Masculinity in the Media* (London: Arnold, 2003), 15.
80 David Savran, "The Sadomasochist in the Closet: White Masculinity and the Culture of Victimisation," *Differences: A Journal of Feminist Cultural Studies* 8, no. 2 (1996): 128.
81 Ibid.

discourse as "a reverse of the feminist theme of the personal as political, so that the complexities of political and socioeconomic change are made personal."[82] Interestingly, when the US economy went into recession in 2008 and economic inequality rose sharply, many authors began focusing on less privileged Americans, declaring it as a crisis for white America, and especially white male America. Political scientists such as Charles Murray, Robert D. Putnam, and many others pointed to "The American Dream in Crisis,"[83] and saw white male America "Coming Apart."[84] Their research supported media discourses that identified white, less privileged males as the major losers in the most recent economic downturn and the concomitant cultural crisis.

American libertarian Charles Murray and Robert D. Putnam focused on the rise in male unemployment, notwithstanding research by Stephanie Seguino, feminist economist and United Nations, as well as World Bank, advisor. Her research demonstrated that nonwhite females bore the greatest burden of the economic decline after 2008, followed by nonwhite men and white women.[85] Murray and Putnam's sensationalistic book titles and widespread publicity bolstered the idea that white US-American men are an endangered demographic, an idea that steadily manifested within public opinion. Stories "about a surge in opiate addiction among white Americans, alongside shocking reports of rising mortality rates (including by suicide) among middle-aged whites"[86] fueled this sentiment, suggesting that the cause of this health crisis was "the perceived and real loss of the social and economic advantages of being white" and male.[87]

But what does Vladimir Putin have to do with these paranoid (or cautiously hopeful) discourses about the decline, or end, of white male America? Arguably, a great deal. Agitators on the Right began referring to Putin's virility

---

82 MacKinnon, *Representing Men*, 15.

83 Robert D. Putnam, *Our Kids: The American dream in crisis that looked at issues of inequality of opportunity in the US* (New York: Simon & Schuster, 2015).

84 Charles Murray, *Coming Apart: The State of White America, 1960–2010* (New York: Crown Forum, 2012).

85 Stephanie Seguino and James Heintz, "Monetary Tightening and the Dynamics of Race and Gender Stratification in the US," *American Journal of Economics and Sociology* 71, no. 3 (2012): 603.

86 Alec Macgillis, "The original underclass: Poor white Americans' current crisis shouldn't have caught the rest of the country as off guard as it has," *Atlantic*, September 2016, https://www.theatlantic.com/magazine/archive/2016/09/the-original-underclass/492731/.

87 Josh Marshall, "You Can't Understand American Politics without Reading This Study," *TalkingPointsMemo*, December 1, 2015, http://talkingpointsmemo.com/edblog/you-can-t-understand-american-politics-without-reading-this-study.

and authority as an enemy threat, and, on occasion, as a positive role model.[88] "The weakness being demonstrated by the West is exposing the crying need for stronger leadership," Gerald Flurry, editor in chief of the *Philadelphia Trumpet,* a Christian monthly magazine, wrote in a cover article in May 2015.[89] He gave voice to the public discourse on the decline of white masculinity in the US, suggesting it would lead to the decline of civilization in the face of hostile "others," such as Putin's Russia and a range of countries with predominantly Muslim populations. In other words, the reference to Putin's (and others') masculinity legitimized the desire for masculine dominance in the US, and dominance by the US of the rest of the world.

The obsession with Putin's masculinity might, indeed, have come from a place of envy on the part of white supremacists and beyond, as Sperling has suggested.[90] *Forbes Magazine* listed Vladimir Putin four times in a row as the most powerful person in the world. *Time* devoted at least ten covers, between 2001 and 2017, to the face or full figure of Vladimir Putin (and a couple more to Russia as headliner). CNN created a photo gallery of "The Cult of Putin" showing Putin working out, hunting a tiger, and so on.[91] Most of these snapshots of a "bare-chested Putin fishing, riding, and climbing trees" were taken on his Siberian vacations in summer 2009 and were part of the aforementioned PR campaign to establish Putin's status as "Russia's ultimate celebrity," in the phrase of Helena Goscilo.[92] Interestingly, the US media continued to disseminate these images over the course of ten years. The last time I saw them was on January 19, 2017 on Comedy Central's *Daily Show with Trevor Noah.*

Indeed, the conservative media was not alone in frequently referring to and showing images of Vladimir Putin. Some of the loudest voices identifying

---

88   Valerlie Sperling, "A Case of Putin Envy: Behind the Obsession with Russia's Leader," *Foreign Affairs,* November 5, 2015, https://www.foreignaffairs.com/articles/russian-federation/2015-11-05/case-putin-envy; Jeremy Diamond, "Timeline: Donald Trump's praise for Vladimir Putin," CNN, July 29, 2016, http://www.cnn.com/2016/07/28/politics/donald-trump-vladimir-putin-quotes/; Travis, "Keith Olbermann: Trump wants to mimic Putin and turn White House press briefings into chaotic circus," *Rawstory,* January 19, 2017, http://www.rawstory.com/2017/01/keith-olbermann-trump-wants-to-mimic-putin-and-turn-white-house-press-briefings-into-chaotic-circus/.

89   Gerald Flurry, "How can leaderless Europe survive in a world of strong men?" *Philadelphia Trumpet,* May–June 2015, 2.

90   Sperling, "A Case of Putin Envy."

91   "The Cult of Putin," CNN, December 25, 2015, http://www.cnn.com/2012/03/02/europe/gallery/cult-of-vladimir-putin/.

92   Helena Goscilo, "Russia's Ultimate Celebrity: VVP as VIP Objet d'Art," in *Putin as Celebrity and Cultural Icon,* ed. Helena Groscilo (London: Routledge, 2013), 6.

Vladimir Putin as the source of all evil, at home and abroad, came from the liberal side of the political spectrum.[93] These commentators also emphasized Putin's masculinity. The othering of Russia as a masculine threat came to the forefront around the 2016 US presidential election, as I have already suggested. A media (including political comedy) that was almost unanimously opposed to or at least critical of Donald Trump began connecting Vladimir Putin to Trump in order to delegitimize him, at the same time casting the Russian's presidency as a danger to the security of the US. Dominic Basulto summarized the situation poignantly, saying that "old Cold War neocons reliving the 1980s and the disappointed liberal supporters of Hillary Clinton, [i]n some bizarre marriage of political convenience," created a Trump-Putin narrative that featured Putin as "the ultimate cartoon villain."[94]

From Putin to Icarus—the *Killing Machine* (2010): Imagining Russian Strong Men[95]

By January 2017, marking the inauguration of Donald Trump as forty-fifth US president, the idea that Russia was being led by a dangerous male aggressor had been sufficiently established. Indeed, it had been so popular in the media and among the political opposition, that the image of Putin was continually used to denigrate and ridicule Trump and to emphasize the danger he posed for the country. Some media outlets used Russian symbols to signify the connection between Donald Trump and the "Evil Empire," to cite Ronald Reagan's famous words. For example, on the title page of its website from November 1, 2016, the *Huffington Post* featured an image of Trump against the background of the iconic St. Basil's Cathedral on Moscow's Red Square. Other news sources, however, were less restrained in visualizing the connection. One image, which went viral in May 2016, was a mural by Lithuanian street artist Mindaugas Bonanu. The mural was commissioned by a Vilnius restaurant owner for the wall of his

---

93 Evan Osnos, David Remnick, and Joshua Yaffa, "Trump, Putin, and the New Cold War: What lay behind Russia's interference in the 2016 election—and what lies ahead?" *New Yorker*, March 6, 2017, http://www.newyorker.com/magazine/2017/03/06/trump-putin-and-the-new-cold-war?mbid=synd_digg.

94 Dominic Basulto, "What the Media Gets Dangerously Wrong about the Trump-Putin Narrative," December 18, 2016, https://medium.com/@dominicbasulto/what-the-media-gets-dangerously-wrong-about-the-trump-putin-narrative-45771aa5f9e4#.s2ciclp8b.

95 A version of this chapter has been published as Katharina Wiedlack, "Enemy number one or gay clown? The Russian president, masculinity and populism in US media," *Norma* 15, no. 1 (2020): 59–75, https://doi:10.1080/18902138.2019.1707459.

business. Various reproductions of the mural were distributed through social, as well as global, news media—*Buzzfeed News*,[96] *Esquire*,[97] the *Huffington Post*,[98] the *Washington Post*,[99] and many others—almost immediately after its completion.

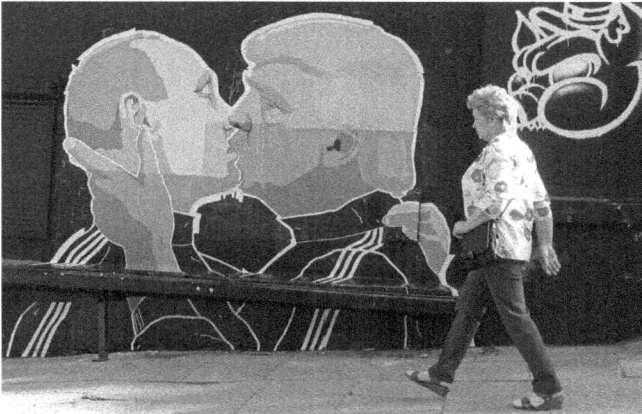

Figure 2. Trump and Putin kissing in a mural by Lithuanian street artist Artist Mindaugas Bonanu, Vilnius. Photo by Mindaugas Kulbi, Associated Press.

The image alludes to the famous 1979 photograph of Soviet leader Leonid Brezhnev kissing Erich Honecker, then leader of East Germany, on the mouth, which was customary for Soviet men at the time. "This 'fraternal kiss' between the two Cold War-era communist leaders was immortalized in a famous piece of graffiti on the East Side gallery of the Berlin wall."[100] The picture of Trump and Putin draws on this historic representation, which was symbolically so central for the remembrance of the Cold War, thereby reactivating Cold War thinking. Simultaneously, it draws on the far more recent history of homophobia in

96 Tasneem Nashrulla, "Trump and Putin Kiss Passionately on A Wall. Not that kind of wall," *BuzzFeed News*, May 14, 2016, https://www.buzzfeed.com/tasneemnashrulla/putin-out?utm_term=.hfAOnJANL#.booldDYex.

97 Elizabeth Griffin, "Here's Donald Trump and Vladimir Putin Kissing," *Esquire*, May 15, 2016, http://www.esquire.com/news-politics/news/a44886/political-street-art/.

98 Jan M. Olsen, "Trump and Putin: Lithuanian Artist Makes Massive Poster of Two Leaders Smooching," *Huffington Post*, May 14, 2016, http://www.huffingtonpost.ca/2016/05/14/trump-kissing-putin_n_9973944.html.

99 Adam Taylor, "The Putin-Trump Kiss Being Shared around the World," *Washington Post*, May 13, 2016, https://www.washingtonpost.com/news/worldviews/wp/2016/05/13/the-putin-trump-kiss-being-shared-around-the-world/?utm_term=.0f3d8c6433ef.

100 Red iLyke, "Donald Trump Kisses Vladimir Putin on Wall of Lithuanian Restaurant," iLyke, May 16, 2016, http://ilyke.com/donald-trump-kisses-vladimir-putin-on-wall-of-lithuanian-restaurant/79893#ixzz4ZGnPNPdk.

Russia, and the 'queering' of its president, in order to reject him and 'the anti-gay propaganda laws' through various activist actions; for example, through the creation of the 'Vladimir Pu$$y' image.

Figure 3: "Vladimir Pu$$y," posted on the Claude Charlier's blog *Musicologie.org,* August 18, 2012, https://www.musicologie.org/actu/2012/08/18.html.

Sadly, these and other images circulated on social media, demonstrations, and other street protests, drawing on a transphobic visual language that uses feminization and gender transgression as means of denigration. As much as they ridicule the Russian president, they also generate assumptions about Russia, its leader, and, in the case of the Lithuanian mural, his connections to, or, indeed, feelings towards, Donald Trump.

George Gerbner argues that the media is the major producer and provider of images of foreign nationals for American audiences; hence, the knowledge that most Americans have about Russia reflects the view created by the media. In his study of the US media views on Russia from the end of World War II to the 1990s, Gerbner concludes that the depictions of foreign countries in US media outlets by and large conformed to those of US government policy, using government sources as the main source of information.[101] According to

---

101 George Gerbner, "The Image of Russians in American Media and the 'New Epoch,'" in *Beyond the Cold War: Soviet and American Media Images,* ed. Everette E. Dennis, George Gerbner, and Yassen N. Zassoursky (London: Sage Publications, 1991) 31–35, 32.

the official Cold War perspective on Russia, the mainstream media and its audiences viewed Russia as an enemy country. While the origin and use of sources changed significantly in the course of the 2000s, the media still reflected the government's stance on Russia before and during the leadership of Barack Obama. References to Russia were increasingly used to signify undemocratic, corrupt, or just plain 'bad' tendencies or people within the US by the administration and media. This media tendency was evident, as already mentioned, in the connections drawn between Donald Trump and Vladimir Putin. Shortly before leaving office in January 2017, Obama imposed unprecedented sanctions on Russia in response to the Russian interference in the 2016 election. The Obama administration deemed Russia's involvement to be "Significant Malicious Cyber-Enabled Activities," according to CNN, and "ordered 35 Russian diplomats to leave the country and two Russian compounds [on US soil to be] closed."[102] This measure was widely covered, and, indeed, applauded, by all major media outlets, from the highbrow media such as the *New York Times*,[103] to the lowbrow media such as *USA Today*;[104] and from very liberal media such as *Politico*,[105] to the conservative Fox News.[106] The incident, however, was just a preliminary surge in the ongoing demonization of Russia.

When Donald Trump's campaign for the presidency became more earnest, and his eventual win more likely, the press used references to Putin to undermine Trump's legitimacy and underline his potential to jeopardize the well-being of the nation. Already in December 2015, Republican politician John Kasich posted a—perhaps involuntarily comical—campaign advertisement that juxtaposed past video material of Putin and Trump saying favorable things about each other, suggesting that Putin would be Trump's running mate in

102 Evan Perez and Daniella Diaz, "White House announces retaliation against Russia: Sanctions, ejecting diplomats," CNN, January 2, 2017, http://www.cnn.com/2016/12/29/politics/russia-sanctions-announced-by-white-house/.

103 David E. Sanger, "U.S. Punishes Russia Over Election Hacking," *New York Times*, December 30, 2016, A1.

104 David Jackson, "Obama sanctions Russian officials over election hacking," *USA Today*, December 29, 2016, http://www.usatoday.com/story/news/politics/2016/12/29/barack-obama-russia-sanctions-vladimir-putin/95958472/.

105 Louis Nelson, "Obama pushes back against Trump's suggestion on Russia sanctions," *Politico*, January 18, 2017, http://www.politico.com/story/2017/01/obama-last-press-conference-trump-russia-sanctions-233784.

106 "Trump responds to sanctions against Russia, says it's time to 'move on,'" Fox News, December 29, 2016, http://www.foxnews.com/politics/2016/12/29/obama-orders-sanctions-against-russia-expels-operatives-in-response-to-hacking.html.

the upcoming election.[107] The following year, the attention of the media was riveted by Russia's reactions during and after the US elections. "A conspiracy-toned discussion of an alleged connection between Donald Trump and the Kremlin, Russia's center of power, [. . .] quickly [became] mainstream."[108] *New York Times* columnist Andrew Rosenthal suggested that Trump was obsessed with Putin and Russia.[109] Jeffrey Goldberg, editor in chief of the *Atlantic*, quipped: "Hillary Clinton is running against Vladimir Putin."[110] Foreign affairs correspondent Max Boot referred to Trump as the "New Modern Marchurian Candidate,"[111] while liberal economist and *New York Times* columnist Paul Krugman labeled him the "Siberian candidate,"[112] and Franklin Foer called him "Putin's Puppet" in *Slate Magazine*.[113] When an unidentified Russian hacker leaked Hillary Clinton's private emails to WikiLeaks in October 2016, much of the American media took it for granted that Russia and Vladimir Putin were behind the hacking. The *Washington Post* ran a headline that read, "Russia meddled in election by hacking, spreading of propaganda,"[114] referring to the opinions of national intelligence officials as evidence, rather than just opinions, as did many other media outlets. According to a Fox News headline on

---

107 John Kasich, "Kasich Ad: Trump/Putin 2016, 'Make Tyranny Great Again'," *Real Clear Politics*, December 19, 2015, http://www.realclearpolitics.com/video/2015/12/19/kasich_ad_trumpputin_2016_make_tyranny_great_again.html.

108 Maxim Trudolyubov "Russia's Culture War," *International New York Times*, February 8, 2014, http://www.nytimes.com/2014/02/08/opinion/trudolyubov-russias-culture-wars.html.

109 Andrew Rosenthal, "Is Trump Obsessed with Putin and Russia?" *New York Times*, July 20, 2016, https://www.nytimes.com/2016/07/20/opinion/campaign-stops/is-trump-obsessed-with-putin-and-russia.html.

110 Jeffrey Goldberg, "It's Official: Hillary Clinton Is Running against Vladimir Putin," *Atlantic*, July 21, 2016, https://www.theatlantic.com/international/archive/2016/07/clinton-trump-putin-nato/492332/.

111 Max Boot, "Donald Trump: A Modern Manchurian Candidate?" *New York Times*, January 11, 2017, A31.

112 Paul Krugman, "Donald Trump, the Siberian Candidate," *New York Times*, July 22, 2016, https://www.nytimes.com/2016/07/22/opinion/donald-trump-the-siberian-candidate.html?_r=0.

113 Franklin Foer, "Vladimir Putin Has a Plan for Destroying the West, and It Looks a Lot like Donald Trump," *Slate*, July 4, 2016, http://www.slate.com/articles/news_and_politics/cover_story/2016/07/vladimir_putin_has_a_plan_for_destroying_the_west_and_it_looks_a_lot_like.html.

114 Ellen Nakashima, Karoun Demirjian, and Philip Rucker, "Top U.S. intelligence official: Russia meddled in election by hacking, spreading of propaganda," *Washington Post*, January 5, 2017, https://www.washingtonpost.com/world/national-security/top-us-cyber-officials-russia-poses-a-major-threat-to-the-countrys-infrastructure-and-networks/2017/01/05/36a60b42-d34c-11e6-9cb0-54ab630851e8_story.html?utm_term=.b61fb3369487&wpisrc=nl_most-draw10&wpmm=1.

January 6, 2017, an "Intel report says Putin ordered campaign to influence US election."[115] "Putin wanted him," summarized the *Huffington Post* on their front page on January 7, 2017, spelling out in bold black letters what almost all the other media sources had only suggested.

Despite the fact that the report[116] about the investigation ordered by the Office of the Director of National Intelligence, and conducted by the FBI, the CIA, and the NSA, among others, which was released by Congress in 2017, was rather inconclusive, the media and politicians were convinced of the existence of "strong evidence" against Russia.[117] Though more cautious in their wording in reference to the report, the *New Yorker*[118] and *New York Times*[119] insisted that Russia had interfered in the US elections with the intention of helping Trump to win or to create chaos. Thomas Friedman claimed that the alleged Russian hacking was an "act of war," and "ex-CIA Deputy Director, Michael Morel" described it as "the political equivalent of 9/11."[120] This hyperbolic language was registered by many as sensationalism,[121] but not always because they favored more balanced reporting on Russia. On the contrary, one commentator suggested that "Russia ha[d] weaponized the American press."[122]

The threat posed by Russia was often symbolized by the image of its president, and occasionally references to the nation and to its president were used interchangeably. Perhaps not coincidentally, political comedies, satire, and caricatures picked up the news media's representations of Putin's virile masculinity—best

---

115 Catherine Herridge, Matthew Dean, and the Associated Press, "Intel report says Putin ordered campaign to influence US election," Fox News, January 6, 2017, http://www.foxnews.com/politics/2017/01/06/trump-to-be-briefed-on-russia-hacking-report-as-unclassified-version-set-for-release.html.

116 Office of the Director of National Intelligence, "Background to 'Assessing Russian Activities and Intentions in Recent US Elections': The Analytic Process and Cyber Incident Attribution," January 6, 2017, https://www.dni.gov/files/documents/ICA_2017_01.pdf.

117 Zack Beauchamp, "Russia has weaponized the American press," *Vox*, October 17, 2016, http://www.vox.com/world/2016/10/17/13245200/russia-wikileaks-american-press-democracy.

118 Osnos, Remnick, and Yaffa, "Trump, Putin, and the New Cold War."

119 David E. Sanger, "U.S. Reacting at Analog Pace to a Rising Digital Risk, Hacking Report Shows," *New York Times*, January 8, 2017, A14.

120 Richard Falk, "The Confused Russian Hacking Debate, Trump Victory, and U.S. Global State," *Foreign Policy Journal*, December 20, 2016, http://www.foreignpolicyjournal.com/2016/12/20/the-confused-russian-hacking-debate-trump-victory-and-u-s-global-state/.

121 Basulto, "What the Media Gets Dangerously Wrong about the Trump-Putin Narrative"; Beauchamp, "Russia has weaponized the American press"; for warnings against the danger of demonizing Russia, see also Seumas Milne, "The demonization of Russia risks paving the way for war," *Guardian*, March 4, 2015, https://www.theguardian.com/commentisfree/2015/mar/04/demonisation-russia-risks-paving-way-for-war.

122 Beauchamp, "Russia has weaponized the American press."

and most often represented by the horse-riding, half-naked Putin—associating them with Russia's increasing strength as a world power posing a threat to the US. What followed was a plethora of Putins, cartoonish and satirized.

"The Emperor's New Clothes," or, Why the Media Likes Putin Topless

Vladimir Putin is, of course, nothing like the vain king in Hans Christian Andersen's fairy tale. Yet the way the US media has presented the Russian president as a despotic czar (occasionally, even explicitly; for example, on the cover of *Time* in May 2014), while also continually churning out pictures of him (or a cartoonish version of him) with a naked torso, makes the reference to Andersen irresistible. In an attempt to ridicule Putin and suggest, again, that he is, indeed, a closeted queer, or rather 'queen,' the Dutch fashion designer Kristof Buntinx created a video game that allows the user to dress up Putin in gay fashion attire. Needless to say, it garnered much attention within the US and beyond.

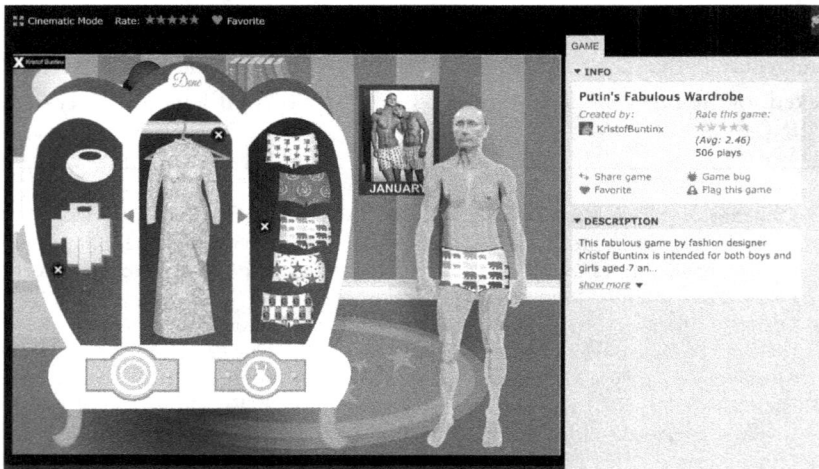

Figure 4. Screenshot/still of Kristof Buntinx, "Putin's Fabulous Wardrobe," Kongregate, February 16, 2014, http://www.kongregate.com/games/kristofbuntinx/putins-fabulous-wardrobe.

Various versions of the same image of Putin as a manly, evil genius appeared in satires and comedy shows. *The Simpsons*'s "Homer Votes 2016," picked up the hacking allegations during the election, showing a horse-riding Russian president voting in Springfield. A "Cartoon Putin" and a "Cartoon Trump" passionately made out on Colbert's *Late Show* on CBS on November 16, 2016. In season 42 of NBC's *Saturday Night Live*, Beck Bennett regularly lost his shirt in an impersonation of the Russian president. In a sketch titled "Valdimir Putin Cold Open" on January 21, 2017, for example, he makes a speech to the American people, reassuring them that everything will be fine under the leadership of 'his friend' Donald Trump.

Figure 5. Screenshot of Homer Simpson and Vladimir Putin on a horse in "Homer Votes 2016," a short about the 2016 presidential election released on the YouTube channel Animation on FOX aired on October 14, 2016, https://simpsons.fandom.com/wiki/Homer_Votes_2016?file=Homer_Votes_2016_Season_28_THE_SIMPSONS.

The image of president Putin shirtless seems to be irresistible; and even more irresistible is the picture of Putin on horseback. *The Tonight Show*, starring Jimmy Fallon, "zoomed in" on a real photo of "Vladimir Putin Riding a Horse" on April 14, 2016. Fox News ironically labeled the promotion campaign that included the horse-riding stunt as "MUST WATCH: Highlight Reel of Vladimir Putin Doing Macho Things."[123] And the Daily Squat, a political satire site, published a photomontage titled "Donald Trump and Vladimir Putin enjoy riding bareback together."[124]

---

123 "MUST WATCH: Highlight Reel of Vladimir Putin Doing Macho Things," Fox News, March 6, 2014, http://nation.foxnews.com/2014/03/06/must-watch-highlight-reel-vladimir-putin-doing-macho-things.

124 David Marrs, "Donald Trump and Vladimir Putin enjoy riding bareback together," *Daily Squat*, August 2, 2016, http://www.dailysquat.com/donald-trump-vladimir-putin-enjoyriding-bareback-together/.

The number of representations of Putin in the US media, with or without his shirt, is indeed impressive. They range from comical and satirical to demonizing; sometimes they are both. Illustrator Roman Genn provided a vampire version of Putin for David Satter's *National Review* article on "The Unsolved Mystery Behind the Act of Terror That Brought Putin to Power."[125] The picture shows a very lean and aged Putin with visible fangs in black and blue tones with occasional blood-red spots. Other visual strategies marking Putin as evil and ruthless involve male stereotypes of him as a gangster or a super spy, for example. On the cover of *Newsweek* on August 1, 2014, he resembles Daniel Craig as James Bond, under the heading: "Inside the Bullet-Proof Bubble of the West's Public Enemy Number One—The Pariah." In a later edition, *Newsweek* added another frightening male stereotype: Putin as a hacker with hoody and laptop.[126]

Disliking Putin is as easy as disagreeing with his political views and policies. His use of homophobic and misogynist rhetoric to dismiss his political opponents,[127, 128] and the repression of the Russian political opposition under his leadership,[129, 130, 131, 132] is well documented and analyzed. But this does not sufficiently explain the US obsession with him. One explanation for the intensity of the media focus on Putin is the easy availability of a cultural register inherited from the Cold War, which emphasizes the threat of Russia to the common American. Another important factor, however, is Putin's easily readable masculinity, which signfies male dominance. This male dominance is clearly identifiable and easy to reject by liberals, as well as conservatives. Rejecting it does not violate any visible racial boundaries because Putin embodies a white masculinity

---

125 David Satter, "The Unsolved Mystery behind the Act of Terror That Brought Putin to Power," *National Review*, 17 August 2016, http://www.nationalreview.com/article/439060/vladimir-putin-1999-russian-apartment-house-bombings-was-putin-responsible.

126 *Newsweek*, cover, September 9, 2016.

127 Sperling, *Sex, Politics, and Putin*, 78–80.

128 Antonina Vikhrest, "Putin's tactical misogyny: A Kremlin-backed TV channel degrades Ukrainian women as part of Putin's wider culture wars," *Aljazeera America*, August 20, 2014, http://america.aljazeera.com/opinions/2014/8/putin-s-tacticalmisogyny.html.

129 Masha Gessen, *The Man without a Face: The Unlikely Rise of Vladimir Putin* (London: Penguin Books, 2012).

130 Julia Ioffe, "'Tomorrow, They'll Shoot Us,'" *New Yorker*, December 9, 2011, http://www.newyorker.com/news/news-desk/tomorrow-theyll-shoot-us.

131 AFP, "Exile or repression: Russian opposition members face tough choice," *Malaymail*, May 7, 2015, http://www.themalaymailonline.com/features/article/exile-or-repression-russian-opposition-members-face-tough-choice#sthash.EJdDiRFv.dpuf.

132 Mikhail Shishkin, "Poets and Czars: From Pushkin to Putin: the sad tale of democracy in Russia," *New Republic*, July 1, 2013, https://newrepublic.com/article/113386/pushkin-putin-sad-tale-democracy-russia.

and his othering as "Russian" or "Slavic man" can easily be dismissed or ignored. In other words, in demonizing and ridiculing Putin, one does not run the risk of being identified as racist or culturalist. In this sense, Putin embodies the ideal opponent for various US-American leaders; he is distinguishable from them only in terms of his values, not the color of his skin or his religion. (Russian Orthodoxy is arguably perceived as simply another variety of Christianity.) The US leadership can mount a fight against Putin, and by association Russia, thereby reaffirming its hero status as that which saves the feminine/victim/nation.

James Messerschmidt analyses local, regional, and global hegemonic and dominating masculinity, as exemplified by both Bush and Obama, in his latest book *Masculinities in the Making*.[133] He argues that both presidents constructed a hero-victim-villain discourse through their public speeches, masculinizing themselves and signifying themselves as protectors. The citizens of the United States and elsewhere become feminized, depicted as innocent, vulnerable, and in need of protection from foreign racialized dangers such as Al-Qaeda, the Taliban, and Saddam Hussein.[134] Such discourses were intelligible within the realm of heterosexual kinship, with the presidents as patriarchal head, and the citizens as women and children. Messerschmidt argues that by implementing military actions against terrorism, which involved killings and torture, Bush and Obama constructed a global dominating masculinity, rather than hegemonic masculinity, because they were "not legitimating unequal relations between men and women, masculinity and femininity".[135]

Yang Shen contests Messerschmidt's thesis, noting that military actions are highly masculine, and their masculinity implies a positioning above femininity in the gender hierarchy. "[Such] actions reproduce and reinforce male dominance/unequal gender relations not only in military forces but also in society."[136] Although Shen's emphasis on the masculinity of military actions, and the military as such, is compelling, I agree with Messerschmidt that the dominance of hegemonic masculinity, understood as white, virile, muscular masculinity, began to unravel, if only slightly, in the age of metrosexuality and "homonationalism." Within homonationalism,[137, 138] and the normalization of some homosexual

---

133 Messerschmidt, *Masculinities in the Making*, 145.
134 Ibid., 147.
135 Ibid., 157.
136 Yang Shen, "Book Review: Masculinities in the Making: From the Local to the Global by James W. Messerschmidt," *Gender & Society* 31, no. 1 (2017): 139.
137 Puar, "Rethinking Homonationalism."
138 Puar, *Terrorist Assemblages*.

bodies[139] as "normal" and "modern," as well as their inclusion into the idea of nations and states, new or alternative versions of masculinity have become increasingly prevalent. The gay white man is no longer abject. In some cases, he might even be recognized as a sex symbol; for example, in the case of the English singer George Michael or the Puerto Rican singer and actor Ricky Martin. Moreover, metrosexual men, such as the former football star David Beckham or the "sexiest man alive" actor George Clooney, are celebrated for their embodiment of beauty and sophisticated self-imaging.

Perhaps the return to the traditional virtues of the Cold War in the form of a re-vilification or re-demonization of Russia through focusing on the macho Vladimir Putin is the most visible sign of a crumbling white hegemonic masculinity in the United States. Against the white, hyper-masculine enemy, a (white) masculine heterosexual hero can reappear to rescue the nation, without any real resistance. Offering further legitimization of the (white) heterosexual hero figure, the US media identified "another"—threatened, but valuable—masculinity in Russia: that of handsome, young, white, gay victims of increasingly homophobic violence. Before analyzing representations of Russian gays, I will take a closer look at cultural imaginaries of "Russian-masculinity-as-threat" beyond the realm of real life. I will look at the recent cultural history of Russian gangsters, villains, and cons in Hollywood films, as well as TV shows.

Hollywood's Eastern Promises: How Russian Bad Guys Got Tattooed

The history of Russian villains in US-American popular culture is long and rich. According to James Chapman, the presentation of Russians as a geopolitical threat to the West in popular literature and film goes back to a time before the Cold War.[140] "But [that stereotyping] takes on a particular ideological inflection during the Cold War when you get the association [with] not just Russia but also Soviet communism."[141] While the 1990s and early 2000s arguably saw a slight decline in the proliferation of Russian enemies in literature and film, starting in the mid-2000s the population of male Russian evildoers on US screens, both small and large, grew exponentially. The rise of dangerous Russian men

---

139 Ibid., 337.
140 Tom Brook, "Hollywood stereotypes: Why are Russians the bad guys?" BBC, November 5, 2014, http://www.bbc.com/culture/story/20141106-why-are-russians-always-bad-guys.
141 Brook, "Hollywood stereotypes."

transgressed genre boundaries, as well as cultural forms. In season 5 (2006–) of the highly acclaimed Fox television drama 24,[142] Jack Bauer (Kiefer Sutherland) has to fight the Russian businessman and uber-villain Vladimir Bierko, played by Julian Sands. In season 8 (2010–), he prevents a Russian assassin from fulfilling his mission, and in season 9 (2014), he fights his old enemy, now a Russian diplomat, from sparking a war between the US and China. The fantasy film *The Golden Compass*[143] introduced an enemy "looking like Grigory Rasputin and shouting in Russian,"[144] and the fantasy/superhero film *Hellboy II: The Golden Army*[145] featured an evil character actually named Rasputin.

Marvel Comics films frequently feature Russian bad men. Mickey Rourke embodied a mad, vicious, traumatized Ivan Vanko in the *Iron Man 2*.[146] *X-Men: First Class*[147] revolves around an alternative history of the 1962 Cuban Missile Crisis, and introduces Azazel (Jason Flemyng) as a Russian who takes pleasure in killing CIA agents.

FX's animated spy sitcom *Archer*[148] introduces Nikolai Jakov, head of the KGB, as a vicious villain. DreamWorks Animation presents Vitaly, the Russian circus tiger, in *Madagascar 3*;[149] he is, admittedly, not a man, but is wicked, nevertheless.

Dolph Lundgren plays the blond Russian hitman in the thriller *Icarus*.[150] *Salt*[151] portrays several vodka-drinking Russian men who infiltrated the US in their youth in order to finally fulfill the long-term goal of destroying the country. The thriller *Limitless*[152] stars Gennady (Andrew Howard) as a Russian loan shark. Sebastian Koch plays the Russian terrorist Yuri Komarov in the action movie

142 *24*, season 5, episode 1, "Day 5: 7:00 a.m.–8:00 a.m.," created by Joel Surnow and Robert Cochran, written by Howard Gordon, aired November 6, 2001, FOX, TV show.

143 *The Golden Compass*, directed by Chris Weitz (UK: New Line Cinema, 2007), film.

144 Nina Khrushcheva, "Hollywood Made Him Do It?" *Nina Khrushcheva* (blog), September 8, 2014. https://ninakhrushcheva.wordpress.com/2014/09/08/hollywood-made-him-do-it.

145 *Hellboy II: The Golden Army*, directed by Guillermo del Toro (US: Universal Pictures, 2008), DVD.

146 *Iron Man 2*, directed by Jon Favreau (US: Marvel Studios/Fairview Entertainment, 2010), DVD.

147 *X-Men: First Class*, directed by Matthew Vaughn (US: Marvel Entertainment/20th Century Fox, 2011), film.

148 *Archer*, season 1, episode 1, "Mole Hunt," created by Adam Reed, aired September 17, 2009, FX, TV show.

149 *Madagascar 3: Europe's Most Wanted*, directed by Eric Darnell, Conrad Vernon, and Tom McGrath (US: DreamWorks Animation, 2012), film.

150 *Icarus*, directed by Dolph Lundgren (Canada: CineTel Films/Corus Entertainment Inc, 2010), film.

151 *Salt*, directed by Phillip Noyce (US: Columbia Pictures/Di Bonaventura Pictures/Wintergreen Productions/Rainmaker Digital Effects, 2010), film.

152 *Limitless*, directed by Neil Burger (US: Virgin Produced/Rogue, 2011), film.

A Good Day to Die Hard.[153] Kenneth Branagh plays a sinister Russian billionaire in the political thriller *Jack Ryan: Shadow Recruit.*[154] And video games frequently feature Russian bad guys; for example, the deeply evil Niko Bellic in *Grand Theft Auto IV*[155] for PlayStation 3 and Xbox 360.

The list of films in which US heroes fight Russian enemies is endless. One that must be mentioned as providing the most drastic and extreme images is, of course, the action-spy film *Mission: Impossible—Ghost Protocol,*[156] in which a bomb destroys the Kremlin. Nina Khrushcheva argues that the prevalence of Russians as villains never really abated after the Cold War.[157] Like Chapman, Khrushcheva sees a connection between the visibility of Vladimir Putin on the terrain of global politics, increasing conflicts between Russia and its neighboring countries, especially Ukraine, and disputes with NATO with the specific portrayals of Hollywood and other pop culture enemies as Russian.[158] In her blog, Khrushcheva makes the ironic claim that "that villainous image that was presented by Hollywood of Russia or Russian leaders"[159] inspired Vladimir Putin to change his image and indeed become a macho enemy to the Western world. Whether it was Hollywood that was inspired by Putin to reintroduce the Russian villain or Hollywood that influenced Putin's self-fashioning, Russian bad guys populated the screens to such a degree that Russian officials considered a ban on Hollywood movies on the Russian market in 2014.[160, 161, 162]

Most of the aforementioned "bad guys"—perhaps with the exception of circus tiger Vitaly—embody either a version of the Soviet boxer Ivan Drago

---

153 *A Good Day to Die Hard*, directed by John Moore (US: 20th Century Fox, 2013), film.
154 *Jack Ryan: Shadow Recruit*, directed by Kenneth Branagh (US: Paramount Pictures/Skydance Productions, 2014), film.
155 *Grand Theft Auto IV*, developed by Rockstar North (US: Rockstar Games, 2008), PlayStation 3/Xbox 360.
156 *Mission: Impossible—Ghost Protocol*, directed by Brad Bird (US: Bad Robot Productions/Skydance Productions/Paramount Pictures, 2011), film.
157 Khrushcheva, "Hollywood Made Him Do It?"
158 Brook, "Hollywood stereotypes."
159 Khrushcheva, "Hollywood Made Him Do It?"
160 Vladimir Kozlov, "Russian Officials Push for a Ban on Films That 'Demonize' Their Country," *Hollywood Reporter*, August 26, 2014, http://www.hollywoodreporter.com/news/russian-officials-push-a-ban-728056?mobile_redirect=false.
161 Ben Child, "Moscow may ban anti-Russian films from cinemas in new censorship threat," *Guardian*, August 27, 2014, https://www.theguardian.com/film/2014/aug/27/russia-ban-anti-russian-movies.
162 Brook, "Hollywood stereotypes."

(played by Dolph Lundgren) of the 1985 film *Rocky IV*[163]—a body-builder type of masculinity, with blond short hair and a square face; or a version of ex-KGB agent Vladimir Putin—the slick, pokerfaced suit-type (for example Viktor Petrov, the fictional president of Russia in the Netflix series *House of Cards*[164] or Viktor Cherevin, played by Kenneth Branagh in *Jack Ryan: Shadow Recruit*, who occasionally undresses to fight his enemies). But there is a third type of Russian villain: the Russian mobster, also known collectively as *Vory*. In what follows, I will discuss *Vory* as a (body) type. In contrast to the previously mentioned types, it is not only the most interesting, multidimensional or multilayered, but it also seems to contain, in one body, the conflicting myths about Russian masculinity: the physical vulnerability that has been created through emasculation and oppression under Soviet rule, as well as the threat of danger, instability, and power that needs to be contained.[165]

Tattoos, Violence, and Pain: The Russian *Vor*

Cronenberg was not the first to make a movie about Russian mafia activity in the North/Western hemisphere. "[S]ince the collapse of the Iron Curtain in the late 1980s," the Russian "underworld" has become "the epicenter of much discussion. For the politicians, law enforcement authorities, and the media of the Western world, the Russians have been identified with hordes of invading 'organized criminals' ready to take over the criminal business from local illegal entrepreneurs or import forms of criminal activities that supposedly were previously unknown."[166] Morally damaged Russian men out to destroy Western civilization from within through drugs and violence have held a recurring fascination for film directors, TV producers, comic artists, and novelists. During the 1990s and early 2000s, Brighton Beach, where a large part of the Jewish Russian American community still lives today, was the focus of many films about the Russian mafia, for example in the Russian-American co-production *Weather Is Good on Deribasovskaya; It*

---

163 *Rocky IV*, directed by Sylvester Stallone (US: MGM/UA Entertainment Company, 1985), film.

164 *House of Cards*, season 3, episode 3, "Chapter 29," directed by Tucker Gates, written by Frank Pugliese, aired February 27, 2015, Sony Pictures, 2015, DVD.

165 Alan Nadel, *Containment Culture: American Narratives, Postmodernism, and the Atomic Age* (Durham, NC: Duke University Press, 1995).

166 Georgios A. Antonopoulos, "Book Review: Russian Criminal Tattoo: Encyclopaedia Volume III: Danzig Baldaev, Sergei Vasiliev and Alexander Sidorov," *Crime, Media, Culture* 5, no. 2 (2009): 232.

Rains Again on Brighton Beach;[167] *Little Odessa*;[168] Andrew Niccol's *Lord of War*;[169] and *We Own the Night*,[170] starring Joaquin Phoenix. The New York-based Russian mafia also plays a role in *Maximum Risk*,[171] in which the protagonist (played by Jean-Claude Van Damme) discovers that he has a deceased twin brother and sets out to avenge his death at the hands of Russian mobsters.

More Russian mafia appeared in James Bond *Golden Eye*[172] and *The World Is Not Enough*[173] and the action thrillers *Fair Game*,[174] *Eraser*,[175] and *Ronin*.[176] The drama *Rounders*[177] evolves within a Russian mafia milieu and the vigilante crime film *The Boondock Saints*[178] portraits a Boston-based mafia clan.

But it is not only dramas, thrillers and action films that feature the Russian mob. The Walt Disney comedy film *Jungle 2 Jungle*[179] features the Russian mafia in New York City; and in Guy Ritchie's British-American crime comedy *Snatch*,[180] the Serbian actor Rade Šerbedžija stars as Boris 'The Blade' Yurinov, aka Boris 'the Bullet Dodger,' an ex-KGB, Russian Uzbek arms dealer. Denzel Washington is hunted down by the Russian mob in *Training Day*,[181] and it remains to be seen if the CBS TV show *Training Day*,[182] a sequel to the film, will have Russian bad guys as well. A particularly interesting Russian mafiosi appeared in two episodes of the highly acclaimed HBO TV series *The Sopranos*. In "Pine Barrens," episode eleven of the third season (premiering May 6, 2001),

---

167 *Weather Is Good on Deribasovskaya, It Rains again on Brighton Beach*, directed by Leonid Gaidai (Russia/US: Mosfilm, 1992), film.

168 *Little Odessa*, directed by James Gray (US: Fine Line Features, 1995), film.

169 *Lord of War*, directed by Andrew Niccol (US: Entertainment/Manufacturing Company/Ascendant Pictures/Saturn Films, 2005), film.

170 *We Own the Night*, directed by James Gray (US: Columbia Pictures/2929 Productions, 2007), film.

171 *Maximum Risk*, directed by Ringo Lam (US: Bill Pankow/Columbia Pictures, 1996), film.

172 *GoldenEye*, directed by Martin Campbell (UK: Eon Productions, 1995), film.

173 *The World Is Not Enough*, directed by Michael Apted, (UK: Eon Productions, 1999), film.

174 *Fair Game*, directed by Andrew Sipes (US: Silver Pictures/Warner Bros, 1995), film.

175 *Eraser*, directed by Chuck Russell (US: Kopelson Entertainment/Warner Bros. Pictures, 1996), film.

176 *Ronin*, directed by John Frankenheimer (US: FGM Entertainment/United Artists, 1998), format/media.

177 *Rounders*, directed by John Dahl (US: Spanky Pictures, 1998).

178 *The Boondock Saints*, directed by Troy Duffy (US: Franchise Pictures/Brood Syndicate/Fried Films/Lloyd Segan Co./Chris Brinker Productions, 1999), film.

179 *Jungle 2 Jungle*, directed by John Pasquin (US: Walt Disney Pictures/TF1 International, 1997), film.

180 *Snatch*, directed by Guy Ritchie (UK/US: Columbia Pictures/Screen Gems, 2000), film.

181 *Training Day*, directed by Antoine Fuqua (US: Village Roadshow Pictures/Outlaw Productions, 2001), film.

182 *Training Day*, developed by Will Beall (US: CBS, 2021), film.

two Russian mafiosi are emphatically juxtaposed to Italian American organized criminals. The episode simultaneously addresses and caricatures the existing cultural clichés for Russian criminals. Frank Ciornei, as Slava Malevsky, and Vitali Baganov as Valery are former Russian special forces in the Chechen war, who now run a money-laundering business in New Jersey, where they peacefully co-exist with the Italian American mafia led by Tony Soprano. While Slava Malevsky, a smart and gentle man, is the boss of the operation, another character, Valery, acts as the henchman for the Russian and the Italian American mafia. He is built like a house, strong and resilient, violent, brutish, and an alcoholic and drug addict. Valery finally escapes, or disappears, in the snowy Pine Barrens of South New Jersey, still alive despite having been severely beaten and suffering a gunshot wound; and, on top of all that, wearing only his pajamas in the icy cold weather. "Fuckin' Rasputin, this guy," Paulie Gualtieri, played by Tony Sirico, says, summing up the Russian man's character and physical strength, while he and his younger companion lose their way in the white suburban woods and almost freeze to death in their smart leather jackets, and, no doubt, custom-made, Italian designer shoes. The contrast between the Russian 'tank,' who is insensitive to cold, violence, or pain, and the slender, idly smoking crooks with their oily black hair could not be more pronounced, despite the fact that they are all gangsters. In *Batman Begins*[183] and *The Dark Knight*,[184] the DC comics anime superhero films, the Russian mob and their leader Yuri 'The Russian' Dimitrov encounter an Italian American crime family: the Sal Maroni clan. In the DC comics *Superior Spider-Man*, the hero fights against Russian mobsters in tracksuits, as does *Hawkeye* in the Marvel comic books series.

Among this plethora of Russian organized criminals, the depictions of Russians in Cronenberg's *Eastern Promises*[185] are, however, unique. One reason is that Cronenberg allows the viewer to identify with some of the Russian bad guys. He cares enough about authenticity to introduce the term *Vor* to an English-speaking audience, as well as the tattoos that signify membership and rank within the organization. Moreover, Cronenberg focuses on every aspect of the men's embodiment of a Russian mafia-type, using every cliché about

183 *Batman Begins*, directed by Christopher Nolan (US: Warner Bros. Animation/Warner Premiere/DC Comics/Syncopy Inc., 2008), DVD.
184 *The Dark Knight*, directed by Christopher Nolan (US: Warner Bros. Animation/Warner Premiere/DC Comics/Syncopy Inc., 2008), DVD.
185 *Eastern Promises*, directed by David Cronenberg (UK/Canada/US: BBC Films/Astral Media/Corus Entertainment/Telefilm Canada/Kudos Pictures/Serendipity Point Films/Scion Films, 2007), film.

Russian men available within the realm of North/Western culture. He thereby not only creates visibility for their existence, but also makes them available for future cultural productions.

The Russian *Vor* is "a-thief-in-law" (вор в закóне/*vor v zakone*),[186, 187] an elite professional criminal. Although *Vory* can come from all the post-Soviet states, Hollywood prefers to depict them as ethnically Russian, as does the model or type of the Russian *Vor* presented in David Cronenberg's *Eastern Promises*. Since the release of *Eastern Promises*, other Hollywood versions of tattooed, muscular, Russian mafia bodies have appeared: for example, in the action films *One in the Chamber*[188] and *Rage*;[189] the neo-noir vigilante action thriller *The Equalizer*;[190] and *Our Kind of Traitor*.[191] Indeed, tattooed Russian mafia bodies show up in TV shows such as Showtime's *Shameless US*,[192] Netflix's *Sense8*,[193] and even in comic books such as the two Marvel *Black Widow* issues "Public Enemy"[194] and "Foliage."[195]

David Cronenberg is, of course, not just any director, but the master of "body horror" or "biological horror." Body horror is a popular horror genre, characterized by the manipulation and warping of the normal state of bodily form and function. It plays "on the fear not of death but of one's own body and its potential destruction."[196] Cronenberg is known for showing bodies infested with

---

186 James O. Finckenauer and Elin J. Waring, *Russian Mafia in America: Immigration Culture and Crime* (Boston, MA: Northeastern University Press, 1998), 13.

187 Michael Schwirtz, "Vory v Zakone has hallowed place in Russian criminal lore," *New York Times*, July 29, 2008, http://www.nytimes.com/2008/07/29/world/europe/29iht-moscow.4.14865004.html?pagewanted=all&_r=0.

188 *One in the Chamber*, directed by William Kaufman (US: Mediapro Studios/Motion Picture Corporation of America, 2012), film.

189 *Rage*, directed by Paco Cabezas (US/France/UK: Patriot Pictures/Hannibal Classics, 2014), film.

190 *The Equalizer*, directed by Antoine Fuqua (US: Village Roadshow Pictures/Escape Artists, 2014), film.

191 *Our Kind of Traitor*, directed by Susanna White (UK: Film4/The Ink/Factory/Potboiler Productions/StudioCanal, 2016), film.

192 *Shameless*, produced by Paul Abbott, developed by John Wells, aired January 9, 2011 to April 11, 2021, Showtime, 2021, TV show.

193 *Sense8*, created by Lana Wachowski, Lilly Wachowski, and J. Michael Straczynski, 2015, Netflix, TV show.

194 *Black Widow—Public Enemy*, issue 4, written by Nathan Edmondson, art by Phil Noto (US: Marvel Comics, 2014), comic book.

195 *Black Widow—Foliage*, issue 3, written by Nathan Edmondson, art by Phil Noto (US: Marvel Comics, 2014), comic book.

196 Ronald Allan Lopez Cruz, "Mutations and Metamorphoses: Body Horror Is Biological Horror," *Journal of Popular Film & Television* 40, no. 4 (2012): 161.

parasites, severely mutilated, or in various stages of decay. *Eastern Promises* horrifies by focusing intensely on bodies in the process of being mutilated, in a state of heightened vulnerability—naked, outnumbered, without defense. It offers amplified imaginations of Russian bodies—both the violence they can produce and the violence that penetrates them. (By the way, none of the Russian figures in the film is played by an ethnically Russian actor.) The most shocking and horrific aspect of *Eastern Promises* is possibly its "terrible beauty": the "positive aesthetic response" of viewers to the most "shocking, devastating, and horrific"[197] physical violence.

The film tells the story of an innocent female nurse (Naomi Watts as Anna Ivanovna Khitrova), a blond, blue-eyed, UK citizen with Russian ancestry, who accidentally stumbles upon a sex-trafficking and prostitution ring led by the Russian mafia and an FSB (formerly KGB) officer who infiltrates this London-based clan. In the course of the drama, the viewer is presented with multiple differently gendered, sexualized, classed, and racialized Russian immigrant bodies. Moreover, these bodies undergo alteration through (prison) tattoos, sexual acts and rape, and mutilations such as stabbings or shooting. Through, and on, these bodies, the whole gamut of underlying North/Western assumptions about the Russian mafia, and Russians in general, is performed: misogyny, sex trafficking, homosociality, homophobia, alcoholism, cruel violence and torture, as well as the valuing of kinship and family. Even cultural practices, such as feasting at enormous Russian banquets or going to the *banya*, the Russian public bathhouse or sauna, are enacted by bodies rather than narrated as stories. In addition, the fact that none of the actors in the movie is able to speak authentic Russian signifies Cronenberg's preference for embodiment and bodily performance. Although the dialogues reveal some important details, for example, the significance of tattoos within the hierarchy of the *Vory*, this knowledge is equally or better communicated through the scenes in which the undercover FSB agent, Nikolai Luzhin, played by the not-at-all Russian Viggo Mortensen, becomes identified with the eight-pointed stars tattooed on his chest, signifying his new and very high rank among the Russian *Vory*.

Adam Lowenstein argues that the broader meaning of *Eastern Promises* is equally to be found in or on the bodies of the film's characters. He argues that

---

197 Cynthia Freeland, "Tragedy and Terrible Beauty in a *History of Violence* and *Eastern Promises*," in *The Philosophy of David Cronenberg*, ed. Simon Riches (Lexington: University Press of Kentucky, 2012), 27.

the film is a "critical reflection on globalization,"[198] which "extends the history of violence to London, Russia, Afghanistan, Chechnya, and elsewhere, [and] America's role in contemporary geopolitics. Eastern Promises insists that when Americanization both gives birth to and gives way to globalization, intertwined histories of violence become the global condition."[199] The history of violence—which was also the title of Cronenberg's last film before Eastern Promises—"haunts"[200] Nikolai's body in the bathhouse scene, where he is attacked by two Chechen clan members. In this iconic scene, two assassins ambush Nikolai because they mistake him for the Russian boss Semyon's son (played by Vincent Cassel). Semyon, played by Armin Mueller-Stahl, has tricked the Chechens, who were out to avenge their brother's murder, previously ordered by his son Kirill. He had Nikolai take over Kirill's rank in the organization and had the visible marks, that is, the Vory stars, tattooed on his chest. Realizing he has walked into an ambush, Nikolai manages to exercise a set of breathtaking physical maneuvers while completely naked and unarmed, and finally kills the two clothed and armed Chechens. "Cronenberg's images of Nikolai stripped to his essence, both literally naked and metaphorically pure, through his complete immersion in violence, pack an embodied shock."[201] His body "speaks with a power and a subtlety toward which the mind can only stumble,"[202] Lowenstein contends.

But which truth does Nikolai speak? The scene is far from heroic; nor is it very realistic. Through its slow motion, the clumsiness with which the two "cartoonish Chechens," dressed in leather jackets, do the job seems grotesque, and Nikolai seems more irritated than threatened. "There is nothing glamorous or romanticized about the fight, or about Mortensen's body, which at fight's end is sprawled on the floor like something out of an Egon Schiele painting," as Dunlap and Delpech-Ramey remark.[203] I generally agree with Lowenstein's claim that Eastern Promises speaks to the globalization of violence. However, the marks of violence left on the male, and, to a lesser extent, female bodies (because most of them are dead), is too intimate and too strongly gendered to understand global violence as the primary message or topic of Eastern Promises. "Cronenberg appears to have pursued the aim of showing violence that is personal, intimate,

198 Adam Lowenstein, "Promises of Violence: David Cronenberg on Globalized Geopolitics," Boundary 2, 36, no. 2 (2009): 200.

199 Ibid.

200 Ibid.

201 Lowenstein, "Promises of Violence," 206.

202 Ibid., 207.

203 Aron Dunlap and Joshua Delpech-Ramey, "Grotesque Normals: Cronenberg's Recent Men and Women," Discourse 32, no. 3 (2010): 330.

and physical," Cynthia Freeland notes.[204] The director himself explained that he has "a very existential approach to the human body. I take bodies seriously, [as if] I'm actually photographing the essence of this person."[205] Taking this testimony into account, I argue that the traces of violence left on Nikolai, Kirill, and the dead Tatiana (the trafficked, raped, and drugged teenager who sets the entire story of the film in motion by giving birth and dying at the very beginning of the film), tell the Russian history of violence and the dual nature of Russian masculinity, as it is conceptualized by the North/Western world.

The male bodies in *Eastern Promises* speak; and Nikolai's body speaks most directly of all. His various tattoos are "a number of coded images that tell his criminal history for those conversant in the subculture of *vory v zakone*: the prisons where he was incarcerated, the length of the sentences he served, the kinds of crime he committed."[206] Most important for the storyline are the already mentioned stars on his chest. The most impressive tattoo, however, covers the largest part of his back and shows a Russian Orthodox church with three towers crowned with cupolas and Orthodox crosses. "Although the significance of this tattoo for *vory v zakone* most likely relates to chronicling prison terms (three towers = three terms), the tattoo's immediate iconic reference [is] the Kremlin," Lowenstein argues.[207] He reads the reference as prompting a connection to "the highly publicized murder of Russian exile (and former KGB agent) Alexander Litvinenko in London in November 2006."[208] Perceiving Litvinenko's death in London to be "a deadly aspect of globalization, especially when paired with Litvinenko's particularly vocal criticism of Russia's own 'war on terror' with Chechnya,"[209] Lowenstein concludes that the two assassins in *Eastern Promises* further hint at a possible reading of the film as a criticism of the geopolitical power plays of the era, the "American and Russian 'wars on terror.'"[210]

Although I agree with Lowenstein that the globalization of violence is one subject of the film, another, much more elaborate, topos is Cronenberg's comment on masculinity. On the broadest level, the Russian men in *Eastern Promises* align with Pete Deakin's diagnosis of *fin de millennial* Hollywood cinema, the most significant feature of which is that it "perpetuate[s] male paranoia over a

204 Freeland, "Tragedy and Terrible Beauty," 32.
205 Ibid., 32.
206 Lowenstein, "Promises of Violence," 207.
207 Ibid., 207.
208 Ibid.
209 Ibid.
210 Ibid.

feared loss of patriarchal power."[211] While Viggo Mortensen as Nikolai Luzhin and Vincent Cassel as Kirill are well positioned in the ranks of Deakin's examples (Edward Norton played by Brad Pitt in David Fincher's *Fight Club* or the hacker Neo played by Keanu Reeves in the Wachowski siblings' *The Matrix*), Nikolai Luzhin's and Kirill's bodies and minds are presented to fit a much more specific embodiment of Russian masculinity, gesturing back to the Soviet ideal of the "New Man." This image also enjoyed significant popularity in the history of Hollywood cinema. In her book *How the Soviet Man Was Unmade: Cultural Fantasy and Male Subjectivity Under Stalin*, Lilya Kaganovsky shows how novelists and other cultural protagonists promoted a contradictory cultural image of the Soviet man. "[T]he New Soviet Man (novyi sovetskii chelovek)," in literature and film, had a "square jaw[. . .], broad shoulders, [and a] "halo" [. . .] emanates in and around his presence,"—he symbolized "the hero of socialist labor."[212]

From the 1980s onward, at least up until today, Hollywood has referenced this Stalinist idea of the Soviet man. Armie Hammer, the blond and buff actor who played the Russian spy Ilya Kuryakin in the 2015 remake of *The Man from U. N. C. L. E.*, fits the profile, as does Richard Lynch, who played the Russian antagonist Mikhail Rostov, in *Invasion U.S.A.*[213] Arguably, the preeminent embodiment of the Soviet man was provided by Dolph Lundgren, who has played several Russian enemies over the course of his ongoing career. He played, for example, a KGB henchman in the James Bond film *A View to a Kill*;[214] and most iconically, Ivan Drago in *Rocky IV.*[215] He also played also Nikolai Cherenko in *The Mechanic*[216] and Edward 'Icarus' Genn in *Icarus.*[217] Viggo Mortensen and Vincent Cassel, both far from being Russian, represent the square-jawed, broad-shouldered masculinity that a Soviet, or, here,

211 Pete Deakin, *White Masculinity in Crisis in Hollywood's fin de Millennium Cinema* (London: Lexington Books, 2019), 121.

212 Lilya Kaganovsky, *How the Soviet Man Was Unmade: Cultural Fantasy and Male Subjectivity under Stalin* (Pittsburgh, PA: University of Pittsburgh Press, 2008), 2.

213 *Invasion U.S.A.*, directed by Joseph Zito (US: Cannon Films, 1985), film.

214 *A View to a Kill*, produced by Albert R. Broccoli and Michael G. Wilson (UK: Eon Productions/United Artists, 1985), film.

215 *Rocky IV*.

216 *The Mechanic*, directed by Dolph Lundgren (Germany/US: Martien Holdings A. V. V., 2005), film.

217 *Icarus*, directed by Dolph Lundgren (Canada: CineTel Films/Corus Entertainment Inc., 2010), film.

post-Soviet, man should embody. Their power, strength, and virility, in short, their masculinity, is just a façade, however.

It is as if Cronenberg wants to underline Kaganovsky's point that the characteristic features symbolizing power, leadership, strength, and virility are always transparent, amounting to a kind of "rhetorically constructed figure"[218] or façade. Importantly, a significant aspect of their masculinity is that "they are wounded and maimed, proudly offering to show off [their] 'decorations lower down.'"[219]

If we revise Cronenberg's gaze on the Russian *Vor* with a view toward history, the image seems to be a nearly perfect visual embodiment of Kaganovsky's description of the Soviet man's "naked body, 'knotted and scarred', [which] appears precisely at the moment when we expect it the least: ready for a display of virility, we [. . .] are unprepared for the vision of the 'pallid and purple scars that cover his chest, neck, and side.' What begins seemingly as a play of muscles, pointed to by [the] invitation to 'come and touch them,' turns instead into an exhibition of wounds."[220]

Kaganovsky is not speaking, of course, about the North/Western or US-American depiction or perception of Russian masculinity. Rather, she identifies "[t]his conflict of tropes—the muscular body of the hero lacerated by scars; pride taken in the possibility of castration" in Fedor Gladkov's 1926 novel *Cement*.[221] But her point that the imagination of 'iron and steel' of Soviet masculinity produced a "circumscribed masculinity, a masculinity that openly acknowledges and privileges its own undoing,"[222] is worth considering with regard to *Eastern Promises*. Soviet literature, in particular, described woundedness "vividly and at length."[223] It "revel[led] in the pain and damage sustained by their heroic subjects, describing in excruciating detail the nature of their heroes' suffering and inviting not only the female characters, but also the readers, to acknowledge and fetishize the damaged male body as a model of exemplary masculinity."[224] Like the Russian Stalinist novelists, in *Eastern Promises* Cronenberg seems to dwell equally on the suffering of his protagonists, not so much in a sentimental manner but in the crude display of the penetration of their bodies through violence. He equally acknowledges or recreates the

---

218 Kaganovsky, *How the Soviet Man Was Unmade*, 2.
219 Ibid.
220 Ibid.
221 Fedor Gladkov, *Cement*, trans. A. S. Arthur and C. Ashleigh (Evanston, IL: Northwestern University Press, 1980).
222 Kaganovsky, *How the Soviet Man Was Unmade*, 10.
223 Ibid.
224 Ibid.

physical and mental trauma the Soviet body is imagined to have suffered, mimicking the fetishizing of the Russian "damaged male body as a model of exemplary masculinity."[225]

One might say that Cronenberg visualizes the cultural imaginary of Russian masculinity, serving it to a North/Western audience. He wants us to 'see' the violence that penetrates these Russian migrant bodies and constitutes their masculinity. At the end of the bathhouse scene, Nikolai stabs one of his attackers directly in one eye. "This action shocks us, viscerally—we feel this assault on vision with an embodied literalism that characterizes Cronenberg's work from its beginnings to the present. This director always stabs us in the eye," Lowenstein eloquently points out.[226] Lowenstein understands "Cronenberg's embodied cinema" as "a newly concrete political sophistication to match its wide-ranging philosophical ambitions,"[227] that is to 'show' the viewer that "we risk the worst kinds of political and ethical blindness"[228] if we do not 'see' the violent effects of globalization, and continue to deal with the different forms of violence on a national level. I would argue, however, that what Cronenberg wants to show is not this state-orchestrated, and, indeed, globally connected, violence. Rather, he presents the violence that constitutes masculinity, especially Russian masculinity, as something ordinary and routine.

Of course, the issues that Cronenberg deals with are global in scale: sex trafficking and coerced sex work, for example. But the way he confronts the viewer with this violence is on the most personal, often private, individual level. We can watch Semyon (Armin Mueller-Stahl's character) raping Tatiana to break her will. We watch every detail when Ekrem, the Kurdish young man with a disability—who 'was touched by an Angel,' as his Uncle Azim, the Kurdish barber, associate to Semyon and henchman to Kirill, frames it with a Russian metaphor—must kill the rival Chechen *Vory* leader, who spread the rumor that Kirill was gay. Later, we can almost feel how the Chechens avenge their brother's death by slowly slitting open Ekrem's throat. The subject of Russian alcohol abuse is graphically brought home as we follow every step of Kirill's self-destructive habit. We see him stumbling over his own feet and witness him crawling over the rug like a toddler, groveling before his father, who kicks him so he can enjoy his embarrassment. We see how Nikolai disassembles the killed Chechen's fingers, removing evidence—the disintegrated body will later surface

---

225 Ibid.
226 Lowenstein, "Promises of Violence," 208.
227 Ibid.
228 Ibid.

on the shore of the River Thames. The motives behind the murder, as well as Kirill's own alcoholism, are deeply bound up in Russian hegemonic masculinity: competition for the favor of the patriarch; the need to preserve and protect male honor and the family name; and homophobia. The Russian *Vory* milieu is highly homosocial. The male bodies the story revolves around are often unusually close—unusually, that is, for the North American viewer. There is a suggestion that Russian men touch each other, take baths with each other, watch each other fucking.

Kirill, however, constantly transgresses the boundaries of what is considered appropriate and feels the need to take drastic action to hide his transgressions afterwards. The scenes in which Kirill gives in to Nikolai's simmering flirtations explode into physical violence. In the character of Kirill, "Cronenberg's [. . .] recurring fascination with bodies and minds at war over identity" is most visible.[229] "[T]he promise of violence lives on in the body, even if the mind surrenders to tortured uncertainty about identity. [. . .] this violent body and defeated mind form a vision of external aggression cut off from internal reflection—of contemporary geo-politics as a sleepwalk from one destructive act to the next."[230] Kirill is presented as self-regarding narcissist with many problems and insecurities, abused and abusive, longing for his father's recognition and Nikolai's friendship—or maybe more. Kirill can be understood as damaged by his father's violent occupation, his lack of respect and compassion for his son. His drug taking and drinking, as well as his violent outbursts and mood-swings, are caused by his traumatic experiences of growing into the skin of a Russian *Vor*. Yet his trauma and wounds are channeled into violence, a display of masculine power. "Cronenberg claimed he wanted to understand things 'from the disease's point of view.'"[231] But what is the disease in *Eastern Promises*? Is it alcoholism and drug abuse? Is it capitalist globalization, as Lowenstein claims? Is it homophobia? Sexism? Or is it post-Soviet or Russian masculinity that is the disease?

Aron Dunlap and Joshua Delpech-Ramey argue that the "disease in Cronenberg films is not essentially physical. What is ill, in Cronenberg, is a series of conflicts between man and woman, nature and machine, science and society that seem somehow to traverse and manifest the grotesque."[232] The grotesque in *Eastern Promises*—the exaggerated violence, the slowing down of the violent deed or act, the un-real action—following Dunlap's and Delpech-Ramey's line

---

229 Ibid., 206.
230 Ibid.
231 Cronenberg qtd. In Dunlap and Delpech-Ramey, "Grotesque Normals," 322.
232 Ibid.

of thought—reveals the limits of the human body and material existence in the face of mental and physical hardship and violence. "In Cronenberg's films, the grotesque is almost always located at the place where love should be but is not, seeming to signify that love, insofar as love involves caring for the body of the other, is impossible."[233] Accordingly, *Eastern Promises* showcases in the most drastic form that the end of the Soviet Union did not suddenly cure post-Soviet man from trauma and suffering, but rather, that the post-Soviet transition to global capitalism added traumas and scars to their already wounded and vulnerable minds and bodies, pushing their bodies to their physical limits, destroying their capacities for love, and erasing their identities.

Nikolai's body speaks most literally to the traumas of the post-Soviet experience: the economic hardship that forced many into criminality, incarceration, and other forms of systemic and personal male violence, already alluded to. "[T]he violence is not actually committed by [him] but suffered by him."[234] His many tattoos, the scars from knife wounds, his porous skin and scarred face, all of these markers report incredible violence and suffering, and signify his body as a post-Soviet one. Yet Nikolai is, at the same time, "purposefully unreadable."[235] Moreover, the tattoos are not straightforward speech. His tattoos convey the position he holds among the *Vory* hierarchy and tell us that he was in prison; but what his crimes were is unknown. When we learn that Nikolai is an FSB undercover man, how can we trust his prison tattoos? And when Semyon offers Nikolai full status as a *Vor*, not in return for his loyalty and valor, but to trick the Chechen warlord assassins, we must question the integrity of the *vory v zakone* as such. "For *vory v zakone*, your life is written on your body," Dunlap and Delpech-Ramey note.[236] "The *vor* have a saying, 'we are marked for life and our stories tell the truth.'"[237] Before Nikolai receives his tattoo stars that mark him a *vor*, he also has to tell the true stories about the ones he already has. But knowing that Nikolai is not who he says he is and after we learn about Semyon's intentions later in the plot, the viewer can no longer trust the truth that is told. In a very twisted gesture, the body, the one thing that "is supposed to tell the ultimate truth [. . .] is itself a lie. This lie undermines the stereotypically masculine

233 Ibid., 324.
234 Freeland, "Tragedy and Terrible Beauty in a *History of Violence* and *Eastern Promises*," 28.
235 David Edelstein, "Post-Traumatic Mystery," *New York Times*, September 17, 2007, 68.
236 Dunlap and Delpech-Ramey, "Grotesque Normals," 329.
237 Ibid.

sense of authenticity and heroism associated with the survival of painful ordeals and danger."[238]

Cronenberg's artful but brutal deconstruction of the illusion of the truthful body becomes even more significant when Nikolai confesses that he "lost his identity" in prison. "'I died then,' he says."[239] His loss of identity, and the lack of visible emotional responses throughout the film, even "to nasty aspersions against his own father and mother,"[240] make Nikolai appear stoic and empty. Stripped of his clothes again, he shows no response when the council of *Vory* leaders 'read' his tattoos and "test his character and allegiance by insulting his father and mother. Nikolai responds not only that they meant nothing to him, but adds, 'I died when I was fifteen.' This is an intriguing statement that seems to shed light on this man's somewhat elusive, empty character. [...] Nikolai is a person who seems to have erased or denied his own identity."[241] Nikolai's emptiness contrasts with the fullness of the messages on his body. Written on the body's surface is the history of intense violence he has been subjected to: "forced sex (almost as much as the prostitute [sic] is) and also, of course, to the brutal attack against him in the bathhouse."[242]

But there is no real reward for having endured this violence at the end. Nikolai has lost his identity and he can no longer answer the question of who he is. It is entirely unclear to the viewer whether he is still an FSB undercover agent working to undermine *vory v zakone* or whether he has become the "underworld boss whose Scotland Yard connections provide a convenient rationalization for his need to be 'king.'"[243] We do not know whether he is good or bad; loving and caring towards the nurse, Anna; or whether his act of sparing the lives of her and her family was just a calculated decision to keep the trust of Scotland Yard. He rescues the baby girl from her abductor, Kirill, and returns it to Anna. He defeats Semyon, who, as he knows from Tatiana's diary, had raped her, "as a lesson to Kirill, who had been unable, in his impotency, to perform the deed himself."[244] "Nikolai is able to have Semyon arrested for statutory rape if they get his DNA matched to that of the baby. 'For poetic reasons, I suggest you take his blood,' he

238 Ibid., 330.
239 Freeland, "Tragedy and Terrible Beauty," 28.
240 Ibid.
241 Ibid., 34.
242 Ibid., 28.
243 Lowenstein, "Promises of Violence," 204.
244 Dunlap and Delpech-Ramey, "Grotesque Normals," 330.

instructs the police."[245] But his righteous acts could just be part of an intrigue to make Kirill take his father's place as the head of the *Vory*. "This effectively installs Nikolai at the highest level of the London mafia, where he can complete his FSB mission."[246] Even Nikolai's "heroism is itself an ironic ruse: Nikolai pretends to have survived a violent past, but only in order to wait out the mob. The passion of Nikolai is a comic rather than a tragic heroism."[247]

In the final scene of the film "we watch him sitting alone in the Russian restaurant with an ambiguous expression."[248] Maybe this is the real conclusion of the film—that the post-Soviet man is all alone. He no longer knows who he is, no longer has an identity, and no longer has morals or values; all he is left with is a history and future of violence. Having recourse to psychoanalytical theory, Dunlap and Delpech-Ramey read Nikolai as "hystericized male, a male who [. . .] remains committed, even overcommitted, to the impasses of the symbolic order (here, the web of power relations that enable Nikolai, by becoming fully part of it, to authentically act)."[249]

Eastern Promises concludes with the image of Nikolai "as a pater familias, a patriarch sitting at the head of a dinner table,"[250] the quintessential image of the symbolic order. But he is also completely alone—"emotionally abandoned and physically isolated."[251] He will never be "able to return to a 'normal' family and always hav[e] the moral implications and social consequences of the violence he has used restrain his further life—shackle him as it were. What was broken can be fixed, but never truly healed or made undone."[252] The final image of Nikolai "is extremely powerful in [its] contemplative resignation, reinstating ambiguity into narratives that only seconds before seemed to end happily."[253] Nikolai's commitment to the Symbolic order leaves him completely isolated and alone, "with nothing else than his fake tattoos."[254] This ending evokes

---

245 Ernst Mathijs, *The Cinema of David Cronenberg: From Baron of Blood to Cultural Hero* (New York: Wallflower Press, 2008), 241.
246 Ibid.
247 Dunlap and Delpech-Ramey, "Grotesque Normals," 331.
248 Freeland, "Tragedy and Terrible Beauty," 34.
249 Dunlap and Delpech-Ramey, "Grotesque Normals," 331.
250 Mathijs, *The Cinema of David Cronenberg*, 227.
251 Ibid.
252 Ibid.
253 Ibid.
254 Dunlap and Delpech-Ramey, "Grotesque Normals," 332.

his castrated position, unable to ride away with his woman, and living in a very precarious state on the side of the law. But even though the tattoos are fake, his castration is completely real. Lacan claimed that all men (and women) who enter into the Symbolic must suffer castration, the problem not really being the castration but the neurotic (or perverse) refusal to accept the situation, to accept the limitation of one's powers. Full acceptance of castration is full entrance into the Symbolic, and Nikolai's castration is the condition of heroic action.[255]

The problem for the post-Soviet man, then, is that the Symbolic order, and the hierarchies in place, no longer provide him with identity or stability, while the neoliberal, capitalist, globalized world depends on individuality and individual fluid identities. In this vein we could interpret Semyon's utterance about his son towards the end of the film: "You know it never snows in the city, it's never autumn, London the city of wars and queers. I think London is to blame for what he is."

With his scarred mind and body, the post-Soviet man is not fit to comply with the demands of capitalism. What remains of his masculinity is violence and pain, a grotesque transformation of what is supposed to be internal—the meaningful—turned inside out, into tattoos. Cronenberg shows us masculinity at its most grotesque. "[I]t is a powerful gesture to show a male that can assume or ingest the grotesque as something internal to his own life, as symbolized in Nikolai's tattoos,"[256] Dunlap and Delpech-Ramey further argue in their psychoanalytical reading. They understand Nikolai's actions as comical "embracing (rather than tragically alienating) the death (drive) represented by the uncanny persistence of the grotesque, new relationships of power become possible."[257]

While Dunlap and Delpech-Ramey detect the death drive in the grotesque, I argue, rather, that the death drive is inherent in the very embodiment of post-Soviet masculinity (and perhaps every known hegemonic masculinity), and is the subject of Cronenberg's gaze. Male competition, masculine violence, the drinking, fucking, and raping—all of these performances of masculinity are destructive/self-destructive. Certainly, we can read Mortensen's detached, highly choreographed performance of masculinity and maleness as Nikolai, best

255 Ibid.
256 Ibid.
257 Ibid.

exemplified in his fight scenes, as "postmasculine," in the words of Dunlap and Delpech-Ramey; a form of "analytic remembrance: yes the emotions are there, yes the correct actions are executed, but there is a lack of immediacy."[258] But we can also read it as mimicry of a heroic post-Soviet masculinity, a dwelling on the wounds and traumas of the past, faced with the lack of a future.

The significance of Cronenberg's imaginary of Russian masculinity is not to be overstated. Judging only by the money the film made at the box offices—as of November 4, 2007, *Eastern Promises* had grossed $56,106,607 worldwide, $17,266,000 of that in the US alone,[259]—a huge audience must have watched the film. Most importantly, as already mentioned, his imaginary inscribed itself deeply into cinematic memory and became a staple of contemporary Hollywood films and TV shows.

Three other compelling examples of contemporary Russian *Vory* are Stellan Skarsgård as Dima in the movie *Our Kind of Traitor*;[260] Anton, in the Netflix series *Sense8*; and Yvon, in the Showtime comedy-drama *Shameless US*. In the first film, *Our Kind of Traitor*, the character Dima is a jovial and impetuous character with a photographic memory, dedicated to saving his family from assassination. On a vacation in Morocco, Dima sets a plot in motion that should safeguard his life and future, by involving literature professor Perry MacKendrick and his lawyer wife Gail in a trade, offering mafia secrets to the British MI6 in exchange for asylum in the UK for him and his family. He holds valuable information about the connections between the head of the Russian mafia, called "the Prince," and British politicians and bankers. Unsurprisingly, things do not proceed as planned, and Dima, his family, as well as the two British civilians, suddenly find themselves hunted by the Prince's assassins. In the last part of the film, the hitmen manage to target Dima, killing him in a spectacular helicopter explosion over the French Alps. But he has already managed to arrange for his family to receive asylum in the UK, and with the help of the young professor MacKendrick, the Prince and his British money laundering network are exposed.

Our Kind of Traitor is a nicely crafted film, but not exceptional or artistically revolutionary. Naturally, it was not nearly as successful or important as *Eastern Promises*. It opened on July 1, 2016 in the US and Canada, and has grossed $3,153,157 domestically and $10,711,027 worldwide as of

---

258 Ibid., 334.
259 "Eastern Promises," Box Office Mojo, November 4, 2007, http://www.boxofficemojo.com/movies/?id=easternpromises.htm.
260 *Our Kind of Traitor*, directed by Susanna White, written by Hossein Amini (UK: Film4, 2016) DVD.

February 26, 2017.[261] However, it is nevertheless worth considering, for several reasons. First, it is a cinematic adaptation from John le Carré's[262] novel of the same name. Le Carré is an author who has influenced the imaginary mythscape of Russia, Russian bad guys of past generations, but also generations to come, particularly in the English-speaking world. Joe Weisberg, producer of the TV spy series *The Americans*, for example, frequently referred to John le Carré's books as inspirations for both writing the script and his attempt to become a CIA agent and fight the Soviets in the late 1980s and early 1990s.[263] Second, *Our Kind of Traitor* reveals many clear visual references to *Eastern Promises*, and not just in the choice of London as global reference point.

Dima, the protagonist, embodies a type and masculinity that could be an older version of Nikolai. His grey-and-white, slightly curly hair reaches down his neck and is often stuck with gel to the back of his head. He wears expensive black, grey, and dark-blue suits. He has expensive style. His body is muscular and arguably good-looking. Like *Eastern Promises*, *Our Kind of Traitor* has a bathhouse scene in which we see Dima fully naked. Although it has a very different setting and outcome from *Eastern Promises*, it is quite interesting that we get to have a peek at this nude man and can admire the many tattoos on his chest. Most importantly, Dima wears the eight-pointed star that signifies his position as a Russian *Vor*. He also has a church with four onion-domed towers and a Madonna with a Child on the chest. "Monasteries, churches, cathedrals, the Virgin Mary, saints and angels on the chest or back display a devotion to thievery,"[264] according to Arkady Bronnikov, who collected and published Russian prison files decoding their prisoners' ink. "The Madonna and Child is a thieves' talisman, acting as a guardian from misfortune and misery. It also means that the bearer has been a thief from an early age: 'A child of prison.'"[265] Although an informed viewer versed in criminal body art could learn all this from Dima's chest tattoos, and although Dima explains his tattoos in the beginning of the film,[266] they play no

---

261 "Our Kind of Traitor," Box Office Mojo, February 26, 2017, http://www.boxofficemojo.com/movies/?page=main&id=ourkindoftraitor.htm.

262 John le Carré, *Our Kind of Traitor* (New York: Viking Press, 2010).

263 Olivia B. Waxman, "Q&A: The CIA Officer Behind the New Spy Drama The Americans," *Time*, January 30, 2013, https://entertainment.time.com/2013/01/30/qa-the-cia-officer-behind-the-new-spy-drama-the-americans/.

264 Arkady Bronnikov, "Decoding Russian criminal tattoos—in pictures," *Guardian*, September 18, 2014, https://www.theguardian.com/artanddesign/gallery/2014/sep/18/decoding-russian-criminal-tattoos-in-pictures.

265 Ibid.

266 "Dima explains tattoos," *Our Kind of Traitor*.

further role later on. Nevertheless, they arguably mark Dima as 'real' Russian *Vor* to the Western audience, which knows just as much about this culture—namely, that it exists.

Other aspects of Dima that mark him not only as Russian, but as "outlaw," are his raucous voice and Skarsgård's accent, which, though not quite Russian, gives his character an ambiguous aura of rough gentleness, or gentle roughness. Unlike Nikolai in *Eastern Promises*, Dima seems not to have lost his soul or identity. On the contrary, he is strongly committed to his family and he is kind to his friends, which, arguably, also signifies his Russianness. Director White seems much more interested in the development of the plot and in telling a story than Cronenberg, who artfully deconstructs his characters in order to get to their core. The viewer is encouraged to feel sympathy for the murderous Russian thug Dima, and to develop, rather, a concern for the morality of international banking. Accordingly, Dima is a likeable, if not loveable figure, more an unfortunate child of his circumstances than a morally objectionable bad guy. His particular masculinity, his willingness to kill and use violence, and his function as patriarch, head of the family and a criminal organization, do not diminish his likeability, but rather increase it—for it seems he just wants to protect those he loves. Although we see him engaging in violence, its purpose is only to protect him or the innocent. The real evils are the Russian oligarchs and international bankers.

Before moving on to the vulnerable Russian gay man and delineating the final type of Russian masculinity that concerns me here, I want to introduce briefly two Russian *Vory* from two very different TV shows. Both figures are interesting to me because they bear significant parallels to characters in *Eastern Promises*. Moreover, they do so although the genres of their respective shows are very different—one a comedy drama, the other a science fiction drama. The first character is Anton Bogdanow of *Sense8*. Anton does not play a big role in the show, but he haunts his son, Wolfgang Bogdanow, played by Max Riemelt, who is one of the main protagonists. Anton, a tattooed safecracker, is a Russian immigrant to Germany. He is an alcoholic, a brute, and an abuser. No longer able to put up with the physical and verbal abuse inflicted upon him, the young Wolfgang strangles his father to death. He then places the lifeless body in a car and sets it on fire. This history of abuse, the trauma of killing his father, the organized crime or belonging to a criminal family, haunts Wolfgang. He believes that he is damaged, unable to be good, or do good, despite the fact that throughout the first season of *Sense8*, he is just that—a caring and loving member of the "Sense8" network. Interestingly, we quite often see Wolfgang naked.

The last Russian *Vor* I will examine is Yvon, played by Pasha D. Lychnikoff, in *Shameless US*. Lychnikoff is one of the rare authentic Russians portraying

Russians on US TV shows, on stage, and in cinema. *Shameless US* is a comedy drama that bases its satire on the presentation of all possible racial and racist, cultural and culturalizing, stereotypes of all ethnic groups living in the US, including migrant Russians. The comical exploitation of these stereotypes is the source of the show's humor. In the seventh season of *Shameless US*, Yvon lives with the threesome Kevin, Veronica, and Svetlana, and their three children, over the course of five episodes. Much like, or even more than, other characters in the show, Yvon is a Russian cliché. Everything that the US-imaginary mythscape 'knows' about Russian criminal men or Russian criminal activities[267] seems to intersect in his character and body. He does not speak English and Svetlana presents him as her father when he first arrives, literally full of excrement, after being human trafficked in an animal transporter from Russia to the US.

Yvon is loud, brutal, a drunkard, and a thug. He frequently runs around naked or half-naked, and the audience can see that he wears the *vory* stars on his chest. He does not shy away from physical violence or the abuse of women. He regularly picks fistfights with his daughter Svetlana, who later turns out to be his wife. He is portrayed as barbaric and uncivilized. He cuts apples with a huge, terrifying hunting knife that he even uses to feed the toddlers. In season 7, episode 6 "The Defenestration of Frank," he smashes potatoes with a hammer, probably for the production of vodka, while listening to Russian folk music, drinking vodka, and watching the three babies. Later in the episode, the camera assumes Kevin's perspective, watching Yvon from behind as he's fucking a woman, while Russian president Putin gives a speech on the TV next to him. It will turn out that this woman is Svetlana, which leads Kevin and Veronica to believe that he rapes his own daughter.

The idea that Yvon is a rapist, pimp, and human-trafficker is outspoken or implicit, in the air, each time the viewer watches him take care of Veronica's and Kevin's little twin girls. As rough and brutish as Yvon appears in his interactions with adults, he is invariably gentle and caring with the three kids. Although he frequently handles knives and other dangerous equipment around them, and allows them to carry bottles of vodka for him, these acts serve a comical purpose. They play on his simplicity, savage character, and backwardness, and do not really endanger the children. Moreover, his actions are carried out with a loving and caring attitude, never in rage or accompanied by negative emotion. Nevertheless, Kevin and Veronica do not trust him around the kids. Their sentiment derives mainly from Svetlana's story, convincingly told, that her father had

---

267 Williams, *Imagining Russia*.

sold her into sexual slavery back in Russia. In Episode 4 "I Am a Storm," the two even call the police on Yvon, thinking he has kidnapped their daughters to sell them into sex slavery, when in reality he just took them out for a walk.

The comedy format of *Shameless US* allows it to intensify the stereotypical attributes of the Russian *Vor*. However, Yvon's visible, embodied signifiers—the broad, muscular build, heightened through body posture, such as the 'cowboy walk' or squat neck buried in the shoulders, the square face with the crooked nose (probably a result of fistfights), the constant handling of dangerous tools, such as hammers or knifes—all these physical signs and marks, most especially the tattoos, recall the characters of the previously analyzed films in one way or the other: Anton (*Sense8*); Dima (*Our Kind of Traitor*); and Nikolai, Semyon, and Kirill (*Eastern Promises*)—characters who introduced the image of the internally conflicted, contradictory Russian *Vor* to the US-American or North/Western mythscape about Russian men.

Conclusion

In this chapter, I have shown how the constructs of Russian man and embodied Russian masculinity operate in different North American, particularly US, media. Looking at different kinds of media, from the daily news sector to comedy, from animated series to political magazines, I have demonstrated how Vladimir Putin embodies the white, able-bodied masculine macho figure, feared for his archaic aggression, as much as admired. The obsession with Vladimir Putin's naked chest, although most often satirical, signifies the retreat of white, potent masculinity as the hegemonic mode of masculinity within the US. Although white, patriarchal, misogynist masculinity still holds sway in the US, probably to an even greater degree than it did between 2008 and 2017, it is nevertheless severely contested, and alternative masculinities have become normalized. The admiration and simultaneous objectification of the nude Russian president can be read as an attempt to hold on to this kind of masculinity, as much as it can be read as criticism.

In any case, as a stand-in for the Russian nation and state, President Putin gives a human body, if not face, to the new (old) image of Russia as male aggressor and opponent to the US. As such, Putin, Russia, and Russian men are constructed as "other" to the US and US men. This strategy of cultural othering of Russia in the US media serves to re-establish a sense of national unity and moral superiority in times of crisis. It is a crisis not only in terms of masculinity and normative manhood, but also a crisis along the lines of racial, gender, economic, and class inequalities, increasing civic unrest, as well as acts of racist violence.

The new wave of Russian male bodies in cinema and on TV, but also within other spheres of popular culture and different kinds of news media, is simultaneously a sign or result, as well as a discursive product, of this new (old) signification. Focusing on TV shows, as well as Hollywood films, I have shown that aggressive masculinity is a part of the imaginary of the common Russian man, and especially the Russian criminal. The imaginary reserved for the Russian *Vor* is based on the assumption that there are particularly many, especially cunning, Russian criminals, given the history of communism, the dissolution of the Soviet Union, and the residue of trauma in Russian society. The bodies of these Russian *Vory*, accordingly, are as traumatized as they are masculine, potent, and threatening. Russian criminal tattoos, which became a staple within North/Western films and TV series after their introduction by David Cronenberg in 2007, function as an important signifier of this trauma.

CHAPTER 3

Vulnerable Russian Gays, the White Male-Centric Gaze, and the Reaffirmation of the East/West Divide[1]

The Funeral Party, Ludmila Ulitskaya's novel about Russian Jewish émigrés in New York City, revolves around the last days of a character named Alik, a tragic, but fascinating and charismatic Russian-Jewish artist. Ulitskaya poignantly sums up the imaginary around what is believed to be the strongest contrast between Russians and Americans: their attitude towards suffering. In the words of Fima, another character in the novel, who contemplates the meaning of America, "[t]his young, suffering-denying nation had developed whole schools–philosophical, psychological and medical–dedicated to the single problem of how to save people from suffering [. . .]. Fima's Russian brain had difficulty in coping with this concept. The land which had raised him loved and valued suffering and derived its nourishment from it: from pain people grew, developed."[2] The connection between Russianness and suffering, or, rather, the embrace of suffering as sign of a deep Russian soul, душа/dusha, is crucial for understanding not only ideas around Russian citizenship among Russian intellectual elites—including queer-identified Russians—but also the Anglophone media.

Brian Baer, in his monograph *Other Russias: Homosexuality and the Crisis of Post-Soviet Identity*, argues convincingly that gay or queer-identified Russian

---

1 An earlier version of this chapter was published as "Gays vs. Russia: media representations, vulnerable bodies and the construction of a (post)modern West," *European Journal of English Studies* 21, no. 3 (2017): 241–257, https://doi.org/10.1080/13825577.2017.1369271.

2 Ludmila Ulitskaya, *The Funeral Party*, trans. Cathy Porter (London: Weidenfeld & Nicolson, 2015), 106.

individuals and groups continue to gravitate towards the embrace of suffering as a marker of their belonging to the Russian nation and its cultural traditions. He identifies the Russian embrace of the Irish gay poet and playwright Oscar Wilde as one of the first cases historically in which discourses of gay suffering emerged as point of such a trans-cultural relations. While Russian audiences were not particularly fond of Wilde and his writing before his criminal conviction for "gross indecency with men," "[h]is public humiliation and imprisonment, it seems, earned the writer honorary citizenship in the Russian nation, insofar as they allowed the writer's fate to be situated very neatly into deeply engrained Russian cultural scripts or narratives of the suffering artist, torn between passion and spirituality."[3] What follows from this observation, according to Baer, is that Wilde's case, while it "marked in a very dramatic way a major shift in the social construction of homosexuality in the modern construction of the homosexual as an essentializing identity, [Wilde] is not typically associated with the birth of the modern era or with the birth of the modern homosexual. Instead, he is understood within very traditional and very Russian cultural narratives."[4]

In this chapter, I turn to the signification of the suffering purported to structure the imaginary of Russians in general, and Russian LGBTIQ+ in particular. Analyzing the representation of Russian LGBTIQ+ within the US-American media from 2013 onwards, I argue that suffering, endurance of pain, and physical vulnerability are the most visible and significant traits structuring their representations and meanings within this context, and that the focus on public displays of vulnerability privileged young gay men within the wider LGBTIQ+ solidarity discourses. I would suggest that Russian LGBTIQ+ people can be said to embrace or reproduce notions of gay suffering to mark their belonging to Russian culture and intellectual citizenship in the tradition identified and described by Baer. This form of agency and self-positioning, however, is lost in translation in the Anglophone media representations of the very events in which Russian LGBTIQ+ individuals insert their suffering into scene. By focusing on the suffering of young, white (male) queers, rather than emphasizing their agency and self-identification as a Russian intellectual national elite, Anglophone discourses have reaffirmed the East/West divide, firmly positioning themselves on the side of liberal progress, while placing Russia on the side of conservative backlash. This serves to both victimize Russian LGBTIQ+ people and to ignore their agency.

---

3   Brian James Baer, *Other Russias: Homosexuality and the Crisis of Post-Soviet Identity* (New York: Palgrave Macmillan, 2009), 91.
4   Ibid., 93

It is important to note that this occurred at a time when the US and many Western countries were struggling with increasing discursive and public violence connected to the so-called culture wars. The Supreme Court's decision to overturn *Roe v. Wade*[5] in June 2022, and to leave the decision to allow or forbid abortion to individual states, was a landmark decision. It brought the cultural divide between conservative and progressive ideologies to the fore, and significantly challenged the image of the US as global spearhead of progressive politics. Before and after this decisive ruling, many US states had already introduced anti-trans laws, in particular, and anti-LGBTIQ+ laws in general—from laws restricting pro-LGBTIQ+ content in public education,[6] to those forbidding transgender health care to minors.[7]

In what follows, I will trace Anglophone discourses on Russian LGBTIQ+ issues, prompted by the introduction of the so-called 'anti-homosexual propaganda law,'[8] in daily news media, magazines, social media, and popular culture. I address the nationalistic politics of these discourses, and their connection to the conceptualizations of modernity, progress, and values, as well as the New Cold War, to focus on the visual construction of the young (male) queer body as "the vulnerable Russian" body. Tracing the news reports over a period of ten years, from 2013 to 2023, and contextualizing them within both US-American and Russian politics, as well as global changes, I show how the preoccupation of the Anglophone media with the dilemmas and suffering of Russian LGBTIQ+s declined over time, despite the fact that the situation for the local individuals and groups worsened dramatically

---

5   In Roe v. Wade (410 U.S. 113 [1973]), the US Supreme Court ruled that the United States Constitution protected a right to have an abortion.

6   In Florida, the so-called "Don't Say Gay" policy prohibits "classroom discussion about sexual orientation or gender identity" and states that "classroom instruction by school personnel or third parties on sexual orientation or gender identity may not occur" (Matt Lavietes, "Here's what Florida's 'Don't Say Gay' bill would do and what it wouldn't do," NBC News, March 16, 2022, https://www.nbcnews.com/nbc-out/out-politics-and-policy/floridas-dont-say-gay-bill-actually-says-rcna19929).

7   As of May 19, 2023, "At least 17 states have enacted laws restricting or banning gender-affirming care for minors: Alabama, Arkansas, Arizona, Florida, Georgia, Idaho, Indiana, Iowa, Kentucky, Mississippi, Montana, North Dakota, Oklahoma, Tennessee, Utah, South Dakota and West Virginia. Federal judges have blocked enforcement of laws in Alabama and Arkansas, and several other states are considering bills to restrict or ban care. Proposed bans are also pending before the governors of Texas, Nebraska and Missouri" (Andrew Demillo, "Here are the restrictions on transgender people that are moving forward in US statehouses," *Associated Press*, May 19, 2023, https://apnews.com/article/restrictions-targeting-transgender-people-legislative-updates-df66b5a86be47b03dd5a50449d239275).

8   The Russian federal law "On Protecting Children from Information Harmful to Their Health and Development" forbids the "propaganda of nontraditional sexual relationships" among minors was introduced in summer 2013, and has been circulated in US media discourse as the "Russian anti-gay law" or "anti-homosexual propaganda law."

during the same period. While some of the loss of interest may be owing to the fact that the attention span of the media is notoriously short, and that more novel topics emerged, I would suggest that the decline in reporting is also connected to the increasing anti-LGBTIQ+ backlash in the US, as well as in Europe. This makes it more difficult to claim to be progressive and enlightened, based on a favorable stance towards sexual minorities, in contrast to the anti-LGBTIQ+ politics of Russia. Despite the fact that LGBTIQ+ individuals and groups are no longer the preferred symbols of progressive Western superiority, it is important to understand why they once were, and to demonstrate how this discursive signification supported not only Russian conservative discourses, but conservative politics globally.

Summer 2013

In the summer of 2013, the Russian federal law On Protecting Children from Information Harmful to Their Health and Development, which forbids the 'propaganda of nontraditional sexual relationships' among minors, was introduced. It was circulated in the US-media discourse as the 'Russian anti-gay law' or 'anti-homosexual propaganda law.' While the initial federal version of the law was limited to prohibiting the exposure of minors, that is youth below their eighteenth birthday, to pro-LGBTIQ+ discourses, the Anglophone media often omitted this restriction. In doing so, they anticipated the expansion of the law to any public content "about 'nontraditional sexual relations' in all media, including social, advertising and movies."[9]

From the start, to illustrate their cases, reports, and other discourses on LGBTIQ+ issues in Russia presented victimized bodies of Russian dissidents. They seemed to prefer showing beaten and frightened young gays, and, much more seldom, lesbians. The representations of these bodies were almost exclusively in relation to the Russian nation and Russian state politics. Perhaps with the exception of Alexander Kargaltsev's depiction of nude Russian gay asylum seekers in the US Northwest, in his photography collection *Asylum*,[10] these visual representations of male white bodies were strongly victimizing and objectifying. It can be argued that in circulating these images, the media, in its turn, victimized gay Russian men, presenting them as the primary recipients of North/Western compassion and solidarity. I examine the

9   Emma Bubola, "Putin Signs Law Banning Expressions of L.G.B.T.Q. Identity in Russia," *New York Times*, December 5, 2022, https://www.nytimes.com/2022/12/05/world/europe/russia-ban-lgbtq-propaganda.html?smid=nytcore-ios-share&referringSource=articleShare.

10   Alexander Kargaltsev, *Asylum* (Engels: Studio Van Stralen, 2013).

motives, cultural significance, goals, and effects of these representations of young gay bodies, and propose that not only does the media concentrate the power of its attention on the bodies' vulnerability, but it also reduces the subjects to this vulnerability, for the sake of demonstrating or promoting larger moral (as well as political) issues. Thus, the media draws a connection between vulnerability and questions of values, modernity, and progress.

The explicit and implicit adversaries of these vulnerable Russian bodies are the Russian state, the Orthodox Church,[11] and other, mostly male, segments of mainstream society. The pictures I analyze were published in the daily news, photo reports of news magazines, photo documentaries, social media, and on NGO and activist webpages. Analyzing these visual representations, I ask what role Russia's most vulnerable citizens play in constructing nations and people, as well as the reaffirmation of concepts like 'The East' and 'The West.' Most importantly, I question the construction of values such as 'tolerance' and 'acceptance,' and evaluations such as 'progressive' and 'modern,' in reference to 'vulnerability,' 'security,' and 'nonnormativity.' I will try to show how mainstream US media discourses locate gays in the center of the negotiation of cultural values between Russia and the North/West, and, more specifically, the US. The preoccupation with the physical vulnerability of Russian gays allows them to portray Russia unfavorably, creating the impression that it is brutal, backward, and antimodern. Moreover, the media constructs Russia as distinctly and decidedly different from the North/West, which in turn appears to be united by its shared values of tolerance and the appreciation of diversity—reducing tolerance and diversity to the social and political inclusion of some (white) lesbians and gays.

Case Studies

David against Goliath

During the period just before the introduction of the federal law On Protecting Children from Information Harmful to Their Health and Development in June 2013, until the Sochi Winter Olympics in February 2014, several dozen

---

11 Western media as well as many Russian analysts understand the contemporary Russian Orthodox Church and its leadership as in very close alliance with the government. Critical voices see the Church increasingly as strongly influencing official state policies; others argue that the Putin government uses the Church and its growing popularity to create greater approval of national policies and state actions.

photographs of Russian gays and lesbians appeared in political news outlets and magazines, as well as on social media sites, such as Facebook, Vkontakte, Twitter, and others, thanks to prominent photographers and journalists, NGOs and activists, and the general interest in Russian homophobia within the US mainstream.

Two of the pictures most frequently posted, published, and commented upon showed the Russian LGBTIQ+ activist Kirill Fedorov, who was beaten bloody at a Gay Pride rally in St. Petersburg on June 29, 2013. The two pictures are taken from a strikingly similar perspective, showing almost exactly the same situation: a handsome, young, white gay man, hurt and visibly frightened, shielded by two or three friends. We glean information about their relationship from the captions under the various pictures. The pictures convey a situation that signifies extreme physical danger through the presence of a violent crowd of people in the background.

Arguably the more famous of the photographs, taken by Norwegian photographer Mads Nissen, was published in his *Newsweek* "Photo Essay: The Dangers of Being Gay in Russia."[12] The second photograph was taken by photographer Olga Maltseva and distributed through the American Free Press (AFP) and the American stock-photo agency, Getty Images, Inc. I will offer a close analysis of Maltseva's iconic picture of Fedorov a bit later in the chapter. First, however, I wish to draw attention to yet another of Maltseva's press photographs, one taken on August 2, 2013 (Paratroopers' Day) showing an LGBTIQ+ activist from St. Petersburg,

Like the picture of Fedorov, the photograph of Kirill Kalugin conveys and consolidates the simplified view of Russian public and legal homophobia expressed by US-American and other Western commentators. Moreover, Kalugin's picture is an ideal example of how the highly selective visual representations of homophobic violence against Russian men become decontextualized from their original historic context. Most importantly, the snapshot shows how able-bodied, young, white cis-gendered gay men become constructed as victims of homophobic violence and how this violence is visualized as embodied by 'other' Russian men. These 'other' Russian men are depicted as nationalistic, brutal, backward, violent, and physically marked by their demeanor. Conveniently, they

---

12   Mads Nissen, "Photo Essay: The Dangers of Being Gay in Russia," *Newsweek*, February 10, 2014, http://www.newsweek.com/being-gay-russia-just-got-harder-228592. Additional photos of suffering queers in Russia were published in "These Photos Show the Brutal Violence Inflicted on LGBT People in Russia," Newsflow24, August 3, 2015, http://www.newsflow24.com/these-photos-show-the-brutal-violence-inflicted-on-lgbt-people-in-russia-bitk; and James Michael Nichols, "Here's What Happens When Two Men Hold Hands While Walking the Streets of Russia," *Huffington Post*, July 14, 2015, http://www.huffingtonpost.com/entry/heres-what-happens-when-two-men-hold-hands-while-walking-the-streets-of-russia_us_55a5206ae4b0ecec71bcf80b.

are wearing the blue-and-white striped jersey T-shirts that are not only part of their military uniform, but also a commercialized national product, available for purchase in any souvenir shop, throughout Russia and beyond.

Figure 6. Russian paratroopers scuffle with gay rights activist Kirill Kalugin (center), who conducted a one-man protest against LGBT rights violations in St. Petersburg on August 2, 2013 during the celebration of Paratroopers Day. Photo by Olga Maltseva for AFP/Getty Images.

Kalugin's actual, unfortunate encounter with a group of Russian paratroopers on their national day of celebration was reported only in a very limited range of news sites, such as the *Advocate*,[13] *PinkNews*[14] and the *Baltimore Sun*,[15] and human rights forums such as Amnesty International.[16] However,

---

13 Daniel Reynolds, "WATCH: Former Russian Paratroopers Attack Gay Activist," *Advocate*, August 2, 2013, http://www.advocate.com/politics/military/2013/08/02/watch-former-russian-paratroopers-attack-gay-activist.

14 "Video: Russian paratroopers violently attack lone gay rights activist in St Petersburg," PinkNews, August 5, 2013, http://www.pinknews.co.uk/2013/08/05/video-russian-paratroopers-violently-attack-lone-gay-rights-activist-in-st-petersburg/.

15 Michael Gold, "Russian paratroopers attack gay rights activist during one-man protest," *Baltimore Sun*, August 2, 2013, http://darkroom.baltimoresun.com/2013/08/russian-paratroopers-attack-gay-rights-activist/#2.

16 "'My freedom defends yours': Propaganda and truth about homophobia in Russia," Amnesty International, October 11, 2014, https://www.amnesty.org/en/latest/news/2014/10/my-freedom-defends-yours-propaganda-and-truth-about-homophobia-russia/.

Maltseva's photographic documentation of the event appeared in many articles and news media that discussed the recent homophobic legislation, homophobia in connection with the Sochi Winter Olympics, and other issues. The *Huffington Post*, for example, used the picture to emphasize why the International Olympics Committee requested that "Russia Must Explain Its Anti-Gay Law"[17] in the wake of the upcoming Sochi Olympics. The *Windsor Star* presented it to shame the Olympic Committee for its lack of action after the questionings.[18] And the *Ottawa Citizen* illustrated the Russian context through a picture with a caption that read: "Russia's world champion [in track and field athletics] Yelena Isinbayeva condemns homosexuality,"[19] apropos her Swedish competitor's "'rainbow' nails"[20] during the 2013 World Championships.

One might assume that the reason the news media decided to run Kalugin's picture is because it conveys most graphically the alleged impotence or powerlessness of a member of the Russian LGBTIQ+ community in the face of statesanctioned homophobia. For Amnesty International, it is a scene reminiscent of "the standoff between David and Goliath."[21] The scene, frozen in time photographically, is infused with a certain nostalgia. The time-honored uniform of the blue beret and striped shirt, "Russian paratrooper regalia," worn by "musclebound men, who locked elbows and cornered [Kalugin] as they hurled verbal abuse and shoved him around,"[22] might have prompted the Amnesty activists to draw this parallel.

In referring to the biblical story about the vulnerable young David, future king of the ancient Israelites, in his combat with the giant Philistine warrior in the books of Samuel, however, Amnesty amplified the racialized composition of this picture. The history of European visual art is rich in representations

17 Justin Palmer, "Russia Must Explain Its Anti-Gay Law, Says International Olympics Committee," *Huffington Post*, August 9, 2013, updated February 2, 2016, https://www.huffpost.com/entry/russia-gay-olympics-committee_n_3730925.

18 Daphne Bramham, "Toothless International Olympic Committee ensures that Russia can get away with anti-gay law," *Windsor Star*, August 2, 2013, http://www.windsorstar.com/opinion/columnists/Toothless%2BInternational%2BOlympic%2BCommittee%2Bensures%2Bthat/8744020/story.html.

19 Chris Lehourites, "Russia's world champion Yelena Isinbayeva condemns homosexuality, rips Swedes for 'rainbow' nails," *Ottawa Citizen*, August 15, 2013, http://www.ottawacitizen.com/sports/Russia%20world%20champion%20Yelena%20Isinbayeva%20condemns%20homosexuality/8794161/story.html.

20 Ibid.

21 Amnesty International, "'My freedom defends yours.'"

22 Ibid.

of a golden-haired, white-skinned David and a racialized Goliath. Mannerist pictures like Daniele da Volterra's famous *David and Goliath* (ca. 1550) is just one of the many works that inform our thinking with images. The reference, accordingly, underlines the fragile photographic "statue" of "the slender, red-haired activist" Kalugin, as well as his frightened white face. The broad-shouldered, brown-haired, bearded men to his left and right contrast starkly with Kalugin and convey the impression that the men are in some way ethnically marked.

The Amnesty International text also explains that Kalugin is a "university student," emphasizing his intellectual superiority, separating him off from the backward roughness of the perpetrators. The idea of backwardness resonates with the uniforms of the men. The blue berets signify both membership in the armed forces and the nation of Russia. The Soviet star with the hammer and sickle is a patriotic, nostalgia-inducing reference to the past. The white and blue, horizontally striped undershirts additionally carry connotations of nostalgia: the 'Russian' Breton shirt, the Russian *telnyashka* (тельня́шка), is not only an iconic garment worn by the Russian Navy, the Russian Airborne Forces (paratroopers), and the Russian Marines, but it is also a remnant of the past. The *telnyashka* dates back to the tsarist navy (Russian Imperial Navy) and was subsequently worn by Soviet troops. Moreover, it has the connotation of a specific patriotic, hegemonic masculinity. "A popular saying presents *telnyashkas* as an attribute of "real men": "'Нас мало, но мы в тельняшках!' (Nas malo, no my v telnyashkakh—We are few in number, but we wear *telnyashkas*!)"[23]

Today, the frequency with which one can see the garment among young hipsters in St. Petersburg and Moscow suggests that it is a fashion statement as well—one with a decidedly national character. In Maltseva's photograph, the *telnyashka* heightens the contrast between Kalugin, dressed in multiple layers of clothes, and the military men surrounding him, who wear the bare minimum—the *telnyashka* is, in fact, an undershirt. The *telnyashka* here does not simply explain who they are, or used to be, professionally; it signals their masculinity and the morals and values connected with it. Because they are depicted as engaging in a violent act against a clearly inferior and vulnerable-looking young man, with a look of affliction on his face, and because the viewer knows not only that the man is a gay activist, but that the act was

---

23   Daan Kolthoff, "Telnyashka's," *I Sea Stripes* (blog), April 5, 2010, http://iseastripes.blogspot.com/2010_04_01_archive.html.

inspired by homophobia, we understand the patriotic values of the four men as a reflection of the national idea, as well as an expression of Russian national homophobia. The official flags of the airborne forces in the center and on the side offer another cue for reading the scene in the photo as representative of the Russian context per se, apart from the journalistic reporting of a specific incident.

In the Amnesty International text, a reference to the historic prohibition and persecution of homosexuality during the Soviet era is a redundant reminder that the recent introduction of the 'anti-homosexual propaganda law' must be seen as backward. The association of the *telnyashka* with the Soviet past, and the implication that homophobia is backward and at the same time traditional in the Russian territory (because it is connected with the past), mark the four figures surrounding Kalugin as backward. The focus on their embodiment and expression of muscular masculinity establishes the violent (homophobic) male body as a backward body. This is once more emphasized through the clearly visible missing teeth of the paratrooper facing the viewer, as well as the red scratch marks on shoulder of the person to the left, not to mention the mark, which could be a long, deep scar, on the face of the bearded person, whose gaze we cannot meet, who visibly grabs Kalugin by his jacket.

The contrast of the paratroopers with Kalugin, his eyes downcast as though he is trying to avoid the paratroopers' hostile gaze as much as their shoves and blows, is striking. He gives the impressin of being a complete victim, but only through the stories in the *Advocate*,[24] *PinkNews*[25] and the *Baltimore Sun*[26] is it possible to deduce that his actions were not absolutely innocent or naïve; his was a conscious provocation, considering the context he chose for displaying his pride. This remark is not meant to judge or criticize Kalugin's action in any way. I believe, however, that it is worth considering that Kalugin must have at least been aware that a violent reaction would follow when he unfurled "a rainbow flag with the words 'This is propagating tolerance' painted across the front"[27] on St. Petersburg's Palace Square, one of the busiest places during Paratroopers' Day celebrations.

---

24 Reynolds, "WATCH."
25 PinkNews, "Video: Russian paratroopers."
26 Gold, "Russian paratroopers."
27 Amnesty International, "My freedom defends yours."

One could argue, however, that Kalugin did not just 'brave' the homophobia of the paratroopers, as Amnesty International's and other reports suggest,[28] but provoked the men to display their homophobia. I do not mean to suggest that their homophobia is in any way legitimate. Nevertheless, it is worth reflecting on who faces what kind of violence in Russia, and what kind of violence becomes recognized by the North/Western media, thus generating solidarity among people, as well as North/Western governments. Such considerations are crucial, not least because press photographs are used to build asylum cases and public discourses inform policymaking. North/Western governments should by all means grant asylum to these young men. The problem, however, is that photographs of Kalugin and other young white men, who are brave enough, and perhaps privileged enough, to face violence publicly, to document this violence and 'show' it to the world, became *the* images for "many in the LGBT community,"[29] and the forms of physical violence they have had to face has become the sole signifier for many forms of oppression.

It is possible that as a consequence of these widely circulated images, the North/Western media, as well as the general public and institutions, did not consider other victims as worthy of solidarity, help, or asylum. Empirical research, however, demonstrates that the oppression many LGBTIQ+ identified people must face takes many different forms. In a study conducted between September 2012 and August 2013, the Russian LGBT Network documented that 15 percent of the 2,007 respondents reported experiencing physical violence, while 50 percent reported experiencing psychological abuse.[30] More recently, public health studies researcher Emily Hylton and her colleagues published a study showing that depression is a major and growing problem for Russian men who have sex with men.[31] They interviewed 1367

---

28   Reynolds, "WATCH"; PinkNews, "Video: Russian paratroopers"; Gold, "Russian paratroopers."
29   Amnesty International, "'My freedom defends yours."
30   Russian LGBT Network, "Narusheniia prav I diskriminatsiia v otnoshenii LGBT v Rossii s sentiabria 2012 g. po avgust 2013 g. [Human rights violations and discrimination against LGBT people in Russia from September 2012 to August 2013]," Russian LGBT Network, 2014, http://lgbtnet.ru/sites/default/files/monitoring_2013.pdf. Unfortunately, as of August 2023, the website where the report used to be is no longer accessible from a Western server. Similar results can be found here: "License to Harm—Violence and Harassment against LGBT People and Activists in Russia, Report," Human Rights Watch, December 15, 2014, https://www.hrw.org/report/2014/12/15/license-harm/violence-and-harassment-against-lgbt-people-and-activists-russia.
31   Emily Hylton et al., "Sexual Identity, Stigma, and Depression: the Role of the 'Anti-gay Propaganda Law' in Mental Health among Men Who Have Sex with Men in Moscow, Russia," *Journal of Urban Health* (2017): 1–11.

men from "Russian provinces, municipalities, and in neighboring Ukraine on depression."[32] They found that almost 40 percent of the participants were depressed, and that the "[d]epressive symptoms are [. . .] exacerbated by stigma and laws that deny homosexual identities."[33] In her study on lesbian lives in the Soviet Union and Russia, Francesca Stella shows that lesbians face more psychological violence and emotional abuse within their different private spheres, in their families, and from their neighbors and their friends, than in public discourses, or physical violence in public.[34] Moreover, their responsibilities for family members in their care reduce their opportunities to be publicly out, and involved in activism.[35]

Trans*gender people,[36] and intersex people[37] in particular, have a long history of being subjected to various forms of pathologization and medical violence, as well as psychiatric abuse, by medical professionals and institutions. A psychological study from November 2019 of 588 trans*gender adults living in all federal districts of Russia "found that 45.1 percent (n = 265) and 24.0 percent (n = 141) of transgender people had clinically significant levels of anxiety and depression, respectively."[38] Another psychological study,[39] from the year 2020, concluded with a strong warning that homo- and transphobic structural and psychological violence would lead to a drastic decrease of mental health and well-being. Unfortunately, it must be assumed that the situation will worsen, due to a new directive issued by the Russian health ministry that went into effect on July 1, 2023, requiring public medical clinics

32 Hylton et al., *Sexual Identity*, 1.
33 Ibid.
34 Francesca Stella, *Lesbian Lives in Soviet and Post-Soviet Russia: Post/socialism and Gendered Sexualities* (London: Palgrave Macmillan, 2015), 22ff.
35 Die 12 Opossums, "Gekommen, um zu bleiben! Und das Lied/Leid der Solidarität," *Migrazine: online Magazin von Migrantinnen für alle* 1 (2016), http://migrazine.at/artikel/gekommen-um-zu-bleiben-und-das-liedleid-der-solidarit-t.
36 Yana Kirey-Sitnikova, "Psychiatric abuse of transgender people: a case from Russia," Transadvocate, November 14, 2016, http://transadvocate.com/psychiatric-abuse-of-transgender-people-a-case-of-russia_n_15245.htm.
37 Aleksander Berezkin, "Breaking the ice: the intersex movement in Russia," Intersex Day Project, November 7, 2016, http://intersexday.org/en/breaking-ice-intersex-berezkin/.
38 Egor M. Chumakov et al., "Anxiety and Depression among Transgender People: Findings from a Cross-Sectional Online Survey in Russia," *LGBT health* 8, no. 6 (2021): 412–419, https://doi:10.1089/lgbt.2020.0464.
39 Sharon G. Horne and Lindsey White, "The return of repression: Mental health concerns of lesbian, gay, bisexual, and transgender people in Russia," in *LGBTQ mental health: International perspectives and experiences*, ed. N. Nakamura and C. H. Logie (Washington, DC: American Psychological Association, 2020), 75–88, https://doi.org/10.1037/0000159-006.

to be staffed "with sexologists to help patients 'overcome' homosexuality and various sexual 'mental disorders' [. . .], and 'violations of sexual behaviour such as fetishism, masochism and sadism.'"[40]

To the Western and Russian public, most trans*gender, intersex people, and lesbians have been invisible. Due to the increase in social stigma, more and more LGBTIQ+ people are prevented from outing in public and taking part in visibility activism. Accordingly, they are less likely to be photographed during violent actions against them. Producing visual photographic evidence or documentation for the forms of emotional and psychological violence that victims of homophobia and transphobia have to survive is difficult, perhaps even impossible. Making a case for a successful asylum application is even more challenging if the applicant cannot produce such documentation.

Returning to Maltseva's image of gay rights activist Kirill Kalugin when he was attacked by Russian paratroopers in St. Petersburg on August 2, 2013, it must be mentioned that one of the probable reasons this image was so frequently used to visualize Russian homophobic violence was because the patriotic paratroopers fit so neatly into the idea of the Russian oppressor and his specific form of embodied masculinity: rough, beefed-up, brutish, vulgar, and often drunk. Moreover, this kind of masculinity is seen as representative of Russia and renders contestations of the same masculinities invisible. Without going into this subject in detail, I would like to mention that the 'Blue Berets,' the Russian Airborne Forces or VDV (Воздушно-десантные войска России/Vozdushno-desantnye voyska Rossii, ВДВ), are frequently ridiculed as 'faggots' or homosexuals because of their blue headgear and because they display a very particular kind of homosocial behavior during their national day of celebration and beyond. Within the Russian-speaking context, light blue, the color of the paratroopers' berets, signifies homosexuality.[41] They are said to display very close friendships, or very close male camaraderie, frequently hugging and touching each other, and so on. Images of such male bonding during VDV Day celebrations, which provoked ridicule as being 'gay,' circulated frequently in the Russian, and to a lesser extent the US, media, between 2007 and 2010.

---

40 Reuters Europe, "Russian sexologists to target homosexuality, other 'disorders' under new rules," *Reuters*, June 29, 2023, https://www.reuters.com/world/europe/russian-sexologists-target-homosexuality-other-disorders-under-new-rules-2023-06-29/.

41 Kevin Moss, "Why are these pages blue?" Russian Gay Culture, October 17, 2016, http://community.middlebury.edu/~moss/goluboy.html.

Figure 7. Two paratroopers embracing each other at the Central Market in Lipetsk during a public celebration on August 3, 2007. "Арбузный погром (17 фото)," copypast.ru, accessed Decmber 12, 2024, http://copypast.ru/2007/08/06/arbuznyjj_pogrom_17_foto.html.

Modern Day Jesus(es)

Another widely circulated press photograph of a young gay victim of homophobic violence in Russia was a photo of Dmitry Chizhevsky. Pictures of the wounded face of Dmitry Chizhevsky,[42] a gay asylum seeker to the US who was

---

42   Nora Fitzgerald and Vladimir Ruvinsky, "The fear of being gay in Russia: Putin's state has allowed violence against the Russian LGBT community to spike," *Politico*, March 22, 2015, http://www.politico.com/magazine/story/2015/03/russia-putin-lgbt-violence-116202#ixzz3phdIzSE7.

the victim of a homophobic attack on November 3, 2013[43] at an LGBTIQ+ community gathering at the LaSky HIV charity center in St. Petersburg, accompanied numerous reports about the incident. These reports detailed the dire situation of Russian LGBTIQ+ individuals over a period of several months, if not years, after the incident. Chizhevsky was wounded by a rubber bullet, and lost his eyesight. The pictures taken after the attack, showing his wounded eye covered with white bandages, became internationally distributed pieces of 'evidence' against contemporary Russia. Several newspapers and blogs, and Amnesty International,[44] in particular, introduced the case to an English-speaking Western audience. Soon after, solidarity actions were organized in the US. The first reports included a full-page picture of Chizhevsky in the now defunct St. Petersburg Times on November 4, 2013, as well as a picture and article in the online news magazine LGBTQ Nation,[45] followed by the news blog the Russian Reader[46] only a few days later. These first reports presented Chizhevsky as one victim of a group of LGBTIQ+ people who were now targets of anti-gay hysteria in Russia, which was prompted, or at least supported, by the then-recent introduction of the so-called anti-gay propaganda laws. These pictures and reports most likely reached a limited, but interested, audience. Much later, Misha Friedman's snapshot of Chizhevsky attracted the attention of a much wider audience, following the circulation of the picture through an article titled "The Fear of Being Gay in Russia," by Nora Fitzgerald and Vladimir Ruvinsky, published on March 22, 2015 in Politico Magazine.

Starting in summer 2013, the violence that wounded some Russian men became the motive and target of renewed activist efforts by some nearly defunct US-based activist groups. Before Chizhevsky's unfortunate encounter with homophobic violence in Russia, it had been relatively quiet within the ranks of the activist group Queer Nation NY, for example. In November 2013, however, the group reemerged to combat Russian homophobia. That month on their

---

43 Joe Morgan, "Russian man blinded by anti-gay shooting speaks out," *Gay Star News*, November 5, 2013, http://www.gaystarnews.com/article/russian-man-blinded-anti-gay-shooting-speaks-out051113/#gs.2oEfvCo.

44 Natasha Barsotti, "Amnesty International calls for arrests in St Petersburg," *Daily XTra*, November 5, 2013, http://www.dailyxtra.com/world/news-and-ideas/news/amnesty-international-calls-arrests-in-st-petersburg-73038.

45 "Masked Thugs Invade Russian LGBT Activist Meeting, One Victim May Lose Eye," *LGBTQ Nation*, November 4, 2013, http://www.lgbtqnation.com/2013/11/masked-thugs-invade-russian-activist-meeting-one-victim-may-lose-an-eye/.

46 "Dmitry Chizhevsky: 'I Feel Really Sorry for the Stupid Guys Who Did This to Me,'" *Russian Reader*, November 9, 2013, https://therussianreader.files.wordpress.com/2013/11/dmitry_chizhevsky_russian_gay_activist_blinded_attack.jpg.

homepage, the slogan "This is why we fight" was posted, accompanying an article from the *St. Petersburg Times* that featured a full-page picture of Chizhevsky sitting up in a hospital bed,[47] one eye covered with gauze. The website article called for a boycott of Russian vodka, in solidarity with the Russian LGBTIQ+ community and in support of Queer Nation NY's street protest aimed at the upcoming Sochi Winter Olympics, in February 2014. The pictures and reports that seem to have spurred the US-based activists and other supporters into action focus intensely on Chizhevsky's facial wound.

In a previous article,[48] I analyzed journalistic photographs of Chizhevsky and the activist Kirill Fedorov, to whom I will return later in this chapter in order to show how the North/West comes to represent itself as the ally and savior of their bodies, a sphere in which the vulnerability of LGBTIQ+ bodies is recognized and protection granted. According to this logic, such recognition and protection is not only morally and ethically right for modern and civilized peoples and nations, but is a logical consequence of modern progress. Focusing on the most famous image of Chizhevsky, the photograph by Misha Friedman, photojournalist and post-Soviet migrant to the US, I show how the picture constructs the young man as vulnerable in the most literal sense, showing his face as the surface or locus of his physical wound. The face is what makes us recognizable as individuals, but also as humans among humans; it is what we have in common. Like the face, our individual corporeal vulnerability defines us universally and ontologically as human beings;[49] but the moment vulnerability appears, it signifies us as individuals. The visibility of a specific, individual vulnerability signifies the person's or group's "susceptibility to harmful wrongs, exploitation, or threats to one's interests on autonomy."[50] Most importantly, the visibility or appearance of vulnerability signals social hierarchies. According to this logic "the especially vulnerable are those who, due to inequalities of power, dependency, capacity, or need, are less able than others to protect themselves."[51]

47 "This Is Why We Fight," *Queer Nation New York*, November 14, 2013, http://queernationny. org/post/66984188441/this-is-why-we-fight-the-st-petersburg-times.

48 Katharina Wiedlack, "Gays vs. Russia: Media Representations, Vulnerable Bodies and the Construction of a (Post)Modern West," *European Journal of English Studies* 21, no. 3 (September 2, 2017): 241–57, https://doi.org/10.1080/13825577.2017.1369271.

49 Judith Butler, *Precarious Life: The Powers of Mourning and Violence* (London: Verso, 2006); Paul Ricoeur, *Reflections on the Just*, trans. David Pellauer (Chicago, IL: University of Chicago Press, 2007).

50 Wendy Rogers, Catriona Mackenzie, and Susan Dodds, "Introduction," *IJFAB: International Journal of Feminist Approaches to Bioethics* 5, no. 2 (2012): 3.

51 Rogers et al., "Introduction," 3.

In Friedman's photograph, Chizhevsky's wounded eye occupies the very center of attention, although his face is half-turned away from the viewer. The picture is aesthetically arranged. It is not merely documentation; it is a piece of political art, aesthetic not by accident, but by intention of the author/artist. It is 'aesthetic' in the most archaic sense of the term, as it is a "discourse of the body."[52] "It is a form of cognition, achieved through taste, touch, hearing, seeing, smell—the whole corporeal sensorium."[53] But it is also aesthetic in a more enlightened, modern, Kantian sense, evoking a value judgment, as it reveals the complicated relationship between the representation of 'truth' and art, of values and authorship. Most of all, it is postmodern, as it poses the question not just of the aestheticization of 'any truth,' but of violence, pain and suffering. Yet this question of curation and aesthetics, so pressing to the researcher, can easily be ignored, or rather not raised, by an audience whose affects, empathy, and politics tend toward sympathy with the young gay man. Ignoring the artificiality of this piece of art, a product of arrangement and cropping, the audience is tempted to view the piece as revealing a truth or reality. The article that frames the picture supports such a reading. The truth of the vulnerability of LGBTIQ+ individuals is thus represented through the wounded body of Chizhevsky, although we can only guess at the wound covered by the white gauze. What deepens the impression of vulnerability is that we cannot meet Chizhevsky's gaze, as the bandage itself deprives the photographic subject of the very act of looking.

Vision signifies individuality, a subject position; it is a 'window onto the world,' as well as a 'mirror of the soul.' In his cultural history of vision, Martin Jay points out that "[t]he eye [. . .] is more than the passive receptor of light and color. It is also the most expressive of the sense organs, with the only competitor being touch."[54] The eye signifies agency, because it "can obey the conscious will of the viewer"[55] through its variable modes, "[r]anging from the casual glance to the fixed glare."[56] Since the Enlightenment's privileging of visuality over other sensual forms, sight has become a significant characteristic of and stand in for modernity in general.[57] Furthermore, "perception,

---

52   Eagleton qtd. in Susan Buck-Morss, "Aesthetics and Anaesthetics: Walter Benjamin's Artwork Essay Reconsidered," *October* 62 (1992): 6.
53   Ibid.
54   Martin Jay, *Downcast Eyes: The Denigration of Vision in Twentieth-Century French Thought* (Berkeley: California University Press, 1993), 9.
55   Ibid., 10.
56   Ibid.
57   Ibid., 97.

language, and difference became inextricably connected."[58] In the picture Chizhevsky cannot see and we cannot meet his eye. His inability to face our gaze as spectators deprives him of any ocular agency, and renders him metaphorically speechless.

While he, like so many other young gay men, becomes a 'visually mute' figure in debates about Russian homophobic barbarism and backwardness, the article, which his picture illustrates, speaks for him about his victimhood. The visualized inability to speak for himself, marked through his gauze-covered eye, and the absent stare of the second healthy eye in the picture, looking outside onto the grey courtyard, emphasizes the danger of the Russian environment that Chizhevsky must (literally) face. Additionally, his pose releases the spectator from all responsibility for the process of looking, observing, or gazing. Thus, the picture does not invite reflection on the fact that the Western gaze is informed by cultural ideas and biases, but rather negates this determination by focusing on the dangers that loom in the St. Petersburg context for the young gay man.

Chizhevsky's inability to look back at the spectator, prohibiting him from meeting the benevolent victimizing gaze, may be read as critique of the aims of the viewer's solidarity. If the act of gazing is understood, and critically questioned, as a violent act, ruling out reciprocity, there is a further implication that the spectator's gaze might undermine the desire for agency in Russian LGBTIQ+ lives through the creation of (photographic) visibility, thus frustrating the aims of Western solidarity. However, the text accompanying the pictures does not allow for Western self-critique. Instead, it emphasizes that the West is an environment where LGBTIQ+ lives can thrive, while "Russia's LGBT [*sic*] community [has] been attacked or harassed in what has become an unprecedented crackdown."[59]

In their text, Fitzgerald and Ruvinsky portray Chizhevsky as one of the ultimate victims of violence—one victim among "a growing number." They understand LGBTIQ+ Russians as a "community that was just beginning to organize [and] found itself under assault, the target of a deep-seated Russian homophobia that had now been embedded in law."[60] Their descriptions of the Russian context keep referring back to comparisons with "the West, [where] gay rights have seen startling breakthroughs in the last decade,"

---

58   Ibid., 9.
59   Fitzgerald and Ruvinsky, "The fear of being gay in Russia."
60   Ibid.

only to conclude that "Russia has not just been left behind, but has become demonstrably worse and more dangerous."[61] In this comparative mode, their focus on LGBTIQ+ people allows them to apply a development paradigm that looks to the North/West as a paragon of acceptance and diversity, toward which Russia had previously been moving, until the Russian state and public changed course and embraced bigotry and xenophobia. Friedman's depiction of Chizhevsky transfers these connotations of backwardness onto the visual level by arranging his wounded body in a sparsely lighted room, whose dark corners are in stark contrast with his illuminated face, half-covered by white gauze. Chizhevsky's vulnerability is not only signified by his thin physique and downward-looking gaze, but, most particularly, through the hidden wound. Thus, the picture seems to suggest that he stands in for the vulnerability of Russian LGBTIQ+ bodies in general, bodies endangered by Russian homophobia.

Photographs of Chizhevsky were not uncommon in the Anglophone media during that period,[62] as his case was frequently used to illustrate "Vladimir Putin's attack on homosexuality [that] is shattering the lives of Russians."[63] Furthermore, aesthetically similar photographs were taken and disseminated throughout 2017 and 2018, when the persecution of Chechen people drew much media attention in the Anglophone media sphere.[64] What made the photo of Chizhevsky so significant is that Friedman, the photographer, and the journalist Nora Fitzgerald were both grantees of the Pulitzer Center. Supported by the Arcus

---

61 Ibid.

62 Various pictures of the wounded Chizhevsky circulated in online news (*St. Petersburg Times*, 2013) and other media (#LGBT on Twitter and Facebook). One other very widely distributed shot of Chizhevsky, taken by Yuri Kozyrev appeared in Jeff Sharlet, "Inside the Iron Closet: What It's Like to Be Gay in Putin's Russia," *GQ*, February 4, 2014, http://www.gq.com/story/being-gay-in-russia. Sharlet received the National Magazine Award for Reporting for this article. Chizhevsky was also featured in Mads Nissen, "Photo Essay: The Dangers of Being Gay in Russia," *Newsweek*, February 10, 2014, http://www.newsweek.com/being-gay-russia-just-got-harder-228592; Queer Nation NY; Global Forum on MSM & HIV, "Services Under Siege: Violence against LGBT People Stymies HIV Prevention & Treatment," MSMGF, December 10, 2015, http://msmgf.org/high-levels-of-violence-against-lgbt-people-stymie-hiv-prevention-and-treatment-worldwide/.

63 Sarah Morrison, "Vladimir Putin's attack on homosexuality is shattering the lives of Russians," *Independent*, January 13, 2014, http://www.independent.co.uk/news/world/europe/vladimir-putin-s-attack-on-homosexuality-is-shattering-the-lives-of-russians-9054660.html.

64 James Hill produced similar photographs with Russian gays turning away from the camera for the *New York Times*, for example for the article: Andrew E. Kramer, "'They Starve You. They Shock You': Inside the Anti-Gay Pogrom in Chechnya," *New York Times*, April 21, 2017, https://www.nytimes.com/2017/04/21/world/europe/chechnya-russia-attacks-gays.html.

Foundation, they traveled around the US telling Chizhevsky's story. Together with Chizhevsky himself, they gave a presentation at the Newseum Institute's Religious Freedom Center and at an LGBTIQ+ Conference at Harvard. All of these events were advertised with Friedman's picture of Chizhevsky. Moreover, the photo was shown at a photography exhibit in the Monroe C. Gutman Library Gallery in Cambridge, Massachusettes. It was shown, as well, on September 10–20, 2015, in the Photoville Container Exhibition in Brooklyn Bridge Park, as part of Friedman's photo series *The Iron Closet*. The picture was also featured in a *CBS News* report about the entire Photoville 2015 Exhibition, which included more than forty-eight cargo containers, each designated to an individual artist or topic. The text announcing the *The Iron Closet* series reads: "Being gay in Russia is lonely and extremely dangerous. Being different is not celebrated. It is prosecuted."[65]

Another photograph of the wounded Chizhevsky was taken by Norwegian photojournalist Mads Nissen, and published as part of a *Newsweek* photo essay on "the dangers of being gay in Russia."[66] However, it was not Chizhevsky's photo, but another from Nissen's series that achieved iconic status within North/Western news and social media—a picture of Kirill Fedorov, the injured LGBTIQ+ activist from St. Petersburg. Fedorov is a well-known figure within Russian LGBTIQ+ and human rights activism circles. At the time Nissen took his picture, Fedorov was aligned with the NGO Coming Out (Выход). On June 29, 2013, he was attacked while participating in a street action in the form of a pride rally, in St. Petersburg.

Nissen's pictures of the wounded Fedorov, and a very similar one taken by Olga Maltseva, were distributed widely in the US and other international media.[67] Although it did not achieve the fame that Nissen's shot of Fedorov enjoyed,

---

65   "Pulitzer Center," last modified February 25, 2015, https://pulitzercenter.org.

66   Nissen, "Photo Essay: The Dangers of Being Gay in Russia."

67   Nissen's pictures appeared in: Hannah Levintova, "From Russia with Love: Photos of Brave Gay Activists Fighting Homophobia," *Mother Jones*, January/February 2014, https://www.motherjones.com/media/2014/02/russia-love-gay-propaganda-photos-wedding/ and Julia B. Chan, "Capturing the rage and resilience of Russian homophobia," *Reveal*, September 30, 2016, https://revealnews.org/article/capturing-the-rage-and-resilience-of-russian-homophobia/. Moreover, it continues to be used to raise awareness for Russian human rights violations, for example in the context of the 2018 Football World Champion Ship by QueerArt (@art_queer): "Kirill Fedorov, 21, after extremists attacked him at a Gay Pride rally in St. Petersburg. The march was declared illegal under the law against 'gay propaganda' and Fedorov was later arrested with other LGBT activists," Twitter, June 19, 2018, https://twitter.com/art_queer/status/1009164340749045761.

Maltseva's image did receive considerable public attention,[68] as it was distributed through the American Free Press and the American stock photo agency, Getty Images, Inc. Moreover, Maltseva's picture became a frequent point of reference within Russian activism and art circles commenting on the international and US-led Western gaze on the Russian LGBTIQ+ community. Like Friedman's shot of Chizhevsky, the photos of Fedorov represented young gay male Russian bodies, in juxtaposition to a brutal Russian public and state apparatus. As can be seen here in Maltseva's photograph, the images present the embodied innocence, beauty, and fragility of white male youth, which is seriously threatened by the Russian people, with their brutal Russian mentality, morals, values, and so on.

Figure 8. Gay rights activists embrace each other after clashes with anti-gay demonstrators during a gay pride event in St. Petersburg on June 29, 2013. Kirill Fedorov is the second person from the right, wearing a black T-shirt. Photo by Olga Maltseva for AFP/Getty Images.

---

68   One fan even produced a video as a tribute to Mads Nissen's photo essay that begins the slide show with Fedorov's iconic picture paired with the great pathos of Wolfgang Amadeus Mozart's and Herbert von Karajan's music (Julien Davenne, "Homophobia in Russia," *Vimeo*, January 21, 2016, https://vimeo.com/152622170). Mainstream news equally celebrated Nissen by presenting the photograph of Fedorov, including the Weekly Photography corner on *Culture Magazine*, i24news (Michal Mika Gurovich, "World Press Photo-Winner—Mika Photography at the Culture Magazine at i24NEWS," i24NEWS, February 24, 2015, https://www.youtube.com/watch?v=kZ1gnewaacw). The occasion for a report on Nissen's work was his winning the World Press Photo of the Year award in 2014.

In this picture, Fedorov's body, with his bleeding (nose), pale face, three-day beard, and wavy brown hair, surrounded by three figures, is reminiscent of a Christian martyr. In fact, it could be read as a contemporary depiction of the passion of Christ in the Christian iconographic tradition, with Fedorov as Jesus in the middle and the two persons to his left and right, who could be read as women: Mother Mary and Mary Magdalene. The first text that accompanied and explained the picture, written by Dylan C. Robertson in the *Toronto Star* newspaper, does not reveal the activists' names.[69] In the subsequent twenty-seven or more publications that reported on the violence against Fedorov, and/or used Maltseva's image to illustrate Russian public violence against LGBTIQ+ people, similar to the dissemination of the shot taken by Nissen, only the wounded figure Kirill Fedorov is named, while the people surrounding him remain anonymous, mentioned only as his friends. Maltseva's photograph illustrated online news articles and headlines about homophobic violence in Russia appearing in Western news media, from the *Vancouver Sun*[70] and the *New Statesman*,[71] to the *Huffington Post*,[72] the *Los Angeles Times*[73] and *BuzzFeed News*.[74] None of them named Fedorov's female companions. This little detail is very significant, because, when analyzed through a feminist lens, it exemplifies how North/Western LGBTIQ+ solidarity discourses marginalize or completely erase women and lesbians.

---

69 Dylan C. Robertson, "Pride parade in St. Petersburg met with violence, hostility," *Toronto Star*, June 30, 2013, https://www.thestar.com/news/world/2013/06/30/pride_parade_in_st_petersburg_met_with_violence_hostility.html.

70 Tiffany Crawford and Brian Morton, "Vancouver bars boycott Russian vodka after anti-gay law passed," *Vancouver Sun*, June 27, 2013, http://www.vancouversun.com/life/Anti%2BRussia%2Bprompts%2BVancouver%2Bbars%2Bstop%2Bserving%2BRussian%2Bvodka/8713709/story.html.

71 Eleanor Margolis, "When it comes to Russia's draconian anti-gay laws, Nazi comparisons are apt," *New Statesman*, August 8, 2013, http://www.newstatesman.com/lez-miserable/2013/08/when-it-comes-russias-draconian-anti-gay-laws-nazi-comparisons-are-apt.

72 Nancy Wilson, "To Russia with Love," *Huffington Post*, September 11, 2013, http://www.huffingtonpost.com/rev-dr-nancy-wilson/to-russia-with-love_1_b_3894300.html. James Nichols, "'Art Speaks Louder Than Words' Showcases Support for LGBT Russians," *Huffington Post*, October 25, 2013, http://www.huffingtonpost.com/2013/10/25/art-speaks-louder-than-wor_n_4159546.html.

73 Daniel Rothberg, "Will gays be safe at Russia's Winter Olympics?" *Los Angeles Times*, July 26, 2013, https://www.latimes.com/opinion/opinion-la/la-ol-gay-law-russia-winter-olympics-boycott-20130726-story.html.

74 Matt Stopera, "36 Photos From Russia That Everyone Needs To See: It's a scary place for LGBT people in Russia right now," *BuzzFeed News*, July 22, 2013, https://www.buzzfeed.com/mjs538/photos-from-russia-everyone-needs-to-see.

The reason why Maltseva's photograph became widely 'celebrated' in the US and international media seems to be because Fedorov's wounded body offered proof of Russia's malign homophobia, and, simultaneously, revealed its last uncorrupted body of resistance. The wounded figure represented everything in Russia that is good, sane, modern, and so forth. The content of the articles and short news segments that accompanied the photograph varied from reports about the then-new anti-homosexual propaganda law,[75] announcements of a local boycott against Russian products,[76] and so on. All of them, however, contained a reminder and warning that "[i]t's a scary place for LGBT [sic] people in Russia right now,"[77] referring to the photograph as one "That Everyone Needs to See."[78] In Maltseva's picture, Fedorov is transformed from an activist into a gay icon due to the display of his wounded body; gay iconography and Christian iconography become one.

Mieke Bal understands "iconography as a useful yet limited code [that] contains and generates verbality in the very core of art history."[79] She describes iconography as a way of 'reading' a detail in a picture. Such reading connects the "signs with the absent item they stand for."[80] The detail that the spectator is inevitably alerted to, through the iconographic arrangement of Kirill's figure, is his bleeding wound. The 'absent item' that the iconographic representation of Kirill stands for is the sacrifice of being 'true' to oneself, the very mechanism North/Western gay identity is based on. Moreover, it is also the violence against him that we do not see, but that we know about, not least because it caused his bleeding nose. Last, but not least, the 'absent item' is the Russian state itself, which sanctions the violence against LGBTIQ+ people through a lack of police protection and the implementation of anti-LGBTIQ+ laws. Importantly, the picture of the gay martyr Fedorov not only creates discourses based on prior knowledge or the text that accompanies it; it also creates emotional, or rather, affective, responses. It stirs pity, shame, and a desire to help. Together, these affects lead to the spiritual elevation of the spectator as helper in solidarity with Fedorov, despite the fact that the viewer engages in nothing more than the act of looking.

---

75 Margolis, "When It Comes to Russia's Draconian Anti-Gay Laws."
76 Crawford and Morton, "Vancouver bars boycott Russian vodka."
77 Stopera, "36 Photos From Russia That Everyone Needs to See."
78 Ibid.
79 Mieke Bal, Reading "Rembrandt:" Beyond the Word-Image Opposition (Cambridge: Cambridge University Press, 1991), 178.
80 Ibid., 215.

These feelings about the wounded victim, as well as the spectator himself, are as normative as they are sentimental.

The worshipping of queer icons or martyrs has a long tradition in Anglophone contexts. The LGBTIQ+ historian Patricia Juliana Smith argues that the "worship of idols—of 'false' gods—is an integral part of queer culture, particularly in times when homosexuality is most severely proscribed."[81] The cultural studies scholar Dominic Janes argues that Catholic imagery of the martyr played a key role in the evolution of the culture and visual expression of homosexuality and male same-sex desire in the nineteenth and twentieth centuries, and that it continues to influence queer culture today.[82] Janes traces the beginnings of what he calls 'queer martyrdom' back to the nineteenth-century Church of England. He proposes that queer martyrdom provided inspiration for artists looking to communicate their own feelings of sexual "deviance" during Victorian times and beyond. With reference to the work of the gay writer Oscar Wilde and the HIV/ Aids activist Derek Jarman,[83] Janes argues for the persisting significance of the queer martyr as an inspiration for expressions of homoerotic desire. "The life and work of Derek Jarman," Janes writes, is "testimony to some of the ways in which the older model of queer martyrdom recovered relevance and importance in the 1980s."[84] Referring to Jack Babuscio and his essay on "Camp and the Gay Sensibility," Janes discusses camp and its "use of melodrama, posing, and stylization as a way of engaging an audience"[85] in close proximity to the stylization of the martyr in Christian tradition. While he speaks to the context of the UK, scholars such as Smith read the celebration of popular figures by queer audiences during the 1960s as the creation of "martyrs/icons"[86] in the US-American context. Figures such as Andy Warhol, were celebrated for their pain and suffering, deputizing for all suppressed homosexuals.[87] In the case of Warhol, it is easy to see how the campness of pop culture and the macabre aspect of its humor

---

81   Patricia Juliana Smith, *The Queer Sixties* (London: Routledge. 1999), xv.

82   Dominic Janes, *Visions of Queer Martyrdom from John Henry Newman to Derek Jarman* (Chicago, IL: University of Chicago Press, 2015).

83   Derek Jarman was an English film director, stage designer, artist, and author. Jarman, who was diagnosed with HIV in 1986, was a leading campaigner against Britain's Clause 28, which banned the "promotion of homosexuality" in schools during the 1980s (Tony Peake, *Derek Jarman: A Biography* [Woodstock, NY: Overlook Press, 1999]). He was an outspoken gay rights activist; after being diagnosed, he also worked to raise awareness of HIV/AIDS until his death in 1994.

84   Janes, *Visions of Queer Martyrdom*, 27.

85   Ibid.

86   Smith, *The Queer Sixties*, xv.

87   Ibid.

and kitsch, which the figure of the artist embodied, facilitated the popularity and allure necessary for becoming a martyr when he was shot by the writer Valerie Solanas. Due to his eccentric, but substantial fame at the time, which was also built on his status as a queer enfant terrible, his martyrdom—his suffering for art and arguably suffering *as* art—came to be understood as camp.

While the connection to camp made the image of the martyr a fixture of gay and queer artistic repertoire, the queer icon does not necessarily feature any campness. In Maltseva's photograph of Fedorov, the ironic and humorous quality of martyrdom, a martyrdom of political camp, is absent. Yet Janes's explorations are nevertheless useful for analyzing Fedorov's image, as he offers a possible explanation for the appeal of martyrs within Western queer cultures. He argues that the "visual images and imaginary visions of suffering" inherited from "ecclesiastical contexts" were used to "develop concepts of male same-sex desire that projected the self as dutiful and penitent rather than shameful."[88] Subsequently, Anglo-Catholic images of martyrs, or images that followed their aesthetic configuration and pathos, could be used by queer individuals "as a way of reflecting on and contributing to the construction of their own notions of queer sensibility."[89] Thus, the depictions of queer martyrs became interpreted as "queer triumph over adversity, or sad tableaux of sexual failure."[90]

The photograph of the bleeding LGBTIQ+ activist Fedorov conveys both of these qualities to the American audience and to the liberal Western audience at large. It is a celebration of queer resistance and integrity, as well as a sad image of sexual suppression. The picture's "exalted drama around the sufferings and privations of sexual and gender deviants"[91] in Russia signifies Fedorov's social and cultural condition as martyrdom. This kind of martyrdom can be employed by an individual themself, but it can also be "imputed to others."[92] Significantly, "[m]artyrdom is a social formation and requires the witness not just of the martyr but of others who will attest to one."[93] An audience that understands its precarity and vulnerability can make or produce the martyr as martyr; in other words, despite their own intentions. The shocked and painfully contorted faces of the figures surrounding Fedorov in Maltseva's photograph, in their failed attempt to protect and shield him from the hostile crowd, attest to his

---

88   Janes, *Visions of Queer Martyrdom*, 5.
89   Ibid.
90   Ibid.
91   Janes, *Visions of Queer Martyrdom*, 12.
92   Ibid., 9.
93   Ibid.

martyrdom. It can be argued, referring to Baer,[94] that Fedorov actively performed Russian suffering-as-form to mark his national belonging to the Russian nation and culture, with its tradition of showcasing the Russian soul or душа/*dusha*. In the Anglophone cultural realm, however, and for the Anglophone audience, that agency becomes invisible, since it does not resonate in the same way with ideas of LGBTIQ+ identification and experience.

The spiritual, almost religious intensity with which the image of the wounded gay activist came to be celebrated in the West, and its diverging meanings within the Russian context, was captured by an oil painting of the picture, in the style of traditional Russian Orthodox iconography, by Russian artist Blue Iconostasis (Голубой Иконостас/goluboy-ikonostas).

Figure 9. "Ikona: Chetyre LGBT Rossiiane" ["Icon: Four LGBT Russians"], from "*Goluboi Ikonostas* [The Blue Iconostasis], Four LGBT Russians," goluboy-ikonostas.tumblr.com, March 20, 2014, http://goluboy-ikonostas.tumblr.com/post/80220089822/icon-four-lgbt-russians-икона-четыре-лгбт.

---

94 Baer, *Other Russias*, 95ff.

The Blue Iconostasis icon shows the four Russian LGBTIQ+ activists in the configuration of Maltseva's photograph at the bottom-center. Their modern shirts and pants are exchanged for Byzantine garb, which, together with their golden haloes, additionally emphasizes the already striking reference to Christian imagery. As in the original picture, Fedorov's nose and mouth are bloody, and the arm of the woman on Fedorov's left side is stained with his blood. The four figures are surrounded by a cloud, which, according to the artist, is "tear gas used to break up the demonstration."[95]

In addition to the poisonous clouds, black barbed wire fencing with a rainbow flag tied to the back of it encircles the group. The text, written in red Cyrillic letters at the bottom, lower right, and left sides of the painting is a passage from the Russian anti-gay propaganda law. Above the group of LGBTIQ+ protesters rises a St. Petersburg landmark and symbol of the Russian Orthodox Church: St. Isaac's Cathedral. The three figures to the left side represent the "Russian police (полиция) and Maxim Martsinkevich [aka Тесак/Tesak, which can be translated as 'machete'], from the group Occupy Pedophilia, skinhead vigilantes who film themselves torturing unsuspecting gay men."[96] The caption accompanying the picture on Tumbler states that "[t]hey do this with the tacit consent of the government."[97]

The picture offers a multilayered and ironic critical analysis of the high visibility of Kirill and other gay men like him, such as Chizhevsky, in the New Cold War discourses in their general Anglophone and Russian LGBTIQ+ contexts. On the one side, Blue Iconostasis's gay icons or martyrs express the idea that the figure of the Russian homosexual has an "almost privileged relationship to suffering"[98] in the Russian cultural context, which many contemporary Russian intellectuals are acutely aware of. To make the point that "the suffering homosexual abounds in post-Soviet culture," Baer refers to the gay poet Genadii Trifonov, who described homosexuals in 1977 as "the very symbols of Sorrow and Suffering."[99]

At the same time, the picture actively addresses US discourses, implicitly criticizing the victimization and celebration of Russian LGBTIQ+ activists, without acknowledging their agency or the connection between their performances and Russian cultural forms. Additionally, and much more explicitly, it also addresses the failure of reporting in the US media and other activist and public solidarity discourses to acknowledge the connections between US-based and Russian

---

95   *Goluboi Ikonostas.*
96   Ibid.
97   Ibid.
98   Baer, *Other Russias*, 95.
99   Ibid.

homophobia. It does so by depicting the "American anti-gay activist Scott Lively, holding his book *The Pink Swastika*, which claims to prove that militant homosexuals caused the Holocaust and the Nazi regime"[100] in the upper-right corner of the picture. In spring 2014, the artist explains, Lively publicly announced his intention to publish his book in Russian.[101] Lively wears the traditional garb of a clergyman in the oil painting, but the colors and style of the fabric's pattern allude additionally to the Stars and Stripes of the American flag, locating the evangelical pastor firmly within the cultural context of the US.[102] The scroll in his hand quotes Lively: "[t]he battle to protect Russia from homosexualization [*sic*] has only just begun [. . .]. Stand against this scourge."[103]

The strategic ignorance, not only of the explicit and factual export/import of US homophobia to Russia, and vice versa, but also of the systematic denigration of Russia and Russian as homophobic and morally compromised, allowed the media to create homonationalistic discourses that presented the US as a forward-looking, progressive, and good modern country, despite the steady growth of anti-LGBTIQ+ violence there. Scholars such as Michelle Rivkin-Fish and Cassandra Hartblay, who warned early on against this simplistic strategy, have emphasized that North/Western discourses at that time framed "Russia's anti-gay legislation as evidence of Russian authoritarianism," and ignored "the collaborations between U.S. Evangelicals and Russian conservatives" that supported the law, consistently portraying "Putin as a rogue despot, exceptional among contemporary political leaders."[104] Rivkin-Fish and Hartblay promoted an analysis of "Russia's gay politics as yet another example of global cultural politics between religious fundamentalism and secular morality that plays out every day in the West."[105] Since then, many scholars, such as the feminist theorist Elizabeth S. Corredor,[106] feminist political scientists

---

100 *Goluboi Ikonostas.*

101 Ibid.

102 The Center for Constitutional Rights represented Sexual Minorities Uganda (SMUG), a nonprofit LGBTI advocacy organization in Uganda that successfully sued Scott Lively for his role in supporting and disseminating homophobic discourses in Uganda and for the persecution of LGBTI people there: "Sexual Minorities Uganda v. Scott Lively," CCR Justice, October 11, 2019, https://ccrjustice.org/home/what-we-do/our-cases/sexual-minorities-uganda-v-scott-lively.

103 *Goluboi Ikonostas.*

104 Michele Rivkin-Fish and Cassandra Hartblay, "When Global LGBTQ Advocacy Became Entangled with New Cold War Sentiment: A Call for Examining Russian Queer Experience," *Brown Journal of World Affairs* 21, no. 1 (2014): 98.

105 Ibid.

106 Elizabeth S. Corredor, "Unpacking 'Gender Ideology' and the Global Right's Antigender Countermovement," *Signs* 44, no. 3 (2019): 613–38, https://doi.org/10.1086/701171.

Mieke Verloo and David Paternotte,[107] and queer theorist Emil Edenborg[108] have analyzed in great detail how the global far-right activated and used religious and other networks to disseminate anti-LGBTIQ+ and so-called anti-gender discourses promoting homo- and transphobia and agitating against feminism, sexual minority rights, abortion rights, and transgender health care, and so on.

In constructing and using the gay victim without allowing sufficient agency or means to end his victimization in order to legitimize themselves, Western homonationalist discourses have missed or ignored transnational anti-gay discourses that embrace the fact that Western liberalism opposes them. Concentrating on the martyr and its overly powerful adversary within the confines of Russian discourses, they ironically repeat the same sentiments that Russian agitators peddled in their propaganda in support of so-called traditional values and assertion that homophobia is antimodern and anti-liberal.[109]

Returning to Maltseva's photograph of Fedorov, a striking element, not yet fully explored, is the background of a shouting, aggressively gesticulating crowd of Russian people, against which the martyr Fedorov and his three supporters are positioned. The arrangement of the bodies constructs the gay body as vulnerable, as much as it establishes its counterpart—the violent Russian masses of homophobes. Like any photograph, the picture shows only a snippet of a scene, a process frozen in time. Moreover, it is artificially cropped and represents the point of view and focus of the photographer. Yet the text that accompanies the picture in various news media makes claims to the truth, not just of the particular event in St. Petersburg on June 29, 2013, but also the context of the whole of Russia. It generalizes the incident involving Fedorov and further emphasizes the formation we see in the picture: the vulnerability and powerlessness of young (white) gay men in the face of violent Russia.

On the news website Canada.com, the picture accompanied an article about the possible increase of applications for asylum to Canada by members of the Russian LGBTIQ+ community.[110] To make the article and story even more impressive, the

---

107 Mieke Verloo and David Paternotte, "The Feminist Project under Threat in Europe," *Politics and Governance* 6, no. 3 (2018): 1–5, https://doi.org/10.17645/pag.v6i3.1736.

108 Emil Edenborg, "Homophobia as Geopolitics: 'Traditional Values' and the Negotiation of Russia's Place in the World," in *Gendering Nationalism: Intersections of Nation, Gender and Sexuality*, ed. Jon Mulholland, Erin Sanders-McDonagh, and Nicola Montagna (Berlin: Palgrave Macmillan, 2018), 1–388, https://doi.org/10.1007/978-3-319-76699-7.

109 Marlene Laruelle, "Making Sense of Russia's Illiberalism," *Journal of Democracy* 31, no. 3 (2020): 115–29.

110 Erica Lenti, "Gay Russian teen desperate to come to Canada to escape homophobic laws," Postmedia Network, October 9, 2013, http://o.canada.com/news/gay-russian-teen-desperate-to-come-to-canada-to-escape-homophobic-laws.

author not only used Kirill Fedorov's picture, but described the case of a seventeen-year-old gay teenager as a discussion starter, under the headline: "Gay Russian Teen Desperate to Come to Canada to Escape Homophobic Laws."[111]

Journalist Eleanor Margolis goes even further in the *New Statesman*.[112] Like Jay Leno, former host of NBC's *Tonight Show*,[113] she reads the "anti-gay legislation" as "truly reminiscent of the antisemitic Nuremberg Laws. It is paving the way for a state in which LGBT [sic] people are tortured to death, while the authorities do nothing."[114] Robertson emphasizes that gays and lesbians at this specific pride parade in St. Petersburg were not adequately protected from "the violence and hostility of a much larger crowd, and most of their country."[115] Regardless of its grammatical ambiguity, the clear purpose of the sentence is to suggest that the incident in St. Petersburg reflected attitudes in the whole of Russia—that most people in Russia are violent homophobes.

In all these articles, the visibly vulnerable activist Fedorov stands in for the vulnerability of all Russian LGBTIQ+ people, suggesting that they are helpless victims of Russian homophobia and disregarding their agency and choice to perform Russian suffering as a claim to notions of душа/dusha and Russian cultural citizenship. As much as Maltseva's photograph constructs Fedorov as an individual gay martyr, the text constructs him as just one example of a general vulnerability. Feminist and disability scholars focus on vulnerability to theorize the relationship between individuals, society, and nation states. As I have already mentioned, Judith Butler invokes vulnerability as a universal human experience and point of interconnectedness, to argue for solidarity, and social and state responsibility.[116] While Butler understands shared vulnerability as the human condition, Kate Kaul,[117] Sherene Razack,[118] and Martha Fineman[119] focus on the particularity of individual vulnerability to determine what differentiates subjects from each other. They draw attention to the fact that vulnerability is a fundamental category for justifying the need for state

---

111 Ibid.

112 Margolis, "When it comes to Russia's draconian anti-gay laws."

113 Francesca Bacardi, "Jay Leno Compares Russian Olympics to Nazi Germany," *Variety*, December 17, 2013, http://variety.com/2013/tv/news/jay-leno-nazi-olympics-1200969781/.

114 Margolis, "When it comes to Russia''s draconian anti-gay laws,"

115 Robertson, "Pride parade in St. Petersburg met with violence."

116 Butler, *Precarious Life*, 27.

117 Kate Kaul, "Vulnerability, for Example: Disability Theory as Extraordinary Demand," *Canadian Journal of Women and the Law/Revue Femmes et Droit* 25, no. 1 (2013): 81–110.

118 Sherene H. Razack, *Looking White People in the Eye: Gender, Race, and Culture in Courtrooms and Classrooms* (Toronto: University of Toronto Press, 1998).

119 Fineman, "The vulnerable subject."

protection. Human rights lobbying groups such as UNESCO's International Bioethics Committee (IBC) also focus on vulnerability, arguing that recognizing it may build a "bridge to greater solidarity, and that a commitment to respect for vulnerability is a necessary constituent of the political responsibility of states."[120]

Vulnerability also implies dependency, however, as Kaul, Razack and Fineman warn. And although it is crucial that a welfare state identifies the various needs of various people to fulfill its responsibilities, identifying certain groups and individuals as vulnerable is not unproblematic—particularly, but not exclusively, in authoritarian regimes. In general, for the liberal subject, the structural connection of vulnerability and dependency invariably refers to the status of children and the need to restrict their full rights and abilities as citizens, allegedly in their own best interest.[121] Furthermore, vulnerability and dependency evoke pity, catering to what Razack calls an "ableist gaze,"[122] which reduces persons with a visible vulnerability to "icons of pity."[123] Although Razack uses the term "icons of pity" in reference to disabled racialized women, through the ableist and heteronormative North/Western gaze of the US media, the wounded Fedorov and Chizhevsky are produced as just such icons of pity.

The emotional response of pity for their vulnerability further creates the desire to rescue Fedorov, Chizhevsky, and other Russian gays. Although it might be connected to admiration, pity, within the realm of Anglophone culture, is hardly compatible with respect. It stands in stark contrast to the idea of душа/dusha in the Russian context, in which suffering and the endurance of suffering is highly valued culturally as a form and expression of spirituality. In the Anglophone context, the person who feels pity for another's suffering can be viewed as complicit in oppressing them, since it may imply a feeling of superiority, both powerful and able. To put it differently, feelings of pity may prevent the viewer from recognizing any agency in the "gazed upon" individual, reducing the person to an object of their patronizing care. By disseminating pictures of the wounded faces of Fedorov and Chizhevsky, or the frightened Kalugin, mentioned in my earlier chapter, the media sacrifices them again and again, in the interests of demonstrating the authoritarian state's injustice and the Russian public's violence towards sexual minorities. Simultaneous with the reframing of vulnerability as a chance to rethink and reimagine human connectedness, articulated by philosophers such as Butler, media discourses, and

---

120 Wendy Rogers, Catriona Mackenzie, and Susan Dodds, "Introduction," *IJFAB: International Journal of Feminist Approaches to Bioethics* 5, no. 2 (2012): 1–10.
121 Kaul, *Vulnerability*, 102; Fineman, *The vulnerable subject*, 2.
122 Razack, *Looking White People in the Eye*, 132.
123 Ibid.

the discourses of activists, is an insistence on vulnerability as a problem to be solved through the protection of the US, other Western powers, and seemingly more enlightened nations. This sentiment is exemplified by the famous plea of Russian journalist and LGBTIQ+ activist Masha Gessen: "Get Us the Hell Out of Here."[124] This is a plea for protection through asylum in the US for all members of the Russian LGBTIQ+ community; this plea was, of course, never answered fully.

The vulnerability conveyed in the pictures of Fedorov, Chizhevsky, and Kalugin makes the spectator feel that the state is responsible and that citizens of states that are 'good,' morally responsive and conscientious, bear this responsibility. When the vulnerable subject is detached from any agency, what the subject wants is no longer in question; the Western viewer already knows what is best for her/him/them. The media produces vulnerable bodies to point to the injustice of the oppressive forces endangering these bodies.

Yet the specific causes and circumstances of this vulnerability, the concrete source of violence and its political nexus, are not presented. Labelled as gay, their status as sacred figureheads of modernity and modern values is established. The political issues or context that preceded it—that the activist Fedorov was beaten by right-wing activists—is no longer relevant. Nor is it important in which specific context Chizhevsky was shot. The reason why these subjects are vulnerable, according to the media, is rather the general "wrongness" and "backwardness" of the Russian state, because "[u]nder President Vladimir Putin, Russia has been sliding back toward the Middle Ages."[125] Through focusing on their vulnerability, the three individuals, together with all Russian LGBTIQ+ people, become objectified by the discourses on LGBTIQ+ issues in Russia. At the same time, Kalugin, Fedorov, and Chizhevsky become celebrated as martyrs, as holy figures representing values that are good, right, and just. These young white men become true celebrities, not so much within the West, but within Russia, setting a standard for what activism, public actions, and resistance should look like, in order to be recognized by a broader (Western) audience. Within the US media, they are not so much celebrated, but patronized and cared for; they are the 'sacred' figures the North/West needs to "get out of Russia," echoing again Gessen's plea.

---

124 Gessen qtd. in Michelangelo Signorile, "Russian Gay Activist's Plea: 'Get Us the Hell Out of Here.'" *Huffington Post*, June 9, 2013, http://www.huffingtonpost.com/michelangelo-signorile/russian-gay-activists-plea-get-us-the-hell-out-of-here_b_3881059.html.
125 Anna Nemtsova, "Russia Slides Back to the Middle Ages," *Daily Beast*, June 8, 2015, http://www.thedailybeast.com/articles/2015/08/07/russia-slides-back-to-the-middle-ages.html.

The Russian Blue Iconostasis/Голубой Иконостас produced another oil painting, which addresses the construction of gay martyrs in Russian discourses, as well as US-American contexts, and their exchange in July 2014. It is in direct conversation with the previous oil painting based on Maltseva's photograph of Fedorov and his three anonymous activist colleagues. The icon depicts Fedorov standing alone in St. Petersburg, signified by the General Staff arch on one side of Palace Square and Saint Isaac's Cathedral. Again, he is wearing a kind of a Latin garment, in white and blue, with a tunic in rainbow colors around one shoulder, a style that alludes to the dress of Christian icons.

Figure 10. "*Goluboi Ikonostas* [The Blue Iconostasis], Kirill Fëdorov—One of the Pride Marchers of St. Petersburg," Goluboy-ikonostas.tumblr.com, July 6, 2014, http://goluboy-ikonostas.tumblr.com/post/91003436038/kirill-f%C3%ABdorov-one-of-the-pride-marchers-of-st.

The halo, the beard and long hair, the sober but serene facial expression, and the gesture of his hand particularly recall portraits of Jesus in traditional Orthodox iconographic paintings. In Russian Orthodoxy, Jesus is frequently depicted holding a holy book in one hand and making a sign or gesture with the other (Christ Pantokrator, Greek for "Christ Almighty"). In Russian Orthodox iconography, the raised hand of Christ Pantokrator is usually the right one, signifying the bestowal of a blessing. The book with a painted cross on the cover, which identifies it as the Gospels, is held in Christ's left hand.[126] The halo "denotes a sanctified state"[127] in Russian Orthodox iconography.

In Fedorov's case, in addition to the reference to Christian iconography, it has yet another meaning. It alludes to the status that Fedorov has acquired within Russian social media and social activism. Moreover, it makes reference to his status as a martyr in the US and international media. The visibility of his martyrdom is also suggested by the text on the parchment scroll in his hands. The script is "a quote [. . .] from an interview that was posted by Children-404 on Facebook."[128] In the interview, Fedorov says, regarding the anti-gay protestors who attacked him, "I do not hate them. They are the same people."[129] This peaceful attitude suggests endurance rather than fighting back. It is reminiscent of the passivity of Christian martyrdom, the brave endurance of imprisonment or torture. In the Russian cultural context, this endurance of suffering signifies "an ahistorical feature of homosexual desire itself."[130] The idea that the "acute artistic sensibility" is not only connected to suffering and Russianness, but also to homosexuality, again highlights notions of Russian national and cultural belonging. In contrast, in the US or North/Western view, the martyr Fedorov endures violence because he has 'witnessed' liberation and freedom like the first Christian martyrs, the Apostles, who witnessed Jesus or God:

> The Greek word *martus* signifies a witness who testifies to a fact of which he has knowledge from personal observation. It is in this sense that the term first appears in Christian literature: the Apostles were "witnesses" of all that they had observed in the public life of Christ, as well as of all they had learned from His teaching.[131]

Translating the Christian concept of the martyr to LGBTIQ+ people in Russia marks them as 'knowing' individuals who are already of the future, a future that

---

126 Solrunn Nes, *The Mystical Language of Icons* (Cambridge: Wm. B. Eerdmans Publishing, 2005), 23.
127 Ibid.
128 *Goluboi Ikonostas* [The Blue Iconostasis].
129 Fedorov qtd. in *Goluboi Ikonostas* [The Blue Iconostasis].
130 Bear, *Other Russias*, 96.
131 Maurice Hassett, "Martyr," in *The Catholic Encyclopedia*, vol. 9 (New York: Robert Appleton Company, 1910), 12.

has yet to come to Russia, which is "sliding back toward the Middle Ages,"[132] away from North/Western modernity and progress.

In and through their vulnerability and their status as gay martyrs, Kalugin, Fedorov, and Chizhevsky become central figures in the New Cold War between Russia and the North/West. In this media war, the old Cold War rhetoric, as well as the hegemonic orientalist ideologies of past decades, are resuscitated. The subjects and figures in which developmental discrepancies become marked, however, have changed significantly from the old to the New Cold War. Russian LGBTIQ+ issues are among the subjects in current discourses, and the framework within which the evaluation takes place is modernity itself. Although Enlightenment notions of Russia prevail up until today, the definitions of modernity and Enlightenment have altered over time. Jasbir Puar, the queer postcolonial studies scholar, argues, as I have already discussed in the previous chapter, that the transformed or actualized contemporary versions of the concepts of civilization, progress, and modernity now include an aspiration to gay rights.[133] In other words, nations and states today which want to be called modern and progressive need to demonstrate legal and social recognition of (some) homosexuals. This change of narrative, however, is "built on the back of racialized others, for whom such progress was once achieved, but is now backsliding or has yet to arrive."[134] The positive, progressive attitude towards (some forms of) homosexuality is constructed in opposition to racialized populations, who allegedly threaten its continuation. These racialized "others" become signified through their heritage, their racialization, their culture, and their presumed 'different' values.

Whereas Puar's concern focuses on the construction of racialized Muslim bodies as a threat to North/Western civilization, Russian studies scholars Brian Baer[135] and Francesca Stella[136] view the discursive field of (homo)sexuality as an ideological site where Russian 'others' delineate the flipside of a North/Western paradigm of progress and values. They criticize previous works on Russian sexualities as contemporary reiterations of the Enlightenment's "development" paradigm. Such representations situate Russia "on the periphery of Western

---

132 Nemtsova, *Russia Slides Back.*

133 Jasbir Puar, "Rethinking Homonationalism," *Middle East Studies* 45, no. 2 (2013): 336–339; Jasbir Puar, *Terrorist Assemblages: Homonationalism in Queer Times* (Durham, N.C.: Duke University Press, 2007).

134 Puar, *Terrorist Assemblages*, 337.

135 Brian James Baer, "Russian Gays/Western Gaze: Mapping (Homo)Sexual Desire in Post-Soviet Russia," *GLQ: A Journal of Lesbian and Gay Studies* 8, no. 4 (2002): 499–521.

136 Stella, *Lesbian Lives in Soviet and Post-Soviet Russia.*

Europe."[137] In contrast to the peripheral Russia, North/Western Europe appears to be modern because of its seemingly "egalitarian sexuality (the global gay)."[138]

The evaluation of Russia by the media on the basis of LGBTIQ+ issues is not restricted only to public discourse. Indeed, positive changes in the sectors of gender equality and sexual citizenship rights are frequently attended to and examined by North/Western hegemonic institutions like the EU or UN, in order to evaluate a country's successful modernization or transition.[139] In their elaborations on the geo-temporal paradigm of postsocialist contexts, Robert Kulpa and Joanna Mizielińska show that the invocation of LGBTIQ+ people often produces a problematic concept of time and progress in which the North/Western model can only ever be seen as forward or "ahead," while the Eastern counterpart can only ever appear to lag behind, requiring that it perpetually try to catch up. The East appears as a 'poor cousin' to the West, which "is now, supposedly, catching up with normality (a.k.a. the 'West')."[140] Kulpa and Mizielińska emphasize the ambivalence of the "'Western' structural enclosing of [Eastern Europe] in toxically imbalanced relations of passivity and (expectations of) activity."[141] Moreover, they highlight the nonrecognition of Eastern European "geo-temporality in hegemonic Occidentalist discourses [for example] through the rejection of state communism as Modernity, one of its many projects, and alternative to the 'Western.'"[142]

The negotiation of cultural values, however, is neither played out within the sphere of the legal or theoretical debates, nor on the level of anonymous populations, Russian majorities and minorities; rather, it takes place in the midst of a culture war, where real, as well as fictional figures emerge, marked by their vulnerability in the face of ill-treatment by Russian forces, President Putin, and his "minions."[143] A focus on LGBTIQ+ rights comes up frequently in references to modernity. The liberal media, in particular, such as the *Huffington Post*,

---

137 Baer, "Russian Gays/Western Gaze," 502.
138 Ibid.
139 See Stella, *Lesbian Lives in Soviet and Post-Soviet Russia*; John Binnie, *The Globalization of Sexuality* (London: Sage, 2004); John Binnie and Christian Klesse, "The Politics of Age, Temporality and Intergenerationality in Transnational Lesbian, Gay, Bisexual, Transgender and Queer Activist Networks," *Sociology* 47, no. 3 (2013): 580–595; Robert Kulpa and Joanna Mizielińska, "Guest Editors' Introduction: Central and Eastern European Sexualities 'in transition,'" *Lambda Nordica: Journal of LGBTQ Studies* (2012): 19–29.
140 Kulpa and Mizielińska, "Guest Editors' Introduction," 23.
141 Ibid.
142 Ibid.
143 Steven Lee Myers, "Putin's Olympic Fever Dream," *New York Times*, January 22, 2014, MM18.

frames the political struggles in Russia as a question of "Modernity vs. Forces of Yesteryear."[144] In this equation, LGBTIQ+ people are increasingly conceptualized not only as vulnerable to Russian violence, but as carriers of culture and sophistication. Within homonationalism, "Western-style gay liberation,"[145] as well as gender equality, "represent [...] the high point of modernity,"[146] and gays and lesbians are, accordingly, created as visible signs of modernity and progress. Given the opportunity, through their country's development, which means "[l]iberated from the pressures of discrimination, [the LGBTIQ+ community] will be able to exercise their creative power to the maximum."[147] The icon of Fedorov by Blue Iconostasis speaks to this signification of queer figures as being ahead of their time and circumstances, 'witnesses' of a future that has yet to arrive for Russia. To consider Fedorov as representative martyr and icon, and a stand-in for the Russian LGBTIQ+ community in general, however, also means to consider his youth, his whiteness, and his able-bodiedness.

Using Puar's concept of homonationalism to analyze US-Russian discourses, academic scholars, such as Helen Lenskyj,[148] Fred LeBlanc,[149] and I[150] identify the ways in which North/Western public discourses idealize the West as modern and progressive, over and against Russia and Russian culture, ignoring the failure of some Western states to grant full rights to LGBTIQ+ people. Different media reproduce "pro-national, pro-Western"[151] scripts, which function as "anti-Othering" tools towards some gay bodies and identities; yet these same scripts "continually (re)produce the [Russian] Other as intolerant, sexually repressed, and uncivilized."[152] LeBlanc goes so far as to say that "in 2013

---

144 András Simonyi, "LGBT Rights—Modernity vs. Forces of Yesteryear," *Huffington Post*, May 11, 2015, http://www.huffingtonpost.com/andras-simonyi/lgbt-rights-modernity-vs-forces-of-yesteryear_b_7256178.html.

145 Stella, *Lesbian Lives in Soviet and Post-Soviet Russia*, 138.

146 Binnie, *The Globalization of Sexuality*, 85.

147 Ibid.

148 Helen Jefferson Lenskyj, *Sexual Diversity and the Sochi 2014 Olympics: No More Rainbows* (New York: Palgrave MacMillan, 2014).

149 Fred Joseph LeBlanc, "Sporting Homonationalism: Russian Homophobia, Imaginative Geographies and the 2014 Sochi Olympic Games," in *Sociology Association of Aotearoa New Zealand Annual Conference 2013*, 1–14.

150 Katharina Wiedlack. "Gays vs. Russia: Media Representations, Vulnerable Bodies and the Construction of a (Post)Modern West," *European Journal of English Studies* 21, no. 3 (September 2, 2017): 241–57, https://doi.org/10.1080/13825577.2017.1369271; Katharina Wiedlack, "'Quantum Leap' 2.0 or the Western Gaze on Russian Homophobia," *Adeptus*, no. 11 (July 10, 2018), https://doi.org/10.11649/a.1662.

151 LeBlanc, "Sporting Homonationalism," 7.

152 Ibid.

Russian homophobia seems to have momentarily trumped Arab homophobia in the media's discussion."[153] By making this reference to media representations of "Arab homophobia," LeBlanc implicitly brings the brown and Black bodies, about whom Puar developed her concept in the first place, into the discussion of North/Western homonationalism towards Russia again.

Recalling that Puar developed her concept in order to understand how US xenophobia and Islamophobia structure racialize Muslim subjects, and delegitimize their cultural and territorial environment, the mechanisms of othering and delegitimization through an identification and rejection of homophobia in the 'Other' raises several, not just methodological, questions. The question of why North/Western, and especially the US-American media, NGOs, activists, public figures, and so on have focused so intensively on these particular Russian gays needs to be raised again, with regard to Russian embodied masculinity. As I explained in the Introduction, this form of US homonationalism can be framed as an actualization of Iver Neumann's[154] and Larry Wolff's[155] Enlightenment paradigm, which positions Russia in-between the enlightened and civilized North/West and the backward and racialized Orient. As such, current discourses cement the signification of the bodies of ordinary Russian people, and especially Russian heteronormative men, as hegemonically masculine and caught in (regressive) transition, leaning towards backwardness, authoritarianism, and antimodernity. They are signified as conservative, misogynist, brutal, uncivilized, homophobic, and so forth.

Moreover, Russian homophobia is often related to homophobia in racialized countries. While some of these reports emphasize that international religious and other conservative networks designed and pushed the homophobic laws,[156] the fact of the globalization of anti-LGBTIQ+ sentiment and misogyny is all too often obscured in favor of the simplistic claim that Russia, as well as racialized global spheres such as Islamic states, Saudi Arabia, and many African states, are antimodern in comparison with progressive Western nations.[157] Despite the

---

153 Ibid.

154 Iver B. Neumann, *Uses of the Other: "The East" in European Identity Formation* (Manchester: Manchester University Press, 1999).

155 Larry Wolff, *Inventing Eastern Europe: the map of civilization on the mind of the Enlightenment* (Stanford, CA: Stanford University Press, 1994).

156 Max Strasser, "From Uganda to Russia, Homophobia Spreading Worldwide," *Newsweek*, February 27, 2014, http://www.newsweek.com/uganda-russia-homophobia-spreading-worldwide-230358.

157 Eve Hartley, "LGBT Rights: Uganda, Russia And Saudi Arabia Show Why The Fight For Equality Continues," *Huffington Post*, December 26, 2015, 2015, http://www.huffingtonpost.

inclusion of Russia into these homonationalist discourses, which emphasize the progressiveness of (white) Western nations,[158] and rest on an epistemology of racialized 'barbarism,' the whiteness of Russian homophobes is never questioned. The fact that Russia is a multiethnic country with many racialized minorities, as well as a country of immigrants, hosting people from Central Asia, China, the continent of Africa, and other racialized spheres is completely ignored.

The identification of whiteness in Russian homophobes is, however, interesting when seen in the framework of the white masculinity of the vulnerable bodies of Russian gay men. The fragility and vulnerability of these young men's bodies comes to be emphasized for the purpose of revealing the brutality and severity of Russian homophobia, as I have already shown. The question then becomes: What is at stake in dwelling on the suffering of white, young, able-bodied gay men in times of racial tensions, the Black Lives Matter movement,[159] increasing anti-Muslim,[160] anti-Mexican,[161] anti-immigrant sentiment, violence, and even

---

co.uk/2015/12/26/reasons-why-this-wasnt-the-year-for-lgbt-rights_n_8812534.html; Shannon Greenwood, "Uganda on their anti-gay legislation: It was all for the Children," Think Progress, July 7, 2014, https://thinkprogress.org/uganda-on-their-anti-gay-legislation-it-was-all-for-the-children-ec5a27313daa#.4x11q3bjt; Anna Kordunsky, "Russia Not Only Country with Anti-Gay Laws: Many other countries, from Iran to Cameroon, have harsh anti-gay laws," National Geographic, August 15, 2013, http://news.nationalgeographic.com/news/2013/08/130814-russia-anti-gay-propaganda-law-world-olympics-africa-gay-rights/.

158 It is important to note that the whiteness of the Western Enlightenment was never questioned in these discourses, even though the US president and one of the strongest proponents and promoters of LGBTIQ+ rights at that time was Barack Obama.

159 Ryen W. Miller, "Black Lives Matter: A primer on what it is and what it stands for," USA Today, July 11, 2016, http://www.usatoday.com/story/news/nation/2016/07/11/black-lives-matter-what-what-stands/86963292/; Rebecca Greenfield, "Patrisse Cullors, Alicia Garza, and Opal Tometi, Activists Against Racial Injustice," Bloomberg, December 3, 2020, https://www.bloomberg.com/news/features/2020-12-03/blm-activists-patrisse-cullors-alicia-garza-and-opal-tometi-bloomberg-50-2020#xj4y7vzkg.

160 Katayoun Kishi, "Anti-Muslim assaults reach 9/11-era levels, FBI data show," Pew Research Center, November 21, 2016, http://www.pewresearch.org/fact-tank/2016/11/21/anti-muslim-assaults-reach-911-era-levels-fbi-data-show/; Eric Lichtblau, "Attacks against Muslim Americans Fueled Rise in Hate Crime, F.B.I. Says," New York Times, November 15, 2016, A13; Clare Foran, "Donald Trump and the Rise of Anti-Muslim Violence: Research suggests that extreme political rhetoric can contribute to a spike in hate crimes," Atlantic, September 22, 2016, https://www.theatlantic.com/politics/archive/2016/09/trump-muslims-islamophobia-hate-crime/500840/.

161 Russell Berman, "A Trump-Inspired Hate Crime in Boston," Atlantic, August 20, 2015, https://www.theatlantic.com/politics/archive/2015/08/a-trump-inspired-hate-crime-in-boston/401906/; Dennis Romero, "In the Era of Trump, Anti-Latino Hate Crimes Jumped 69% in L.A.," LA Weekly, September 29, 2016, https://www.laweekly.com/in-the-era-of-trump-anti-latino-hate-crimes-jumped-69-in-l-a/; Tina Vasquez, "I've experienced a new level

killings? What does it mean that activist groups such as Queer Nation focus on the suffering of young, white, gay Russians at a time when Black trans*gender women are speaking up about the systematic violence they must face?[162] When Black trans*gender women demand action against the many transphobic and racist killings of such women?[163] What does it mean that young white martyrs, supposedly enduring their oppression in peace, or even silence, are celebrated at a moment when Black trans*gender people, and Black and brown queers, step up to show their anger and articulate their pain?[164] Of course, no one should question the fact that those young, white, and able-bodied gay men deserve US-based solidarity and care. However, the decision of the US media, journalists, photographers, public figures, activists, and so on to address Russian homophobia, but not US racialized and class-based, homo-, and, transphobia, needs to be interrogated, particularly in the wake of the Trump presidency.

Donald Trump, with his misogyny, racism, and homophobia, did not come out of nowhere. His hate speech-centered populism is tailored to address and amplify discourses that have been present all along. In this light, the choice by

---

of racism since Donald Trump went after Latinos," *Guardian*, September 9, 2015, https://www.theguardian.com/commentisfree/2015/sep/09/donald-trump-racism-increase-latinos.

162 2014 became known as the year of the so-called "transgender tipping point" due to Laverne Cox' success in the Netflix show *Orange Is the New Black*; and transgender women reached even broader visibility due to Caitlyn Jenner's coming out as transgender woman. See: Katy Steinmetz, "The Transgender Tipping Point," *Time*, May 29, 2014, https://time.com/135480/transgender-tipping-point/; Jessica Diehl, "Caitlyn Jenner: The Full Story," *Vanity Fair*, June 25, 2015, https://www.vanityfair.com/hollywood/2015/06/caitlyn-jenner-bruce-cover-annie-leibovitz. Unfortunately, this hypervisibility has rather increased the vulnerability of transgender people, and Black transgender women in general, as the most recent data suggests (see: Sean Arayasirikul et al., "A global cautionary tale: discrimination and violence against trans women worsen despite investments in public resources and improvements in health insurance access and utilization of health care," *International journal for equity in health* 21, no. 1 [2022]: 32, https://doi.org/10.1186/s12939-022-01632-5). "Our Approach and Principles," Sylvia Rivera Law Project, accessed August 30, 2016, http://srlp.org/about/principles/.

163 André St. Clair, "Stop Killing Us: Black Trans Lives Matter," *Huffington Post*, August 17, 2016, http://www.huffingtonpost.com/entry/stop-killing-us-black-trans-lives-matter_us_57b38d3ae4b03dd538089da9; Mic Kinkead, "Leaving Trans Women out of the Women and Criminal Justice System Convening," Silvia Rivera Law Project, April 9, 2016, http://srlp.org/speaking-about-us-without-us-leaving-trans-women-out-of-the-women-and-criminal-justice-system-convening/.

164 Cody Charles, "Reclaim Anger: I am the Rage Baldwin Speaks of," *Medium*, February 28, 2017, https://medium.com/reclaiming-anger/black-joy-we-deserve-it-1ab8dc7569b1#.rj81nx7ud; "*Angry* Black HoeMo? I absolutely am," Angry Black HoeMo, accessed December 12, 2024, http://angryblackhoemo.com/; Chancellor Agard, "Laverne Cox reacts to Trump lifting transgender student bathroom protections," *Entertainment Weekly*, February 23, 2017, http://ew.com/tv/2017/02/23/laverne-cox-gavin-grimm-transgender-student-bathroom-protections/.

the US media to hold up the US as a positive role model to Russia, is not only evidence of US-centrism in the midst of the contemporary Cultural Cold War, but also of deeply embedded racisms within American and Western LGBTIQ+ discourses, discourses that understand homosexuality and all matters LGBTIQ+ as intrinsically connected to a whitewashed US gay-liberation movement, and an equally whitewashed idea of the Stonewall riots, American gay and queer theory, and so on. This discursive connection explains why the *Washington Post* editorial board interpreted "Russia's war on gays" as explicitly targeting (white, liberal, middle- or upper class, Western) foreigners, who now could be "arrested and detained for up to two weeks should they choose to 'propagandize' homosexuality while visiting"[165] Russia during the Sochi Winter Olympics in 2014.

Moreover, this discursive connection also explains why the same editors were very concerned about another "anti-gay measure" signed into law, "preventing the adoption of Russian-born children by any person living in a country in which same-sex marriage is legal, regardless of that person's sexuality."[166] They confirmed the idea that the social inclusion of LGBTIQ+ people is indeed a US project and that LGBTIQ+ identifications are modern and progressive. A *Nation* article, titled "Gay Pride Versus 'Gay Propaganda,'"[167] operates on the same assumptions, implicitly defining the connection between global location and homosexuality as American even more unequivocally through the use of the US-American signifier "Gay Pride." A CNN broadcast compared US president Obama, who allegedly "has often been referred to as America's first 'gay president' because of his aggressive advocacy of gay rights and same-sex marriage,"[168] with Russian president Putin, suggesting that the former was a modern and protective father of the US nation, while the latter was a dictator, authoritarian and irrational, who had designed a "dangerously open-ended [bill], potentially treating any communication that doesn't portray homosexuality in a negative light as a punishable offense."[169] President Obama's support for the LGBTIQ+ community was arguably never as popular within the public US media as it seemed to

---

165 "Russia's war on gays," *Washington Post*, August 8, 2013, https://www.washingtonpost.com/opinions/russias-war-on-gays/2013/08/08/41721722-0065-11e3-9711-3708310f6f4d_story.html?utm_term=.241f07f5e116.

166 Ibid.

167 Alec Luhn, "Gay Pride Versus 'Gay Propaganda': In Russia, activists struggle against rising homophobia and a government crackdown on LGBT rights," *Nation*, June 28, 2013, http://www.thenation.com/article/gay-pride-versus-gay-propaganda.

168 Michael Martinez, "3 issues that have chilled U.S.-Russia ties," CNN, September 5, 2013, https://www.cnn.com/2013/09/05/world/us-russia-key-issues/index.html.

169 "Russia's war on gays."

be during the introduction of the anti-gay propaganda law in Russia in summer 2013.[170] The election of Trump, as well as recently introduced anti-LGBTIQ+ laws in many US states, suggests that the media significantly overestimated the enthusiasm of legislators, politicians, and the American people. Considering the increasing violence against Black transgender people within the US and beyond, the silence regarding this issue, and the strong focus on Russian gays, must be seen as a race-based, class-based, and gender-based decision, which prefers to show handsome, young, able, white male bodies without agency.

White Russian LGBTIQ+ Vulnerability and the Western Gaze after the Full-Scale Invasion of Ukraine in February 2022

Since the full-scale invasion of Ukraine by Russia in February 2022, LGBTIQ+ issues no longer occupy the center of Western media attention. Yet between reports about the daily attacks and casualties, about the state of combat forces, and the suffering of civilians, the subject of sexual minorities is occasionally addressed. These media reports focus on how the war has only exacerbated the situation for Russian LGBTIQ+ and other vulnerable minorities. Already before the war, Russia had increased its persecution of LGBTIQ+ organizations (now labeled "foreign agents"), individuals, and groups for alleged violations of the anti-gay propaganda law.[171] In December 2022, the anti-gay propaganda law was significantly expanded, making it "illegal to spread 'propaganda' about 'non-traditional sexual relations' in all media, including social media, advertising, and movies,"[172] and allowing for a significant extension of its violence.

In July 2023, the Russian state went even further, introducing legislation, outlawing gender-affirming procedures, banning any "medical interventions aimed at changing the sex of a person, as well as changing one's gender in official

---

170 Edward-Isaac Dovere, "Obama: 'No patience' for Russia's anti-gay laws," *Politico*, August 6, 2013, http://www.politico.com/story/2013/08/barack-obama-russia-anti-gay-laws-095266.

171 "Persecution of LGBTI+ people in Russia: Increasing repressions 2021-2022," Anti-Discrimination Centre, May 18, 2022, https://adcmemorial.org/en/articles/persecution-of-lgbti-2021-22/.

172 Emma Bubola, "Putin Signs Law Banning Expressions of L.G.B.T.Q. Identity in Russia," *New York Times*, December 5, 2022, https://www.nytimes.com/2022/12/05/world/europe/russia-ban-lgbtq-propaganda.html?smid=nytcore-ios-share&referringSource=articleShare.

documents and public records."[173] Not surprisingly, Russian lawmakers justified the legislation by arguing that it would "safeguard Russia against 'Western anti-family ideology.'"[174] In an attempt to unify the Russian nation and heighten its enthusiasm for the war, from the start framed as an effort against Western cultural imperialism,[175] as "shaking off the Western yoke,"[176] Putin has increasingly targeted LGBTIQ+ people. Considering the anti-LGBTIQ+ backlash in the US, with many states introducing similar laws—banning LGBTIQ+ content from schools, public libraries, and restricting or straight-out banning transgender health care—the Anglophone media's insistence on framing Russia's war against Ukraine through the lens of LGBTIQ+ issues might read hollow. Yet many authors, and particularly Western-funded global LGBTIQ+ organizations, still seem to rely on these homonationalistic discourses. When Ukrainian lawmakers "introduced legislation in the country's parliament that would give partnership rights to same-sex couples"[177] in late June 2023, Western journalists read the "legislation, along with a prohibition against anti-LGBTQ hate speech abruptly adopted in December, [as] a sharp rejection of Russia's effort to weaponize homophobia in support of its invasion."[178] While there might be some truth to this interpretation, what was presented as a syllogism—that "Russia's invasion of Ukraine has galvanized Ukrainian society [to] advance [. . .] the rights of LGBTQ people"[179]—might rather be considered sophistry or politicized exaggeration.

Yet commentators celebrated queer visibility among the Ukrainian active forces and praised a Ukrainian news media "that's sympathetically covering

---

173 "Russian president signs legislation marking the final step outlawing gender-affirming procedures," Associated Press, July 24, 2023, https://apnews.com/article/russia-lgbtq-transgender-procedures-banned-21b88f53b9a74a646400d63ce93bde6f.

174 Ibid.

175 Max Fisher, "Putin's Case for War, Annotated," *New York Times*, February 24, 2022, https://www.nytimes.com/2022/02/24/world/europe/putin-ukraine-speech.html; Bobby Ghosh, "An Unarmed Putin Wants a Culture War with the West," Bloomberg, September 14, 2022, https://www.bloomberg.com/opinion/articles/2022-09-14/an-unarmed-putin-wants-to-fight-a-culture-war-with-the-west#xj4y7vzkg.

176 Sergei Karaganov, "We are shaking off the western yoke," Russian International Affairs Council, June 20, 2023, https://russiancouncil.ru/en/analytics-and-comments/comments/we-are-shaking-off-the-Western-yoke/.

177 J. Lester Feder, "How Russia's War against Ukraine Is Advancing LGBTQ Rights," *Politico*, July 3, 2023, https://www.politico.com/news/magazine/2023/03/07/russias-war-ukraine-advancing-lgbtq-rights-00085841.

178 Ibid.

179 Ibid.

queer peoples' contributions to the war effort."[180] These reports refer to Ukrainian LGBTIQ+ rights lobbyists such as Inna Sovsun, the parliamentarian who authored the newly implemented partnership legislation and believes that "'[e]stablishing same-sex partnership rights,' [. . .] is an important step for 'Ukraine to be perceived as a Western democracy.'"[181] Such reports confirm the Western-visibility paradigm and assert that coming out leads necessarily to the acknowledgement and acceptance, if not celebration, of queer people. Importantly, they support nationalism and the idea of the heroic Ukrainian soldier, who "give[s] visibility and legitimacy to the claims for equal treatment."[182] While the Western media celebrates the inclusion of queer people in the image of the heroic soldier as a sign of Western progress, the same images can equally be read as the remasculinization of previously abject, because effeminate or transgressive, masculinities. Social media posts, such as "Ukrainian drag queens destroy Moscovian occupiers!,"[183] ostensibly celebrating the inclusion of queerness into Ukrainian military masculinity, humiliate the enemy forces by pointing out that 'even' a drag queen can defeat them. Moreover, even if queer masculinities are now mainstreamed, the general militarization of gender roles has equally many negative consequences for queer people and women. War always reinstalls binary and hierarchically arranged gender models, and the war in Ukraine is no exception to this rule, as masculinity studies scholars Katarzyna Wojnicka, Ulf Mellström, and Sam De Boise have pointed out.[184] "[Military m]asculinity is mobilized as a rhetorical figure and symbolic resource in the brutal reality for all these young men and women that have to go into a war,"[185] not least by US-American news outlets of all colors, from the "right-leaning Fox News [to the] left-leaning MSNBC."[186] Nevertheless, despite the inclusion of heroic female soldiers in celebratory media portrayals, war historically solidifies polarized gender models and undoes previous gains of gender equality.[187] This sentiment is supported by

---

180 Ibid.
181 Ibid.
182 Sovsun qtd. in ibid.
183 "Ukrainian drag queens destroy moscovian occupiers!" Kyiv Pride, March 30, 2022, https://www.instagram.com/p/CburVxHAG0G/?img_index=1.
184 Katarzyna Wojnicka, Ulf Mellström, and Sam De Boise, "On War, Hegemony and (Political) Masculinities," *NORMA* 17, no. 2 (April 3, 2022): 83–87, https://doi.org/10.1080/18902138.2022.2069856.
185 Wojnicka, Mellström, and De Boise, "On War, Hegemony and (Political) Masculinities," 83.
186 Ibid.
187 Maryna Romanets, "Virtual warfare: Masculinity, sexuality, and propaganda in the Russo-Ukrainian War," *East/West: Journal of Ukrainian Studies* 4, no. 1 (2017): 159, https://doi:10.21226/t26880.

the overwhelming majority of Western sources reporting on the war, offering images of heroic male warriors juxtaposed to vulnerable, yet supportive women caring for the elderly, their children, and their pets, and so forth. Unsurprisingly, structural, mental, and physical violence against transgender,[188] gays, lesbians and bisexuals,[189] women,[190] Black and people of color[191] has surged throughout the war, though only a few Western media sources discuss it.

Focusing on positive queer visibility as progress, while remaining silent about violence against LGBTIQ+ and women, violence viewed as illiberal and backward, solidarity reports further what Olenka Dmytryk, Syaivo, and I have proposed about the East/West divide around queerness[192] that attempts to garner Western sympathy for Ukraine. The evidence of LGBTIQ+ nationalism through the participation of gay soldiers in the war, accompanied by their visibility politics, for example the green "unicorn insignia, a mythical creature that has become a symbol of the LGBTQ community" that some carry on the sleeves of

---

188 Kateryna Farbar, "Trans people are caught in the war in Ukraine," Open Democracy, February 8, 2023, https://www.opendemocracy.net/en/odr/ukraine-trans-people-war-lgbt-gender-identity-documents-hormones-zelenskyy-eu/; Julia Lee, "'Danger everywhere': War and transphobia create perfect storm for trans Ukrainians," NBC News, April 8, 2022, https://www.nbcnews.com/nbc-out/out-news/danger-everywhere-war-transphobia-create-perfect-storm-trans-ukrainian-rcna23567; Patrick Kelleher, "Trans Ukrainians being forced back into closet as cruel despot Putin's bloodthirsty war rages on," Pink News, May 6, 2022, https://www.thepinknews.com/2022/05/06/gay-alliance-ukraine-russia-war-trans/.

189 Finbarr Toesland, "Why tracking anti-LGBT war crimes in Ukraine is so difficult," Open Democracy, May 26, 2023, https://www.opendemocracy.net/en/5050/ukraine-russia-war-crimes-anti-lgbt-violence/; OCHA Service, "Protection of LGBTIQ+ people in the context of the response in Ukraine," Relief Web, May 17, 2022, https://reliefweb.int/report/ukraine/protection-lgbtiq-people-context-response-ukraine.

190 Jessie Williams, "'This War Made Him a Monster.' Ukrainian Women Fear the Return of Their Partners," Time, March 13, 2023, https://time.com/6261977/ukraine-women-domestic-violence/; "Mounting Reports of Crimes against Women, Children in Ukraine Raising 'Red Flags' over Potential Protection Crisis, Executive Director Tells Security Council," UNHCR Meeting Coverage and Press Releases, April 11, 2022, https://press.un.org/en/2022/sc14857.doc.htm; "Ukraine: Women face grave risks as Russia's full-scale invasion enters its second year," Amnesty International, March 8, 2023, https://www.amnesty.org/en/latest/news/2023/03/ukraine-women-face-grave-risks-as-russias-full-scale-invasion-enters-its-second-year/.

191 "Africans in Ukraine: Jessica's story - BBC Africa," BBC Africa, March 1, 2022, https://www.youtube.com/watch?v=ldBKmPsST6A&t=101s; Rashawn Ray, "The Russian invasion of Ukraine shows racism has no boundaries," March 3, 2022, Brookings Institution, https://www.brookings.edu/articles/the-russian-invasion-of-ukraine-shows-racism-has-no-boundaries/; "Supporting Vulnerable Black People," Global Black Coalition, February 2022, https://www.globalblackcoalition.org/.

192 Katharina Wiedlack, Olenka Dmytryk, and Syaivo, "Introduction to Fucking Solidarity: Queering Concepts on/from a Post-Soviet Perspective," Feminist Critique 5 (2022): 10–26, https://doi.org/10.52323/567892.

their military uniforms, inclines one to agree with the New Zealand-based queer theorist Fred Joseph LeBlanc. LeBlanc suggests that this form of homonationalism "can be reconfigured as a survival strategy for LGBT [sic] citizens in Eastern Europe."[193] I am more concerned, however, about the negative effects of this strategy and more doubtful about the positive ones. In perpetuating the idea of a queer-loving West that welcomes Ukraine into its sphere and frames a potential "Russian victory [a]s an existential threat to both the sovereignty of Ukraine and the rights of LGBT[I]Q+ people,"[194] The Anglophone media and global activism support Russian discourses that reject precisely this Western narrative as imperialism and embrace what is constructed as opposed to Western values. This binary configuration aligns itself neatly with Russian imperialism and what gender and political science studies scholar Emil Edenborg calls "[t]he myth that Russia has a divine mission in carrying the torch of true Christian civilization after the West's plunge into ungodly materialism, secularism, and individualism dates back to at least sixteenth-century thinking of "Moscow as the Third Rome" and is prominent in the works of nineteenth-century novelists such as Dostoevsky."[195]

The systematic contrast of a supposedly godless, atomistic, mechanistic, and immoral West to a deeply religious, communitarian, spiritual, and moral Russia, which characterized nineteenth-century Slavophile thinking, was resuscitated by late Soviet and post-Soviet religious nationalist writers. It is not only Western discourses that frame Russian anti-LGBTIQ+ cultural politics through concepts of modernity and progress; Russian discourses actively participate in this discussion from a traditional Slavophile point of view. Russian nationalism, framed as an anti-imperialist desire to free Russia from the "Western yoke,"[196] "is perceived as historically suffering under Western cultural, economic, military, and epistemological hegemony."[197] This idea, which is frequently articulated in conservative sexual and gender politics, is intrinsically connected to Russian

---

193 Fred Joseph LeBlanc, "Between a Rock and a Hard Place: Why the Ukrainian Crisis is a Queer Issue," International Norms and East European Nations Conference, February 5, 2015, https://www.academia.edu/10356627/Between_a_Rock_and_a_Hard_Place_Why_the_Ukrainian_Crisis_is_a_Queer_Issue.

194 Aydan Greatrick, Tyler Valiquette, and Yvonne Su, "Other frontlines: How the war in Ukraine is transforming the LGBTQ+ rights landscape in Europe," *Conversation*, May 10, 2022, https://theconversation.com/other-frontlines-how-the-war-in-ukraine-is-transforming-the-lgbtq-rights-landscape-in-europe-182209.

195 Emil Edenborg, "Putin's Anti-Gay War on Ukraine," *Boston Review*, March 14, 2022, https://www.bostonreview.net/articles/putins-anti-gay-war-on-ukraine/.

196 Karaganov, "We are shaking off the western yoke."

197 Edenborg, "Putin's Anti-Gay War on Ukraine."

imperialist aspirations: "its 'civilizing' mission against peoples seen as culturally and racially inferior, for example in the Caucasus and Central Asia."[198] To put it bluntly, Western discourses co-produce Russian white Slavophile supremacist/imperialist discourses. They reaffirm historical, tried and true (Western) imperialist notions of Russian backwardness through the celebration of (white, male) suffering queers signified as embattled bearers of the Enlightenment torch, views that are easily targeted as Russian anti-imperialism in the pushback against this Western imperialism. Framing Western imperialism as the attempt to corrupt Russia with its 'perversion' of civilization, Russian discourses affirm a notion of 'innocence' that "permits Russians to imagine their nation as universally, naturally, and purely heterosexual,"[199] an "in-between space of sexual morality and innocence, neither part of the 'decadent' West or the 'primitive' Orient."[200] Queer figures and groups are produced at the juncture of Western and Russian imperialism, co-produced by their respective discursive politics, which only seem to be at odds.

Moreover, by framing Russian anti-LGBTIQ+ violence in terms of progress and Enlightenment, thereby constructing young gay men such Dmitry Chizhevsky, Kirill Kalugin, and Kirill Fedorov, as I have already demonstrated, as martyrs, the class-based, racialized, age-based, ableist, and gendered structures that privilege (what is perceived as) white, cultured Russianness are rendered invisible and unspeakable.

The problem with this view became particularly evident in the context of the so-called gay purges in the Russian region of Chechnya. When the Russian newspaper *Novaya Gazeta* broke the news that up to one hundred gay men had allegedly been detained, tortured, and some of them killed in the province of Chechnya in April 2017, the Anglophone media described the events using orientalist language, signifying the violence as the barbaric deeds of Chechen Muslims.[201] The reports connected homophobic violence to the backward or ret-

---

198 Ibid.
199 Dan Healey, *Homosexual Desire in Revolutionary Russia: The Regulation of Sexual and Gender Dissent* (Chicago, IL: University of Chicago Press, 2001), 253.
200 Edenborg, "Putin's Anti-Gay War on Ukraine."
201 "British government calls abuse of gay men in Chechnya 'utterly barbaric,'" *Pink News*, last modified April 20, 2017, www.pinknews.co.uk/2017/04/20/british-government-calls-abuse-of-gay-men-chechnya-utterly-barbaric/; Dave Burke, "Chechnya 'is attempting to eliminate its gay community by the start of the Muslim holy month of Ramadan,'" *Daily Mail*, April 25, 2017, www.dailymail.co.uk/news/article-4443890/Chechnya-attempting-eliminate-gay-community.html#ixzz4fkdAsMaP; Harriet Agerholm, "Theresa May condemns Chechen persecution of gay men as 'utterly barbaric,'" *Independent*, May 10, 2017, www.independent.co.uk/news/

rograde *Otherness*[202] of religious fundamentalism. Moreover, they suggested that the violence not only originated in religious fundamentalism, but also that it was alien to "Western" contexts, in the "remote" region of the half-civilized East.[203] In doing so, the Western solidarity discourses in all of these news articles signified anti-gay violence, as well as religious fundamentalism, as signs of racialized inferiority and backwardness, in contrast to forward-thinking Western tolerance and justice marked as gay liberation and secularism. Only a very few voices in the media noted that the situation in the southern Russian region was created and upheld by Russian imperialism.[204] No one, to my knowledge, noted that the racialized othering of Chechen homophobia by the Western media supported Russian imperialist discourses, which also signify Chechens as inferior racialized Others. While these Russian discourses, naturally, do not focus on anti-LGBTIQ+ violence, the signification of Muslim barbarism is used in the same way to differentiate this racialized population from its white Russian Orthodox counterpart.[205]

In May 2023, in the context of a PEN America event, an incident occurred that pointed up the need to interrogate how Western homonationalistic imperialism and Russian racist imperialism intersect. Masha Gessen, a Russian American writer, and one of the Russian queers (self-)styled by the Western media as martyrs, was supposed to chair a panel with two other Russian writers at the PEN World Voices Festival. The event was cancelled at the last minute, due to an intervention by two Ukrainian writers, who were both serving in the army at that time, and refused to attend an event featuring Russians. In the aftermath of this cancellation, Gessen resigned from the board of PEN America. In one of the first interviews following their resignation, which appeared in the *Atlantic*,

---

world/europe/theresa-may-chechnya-gay-men-chechen-torture-detain-camps-barbaric-russia-region-a7728641.html.

202 "Chechnya anti-gay violence: Newspaper fears 'retribution' for reports," BBC News, last modified April 14, 2017, www.bbc.com/news/world-europe-39600124; Michelle Garcia, "At least 100 gay men in Chechnya have been abducted by police," *Vox News*, April 18, 2017, www.vox.com/identities/2017/4/18/15326500/gay-men-chechnya-violence-homophobia-antigay-torture; Tim Lister, Maria Ilyushina, and Darya Tarasova, "UN experts condemn reports of violence against gay men in Chechnya," CNN, April 14, 2017, www.cnn.com/2017/04/14/europe/un-chechnya-gay-men/; Dan Healey, "Violence Shows Risks of Being Gay in Chechnya," *Huffington Post*, April 27, 2017, www.huffingtonpost.co.uk/professor-dan-healey/violence-shows-risks-of-b_b_16260984.html.

203 Andrew E. Kramer, "Gay Men in Chechnya Are Killed, Paper Says," *New York Times*, April 2, 2017, A10.

204 Masha Gessen, "The Gay Men Who Fled Chechnya's Purge," *New Yorker*, July 3, 2017, www.newyorker.com/magazine/2017/07/03/the-gay-men-who-fled-chechnyas-purge.

205 Nikolay Zakharov, *Race and Racism in Russia* (New York: Palgrave Macmillan, 2015).

Gessen called the decision to cancel the event by the CEO of PEN as consent to being "blackmailed."[206] Furthermore, Gessen said that they had "felt like [. . .] being asked to tell [the other panelists] that because they're Russians they can't sit at the big table; they have to sit at the little table off to the side [. . .]. Which felt distasteful."[207] They also said allegedly that they understood the Ukrainians' "desire to be cruel to Russians [but that they had] expected a different response from PEN,"[208] calling the decision a 'silencing,' and insinuating that it was an act against freedom of expression. While Gessen later offered a more nuanced take on the issue in the *New Yorker*, admitting that "Ukrainians are constantly confronted with Russian dominance in cultural spheres and academia," they still insisted on the "human victims," by which she meant the Russian curators, Russian musicians, and Russian writers whose cultural productions were in danger of being "erased."[209]

In my view, the problem with Gessen's reaction is that they self-victimize, calling the Ukrainians' wish to not share a public platform as cruel punishment of themselves (and fellow Russian artists and writers) and as retribution, rather than understanding the symbolic power of stepping aside in favor of Ukrainian representation. Arguably, the idea that Gessen is a victim emerged when they emphatically pleaded with Western nations to save Russian LGBTIQ+ people like themself from Russian homophobia in the wake of the first national anti-gay propaganda law. What Gessen did not discuss then (or since) is their own privilege as white Russian intelligentsia from the Russian capital of Moscow (moreover with dual citizenship). A sharing of privileges could have meant not taking the public stage, but rather agreeing to question Russian white urban privilege and supporting the aspirations of Ukrainians for more visibility within PEN. Russian culture and its ethnically Russian writers, musicians, artists, performers have acted—willingly or not—as agents of Russian imperialism throughout the post-Soviet sphere and beyond. "[D]eplatforming Russian culture would benefit Ukraine—and perhaps even Russians themselves,"[210] as some analysts have

---

206 Gal Beckerman, "Masha Gessen Resigns in Protest from PEN America Board," *Atlantic*, May 16, 2023, https://www.theatlantic.com/books/archive/2023/05/what-happens-when-the-free-speech-absolutists-flinch/674069/.

207 Beckerman, "Masha Gessen Resigns in Protest from PEN America Board."

208 Ibid.

209 Isaac Chotiner, "Why Masha Gessen resigned from the PEN America board," *New Yorker*, May 24, 2023, https://www.newyorker.com/news/q-and-a/why-masha-gessen-resigned-from-the-pen-america-board.

210 Yuriy Gorodnichenko and Ilona Sologoub, "The Ukraine-Russia Culture War," Project Syndicate, June 7, 2023, https://www.project-syndicate.org/commentary/ukraine-russia-culture-war-gessen-pen-resignation-by-yuriy-gorodnichenko-and-ilona-sologoub-2023-06.

suggested. But Gessen seems to understand such a suggestion as an insult, which the refusal to "to sit at the little table off to the side" while Ukrainians take center stage, implies. Instead, Gessen is once again styled by the media, such as the aforementioned *Atlantic*, as a martyr and innocent victim in the face of not only the Russian war, but also the 'cruelty' of the Ukrainian writers.

A thorough, much needed examination of Russian imperialism and the colonialism of Russian culture—including (queer) art, literature, music, and performance—is only now emerging. Russian language and Russian culture were used as oppressive tools against ethnic minorities and other nations in the former Soviet republics. Moreover, much like Western empires, Russia has appropriated the talents of oppressed nations, including Ukrainians, and Georgians, claiming them as Russian.

The continued support of "[R]ussian culture today implies financing the war. Watching a Russian movie, listening to Russian music, or attending a Russian theater performance provides Putin's government with royalties and tax revenue. Moreover, [. . .] businesses will believe that it is acceptable to remain in Russia."[211] Russian LGBTIQ+ artists, writers, curators, musicians, and performers need to interrogate their complex entanglement in Russian cultural imperialism, as well as the conjuncture and complicity of Western and Russian imperialisms, in order to find ways to support Ukraine and Ukrainians through their ongoing cultural work.

211 Ibid.

CHAPTER 4

Russian Feminisms and Issues of Whiteness in American Media and Popular Culture

In May 2023, the Russian State Duma discussed "a law labeling feminism as 'extremist.' The lawmaker who drafted the proposed law blamed feminists for the 'destruction of traditional values' and accused them of being 'simply agents of the West,'"[1] bringing once again to the fore the idea that feminism, together with LGBTIQ+ issues, are still at the center of the New Cold War. In this chapter,[2] I analyze how Russian feminisms have been presented within the US-American mainstream media over the last decade. In terms of the discursive purposes or effects of such representations, I speculate about the function of Russian feminisms and their protagonists in the broader context of Anglophone, and particularly US-American, media discourses that present feminism per se as modern and progressive. In doing so, I do not necessarily question the sincerity of feminist politics. Rather, this chapter questions the media representation and celebration of a small group of Russian feminist activists, how they reflect

---

1   Ekaterina Pechenkina, "Are feminists next on Vladimir Putin's list?" *Politico*, April 14, 2023, https://www.politico.com/newsletters/women-rule/2023/04/14/are-feminists-next-on-vladimir-putins-list-00092070.

2   Parts of this chapter are an update of my earlier chapter "The Spectacle of Russian Feminism: Questioning Visibility and the Western Gaze," in *Subcultures, Bodies and Spaces: Essays on Alternativity and Maginalization*, ed. Samantha Holland (Bingley: Emerald Publishing, 2018), 131–49. Some minor points were previously published as Katharina Wiedlack, "'both married, both moms, both determined to keep getting their message out'—The Russian Pussy Riot and US popular culture," in *Marlboro Men and California Gurls: Rethinking Gender in Popular Culture in the 21st Century*, ed. Astrid M. Fellner, Marta Fernández, and Martina Martausová (Newcastle upon Tyne: Cambridge Scholars Publishing, 2017), 131–159.

American-Russian relations, as well as their implications in US nationalism and imperialism, and Russian nationalism and imperialism.

US-American feminisms have a strong presence in contemporary popular culture. Some celebrate the claims to feminism(s) in the music industry, with artists such as Beyoncé Knowles-Carter, Taylor Swift, and Lady Gaga, as well as the genderqueer Janelle Monáe; in comedy, with comedians such as Aly Wong, Margaret Moran Cho, Amy Schumer, Samantha Bee, and Lena Dunham; and in the film business, with actresses such as America Ferrera, Kate McKinnon, Helen Mirren, Issa Rae, and Margot Robbie, who all starred in the recent Barbie movie, directed by feminist director Greta Gerwig. Others, however, lament its commercialization.

In comparison with the hypervisibility of US feminisms, reporting on Russian feminisms and feminists seems marginal, and minimal. Yet the Anglophone media has continuously followed a handful of Russian feminists, their art, performances, and their writing, throughout the last decade. Masha Gessen, the nonbinary journalist and activist, together with Nadya Tolokonnikova and Maria Alyokhina of the protest group Pussy Riot, have formed a steady relationship with the US public. They are frequently featured in the US news media and beyond, which addresses US-Russian relations, Russian illiberalism, and authoritarianism, as well as the war against Ukraine.

My interest in these feminists not only concerns their feminist politics, but also the question of what their Russian feminism 'means' within Anglophone, particularly US, discourses and culture. In other words, I ask: Why them and not others?; and: 'To what purpose and effect?' Building on the thesis that these Russian feminists enter the Anglophone media as spectacular opposition to the Russian administration and political hegemony, I read their actions and personalities, and their feminism, as support of US-American cultural hegemony, through the semantic connection between feminism, equality, homo-tolerance, modernity, and progress. Nadya Tolokonnikova, and to a lesser extent Maria Alyokhina, have arguably mastered the spectacle. Tolokonnikova's feminist videos, in particular, have focused on otherness and marginalization as a media spectacle, as I will show in a close reading of her video "Make America Great Again." As a nonbinary journalist and LGBTIQ+ activist, Masha Gessen, on the other hand, has deployed the spectacularity of victimhood. Beyond the fact that the limited focus on Gessen's or Tolokonnikova's experience lacks nuance, as theirs are not necessarily the typical Russian immigrant and activist stories, another salient issue is that they meet Western expectations too neatly. Yet the media presents them as individual hero*ines, and simultaneously universalizes their individual experiences as 'typically' Russian, thereby rendering many other experiences, approaches, and circumstances invisible.

My analysis of the Anglophone representations and self-representations of Russian feminists and feminisms follows the co-construct of US and Russian values and notions of anti-/modernity, regress/progress, and civilization/barbarism in news articles, interviews, and media discussions of Russian feminist work. I argue that Russian feminists within these discourses embody feminism as something inherently Western, a stable part of enlightened civilization. Not coincidentally, the invocation of Russian feminists as alien to their own backward environment, and their 'naturalization' into forces of US or Western progress, comes at a time when Western anti-feminist groups are becoming more and more visible. Moreover, the discursive construction and signification of feminists as carriers of Western values draws on ideas propagated by Russian discourses that reject feminism as Western. In short, the construction of feminism as Western progress and Russian feminists as defenders of Western enlightenment is a co-construction of Western and Russian nationalisms and imperialisms. Importantly, it constructs feminism as white in times of intensive and intensifying racial inequality, and despite the increasing interventions by Black, Indigenous and Women* of Color throughout North America, Russia, and globally. Analyzing the (self)representations of Tolokonnikova, Alyokhina, and Gessen within the Anglophone media, I will critically discuss the Western gaze, its victimizing strategies, homonationalism, and imperialism. My analysis includes a thorough semiotic analysis of Tolokonnikova's music video "Make America Great Again," which I read as an important part of her representation within the mainstream media. I also, and equally, include a semiotic analysis of Masha Gessen's self-representation, as well as her writing in support of the broader Russian LGBTIQ+ community.

I argue that discourses of spectacular marginalization allow Tolokonnikova and Gessen to completely negate their white class privilege, and that in Tolokonnikova's case this mechanism supports the appropriation of the experience of people of color. In Gessen's and Alyokhina's cases, their victim status makes it hard to discuss their internalized Russian imperialism. Comparing their presence in the media to other voices of Russian dissent, for example, that of the singer Manizha, I will argue that in embracing some Russian feminists and remaining oblivious to others, Western imperial discourses perpetuate notions of feminist whiteness, and, ironically, Russian whiteness. To put it bluntly, while Black and Women* of Color feminists, from the abovementioned Beyoncé and Janelle Monáe, to Viola Davis, Laverne Cox, and Kerry Washington, along with producers such as Shonda Rhimes and Mindy Kaling, and Indigenous women* such as Paulina Alexis and Quannah Chasinghorse, are gaining ground within the still too white popular culture and media landscape, the focus on Russian feminists allows the Anglophone media to see only white feminists. This whitening of Russian feminism, and feminism per se, supports the white nationalism embedded in Russian anti-feminist imperialism. No less important, in the creation of Russian feminists as martyrs who continue to carry the torch of Western Enlightenment in the face of Russia's overpowering misogyny and queerphobia, issues of classism and imperialism within the work of these same 'sacred' feminists have never even been considered.

Pussy Riot and Western Enlightenment Discourses

The Russian feminist group Pussy Riot emerged in October 2011 during the public protests now known as the Snow Revolution,[3] in which people demonstrated for fair elections and criticized the ruling party, United Russia, led by Vladimir Putin, opposing his renewed candidacy for president.

The half-dozen members of Pussy Riot organized anonymous and illegal punk performances on a prison roof in front of the Kremlin on Red Square and on an oil platform. They performed in brightly colored dresses in unusual combinations, wearing equally brightly colored—self-fashioned, DIY—balaclavas over their faces. Their acts protested political persecution, sexism, and homophobia, as well as capitalism, exploitation, and pollution within and by contemporary Russian society, and through and by the state.[4]

In early spring 2012, Pussy Riot were persecuted for a punk performance in the famous Christ the Savior Cathedral in Moscow, a church that was demolished in 1931 then rebuilt and consecrated in 2000. The new cathedral has a shopping mall underneath it, and the Pussy Riot action wanted to highlight the fact that the current Orthodox Church leadership runs a kind of money laundering machinery, with the president as their protector. While this latter aspect was largely missed by the Western media, Pussy Riot's choice of location, one of the main centers of the Orthodox Church, was noticed. With all the attention that followed, Pussy Riot's performance became a global media cause célèbre, and their feminism, in the Western as well as Russian media, became synonymous

---

3 Andrew Osborn, "Bloggers who are changing the face of Russia as the Snow Revolution takes hold," *Telegraph*, December 10, 2011, https://www.telegraph.co.uk/news/worldnews/europe/russia/8948414/Bloggers-who-are-changing-the-face-of-Russia-as-the-Snow-Revolution-takes-hold.html.

4 Henry Langston, "Meeting Pussy Riot," *Vice*, March 12, 2012, http://www.vice.com/read/A-Russian-Pussy-Riot.

with anti-Putinism. US newspapers[5] and television news channels,[6] as well as popular culture magazines,[7] reported every detail about the trial. Very soon, celebrities such as Madonna, Carrie Brownstein, Bryan Adams, the Beastie Boys, Peter Gabriel, Sting, the Red Hot Chili Peppers,[8] Mischa Barton, or Elijah Wood[9] came out in solidarity with the Russian feminists. If their campaigns and actions made anything clear, besides the reemergence of the Cold War, it was that feminism had gained a visible place within the US-American mainstream media.

Although the original group was made up of half a dozen people, only three of them—Nadya Tolokonnikova, Yekaterina Samutsevich, and Maria Alyokhina— were put on trial. From the beginning, however, most of the media attention was focused on the beautiful and media savvy Nadya Tolokonnikova. Moreover, due to her continuous activities in the US, and her collaborations with popular artists and musicians, Tolokonnikova maintained a continuous presence in the North American media.

As a media or pop-cultural phenomenon, Tolokonnikova's popularity differs in significant ways from that of all of the other famous feminists mentioned before. Unlike these women*, who first became famous artists, actresses, and so on, and then came out as feminists, Tolokonnikova became famous for being a feminist. Moreover, she came to be embraced by the mainstream media,

---

5   Thomas L. Friedman, "Pussy Riot, Tupac and Putin," *New York Times*, December 19, 2012, A35; Robert Mackey and Glenn Kates, "Russian Riot Grrrls Jailed for 'Punk Prayer,'" *New York Times Blog*, March 7, 2012, https://archive.nytimes.com/thelede.blogs.nytimes. com/2012/03/07/russian-riot-grrrls-jailed-for-punk-prayer/?searchResultPosition=1; Suzi Parker, "What American women could learn from Pussy Riot, a Russian punk rock girl band," *Washington Post*, April 21, 2012, https://www.washingtonpost.com/blogs/she-the-people/post/what-american-women-could-learn-from-pussy-riot-a-russian-punk-rock-girl-band/2012/04/21/gIQAYr42XT_blog.html.

6   Traci Lee, "Pussy Riot gets prison for Putin protest," MSNBC, August 17, 2012, https://www.msnbc.com/melissa-harris-perry/pussy-riot-gets-prison-putin-protest-msna35545.

7   Jeffrey Tayler, "What Pussy Riot's 'Punk Prayer' Really Said," *Atlantic*, November 8, 2012, https://www.theatlantic.com/international/archive/2012/11/whatpussy-riots-punk-prayer-really-said/264562/.

8   Freya Petersen, "Madonna joins celebrities backing Pussy Riot," *World*, August 19, 2012, https://www.pri.org/stories/2012-08-19/madonna-joins-celebrities-backing-pussy-riot.

9   "Celebrities react on Twitter as Pussy Riot members sentenced," *Toronto Star*, last modified August 17, 2012, https://storify.com/torontostar/celebritiesreact-on-twitter-as-pussy-riot-members.

from glossy magazines such as *Vogue*,[10] *Time*[11] (which nominated Pussy Riot for Person of the Year 2012),[12] and *Rolling Stone*,[13] to daily newspapers such as the *New York Times*,[14] the *Guardian*,[15] and the *Huffington Post*.[16] In the many

---

10   Sara Corbett, "Enemies of the State," *Vogue*, June 30, 2014, http://www.vogue.com/magazine/article/pussy-riot-members-start-new-organization-zona-prava/#1.

11   Raisa Bruner, "Exclusive: How Pussy Riot's Nadya Tolokonnikova Is Using Crypto to Fight for Equality," *Time*, March 3, 2022, https://time.com/6154118/pussy-riot-unicorn-dao-nadya/; Mahita Gajanan, "Pussy Riot's Nadya Tolokonnikova on Resisting President Trump: 'We Have a Ton of Work to Do,'" *Time*, February 21, 2017, https://time.com/4671189/pussy-riot-nadya-tolokonnikova-donald-trump-resistance/; Simon Shuster, "Pussy Riot Unveils a Wildly NSFW Vision of America under Donald Trump," *Time*, October 27, 2016, https://time.com/4547274/pussy-riot-donald-trump-make-america-great-again/; Dan Kedmey, "Pussy Riot Member Detained in Russia for Protest over 'Sadistic' Prison Law," *Time*, June 12, 2015, https://time.com/3919412/pussy-riot-nadya-prison-camp-police-protest/.

12   Daniel Martin, "Pussy Riot members nominated for 'Time' magazine's Person of the Year award," *NME*, November 28, 2012, https://www.nme.com/news/music/pussy-riot-71-1257775.

13   Tessa Stuart, "Pussy Riot's Nadya Tolokonnikova: Trump and Putin Both 'Dangerous Clowns,'" *Rolling Stone*, February 23, 2016, https://www.rollingstone.com/music/music-news/pussy-riots-nadya-tolokonnikova-trump-and-putin-both-dangerous-clowns-92754/; Kory Grow, "Pussy Riot's Nadya Tolokonnikova Added to Russia's Most Wanted Criminals List," *Rolling Stone*, March 29, 2023, https://www.rollingstone.com/music/music-news/pussy-riot-nadya-tolokonnikova-russia-most-wanted-criminals-1234705647/.

14   Nadya Tolokonnikova, "I'm an Activist in Russia. I Can't Believe What My Life Has Become," *New York Times*, August 28, 2020, https://www.nytimes.com/2020/08/26/opinion/navalny-russia.html; Rick Gladstone, "Pussy Riot Members Take Tour to New York," *New York Times*, February 6, 2014, https://www.nytimes.com/2014/02/06/world/europe/pussy-riot-members-say-prison-emboldened-them.html.

15   Amelia Gentleman, "Nadya Tolokonnikova: 'I suppose we have nothing more to lose,'" *Guardian*, September 19, 2014, https://www.theguardian.com/theguardian/2014/sep/19/nadya-tolokonnikova-pussy-riot-interview-nothing-to-lose; Miriam Elder, "Pussy Riot Trial: Closing Statement Denounces Putin's Totalitarian System," *Guardian*, August 8, 2012, http://www.theguardian.com/music/2012/aug/08/pussy-riot-trial-closing-statement; Nadezhda Tolokonnikova, "Pussy Riot's Nadezhda Tolokonnikova: Why I have gone on hunger strike," *Guardian*, September 23, 2013, https://www.theguardian.com/music/2013/sep/23/pussy-riot-hunger-strike-nadezhda-tolokonnikova; Megan Nolan, "Nadya Tolokonnikova: 'I have nightmares about being in prison again,'" *Guardian*, April 20, 2019, https://www.theguardian.com/lifeandstyle/2019/apr/20/this-much-i-know-nadya-tolokonnikova-pussy-riot; Zoe Williams, "Pussy Riot's Nadya Tolokonnikova: 'You cannot play nice with Putin. He is insane. He might open fire on his own people,'" *Guardian*, March 8, 2022, https://www.theguardian.com/artanddesign/2022/mar/08/pussy-riot-nadya-tolokonnikova-interview-putin-nfts-russian.

16   Nina Golgowski, "Pussy Riot Founder Says More Russians Are against Putin's War Than We've Seen," *Huffington Post*, March 6, 2022, https://www.huffpost.com/entry/pussy-riot-nadya-tolokonnikova-russians-oppose-putin-war_n_622513d6e4b012a2628c4b47; Jessica Elgot, "Pussy Riot's Nadezhda Tolokonnikova Describes Depravity of 'Stalinist' Work Camp," *Huffington Post*, September 23, 2013, https://www.huffingtonpost.co.uk/2013/09/23/pussy-riot-work-camp_n_3975953.html.

professional photographs featuring Tolokonnikova, such as the one below, published in the *New York Times* in December 2016, she seems to be nothing less than the living embodiment of feminism—a new and young kind of feminism that is not afraid to be feminine, beautiful, sexy, smart, and marketable.

Figure 11. Photograph of Nadya Tolokonnikova at Miami Beach in 2016 by Casey Kelbaugh for the *New York Times*; first published as part of the article Jim Rutenberg, "A Warning for Americans from a Member of Pussy Riot," *New York Times*, December 4, 2016, https://www.nytimes.com/2016/12/04/business/rutenberg-lessons-in-free-speech-from-pussy-riot.html.

In addition to appearing in the news and other media, Tolokonnikova made guest appearances on the TV show *House of Cards*.[17] At the same time, she was celebrated by subcultural and counter-cultural movements such as the riot grrrl movement and by musicians such as JD Samson, Kathleen Hanna, and Johanna Fateman.[18] US-American feminists, and particularly third wave feminists , previously had little to no knowledge of or interest in Russian feminists or Russian women. One reason for this ignorance was their "insistence on finding

---

17 *House of Cards*, "Chapter 29," directed by Tucker Gates, aired February 27, 2015, Netflix.

18 "JD Samson working with Pussy Riot's Nadya Tolokonnikova and Masha Alyokhina," *Impose*, last modified December 9, 2014, http://www.imposemagazine.com/bytes/news/jd-samson-working-with-pussy-riots-nadyatolokonnikova-and-masha-alyokhina; Joanna Fateman, "Pussy Riot Realness," *ARTNews*, February 27, 2015, https://www.artnews.com/art-in-america/features/pussy-riot-realness-63065/.

expressions of Western-style feminism,"[19] as Jennifer Suchland has pointed out. Pussy Riot offered US-American third wavers pattern recognition.

The continuous and long-term representation in both spheres—the mainstream and the sub- and counter-cultural—is rather exceptional. It seems that Tolokonnikova has aligned herself tightly to a pop-cultural feminism that is political, on the one hand, but very marketable, on the other. Commenting on the US political field through her art, in interviews, opinion pieces, and her book *Read & Riot: A Pussy Riot Guide to Activism*,[20] which oscillates between memoir, punk manual, and political pamphlet, Tolokonnikova has managed to keep up media interest in her. Importantly, the artistic form that Tolokonnikova employs with her group Pussy Riot is the media spectacle, which, according to media scholar Douglas Kellner, is the most dominant and successful form of US-American popular culture.[21] Kellner argues that the spectacle itself has become one of the organizing principles of US-American economy, polity, society, and everyday life. Strongly supported by the internet-based economy, which produces unprecedented amounts of media content and distributes it widely and at a high speed, the spectacle has become essential as a means of the promotion, reproduction, circulation, and selling of commodities.[22] Interestingly, and perhaps coincidentally, Pussy Riot managed to offer US-American and other Anglophone audiences feminism in its most spectacular form, interwoven with New Cold War politics, as well as popular culture politics. The initial images of Pussy Riot and the "Punk Prayer" "fit with the global media market and its use of recognizable 'global' feminist imagery."[23] They were easily recognizable as images of feminist protest and resistance, and were, at the same time, spectacular and novel, because they came out of Russia and were directed against the Russian president and the Russian Orthodox Church.

Pussy Riot's appeal to the US-American artistic elite and popular audiences alike, was due to a combination of their particular version of feminist action; their ability to meet the needs of Western markets together with their appeal

---

19   Jennifer Suchland, "Contextualizing Pussy Riot in Russia and Beyond," E-International Relations, August 28, 2012, https://www.e-ir.info/2012/08/28/contextualizing-pussy-riot-in-russia-and-beyond/.

20   Nadia Tolokonnikova, *Read & Riot: A Pussy Riot Guide to Activism* (New York: HarperOne, 2018).

21   Douglas Kellner, *Media Spectacle* (London: Routledge, 2003).

22   Ibid., 1.

23   Elena Gapova, "Becoming Visible in the Digital Age," *Feminist Media Studies* 15, no. 1 (2014): 22, https://doi:10.1080/14680777.2015.988390.

to New Cold War politics;[24] and homonationalism.[25] Pussy Riot's trial and Tolokonnikova's subsequent emergence as a pop-cultural phenomenon coincided with the presidency of Barack Obama, who was increasingly seen not only as supporter of gender equality, but, particularly during his second term, as a champion for the inclusion of homosexuals into the nation. He famously called, for example, "the Supreme Court decision [of June 2015] requiring states to recognize same-sex marriage 'a victory for America,'"[26] strongly suggesting that to be American means to have liberal values.

The contrast between Obama's publicly uttered sentiments and those of the Russian president could not have been greater. Despite the fact that Putin did not often speak publicly about Pussy Riot, other Russian politicians, public figures, and the Russian Orthodox Church condemned them and their artistic expression as being too closely aligned to Western forms and values, which they deemed antithetical to those of Russia. Indeed, spurred by the controversy over Pussy Riot and their "Punk Prayer,"[27] the Russian media and public fiercely debated the question of what defines 'Russianness' for the Russian nation. Inspired by their example, the Western media attempted to define US-Americanness for the US-American public. The apparently strong disparity of political trends between Russia and the US, along with the resurgence of New Cold War media discourses, made Pussy Riot and feminism, as a cultural politics, appealing to US-American and other Western audiences. It enhanced their compassion because their support for Russian feminists confirmed feelings of Western modernity, progress, and superiority, while also confirming their rightful belonging to the US. That Pussy Riot practiced feminist politics in the form of punk performances, and the negative response of Russian authorities and the hostile public that their performances elicited, made feminism appear newly relevant and contemporary within the mainstream United States, and stabilized

---

24 Richard Sakwa, "'New Cold War' or Twenty Years' Crisis? Russia and International Politics," *International Affairs* 84, no. 2 (2008): 241–267.

25 Jasbir Puar, "Rethinking Homonationalism," *Middle East Studies* 45, no. 2 (2013): 336–339; Jasbir Puar, *Terrorist Assemblages: Homonationalism in Queer Times* (Durham, NC: Duke University Press, 2007).

26 Gregory Korte, "Obama: Gay marriage ruling is 'a victory for America,'" *USA Today*, June 26, 2015, https://eu.usatoday.com/story/news/politics/2015/06/26/obama-gay-marriage-ruling/29328755/; Scott Neuman, "Obama: Supreme Court Same-Sex Marriage Ruling 'A Victory for America,'" NPR, June 26, 2015, https://www.npr.org/sections/thetwo-way/2015/06/26/417731614/obama-supreme-court-ruling-on-gay-marriage-a-victory-for-america.

27 Gapova, "Becoming Visible in the Digital Age," 22; Elena Sineok, "Antipussing v Krasnodare [Antipussing in Krasnodar]," Yuga.ru, March 31, 2012, http://www.yuga.ru/photo/1196.html.

the idea that feminism was indeed a US national value. Additionally, their "Punk Prayer," and other performances that used punk aesthetics, not only in musical, but also in the form of verbal social criticism and mockery of the Russian president Vladimir Putin and the Russian Orthodox Church, through the lyrics and additional statements, actualized Western riot grrrl feminism and brought the seemingly passé pop cultural form of activism back into the international spotlight.[28]

Tolokonnikova and Alyokhina were sentenced to two years of hard labor in a prison colony, where they were ultimately imprisoned for about twenty months before being granted amnesty. Their suffering was highly publicized, not least through Tolokonnikova's correspondence with the philosopher Slavoj Žižek, which was published in the *Guardian*.[29] Through these and other media representations, Tolokonnikova and Alyokhina, came to be styled as feminist martyrs, which seemed to confirm the political potential of pop feminism.

Pussy Riot and Western Enlightenment Discourses

At the same time that the New Cold War discourses grew around Pussy Riot, perpetuating the idea of an illiberal, retrograde Russia and a liberal, enlightened West, illiberal transnational alliances continually propagated misogyny and queerphobia within the allegedly liberal West, and academic literature on the subject grew in volume. By the time Tolokonnikova and Alyokhina had been released, "advanced theoretical perspectives from an array of disciplines—ranging from feminist theory to studies of religion were being applied."[30] Most of the academic analyses focused on the interpretation and sociopolitical context of their lyrics, performances, and political activities,[31] as well as their reception in

---

28   Laura Barton, "Pussy Riot's Kremlin protest owes much to riot grrrl," *Guardian*, February 3, 2012, https://www.theguardian.com/commentisfree/2012/feb/03/pussy-riot-kremlin-protest-riot-grrrl.

29   Slavoj Žižek and Nadezhda Tolokonnikova, "Nadezhda Tolokonnikova of Pussy Riot's prison letters to Slavoj Žižek," *Guardian*, November 15, 2013, https://www.theguardian.com/music/2013/nov/15/pussy-riot-nadezhda-tolokonnikova-slavoj-zizek; Nadya Tolokonnikova and Slavoj Žižek, *Comradely Greetings: The Prison Letters of Nadya and Slavoj* (New York: Verso, 2014).

30   Yngvar B. Steinholt, and David-Emil Wickström, "The Pussy Riot Complex: Entering a New Stage of Academic Research into a Viral Russian Controversy," *Popular Music and Society* 39, no. 4 (2015): 393–395, 394.

31   Anya Bernstein, "An Inadvertent Sacrifice: Body Politics and Sovereign Power in the Pussy Riot Affair," *Critical Inquiry* 40, no. 1 (2013): 220–41, https://doi:10.1086/673233; Jessica

Russia.[32] Only a few explicitly addressed the perception of Pussy Riot within the Western, and particularly US-American, context. Among this work was my own writing on Western Free Pussy Riot solidarity;[33] Sophie Pinkham's short review and contextualization of Masha Gessen's *Words Will Break Cement: The Passion of Pussy Riot*;[34] and Frank Weij's and Pauwke Berkers's analysis of political discourses in YouTube viewer comments to the Pussy Riot videos.[35]

These latter works, which investigate Western imperialism and forms of homonationalism in Anglophone Pussy Riot discourses, identify notions of an "uncivilized Russia"[36] in the tradition of the European Enlightenment.[37] In these discourses, which emerged in the context of European colonialism's attempts to legitimate racist exploitation of othered cultures and territories, Eastern Europe was invented as a cultural and intellectual construct that allowed for a clear(er) delineation of imaginary North/Western superiority and

---

Zychowicz, "The Global Controversy over Pussy Riot: An Anti-Putin Women's Protest Group in Moscow," *International Institute Journal* 2, no. 1 (2012): 13–15; Erin Katherine Krafft, "Punk Prayers Versus Neoliberalism: Pussy Riot and the Fractured Feminist Family Tree," *Canadian-American Slavic Studies* 56, no. 2 (May 10, 2022): 152–77, https://doi.org/10.30965/22102396-05602006; Eliot Borenstein, *Pussy Riot: Speaking Punk to Power* (London: Bloomsbury, 2020).

32 Gapova, "Becoming Visible in The Digital Age"; Valerie Sperling, *Sex, Politics, and Putin: Political Legitimacy in Russia* (Oxford: Oxford University Press, 2014); Regina Smyth and Irina Soboleva, "Looking beyond the Economy: Pussy Riot and the Kremlin's Voting Coalition," *Post-Soviet Affairs* 30, no. 4 (2013): 257–275; Jasmine French, "Pussy Power: Feminism, Protest and the Remasculinisation of Putin's Russia," *Canadian-American Slavic Studies* 56, no. 2 (May 10, 2022): 127–51, https://doi.org/10.30965/22102396-05602005; Marina Vinnik, "Bogoroditsa, Stan' Feministkoi? The Leningrad Feminists and Pussy Riot," *Canadian-American Slavic Studies* 56, no. 2 (May 10, 2022): 178–99, https://doi.org/10.30965/22102396-05602007.

33 Katharina Wiedlack, "Pussy Riot and the Western Gaze: Punk Music, Solidarity and the Production of Similarity and Difference," *Popular Music and Society* 23 (2015), http://www.tandfonline.com/doi/full/10.1080/03007766.2015.1088281; Katharina Wiedlack and Masha Neufeld, "Lost in Translation? Pussy Riot Solidarity Activism and the Danger of Perpetuating North/Western Hegemonies," *Religion & Gender* 4, no. 2 (2014): 145–165.

34 Sophie Pinkham, "Pussy Riot in Translation," *Dissent*, Summer 2014, https://www.dissent-magazine.org/article/pussy-riot-in-translation/; Masha Gessen, *Words Will Break Cement: The Passion of Pussy Riot* (New York: Riverhead Books, 2014).

35 662; Frank Weij and Pauwke Berkers, "The Politics of Musical Activism: Western YouTube Reception of Pussy Riot's Punk Performances," *Convergence: The International Journal of Research into New Media Technologies* (2017): 1–20, https://doi.org/10.1177/1354856517706493.

36 Piotr Dutkiewicz, "Missing in Translation: Re-Conceptualizing Russia's Developmental State," in *Russia: Challenges of Transformation*, ed. Piotr Dutkiewicz and Dmitri Trenin (New York: NYU Press, 2011), 9–40, 10.

37 Wolff, *Inventing Eastern Europe*; Iver B. Neumann, *Russia and the Idea of Europe: A Study in Identity and International Relations* (London: Routledge, 1995); Neumann, *Uses of the Other*.

development.[38] Within this framework, Russia signifies, culturally, a paradoxical locus between similarity and difference, between white Western civilization and the 'barbarian Orient.' The US and other Anglophone media that conceives a narrowly determined Western history to be the scale and criterion for evaluating the developmental state of any country outside of this sphere, applied this colonial and imperialist Enlightenment framework in their reports about Pussy Riot. The *Daily Beast* called their persecution "a form of Russian McCarthyism" and a "witch hunt."[39] The *New Yorker* described the conviction of Alyokhina and Tolokonnikova to hard labor as "a triumph of anti-modern obscurantism over young Russian modernity, the crushing power of the state over the individual, servility over independence."[40]

The pop star Madonna, who even integrated Pussy Riot solidarity slogans and balaclavas into her world tour, was one of the most vocal celebrity supporters of Tolokonnikova and Pussy Riot. The Anglophone media reported enthusiastically on Madonna's actions, particularly when she stripped to her shirt on stage, revealing the words "Pussy Riot" on her back, at concerts in Moscow and St. Petersburg in August 2012.[41] During these performances, she also called on her audience to "show your love and appreciation for the gay community" and criticized the law against "homosexual propaganda,"[42] which at the time had been introduced only locally in St. Petersburg. Through her affirmation of gay rights, gay pride, and her support of Pussy Riot, she firmly re-established the connection between the group and progressive values for the Western viewers. Moreover, Madonna's advocacy of Pussy Riot also promoted (her version of) feminism, which was young, sexy, and committed to social activism. Importantly, Madonna's intervention further established the notion that although this feminism was embodied by young, white, feminine women from Eastern Europe, its ideas were rooted in the Western world, especially the United States.

---

38   Wolff, *Inventing Eastern Europe*; Neumann, *Russia and the Idea of Europe*; Neumann, *Uses of the Other*; Stuart Hall, "The West and the Rest: Discourse and Power," in *The Formations of Modernity*, ed. Stuart Hall and Bram Gieben (Cambridge: Polity, 1993), 275–331.

39   Anna Nemtsova, "Pussy Riot Witch Hunt by Kremlin-Backed 'Youth Movement,'" *Daily Beast*, September 30, 2012, http://www.thedailybeast.com/ articles/2012/09/30/pussy-riot-witch-hunt-by-kremlin-backed-youth-movement.

40   Masha Lipman, "The Pussy Riot Verdict," *New Yorker*, August 17, 2012, http://www.newyorker.com/online/blogs/newsdesk/2012/08/the-pussy-riot-verdict.html.

41   "Madonna Shows Support for Pussy Riot at Moscow Concert—Video," *Guardian*, August 8, 2012, http://www.theguardian.com/music/video/2012/aug/08/ madonna-pussy-riot-moscow-video.

42   Ibid.

In this version of feminism, equality, self-representation, sexual freedom, and financial independence were eclipsed by access to capitalist power and public visibility. Thus, Madonna supported media discourses that signified feminism as a cultural politics strongly embedded in the logic of market capitalism and the US democratic system, and entangled with other liberal rights claims and causes, particularly gay and lesbian rights struggles. Her solidarity was arguably entirely informed by North/Western feminist discourses and universalist human rights rhetoric supporting freedom of speech. Her speeches frequently employed the strategy of paternalistic "shaming"[43] of Russia for its backwardness, advancing the idea that the United States is much more progressive and modern, in comparison. Speaking at the 2014 Amnesty International Benefit Concert, for example, Madonna said that only after coming to Russia had she realized how lucky she was to live in a country that allows her to speak her mind. In this and other speeches, Madonna equated the persecution of Pussy Riot with the homophobic legal constraints on public discussions of homosexuality as human rights violations, implicitly setting human rights as the aim and standard of progress. Importantly, she also equated the United States with human rights.[44]

Read through the works of postcolonial scholars Aihwa Ong[45] and Jasbir Puar,[46] Madonna's acts of solidarity appear to be clearly embedded in US colonial imperialism and (homo)nationalism. US feminists have a long history of entanglement with colonial imperialist and nationalist discourses. Much of this feminism legitimizes itself through the "becoming conscious of oppression from the Other,"[47] as mentioned in Madonna's speech quoted above. It builds on the assumption that women in places other than the West are generally more oppressed than they are in the West, that is, the Western standard is the future and the template that other places need to adopt. This feminism generates national pride based on alleged superiority to the abject Other, measured not least by "'acceptance' and 'tolerance' for gay and lesbian subjects [as] a

---

43 "Madonna Calls for Leniency in Pussy Riot Trial During Russian Leg of World Tour," *Telegraph*, August 7, 2012, http://www.telegraph.co.uk/news/newsvideo/ 9458246/ Madonna-calls-for-leniency-in-Pussy-Riot-trial-during-Russian-leg-of-world-tour.html.

44 Ibid.

45 Aihwa Ong, "Colonialism and Modernity: Feminist Re-presentations of Women in Non-Western Societies," *Inscriptions* 3–4 (1988): 79–93, http://culturalstudies.ucsc.edu/PUBS/ Inscriptions/vol_3-4/v3-4top.html.

46 Puar, *Terrorist Assemblages*.

47 Ong, "Colonialism and Modernity," 79.

barometer by which the right to and capacity for national sovereignty [of the Other] is evaluated."[48]

Tolokonnikova, in particular, added fuel to the media's Enlightenment blaze, confirming the growing cleavage between the modern, progressive, free North/West and barbaric Russia, describing the latter as a "totalitarian machine,"[49] yet again opening up feminism as a platform for New Cold War culture wars. Her statements supported "the dominant conceptualization of the last two decades of [. . .] Putin's regime [as] a new authoritarian empire, within which one can already discern the resurrection of the Soviet Union."[50] These discourses perceived Russia as increasingly threatening "not only the rights and freedoms of ordinary Russian citizens but also the former Soviet republics, East and North/Western Europe, and, in fact [. . .] the entire world."[51] Unfortunately, these discourses did not lead to a serious interrogation of Russia's increasingly militarized cultural imperialism, which led eventually to the military invasion of Ukraine and the support of white Russian Orthodox nationalism for the genocide of Indigenous peoples and violence against many other minorities in Russia. Rather, the focus on President Putin as the single locus of Russian homophobia, sexism, and authoritarianism created panic about Russian infiltration of the West reminiscent of Cold War discourses and the "Red Menace"[52]—though in inverted form. This phenomenon included overstating the role that Russia had played in the US election of Donald Trump as president,[53] which came to be known as "Russia-gate."

Although I do not want to defend or dismiss the harm caused by espionage, hacking, or other criminal activities, I nevertheless view the election of Trump as an entirely American phenomenon, which speaks to the prevalence and evident increase in attitudes and acts of white supremacy, misogyny, queerphobia, racism, and xenophobia within the country. While Russia-gate discourses

---

48 Puar, "Rethinking Homonationalism," 336.
49 Tolokonnikova qtd. in Miriam Elder, "Pussy Riot Trial: Closing Statement Denounces Putin's Totalitarian System," *Guardian*, August 8, 2012, http://www.theguardian.com/music/2012/aug/08/pussy-riot-trial-closing-statement; Dough Stanglin, "Freed Pussy Riot Members Call Russia Amnesty a PR Stunt," *USA Today*, December 23, 2013, 23–24; "Olympics Has Made Russia Totalitarian—Pussy Riot," Newshub, last modified February 21, 2014, http://www.newshub.co.nz/world/olympics-has-made-russia-totalitarian--pussy-riot-2014022106#axzz44zPsZ2nL.
50 Dutkiewicz, "Missing in Translation," 10.
51 Ibid.
52 Steven Heller and Michael Barson, *Red Scared! The Commie Menace in Propaganda and Popular Culture* (San Francisco, CA: Chronicle Books, 2001).
53 Robert Parry, "The Politics behind 'Russia-gate,'" Global Research, March 6, 2017, http://www.globalresearch.ca/the-politics-behind-russia-gate/5578089.

understand Trump to be "Putin's Puppet,"[54] and his indifference "to Western moral values [and] Western moral leadership" to be an attack against Western civilization,[55] in favor of a "post-West world order led by Russia,"[56] I argue that Trump's popularity is a logical consequence of white Western imperialism. Not coincidentally, Trump understands himself as defender of white Western civilization against racialized, and particularly Muslim, Others.[57] Moreover, the racism and white supremacy of Russian imperialism is deployed in similar ways, though from an anti-Western perspective. In other words, both Russian imperialism and "America first" discourses are intrinsically embedded in notions of white civilization and white superiority that legitimize (settler) colonialism and imperial expansionism. Rather than investigating the implication of Western Enlightenment discourses in racism and white supremacy, the Anglophone media preferred to focus on Tolokonnikova as a model of enlightened progressive values, an "emissary from a dystopian political-media environment that seemed to be heading our way, with governmental threats against dissent, disinformation from the presidential level and increasingly assertive propagandists who stoke the perception that there can be no honest arbiter of truth."[58]

Critics of Pussy Riot, and particularly of Tolokonnikova, argue that their cultural productions are "specifically calibrated for the Western media market."[59] While this interpretation was initially, as I have explained elsewhere,[60] a well-meant misinterpretation on the part of Western allies, it became a more concerted effort in the aftermath of Tolokonnikova's and Alyokhina's amnesty. Tolokonnikova continued to feed the US media with interviews, opinion pieces, and other forms of writing, and she released videos under the Pussy Riot brand

---

54 Franklin Foer, "Putin's Puppet," *Slate*, July 4, 2016, http://www.slate.com/articles/news_ and_politics/cover_story/2016/07/vladimir_putin_has_a_plan_for_destroying_the_ west_and_it_looks_a_lot_like.html.

55 Ibid.

56 A. Frank, "The Autumn of Western Civilization," *Today in Politics*, February 21, 2017, accessed March 10, 2023, https://tipolitics.com/the-autumn-of-Western-civilization-5c695fc980f1. Link no longer working.

57 Arianna, "Donald Trump Gives Speech About 'Survival' Of Western Civilization During Poland Visit," Organization for World Peace, July 15, 2017, https://theowp.org/ donald-trump-gives-speech-about-survival-of-Western-civilization-during-poland-visit/.

58 Jim Rutenberg, "A Warning for Americans from a Member of Pussy Riot," *New York Times*, December 4, 2016, https://www.nytimes.com/2016/12/04/business/rutenberg-lessons-in-free-speech-from-pussy-riot.html.

59 Melena Ryzik, "Pussy Riot Was Carefully Calibrated for Protest," *New York Times*, August 22, 2012, https://www.nytimes.com/2012/08/26/arts/music/pussy-riot-was-carefully-calibrated-for-protest.html.

60 Wiedlack, "Pussy Riot and the Western Gaze"; Wiedlack and Neufeld, "Lost in Translation."

long after many of her colleagues had expressed their discomfort with her coop-tation of the name for her personal politics.[61] As I suggested earlier, the market-ability of Pussy Riot was due to the fact that the group "became an international symbol of Mr. Putin's crackdown"[62] on his opposition. Importantly, they offered "a familiar story with a modern twist. Once again, authoritarian Russia was oppressing dissident artists; but this time, instead of being 'grumpy old men' like Solzhenitsyn, retyping dogeared manuscripts in dingy communal apart-ments, the artists in question were young, attractive, charismatic women who invoked riot grrrl and Slavoj Žižek."[63] Pussy Riot functioned as a throwback to a familiar pattern and scale of world power distribution: East against West, Russia against America, bad against good, backward against progressive. By 2016, when "the political-media environment that we smugly thought to be 'over there' seem[ed] to be arriving over here,"[64] in the wake of Trump and his alleged rela-tions to Russia, Tolokonnikova had long become *the Other* of contemporary US-American popular culture. She embraces the position of the immigrant, the othered body, the cultural other, as well as signifying Putin's adversary in her music video titled "Make America Great Again"—her visual commentary on Trump.

Whiteness

The widely held idea that Trump was handed the US presidency by Putin, who paved the way for his backward world leadership, is open to question. One rea-son for this, among others, is that the juxtaposition it implies of bad vs. good, uncivilized vs. progressive, and so on completely overlooks the white-wash-ing of feminism. This problem is highlighted in Tolokonnikova's video "Make America Great Again," released in October 2016,[65] the title of which repeats

---

61 Anonymous members of Pussy Riot, "We wish Nadia and Masha well—but they're no lon-ger part of Pussy Riot," *Guardian*, February 6, 2014, http://www.theguardian.com/ com-mentisfree/2014/feb/06/nadia-masha-pussy-riot-collective-no-longer; Vladimir Kozlov, "Pussy Riot: Anonymous Members Distance Themselves from Two Former Bandmates," *Hollywood Reporter*, February 6, 2014, http://www.hollywoodreporter.com/news/pussy-riot-anonymous-members-distance-677713.

62 Rutenberg, "A Warning for Americans."

63 Pinkham, "Pussy Riot in Translation."

64 Rutenberg, "A Warning for Americans."

65 Elias Leight, "Pussy Riot Slam Trump in 'Make America Great Again' Video," *Rolling Stone*, October 27, 2016, https://www.rollingstone.com/music/music-news/pussy-riot-slam-donald-trump-in-make-america-great-again-video-126889/.

Donald Trump's notorious electoral campaign slogan. The music video clip was intended as an intervention in the US presidential elections of November 2016. It attempted to mobilize voters against Trump by adding to the video the comment: "YOU decide elections, and if we get together, we could blow this shit up, take action and reverse this erosion of rights. Because fuck it," according to *Rolling Stone*.[66] The video is a montage of clips from pro-Trump rallies, scenes of police brutality against rioters, and scenes in which Tolokonnikova plays the parts of both a violent Trump, and herself as his victim. "Under [Tolokonnikova's] imagined Trump regime, American police are shown morphing into a version of the Gestapo, using a hot poker to burn Tolokonnikova's supposed transgressions into her skin before torturing, raping and shooting her dead."[67] The song's chorus targets US-American immigration policies in the line: "Let other people in." According to the Migration Policy Institute, already under Barack Obama's presidency "more than 2.5 million people between 2009 and 2015"[68] were deported. Tolokonnikova's video implies that this record will only worsen, conjuring up Trump's infamous—and now at least partly fulfilled—promise to build a thirty-feet-high wall on the Mexican border.[69] When Tolokonnikova sings, "Listen to your women," she addresses simultaneously the many women who have accused him of sexual harassment and rape and the feminists who have opposed him and his politics. It might also speak to the widely shared view by liberal commentators that Ivanka Trump could have a positive influence on her father[70] or to Tolokonnikova's support of the democratic presidential candidate Hillary Clinton.

The most visible, and at the same time most elusive, subject of "Make America Great Again" is American racism. The line, "Stop killing [B]lack children," can be read as a reference to the fact that "[a]cross the United States, [B]lack infants die at a rate that's more than twice as high as that of white infants."[71] The line

---

66   Ibid.

67   Shuster, "Pussy Riot Unveils."

68   Aline Barros, "Comparing Immigration Raids Under Trump, Obama," Voice of America, February 16, 2017, https://www.voanews.com/a/comparing-immigration-raids-under-trump-and-obama/3727706.html.

69   Alicia A. Caldwell, "Trump wants to build 30-foot-high wall at Mexican border," *Associated Press*, March 18, 2017, https://apnews.com/article/4453616f041f4ebaa49128bd6f390f1c.

70   Natasha Geiling, "The Myth of Liberal Ivanka Trump," ThinkProgress, May 22, 2017, https://archive.thinkprogress.org/liberal-myth-of-ivanka-trump-68195b8039cc/.

71   Zoë Carpenter, "What's Killing America's Black Infants?" *Nation*, March 6, 2017, https://www.thenation.com/article/archive/whats-killing-americas-black-infants/.

additionally addresses the charges of "environmental racism";[72] for example, the case of the Flint, Michigan water scandal that surfaced in 2015. The NAACP and other advocates accused the authorities of ignoring the contamination of Flint's drinking water with lead because it affected a predominantly Black and poor population.[73] Last, but not least, the chorus also addresses the extremely high number of fatal shootings of Black citizens by police. According to a project on police fatalities in the US carried out by the *Guardian,* the "U.S. police killed at least 258 [B]lack people in 2016."[74] In the last scene of the video, Tolokonnikova is shot in the back by a police officer. The depiction of police brutality—the men in uniform beat Tolokonnikova, strip her to her underwear, grab and push her around, and in the end shoot her—are in stark contrast to the upbeat hip-hop music.

The problematic nature of the representation and tropes of border violence, deportation, and anti-Black violence in the video "Make America Great Again," however, rests in the fact that experiences that are in actuality suffered by Blacks and people of color are here embodied by a white woman through a strategy of self-othering. Besides the images that conjure up scenes of border violence and anti-Black police violence, some scenes, such as the one in which Tolokonnikova is brought into a medical examination room that is equipped with a scale, a kind of surgical table, and so forth recall the racist phrenology used by nineteenth-century physicians, biologists, and philosophers to justify slavery and other forms of oppression.[75] White European and American colonists measured body parts to determine racial differences, and concluded from the resulting numbers what 'grade' of morality, civilization, and intelligence the racialized Others demonstrated. These pseudoscientific racist practices might seem to have been abandoned; but, in fact, race-based measurements still persist. A book-length study by the Africana studies and medical science scholar Lundy Braun, for example, shows how racist ideas about bodily difference continue to shape contemporary

---

72 Michael Martinez, "Flint, Michigan: Did race and poverty factor into water crisis?" *New York Amsterdam News,* January 27, 2016, https://amsterdamnews.com/news/2016/01/27/flint-michigan-did-race-and-poverty-factor-water-c/.

73 Ibid.

74 Julia Craven, "More Than 250 Black People Were Killed by Police In 2016," *Huffington Post,* July 7, 2016, https://www.huffpost.com/entry/black-people-killed-by-police-america_n_577da633e4b0c590f7e7fb17.

75 Rachel Walker, "Facing Race: Popular Science and Black Intellectual Thought in Antebellum America," *Early American Studies: An Interdisciplinary Journal* 19, no. 3 (2021): 601–40, https://doi.org/10.1353/eam.2021.0019.

science and technology.[76] The medical surveillance and assessment of bodies through common measures such as Body Mass Index, as well as the establishment of risk factors for, and notions of, obesity, are inherently racist and sexist.[77]

The video "Make America Great Again" alludes unequivocally to racism through the practice of body measurement exercised on Tolokonnikova, whose body, it can be argued, conforms quite strictly to contemporary beauty standards, by two border control policemen. Further, her measurements and body shape are actively compared to a chart behind her, showing the outlines of a female shape, with exaggeratedly large breasts, wide hips, and very pronounced buttocks, as can be seen in the following screen shot.

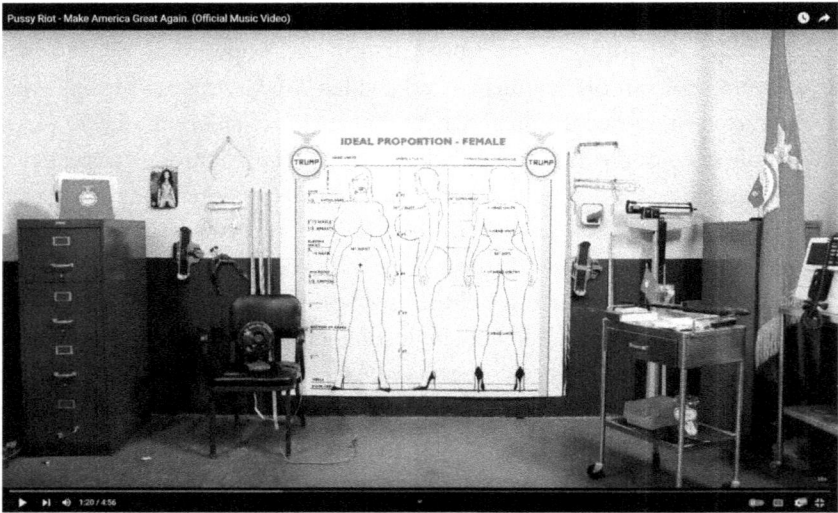

Figure 12. Screenshot of Pussy Riot, "Make Amerika Great Again," dir. Jonas Akerlund, Youtube, October 17, 2016, 1:20, https://www.youtube.com/watch?v=s-bKFo30o2o&t=173s.

This chart, although it is most likely meant to signify the male gaze on women, brings up racist notions identifying Black women with disproportionally enhanced breasts, hips, and buttocks. These features align with historic US-American racial stereotypes in popular culture that objectify Black women

76 Lundy Braun, *Breathing Race into the Machine: The Surprising Career of the Spirometer from Plantation to Genetics* (Minneapolis: University of Minnesota Press, 2014).

77 Rachel Sanders, "The color of fat: racializing obesity, recuperating whiteness, and reproducing injustice," *Politics, Groups, and Identities* 7, no. 2 (2019): 287–304, https://doi:10.1080/21565503.2017.1354039.

"as inferior, dumb and incompetent, [attributing these qualities] to [B]lack female sexuality [as well as] the typically curvaceous buttocks and body."[78] The emergence of "the hyper-sexualized [B]lack female butt" dates back to the early nineteenth century.[79] In her book *Black Looks: Race and Representation*, bell hooks describes how Black female sexuality and bodies have traditionally been associated with sexual deviance, primitiveness, and availability.[80] Ashley Relates traces the sexualization of the exaggerated Black female buttocks from the American antebellum era to contemporary hip-hop culture. Music videos and song lyrics by Black musical artists and performers reproduce the objectification of Black female buttocks through their videos. They "all highlight the importance of a big butt in Black popular culture,"[81] according to Relates. The chart against which Tolokonnikova's body is measured, in combination with the hip-hop style of her song, combines (sexist) Black cultural significations with racial stereotypes and racist practices.

The last imagery of intersecting racialization and injustice that "Make America Great Again" depicts is the prison-industrial complex. Towards the end of the video, Tolokonnikova is incarcerated. The video's visual language addresses the racialized and anti-Black structures of the US-American prison-industrial complex, which disproportionally targets African Americans.[82] Moreover, specifically honing in on Trump and his politics, the video clip addresses anti-Mexican and anti-Muslim racism and immigration policies, and practices of border violence and deportation. By burning the words "visitor" and "freak" into the flesh of her hands with glowing branding irons, these ideas are further connected to the US history of chattel slavery. Yet beyond the line "stop killing [B]lack children" in the aforementioned chorus, Tolokonnikova does not verbally address anti-Black, anti-Mexican, or anti-Muslim racism. Her white, violently mistreated, and partially burned body is the only embodiment of Otherness.

One of the strong visual references that offers a feminist perspective in the video is the iconic Pussy Riot balaclava, in a sparkling and camp fashion version. Together with images that implicitly address multiple forms of racialized violence,

---

78 Ashley Relates, "Closer Look at the Butt: Appropriation and Exploitation of Black Female Sexuality," *Medium*, November 9, 2015, https://medium.com/@ashleyrelates/closer-look-at-the-butt-appropriation-of-black-female-sexuality-1153b1840c9c.
79 Ibid.
80 bell hooks, *Black Looks: Race and Representation* (Boston, MA: South End Press, 1992).
81 Relates, "Closer Look at the Butt."
82 Michelle Alexander, *The New Jim Crow: Mass Incarceration in the Age of Colorblindness* (New York: The New Press, 2010).

Tolokonnikova's video appears to be an example of what Amy Alexander calls "marketable white feminism."[83] This version of feminism, and the "place it holds in the public imagination, is largely occupied by white women" who use the experience of Blacks and people of color to "explain" oppression.[84] The phenomenon of labeling discrimination of migrants from Eastern Europe as racism is not confined to feminist discourses, nor to the US context. The queer theorist Alyosxa Tudor has analyzed how bloggers, social media activists, and journalists, in their struggle to identify and name the "nexus" of anti-Black, anti-Muslim, anti-people of color politics with anti-migrant sentiments against Eastern Europeans in Brexit-era UK, frequently resort to the label "racism." "This use of 'racism', however, is based on methodological nationalism and conceptual whiteness."[85] To identify the overlapping of racist and anti-immigration discursive violence, Tudor suggests using the term "migratism." "If racism is the power relation that racializes (=ascribes race to) people, migratism is the power relation that migratizes (=ascribes migration to) people. [...] Racism and migratism are bound to each other and play a crucial role in organizing the Western nation state."[86] Yet it is important to distinguish them from each other in order to make invisible the white privilege that white Eastern European migrants hold.

Queer Feminist Martyrs

I wish to return to my previously mentioned point, that during their trial and time in prison, Alyokhina and Tolokonnikova were presented in the US and international media as (queer) feminist martyrs, resisting, or rather enduring, the suffering caused by Putin's patriarchal violence. Articles and photographs presented them as heroic dissident figures, embodying everything antithetical to misogynistic and power-hungry Putin: youth, beauty, courage, and innocence. Tolokonnikova's image, in particular, shown below wearing the blue Pussy Riot Solidarity T-shirt, and raising her (feminist) fist, came to be celebrated as an iconoclastic sign for feminist defiance.

---

83 Amy Alexander, "Today's Feminism: Too Much Marketing, Not Enough Reality," NPR, February 21, 2017, http://www.npr.org/sections/codeswitch/ 2017/02/21/515799019/today-s-feminism-too-much-marketing-not-enough-reality.

84 Alexander, "Today's Feminism."

85 Alyosxa Tudor, "Ascriptions of Migration: Racism, Migratism and Brexit," *European Journal of Cultural Studies* 26, no. 2 (2023): 230–48, 230, https://doi:10.1177/13675494221101642.

86 Ibid.

Figure 13. Tolokonnikova on trial/Толоконникова в суде, August 8, 2012, Creative Commons Attribution-Share Alike 3.0, accessed December 12, 2024, https://commons.wikimedia.org/wiki/File:Nadezhda_Tolokonnikova.jpg. Photo by Mitya Aleshkovsky/Митя. Алешковский.

Masha Gessen, who was mentioned earlier in this chapter, and who also styled themself as a Russian martyr, helped significantly increase Tolokonnikova's visibility in US contexts with the book *Words Will Break Cement: The Passion of Pussy Riot.* Although Gessen's popularity cannot compete with Tolokonnikova's fame, they are well known in American liberal circles, and have enjoyed a steady presence within US news media for more than a decade. Gessen has a reoccurring column in the *New Yorker* and frequently writes for the *New York Times,* the *Los Angeles Times,* the *Washington Post, New Republic,* and *U.S. News & World Report.* They are also familiar to readers of *Slate, Vanity Fair,* and *Harper's Magazine,* where they are a recurring guest writer. Like Tolokonnikova, Gessen is best known as a harsh critic of Vladimir Putin and has arguably significantly influenced perceptions of him in the US, the Anglophone sphere, and beyond. Their book *The Man without a Face: The Unlikely Rise of Vladimir Putin,*[87] which details Putin's life from his early years, his marriage, his involvement in the First Chechen War, his relationship with Boris Yeltsin, and his ascent to power was published in 2012 and translated into twenty languages. CIA analyst John Ehrman, who reviewed the book for its intelligence details, wrote in a published review that although it does not offer any new facts, the book

> has its attraction [in publicly] support[ing] the consensus in academic and popular media analyses that, after 13 years, Putin's chief accomplishment has been to create a privileged elite that has systematically enriched itself by stripping Russia of just about any asset that can be stolen. While Gessen's metaphor oversimplifies—a Mafia don, after all, does not have to over-see the administration of a country or deal with the intricacies of international politics—it is easy to grasp and [is] effective as anti-Putin propaganda.[88]

Even before the book's publication, the language Gessen used to describe Putin fell neatly into US-American and Western superiority discourses, calling him

---

87 Masha Gessen, *The Man without a Face: The Unlikely Rise of Vladimir Putin* (New York: Riverhead Books, 2012).

88 John Ehrman, "Intelligence in Public Literature," review of *The Man Without a Face: The Unlikely Rise of Vladimir Putin,* by Masha Gessen, *Studies in Intelligence* 57, no. 4 (2013), https://www.cia.gov/resources/csi/static/Mr-Putin.pdf; John Ehrman, "Intelligence in Public Literature," review of *Mr. Putin: Operative in the Kremlin,* by Fiona Hill and Clifford Gaddy, *Studies in Intelligence* 57, no. 4 (2013), https://www.cia.gov/resources/csi/static/Mr-Putin.pdf.

"an aspiring thug" and characterizing the sociopolitical situation of Russia as "backward evolution."[89]

When it became clear that the Duma would greenlight the first national version of the so-called anti-gay propaganda law, many US media outlets interviewed Gessen or reported on their 'case.' In media appearances, articles, and interviews, Gessen indicated that they had become one of the preferred targets for Russian homophobes, quoting, for example, the ultra-conservative St. Petersburg politician Vitaly Milonov, who promoted the law against adoptions of Russian children by foreigners, saying "The Americans want to adopt Russian children and bring them up in perverted families like Masha Gessen's."[90]

The News media dramatized Gessen's migration to the US as a flight for their life. In an interview she gave to Michelangelo Signorile from the *Huffington Post*, they asked the US to offer asylum to all Russian LGBTIQ+ people with the words "get us the hell out of here."[91] Many other news outlets—particularly US LGBTIQ+ media—echoed this plea.[92] While Dmitry Chizhevsky, Kirill Kalugin, and Kirill Fedorov might have been the most famous visual queer icons, Gessen became the most famous queer voice of Russia. Gessen's spectacularly personal account, although arguably a privileged one, resonated well within US media, appearing in many US national newspapers, and on TV programs, such as *PBS News Hour* and *MSNBC*.

Although Gessen's move to the US was understandable, and although Russian homophobic sentiments and laws must not be trivialized, it is important to note that Gessen was in an extremely privileged position. They not only had the American passport that allowed them and their family to move immediately to the US, but also the necessary funds and (work and activism) connections.

---

89 Masha Gessen, "Dead Soul," *Vanity Fair*, October 1, 2008, 336–343.

90 Masha Gessen "When Putin Declared War on Gay Families, It Was Time for Mine to Leave Russia," *Slate*, August 26, 2013, https://slate.com/human-interest/2013/08/when-putin-declared-war-on-gay-families-it-was-time-for-mine-to-leave-russia.html.

91 Michelangelo Signorile, "Russian Gay Activist's Plea: 'Get Us the Hell Out of Here.'" *Huffington Post*, June 9, 2013, http://www.huffingtonpost.com/michelangelo-signorile/russian-gay-activists-plea-get-us-the-hell-out-of-here_b_3881059.html.

92 "Russian Gay Activist's Plea: 'Get Us the Hell Out of Here,'" Queer Nation NY, last modified September 7, 2023, https://queernationny.org/post/60566127409/russian-gay-activists-plea-get-us-the-hell-out; "Russian Gay Activist's Plea: 'Get Us the Hell Out of Here,'" Women Born Transsexual, last modified September 10, 2013, https://womenborntranssexual.com/2013/09/10/russian-gay-activists-plea-get-us-the-hell-out-of-here/; MNBrewer, "Russian Gay Activist's Plea: 'Get Us the Hell Out of Here,'" Democratic Underground, September 7, 2013, https://www.democraticunderground. com/113731651.

To meet the criteria of Kellner's media spectacle, and thereby stay relevant,[93] Gessen remained mostly silent about the fact that, although born in Moscow, they had immigrated to the United States in the early 1980s and gained US citizenship that decade.[94] Their portrayal of Russian homophobes, and particularly the Russian president, as "an uneducated, unintelligent, uncultured man who has no plan" (Gessen qtd. in Chotiner, 2017), who holds a personal grudge against liberal LGBTIQ+ advocates like themself, fits nicely into Guy Debord's "society of the spectacle," which is, according to Kellner, "a media and consumer society organized around the production and consumption of images, commodities, and staged events."[95] Kellner goes on to say that "media spectacles are those phenomena of media culture that embody contemporary society's basic values, serve to initiate individuals into its way of life, and dramatize its controversies and struggles, as well as its modes of conflict resolution."[96] Gessen's political commentary, in conjunction with their personal story as LGBTIQ+ refugee, spectacularizes contemporary politics. Their rhetoric, for example, in the headline "Time to Panic: It's like the Early Days of AIDS All over Again"[97] (their commentary on Trump's election in 2016), is always alarmist. Yet their words seem to weigh more because their persona embodies spectacular world events, such as the oppression of gays and lesbians and the backlash against human rights.

Like that of Tolokonnikova, Gessen's experience in Russia functions as evidence of what could happen in the United States if liberals do not change track immediately, and if progressive values and morals do not succeed in shaping the future. The problem with Gessen's account of Russia, however, as with Tolokonnikova's, is that they reduce Russia to a backward, authoritarian place, and paint the Russian opposition in exclusively Western terms. In *Words Will Break Cement*, Gessen

> craft[ed] a heroic story[, . . .] easily digestible for Western readers. [They do] not engage with the thornier questions raised by the Pussy Riot affair, such as Russian liberals' disgust with the

---

93 Kellner, *Media Spectacle*, 1.

94 Isaac Chotiner, "Donald and Vlad: Compare and Contrast," *Slate*, February 27, 2017, https://slate.com/news-and-politics/2017/02/how-trump-and-putin-are-similar-and-different-according-to-masha-gessen-and-what-it-means-for-americans.html.

95 Kellner, *Media Spectacle*, 2.

96 Ibid.

97 Masha Gessen, "Time to Panic: It's like the Early Days of AIDS All over Again," *Out*, December 14, 2016, https://www.out.com/news-opinion/2016/12/14/time-panic-its-early-days-aids-all-over-again.

cathedral action, or the claims made by Russian feminists that Pussy Riot members didn't know what they were talking about. *Words Will Break Cement* also seems torn between two competing theses: one about the power of words, indebted to the history of Soviet dissidence, and one about using the body when words have lost their power. This seems a false binary given the close connection, in Soviet history and Russian art, between protest through language and protest with the body. Eager to make its members heroes, Gessen diminishes the complexity of Pussy Riot's art and downplays its largely negative reception within Russia.[98]

Gessen, equally eager to produce themselves as victim-hero, exploits the story of their adopted child to show how wrong the Russian political regime is. In the *Slate* article quoted above, "When Putin Declared War on Gay Families, It Was Time for Mine to Leave Russia," Gessen showcases the opportunities that their son has, thanks to their liberal, US-influenced values. They describe how, when working as an AIDS activist and reporter, they "met Vova, who lived in an orphanage for the children of HIV-positive women, and adopted him. (He was negative.) At the time, no other Russian citizen would have adopted him, so great was the fear of AIDS, and so rare were adoptions generally." Not shying away from disclosing their son's disability, Gessen goes on to describe that "when Vova was 3, he didn't talk. He responded to speech unreliably," until they found out that "music lessons gave him the ability to communicate—and the confidence to do so. In the end, music was also how he learned to speak." Over the years he became proficient at playing musical instruments, and by 2013, "he was practicing for auditions at American high schools."[99]

Here, Gessen exploits an already established American discourse about Russian orphans. In her conference presentation "Global Gays/Local Crips: Or, Why Neoliberalism Needs Russia's (Retarded) Orphans,"[100] Anastasia Kayiatos argues that reactions within the US to Russia's introduction of the first national, anti-gay propaganda law were divided, with unanimous rejection on the part of liberals, and approval on the part of many conservatives and right-wingers. The

---

98 Pinkham, "Pussy Riot in Translation," 88.
99 Gessen, "When Putin Declared War on Gay Families."
100 Anastasia Kayiatos, "Global Gays/Local Crips: Or, Why Neoliberalism Needs Russia's (Retarded) Orphans," paper presented at De-colonizing Disability Theory I—Cripping Development, Prague, September 20, 2013.

ban on the adoption of Russian children by Americans (called the Dima Yakovlev or Anti-Magnitsky Law), however, although partly introduced as an anti-gay measure to prevent Russian children entering queer families, was opposed by a much more heterogenous group, consisting of progressive advocates of gay rights and religious conservatives. People of all political colors warned that "the ones who will suffer most from the law are Mother Russia's disproportionately high number of developmentally-delayed and maladjusted orphans."[101]

Kayiatos, anaylzing US newspaper articles,[102] TV news segments,[103] and public speeches, and applying crip and anti-social queer theory, shows that the focus on what she calls "crip orphans" and "post-communist crips" was not only "an implicit indictment of the failed Russian family and the propitious expansion of American kinship forms," but also a remnant of the "cold-war discourse about the country's own developmental delay under an alternative anticapitalist modernity." Additionally, these discourses "animate homonormative and homonational discourses of futurity embodied in the figure of the Child,"[104] a symbolic figure that queer theorist Lee Edelman has successfully proposed is the antithesis of queerness within the symbolic order of meaning.[105]

Although Gessen's life decisions are certainly admirable, the focus on their developmentally delayed adopted son, besides raising questions about the exploitation of minors through social journalism, conjures up the discourse described by Kayiatos. It positions the secret child, which barely escaped the developmentally delayed country, as a weapon against Putin and the hegemonic political tide within Russia, and simultaneously affirms American values that include transnational adoptions, as well as LGBTIQ+ rights. At the same time, Gessen elevates themselves through this narrative, becoming the hero*ine of the story, as protector of innocent crips/children. In suggesting that Putin's war against Western values is a war against their family—a queer family—they imply that they embody Western values as kind of a martyrdom.

---

101 Ibid.

102 Simon Shuster, "The Blind Girl vs. Putin: A Plea for Russia's Handicapped Orphans," *Time*, January 14, 2013, https://world.time.com/2013/01/14/the-blind-girl-vs-putin-a-plea-for-russias-handicapped-orphans/.

103 Tim Allman, "Blind girl criticises Kremlin over US adoption laws," BBC, January 15, 2013, https://www.bbc.com/news/av/world-europe-21022222.

104 Ibid.

105 Lee Edelman *No Future: Queer Theory and the Death Drive* (Durham, NC: Duke University Press, 2004).

The artist Голубой Иконостас / Blue Iconostasis created yet another icon that critically interrogates Gessen's media performances visually, as can be seen in the image further down.

Figure 14. "*Goluboi Ikonostas* [The Blue Iconostasis]; Icon: Masha Gessen/ Икона: Маша Гессен," Goluboy-Ikonostas.tumrlr.com, April 25, 2014, https://goluboy-ikonostas.tumblr.com/image/83814988411.

Gessen's icon holds the book of gospels, usually carried by saints, with a pink triangle and three blue triangles that form a Star of David. The pink triangle signifies their queer identification and the Star of David symbolizes their Jewish heritage. According to The Blue Ikonostas, the book of gospels "represents the fact that [they are] a writer and [have] published multiple outspoken and risky works." The scroll reads "as a gay parent, I must flee Russia or lose my children." It identifies their rhetoric of self-sacrifice, as well as referencing the innocent children that they must save from Russia.

Circulating in the media, the feminism and queer politics of Pussy Riot and Masha Gessen position Russia as a threat to their lives; meanwhile, the US signifies not only their place of refuge, but a developmental stage that Russia was previously moving towards and is now turning its back to. Thus, their feminism and queer politics confirm US-American liberalism and national superiority. Unsurprisingly, this version of Russian queer politics and feminism inhabits a spectacular place within contemporary US media. Their physical fragility, as women or nonbinary persons in the face of overwhelming authoritarian state power, is made visible and exaggerated in the US media to create a media spectacle. They embody the vulnerability of the liberal opposition to the monstrous, conservative Russian political establishment. Unsurprisingly, media outlets from the Associated Press[106] to *Forbes Magazine*[107] and Billboard[108] reported with gusto that Tolokonnikova had allegedly been put "on the list of Russia's Most Wanted Criminal Suspects."[109]

Through the widespread media presence of Pussy Riot, and especially of Tolokonnikova, strongly identified with Pussy Riot within American discourses, references to the group and their opposition to Putin frequently appear at feminist events that are not directly connected to New Cold War discourses. Anti-Putin signs and slogans, as well as brightly colored balaclavas, appeared, for example, at the various Women's Marches in Washington, DC, New York City, Boston, and other US cities, in January 2017.[110] "There were [. . .] Pussy Riot balaklavas, many depictions of shirtless President Putin, and signs that used historical themes and Stalinist-style posters with photo-shopped faces of Trump and Putin. There was also a great deal of Soviet-era Cold War imagery. The signs linking Russia, Putin, and Trump invoked existing language and memes that

---

106 "Russia puts Pussy Riot member on wanted list for criminals," *Associated Press*, last modified March 29, 2023, https://apnews.com/article/russia-pussy-riot-list-opposition-860d1f1288dca317e4b0783c68b49422.

107 Diane Brady, "Pussy Riot's Nadya on Putin and Being on Russia's Most Wanted List," *Forbes*, May 19, 2023, https://www.forbes.com/sites/dianebrady/2023/05/19/pussy-riots-nadya-tolokonnikova-on-punk-putin-and-being-on-russias-most-wanted-list/?sh=4f21bdbf1109.

108 "Pussy Riot's Nadya Tolokonnikova Added to Russia's Most Wanted List," *Billboard*, last modified March 29, 2023, https://www.billboard.com/music/music-news/pussy-riot-nadya-tolokonnikova-russia-most-wanted-list-criminals-1235294889/.

109 Brady, "Pussy Riot's Nadya."

110 "The depiction of Russia at the Women's Marches [with photos]," PONARS Eurasia, last modified January 30, 2017, http://www.ponarseurasia.org/article/ponars-eurasiadiscusses-depiction-russia-womens-marches-photos.

were often bawdy and hilarious."[111] Many "[p]osters and slogans featured Trump as little more than a sinister stooge of Russian President Vladimir Putin."[112] Such signs are not just about debates over Russian influence on US politics. They point to the symbolic connection between the meaning and concept of feminism and queer politics, and anti-Russian views.

An examination of Masha Gessen's and Nadya Tolokonnikova's media presence indicates, in turn, that Russia has been successfully established as a meaningful trope within Western imperialist discourses and as a point of demarcation for US-American liberalism. This allows for the projection of unified national values and identifications in times of cultural divisions and disunity. In these times of blurred lines and dissension, when, with the support of national and international anti-feminist movements, landmark cases such as *Roe v. Wade* (1973) and the right to an abortion, are undone,[113] the Western, and particularly US-American, media-fueled alliance with a limited number of Russian feminists and queer activists, allows for the continuation of Western superiority discourses through the rejection of Russian authoritarianism. Aside from the occasional report about collective feminist actions in Russia,[114] and beyond the updates about the increasing suppression of feminists,[115] the Anglophone media focuses its attention on individual feminist dissidents, such as Tolokonnikova

---

111 Regina Smyth qtd. in "The depiction of Russia."

112 Mark Kramer qtd. in ibid.

113 *Roe v. Wade*, 410 U.S. 113 (1973) was a landmark ruling of the US Supreme Court that said that the Constitution of the United States generally protected the right to have an abortion before the point of fetal viability. On June 24, 2022, the US Supreme Court overruled both *Roe v. Wade* and *Planned Parenthood of Southeastern Pennsylvania v. Casey* with the release of *Dobbs v. Jackson Women's Health Organization* and returned the question of abortion's legality to individual states.

114 Susie Armitage, "Russian Women Unfurled a Feminist Banner on the Kremlin like It Was NBD," *BuzzFeed News*, March 8, 2017, https://www.buzzfeednews.com/article/susiearmitage/feminists-arrested-for-demonstrating-in-moscow-and-st-peters; Amie Ferris-Rotman, "Putin's War on Women: Why #MeToo skipped Russia," *Foreign Policy*, April 9, 2018, https://foreignpolicy.com/2018/04/09/putins-war-on-women/; Daria Litvinova, Daria, "Russian feminist runs for Duma to take on domestic violence," *Associated Press*, September 15, 2021, https://apnews.com/article/europe-religion-russia-elections-violence-83c6446d2d7813c4f-2900c852e4bf08b; "Feminism in Russia: From Soviet Samizdat to Online Activism," Wilson Center, last modified November 2, 2020, https://www.wilsoncenter.org/event/feminism-russia-soviet-samizdat-online-activism.

115 "The persecution of a feminist Russian artist," *Economist*, last modified October 14, 2020, https://www.economist.com/books-and-arts/2020/10/14/the-persecution-of-a-feminist-russian-artist; "Russia: Artist detained amid clampdown on anti-war feminists," Amnesty International, last modified April 13, 2022, https://www.amnesty.org/en/latest/news/2022/04/russia-artist-detained-amid-clampdown-on-anti-war-feminists/; Robin Ashenden, "Putin's feminist crackdown won't crush the spirit of Russia's women," *Spectator*, April 9, 2023, https://www.spectator.co.uk/article/putins-feminist-crackdown-wont-crush-the-spirit-of-russias-women/.

and Gessen, to create female/non-binary versions of the male martyrs discussed in the previous chapter: young, beautiful, educated, and white.

The dominance of white and middle- or upper-class feminisms in the mainstream media has long been criticized from Black, people of color, and working-class positions. Many writers have argued that the issues presented by women in mainstream popular culture are unrepresentative of the average Black, Indigenous, or Latina women*'s struggle.[116] I believe the critiques of white dominance and inequality among women* are important for understanding contemporary pop culture feminism and queer politics. However, Tolokonnikova's and Gessen's popularity raises additional questions. First, the media-powered visibility of the terms "feminism" and some variant of "(queer) feminism" are not merely a reflection of the relative power of white middle-class women* in American mainstream society. The terms also signify changing notions of the concepts of modernity and progress, and the conceptual inclusion of gender equality and sexual liberty (for white people). In addition, (queer) feminism has advanced to become a popular trope within popular culture. Not coincidentally, the success of individual Black and Latina women in popular music, for example, Beyoncé, J-Lo, Janelle Monáe, and Rhianna propelled feminism as trope into the mainstream. In US society, they have been viewed, and indeed appreciated, as feminists, and "female Others." Indeed, it seems that their presence and worldwide fame is understood as US-American "Otherness" per se. This is not a new phenomenon. The Black experience, for example slavery, but also Black Death at the hands of the police,[117] have been commoditized or carelessly used as metaphors describing other phenomena—for example, coerced sex work.[118] Writers such as Norman Mailer[119] have used the N-word to signify their experience of cultural otherness in the context of the nonconformist hipster, and New York punks, such as Richard Hell, and Patti Smith,[120] have equated their own

---

116 Alexander, "Today's Feminism"; Jessa Crispin, "The Failures of Mainstream Feminism," *New Republic*, February 13, 2017, https://newrepublic.com/article/140248/failures-mainstream-feminismmisogyny-doom-hillary-clinton; Rafia Zakaria, *Against White Feminism: Notes on Disruptio* (New York: W. W. Norton & Company, 2021); Koa Beck, *White Feminism: From the Suffragettes to Influencers and Who They Leave Behind* (New York: Atria Books, 2021).

117 Nia Imara, "The Commodification of Black Death," *Progressive Magazine*, July 27, 2020, https://progressive.org/latest/commodification-of-black-death-imara-200727/;

118 Anca Parvulescu, *The Traffic in Women's Work: East European Migration and the Making of Europe* (Chicago, IL: University of Chicago Press, 2014).

119 Norman Mailer, "The White Negro," in *White Riot: Punk Rock and the Politics of Race*, ed. Stephen Duncombe and Maxwell Tremblay (London: Verso, 2011), 19–22.

120 Katharina Wiedlack, *Queer-Feminist Punk: An Anti-Social History* (Vienna: Zaglossus, 2015), https://doi.org/10.26530/OAPEN_574668.

experience with that of Blacks to position themselves as social outsiders and artists outside the mainstream. Tolokonnikova builds on this questionable legacy of appropriation using imagery of Black and POC oppression to signify white Otherness and anti-immigrant discrimination in "Make America Great Again."

Tolokonnikova and Gessen employ slightly different strategies to demand solidarity and warn against right-wing and conservative politics and politicians. Tolokonnikova appropriates the experiences of Blacks and people of color to show the violence of authoritarian power, putting herself in the role of people of color and African Americans in her videos, thereby ignoring her white privilege. Gessen styles themself as a victim of Russian violence against LGBTIQ+ people, portraying themself as a refugee, thereby ignoring citizenship and class privilege. To my knowledge, neither of them has acknowledged the privilege they enjoy of being white, educated Russians, or their entanglement in Russian imperial discourses at the intersection of US imperialism. US academia has historically, although perhaps partially unknowingly, mirrored Russian imperialist ideas about the superiority of (white) Russian culture over other Eurasian cultures, privileging Russian over other histories, languages, and literary traditions in programs and publications.[121] Moreover, universities and academic circles, from Columbia University to New York University, Middleton College to UC Berkeley, have welcomed and supported Pussy Riot and Gessen, offering them an expansive platform to speak for their political causes. US popular and political culture equated most of Eurasia and the post-Soviet sphere with Russia before and during the Soviet period, and has continued to do so since the fall of the Iron Curtain. Tolokonnikova and Gessen profit from the discursive privileging of (white Russian Orthodox) Russia.

Feminisms Partake in Imperialism, too; and the West Helps Them Do So

Russian feminist scholar Vanya Mark Solovey,[122] who has analyzed the Russian feminist movement over the past twenty years, argues that Gessen and Tolokonnikova are not alone in their lack of awareness about the privileges that

121 Susan Smith-Peter, "What do scholars of Russia owe Ukraine?" *Jordan Center Blog*, April 1, 2022, https://jordanrussiacenter.org/news/what-do-scholars-of-russia-owe-ukraine-today/.

122 Vanya Mark Solovey, "Feminism and Aggressive Imperialism: Russian Feminist Politics in Wartime," *Femina Politica—Zeitschrift Für Feministische Politikwissenschaft* 32, no. 1 (2023): 95–101, https://doi.org/10.3224/feminapolitica.v32i1.08.

their whiteness affords them. He notes that Russian feminists have only recently begun to discuss Russian colonialism and racism and to formulate an anticolonial agenda. Not coincidentally, these debates emerged with the Russian full-scale invasion of Ukraine in February 2022. Already during the first days of the war, the newly formed feminist coalition Feminist Anti-War Resistance (FAR) began their "anti-war protests, countering Russian state propaganda with media campaigns, and providing emergency support to those affected by the war [. . .], condemning Russia's military aggression and supporting Ukraine's right to self-defence [. . .], engaging in practical solidarity by helping forcibly displaced Ukrainians leave Russia and raising funds for humanitarian needs."[123]

In contrast to earlier feminist activist movements, FAR focuses their anticolonial activism on solidarity with Russian national minorities, and connects this political focus to their anti-national critique and their anti-war agitation. Importantly, Russian feminist anticolonial, anti-war initiatives name "Ukraine's anticolonial resistance"[124] as their inspiration. Although it might seem peripheral, this is significant. Within Russian culture, Ukraine has traditionally been signified as a lesser sibling, at best, and corrupted by Western influence, at worst. An indication that the Pussy Riot feminists shared this sentiment was Alyokhina's comment to a solidarity action on their behalf by Ukrainian FEMEN. According to Jessica Zychowicz,[125] feminist researcher and expert in Ukrainian studies, Alyokhina dismissed FEMEN, saying "we may share the same [. . .] general stance against authoritarianism, but we look at feminism differently, especially in our actions. We have never stripped and never will. The recent action in cutting down the cross, unfortunately, does not create any feeling of solidarity."[126] Alyokhina's comment might have resulted, on the one hand, from the fact that when the Western media took an interest in the FEMEN action, it insisted on connecting FEMEN and Pussy Riot to anti-religious sentiments. This did a disservice to the Pussy Riot activists, who stated that they were not criticizing religion as such and argued that they are in fact believers.[127] On the other hand, this comment also carries a certain disdain for the methods of FEMEN, which seems to be overly judgmental. Beginning with their emergence in 2008,

---

123 Solovey, "Feminism and Aggressive Imperialism," 96.
124 Ibid. 97.
125 Jessica Zychowicz, "Performing Protest: Femen, Nation, and the Marketing of Resistance," *Journal of Ukrainian Politics and Society*, April 2015, https://jups.krytyka.com/articles/performing-protest-femen-nation-and-marketing-resistance?page=3.
126 Ibid.
127 Wiedlack and Neufeld, "Lost in Translation."

nude activism, FEMEN's signature feature, has been critically interrogated through the "prostitute archetype."[128] FEMEN embodies, in the truest sense of the word, Ukrainian "nationalized sex products[:] the naked woman for sale."[129] Their message is that the naked woman is "just a naked body when its exchange value is emptied of its symbolic content. [T]he body is shown as the outcome of economic violence acted out upon it by human agents."[130] However, because their normatively beautiful, thin, young bodies fit nicely into the demands of the media market, their critique of the commodification of Ukrainian women has often been ignored and their actions sold as media spectacle. Accordingly, feminists have criticized FEMEN as being pedestrian sellouts. In her comment, Alyokhina, who speaks in the jargon of the cultured St. Petersburg intelligentsia, almost seems to dismiss FEMEN as cheap and unsophisticated. Ironically, Alyokhina seems to have forgotten that Tolokonnikova had staged a naked protest some years before, together with the group Voina (War), in their "Fuck for the Heir—Medvedev's little Bear!" intervention at the State Museum, Moscow, on February 29, 2008.[131] To come back to Alyokhina, viewing FEMEN as tacky sellouts might also derive from the Russian imperialist belief that Ukrainian culture is not as advanced as Russian:

> What hinders Russian intellectuals, particularly those in exile, in reflecting on their own complicity with Russian imperialism is, according to Solovey, their strong disidentification with the [Russian] imperialist regime. [. . .] Self-identification as a "good Russian," someone who supposedly bears no responsibility for the war, results in a self-victimization whereby one's suffering [due to Western sanctions] overshadows the experiences of being bombed, having one's house destroyed or one's family torn apart by the war. What might be called "Russian fragility"—an oversensitivity to any suggestion of responsibility for imperialism—is something self-designated 'good Russians' have in common with the regime they seek to disengage from.[132]

---

128 Jessica Zychowicz, *Superfluous Women: Art, Feminism, and Revolution in Twenty-First-Century Ukraine* (Toronto: University of Toronto Press, 2020), 46.
129 Ibid.
130 Ibid.
131 Paco Barragán, "Voina: A Russian Revolution," *Art Plus*, 2012, http://artpulsemagazine.com/voina-a-russian-revolution.
132 Solovey, "Feminism and Aggressive Imperialism," 97.

This self-positioning as a victim of Russian authoritarianism, and its connected disidentification with Russian imperialism, prompted Masha Gessen to call Ukrainian poets, who did not want to share a public stage with Russian writers, "cruel," as mentioned in the previous chapter.

The reasonable suspicion that the Western media prefers to focus on suffering white Russian feminist exiles is further reinforced by the meager resonance that Manizha's feminist participation at the 2021 Eurovision Song Contest attracted. Despite Manizha's explicitly feminist and anti-racist stance and performance, the Anglophone media focused only briefly on her politics and persona. Arguably, Manizha's embodiment of racialized sociopolitical entanglements is too complicated for the Western media, and does not allow an easy creation of a (white) Russian martyr. This silence is particularly surprising, since Manizha has been very vocal in opposing the Russian war in Ukraine and has suffered a severe backlash because of it within Russia.[133]

Manizha, or the Missed Chance to Challenge Russian Whiteness[134]

Manizha is of Tajik origin, and has been living in Russia since 1994. Identifying as both Russian and Tajik, race, nationality, and ethnicity are frequently addressed in her songs and media comments. She is open about her history as a refugee, and supports refugee organizations in Russia, for example, as Good Will Ambassador for the United Nations High Commissioner for Refugees within the United Nations Refugee Agency.[135] Because she was known as an outspoken feminist, publicly addressing issues such as domestic violence,[136] and as an

---

133 Katy Dartford, "Russian Eurovision star fights back after tour cancelled over opposition to Ukraine war," *EuroNews*, March 7, 2023, https://www.euronews.com/culture/2023/03/07/russian-eurovision-star-fights-back-after-tour-cancelled-over-opposition-to-ukraine-war.

134 An earlier version of this chapter was previously published in Katharina Wiedlack and Iain Zabolotny, "Race, Whiteness, Russianness and the Discourses on the 'Black Lives Matter' Movement and Manizha," in *The Routledge International Handbook of New Critical Race and Whiteness Studies*, ed. Rikke Andreassen et al. (London: Routledge, 2023), 251–264, https://doi.org/10.4324/9781003120612.

135 "Muzykant Manizha stala pervym rossiiskim poslom dobroi voli agentstva OON po pravam bezhentsev" [Musician Manizha becomes the first Russian Goodwill Ambassador of the UN Refugee Agency], UNHCR, December 14, 2020, https://www.unhcr.org/ru/24633-manizha-good-will-ambassador.html.

136 "Manizha выпустила приложение против домашнего насилия," *Wonderzine*, last modified February 28, 2019, https://www.wonderzine.com/wonderzine/life/news/241551-manizha-silsila.

LGBTIQ+ rights advocate,[137] her selection as the Russian representative at the 2021 Eurovision Song Contest was more than unexpected, considering the anti-feminist and anti-LGBTIQ+ politics of the Russian government. Russian audiences reacted in very polarized ways to the choice. While a minority cheered, most rejected it.[138] Her Eurovision song "Russian Woman," in which she explicitly claims a belonging to the Russian nation, was harshly criticized; people argued she was not ethnically (white) Russian and some even questioned her citizenship.

Manizha's case is interesting, as Iain Zabolotny and I have discussed elsewhere, because "it reveals the ways in which current political discourses in Russia proliferate and center on racialized 'othering', the intersection of racism and 'migratism' and a fantasy of Russian (Orthodox) whiteness."[139] Examining her representation in the Anglophone, especially US, media, or, rather, the absence thereof, her case also speaks to the American fantasy of Russia as an exclusively white space.[140] Although there has been some academic interest in the Russian racialization of, and violence against, Indigenous people and people of color from Central Asia and the Caucasus,[141] the US media has only occasionally taken up the topic, most recently due to the public visibility of the above-mentioned Free Buryatia Foundation.[142] Due to the fact that Russia, in contrast to the United States, never implemented racial segregation along color lines, and because of the initial hospitable attitude of Soviet Russia to African American migrants in the early twentieth century,[143] as well as the social, economic, and political successes of some Black people in imperial Russia and the Soviet Union, US-American beliefs about a Russia free of (anti-Black) racism circulated during the better part of the twentieth century. The notion that Russia was not racist

---

137 764. "Равенство– это," *Журнал Открытые*, last modified June 26, 2019, video, https://youtu.be/rWq0UyNXrKM.

138 Anastassia Boutsko, "Eurovision: Tajik singer polarizes Russia," *DW*, May 19, 2021, https://www.dw.com/en/eurovision-manizha-from-tajikistan-polarizes-russia/a-57577536.

139 Wiedlack and Zabolotny, "Race, Whiteness, Russianness and the Discourses on the 'Black Lives Matter' Movement and Manizha," 252.

140 How whiteness is constructed with regards to American immigrants from post-Soviet space is analyzed in detail in Claudia Sadowski-Smith, *The New Immigrant Whiteness: Race, Neoliberalism, and Post-Soviet Migration to the United States* (New York: NYU Press, 2018).

141 Nicolay Zakharov, *Race and racism in Russia* (New York: Palgrave Macmillan, 2015).

142 "Buryats in Bucha: the Biggest Myth of the War," Buryats against War, April 28, 2022, https://freeburyatia.org/en/buryats-against-war/.

143 Kimberly St. Julian-Varnon, "Black skin in the red land: African Americans and the Soviet experiment," *Russian File: A blog of the Kennan Institute*, February 28, 2020, https://www.wilsoncenter.org/blog-post/black-skin-red-land-african-americans-and-soviet-experiment.

was further supported by the Soviet Union's official solidarity with the African American struggle against racism on US territory, especially in the US South,[144] and, later, its support of African decolonization. The self-idealization of the young Soviet Union as ally of racially oppressed African Americans and Central Asians throughout the 1920s and 1930s lingers within US epistemologies,[145] as does the Russian support for decolonizing countries and peoples during the 1960s and 1970s.[146]

Black scholars such as W. E. B. Du Bois, poets such as Langston Hughes and Dorothy West, and feminist activists such as Louise Patterson and Eslanda Goode Robeson, who visited the Soviet Union during the 1930s, served as enthusiastic eyewitnesses to the myth of Soviet racial equality.[147] Without doubting their experience of the absence of anti-Black racism within the Soviet Union at the time, it is highly unlikely that there was no prejudice against racialized minorities of Central Asian decent or against Indigenous peoples. The negative sentiments towards Indigenous groups and ethnic minorities certainly proliferated and expanded from the early 1990s onward, when, for example, skinhead racism became a visible phenomenon throughout Russia.[148] Historical racial prejudices against people of color, Muslims, and Jews existed before, during, and after the Soviet period,[149] and they have become entangled with other global phenomena, such as white (Slavic) pride and neo-Nazi ideologies. The language of racism, antisemitism, and anti-Muslim sentiment does not easily or neatly fit into their Anglophone categories, however. The Russian term "black," for example,

---

144 Astrid Haas, "'To Russia and myself': Claude McKay, Langston Hughes, and the Soviet Union," in *Transatlantic negotiations*, ed. C. Buschendorf and A. Franke (Heidelberg: Winter Verlag, 2007), 111–131; Katharina Wiedlack, "A feminist becoming? Louise Thompson Patterson's and Dorothy West's sojourn in the Soviet Union," *Feminismo/s* 36 (2020): 103–128, https://doi.org/10.14198/fem.2020.36.05.

145 Kate A. Baldwin, *Beyond the Color Line and the Iron Curtain: Reading Encounters between Black and Red, 1922–1963* (Durham, NC: Duke University Press, 2002); Erik S. McDuffie, *Sojourning for Freedom: Black Women, American Communism, and the Making of Black Left Feminism* (Durham, NC: Duke University Press, 2011); Cedric J. Robinson, *Black Marxism: The Making of the Black Radical Tradition* (Chapel Hill: The University of North Carolina Press, 2000).

146 Natalia Telepneva, "Saving Ghana's revolution: The demise of Kwame Nkrumah and the evolution of soviet policy in Africa," *Journal of Cold War Studies* 20, no. 4 (2018): 4–25.

147 Wiedlack, "A feminist becoming?"; Baldwin, *Beyond the Color Line*; McDuffie, *Sojourning for Freedom*.

148 Richard Arnold, "Systematic Racist Violence in Russia between 'Hate Crime' and 'Ethnic Conflict,'" *Theoretical Criminology* 19, no. 2 (2015): 239–56, https://doi.org/10.1177/1362480615581102, 245.

149 Ian Law, *Red Racisms: Racism in Communist and Post-Communist Contexts* (Basingstoke: Palgrave Macmillan, 2012).

although used in a derogatory way, does not primarily refer to people of African descent, but to a range of racialized culturally and religiously "Othered" people, including Muslim minorities from the North Caucasus region,[150] Armenians, and Roma.[151]

Russian racism and violence against ethnically "othered" Indigenous and other minorities is based on the murky and shifting signification of the notion of *russkie* (Russians), which refers to members of a *russkaia kul'tura* (Russian ethno-cultural totality).[152] This category is loosely formed around Russian Orthodox Christianity and distinguishes between white, Slavic Russians (*russkie*) and *rossiiskie*, or the "transnational rossiiskii community" living in the Russian territory.[153] Only *russkie*, white, Slavic Russians, are understood to be the legitimate bearers of Russian citizenship and culture. "Nationality," in this sense, does not mean citizenship, but ethnicity or race. Russian citizens are ordered hierarchically, with white, Slavic Christian Orthodox Russians (*russkie*) at the top, followed by the lesser (white, Slavic) Ukrainians, who comprise the largest ethnic minority grouping in Russia, and (white, Slavic) Belarusians. All other eighty-four nationalities, which include Jewish, Chechens, Armenians, Tatars, Bashkirs, Buryats, Nenets, Chukchi, Roma and Komi, are considered lesser, nonwhite others. Russian state discourses alternate between white, Slavic supremacy, and nostalgia-filled Soviet notions of Russia as the nation of nations (comprising different ethnicities and religious groups). The political opposition seems to be split into groups that advocate for Indigenous autonomy and an eclectic potpourri of right-wingers and liberals promoting Russian whiteness.

The pop singer Manizha contested the whiteness of "Russianness" and what it means to represent the nation through her participation in the Eurovision Song Contest, in which she won third place. She mixes the Russian, Tajik, and English languages in her daily communication and music. She mixes Tajik and Russian folklore elements with US-American and global hip-hop fashion, poses, and dancing, as can be seen in the two screen shots from her performance below.

---

150 Zakharov, *Race and racism in Russia*, 62; Meredith L. Roman, "Making Caucasians Black: Moscow since the fall of communism and the racialization of non-Russians," *Journal of Communist Studies and Transition Politics* 18, no. 2 (2002): 8, https://doi.org/10.1080/714003604.

151 Alaina Lemon, "'What Are They Writing about Us Blacks?'—Roma and 'Race' in Russia," *Anthropology of East Europe Review* 13, no. 2 (1995): 34–40.

152 Sanna Turoma and Kaarina Aitamurto, "Contesting cultural and religious identities in Russia: An introduction," in *Religion, expression, and patriotism in Russia*, ed. Sanna Turoma, Kaarina Aitamurto, and Slobodanka Vladiv-Glover (Stuttgart: Ibidem, 2019), 11.

153 Ibid.

Figure 15. Screenshot of 0:49 of the performance at the first semi-final of Eurovision 2021: Manizha, "Manizha—Russian woman—Russia—Official video—Eurovision 2021," Eurovision Song Contest YouTube channel, March 10, 2021, https://www.youtube.com/watch?v=ajfaz1CKZq0.

Figure 16. Screenshot of minute 2:00 of the performance at the first semi-final of Eurovision 2021: Manizha, "Manizha—Russian woman—Russia—Official video—Eurovision 2021," Eurovision Song Contest YouTube channel, March 10, 2021, https://www.youtube.com/watch?v=ajfaz1CKZq0.

Manizha is not afraid to address racism, xenophobia, refugee rights, sexism, violence against women, and LGBTIQ+ rights in her music and media statements, despite the increasing censorship of these topics. She continues to be an outspoken critic of the war in Ukraine.[154] Why, then, did the Anglophone media omit to report about her more extensively? Why is she not a Russian feminist icon, next to Tolokonnikova and Gessen?

Manizha's songs take on complicated issues, with care and concern. Her song "Mama,"[155] for example, focuses on domestic violence and support for its survivors, and she openly and publicly supports the Russian LGBTIQ+ community. Her contribution to the Eurovision Song Contest "Russian Woman" is a feminist manifesto addressing a plethora of feminist issues, from harmful beauty standards to the pressure to reproduce and become mothers, to the denial of women's subjectivity and their subjugation under the patriarchal order. Moreover, "Russian Woman" wants to empower women to be self-confident, ambitious, and daring.[156] That the song resonated with a large audience in Russia is proven by the fact that forty percent of national TV viewers voted for Manizha to represent Russia at the Eurovision Song Contest.[157] While many supported Manizha, others reacted with open or covert racism and sexism. On social media, in particular, people argued that a Tajikistan-born singer could not legitimately represent the Russian nation in an international contest, or Russian womanhood, for that matter. Manizha's answer to her haters was the satirical video "Can This represent Russia at the Eurovision?"[158] In the video, she plays the role of an investigative journalist with a blonde wig discovering that she is an alien. In contrast to Manizha's social media critics, conservative officials and institutions did not take issue publicly with her ethnicity. Yet they were concerned, and some were even outraged, about her focus on sexism and misogyny, with some even requesting a

154 Mark Savage, "Manizha: Russian Eurovision star faces hate campaign over opposition to Ukraine war," BBC, August 25, 2022, https://www.bbc.com/news/entertainment-arts-62671940.

155 Manizha, "Mama," Manizha, February 28, 2019, video, https://www.youtube.com/watch?v=iCwuW3yClO4.

156 "Manizha—Russian woman—Russia—Official video—Eurovision 2021," Eurovision Song Contest, March 10, 2021, video, https://www.youtube.com/watch?v=l01wa2ChX64.

157 Josh Milton, "Russia's Eurovision act is a fearless feminist and LGBT+ rights campaigner and—shock—Russian bigots are mad," PinkNews, March 15, 2021, https://www.thepinknews.com/2021/03/15/russia-eurovision-2021-manizha-sangin-2021-lgbt/.

158 Manizha, "Mozhet li eto… predstavliat' Rossiiu na Evrovidenii?" [Can it…represent Russia at Eurovision?] Manizha, March 17, 2021, video, https://www.youtube.com/watch?v=g7J4lAGeFKo.

criminal investigation into the song's lyrics, fearing that they might "seriously insult and humiliate the human dignity of Russian women."[159]

Vladimir Solovyov, the journalist and TV host of the state channel Rossiya-1, which broadcast the Eurovision Song Contest and managed all of Manizha's Eurovision-related communications, argued that Manizha was "betraying national culture" by promoting "all this gender bullshit."[160] Furthermore, he asserted that the women* shown in the videos during the performance "have nothing to do with the image of a Russian woman"[161]

Manizha seems to be the target of anti-gender proponents, homophobes, and racists alike. Yet the American media did not feature her extensively. The reason why American and other Anglophone media did not create the kind of hype around Manizha that they had created around Tolokonnikova and Gessen is likely because the singer does not address the West, and particularly the US, as a superior, more progressive and enlightened example that Russia should follow. Rather, she takes up Russian discourses that view the nation as a multinational and multiethnic space—an immigrant country. Rather than mimicking or appropriating Anglophone symbols of diversity, Manizha represented the diversity of Russian women* in her Eurovision performance. Images of 7, 400 women and nonbinary people of different ages, ethnicities, body types, professions, and (dis)abilities recorded singing her song were projected onto a large screen. All the videos were played simultaneously and they provided the backup choir for her. The screen shot below shows some of the videos in the background.

159 "Russia's Eurovision entry to be investigated for 'illegal' lyrics," *Guardian*, March 18, 2021, https://www.theguardian.com/world/2021/mar/18/russias-eurovision-entry-to-be-investigated-for-lyrcs.

160 Krivotulova, Kseniia, "Solov'ev raskritikoval Manizha i nashel v ee pesne 'gendernye hreni,'" [Solovyev criticized Manizha and found "gender crap" in her songs"], Lenta.ru, March 25, 2021, https://lenta.ru/news/2021/05/25/soloviev/?utm_source=yxnews&utm_medium=desktop&utm_referrer=https%3A%2F%2Fyandex.com%2Fnews%2Fsearch%3Ftext%3D.

161 Ibid.

Figure 17. Screenshot of minute 2:47 of the performance at the First Semi-Final of Eurovision 2021: Manizha, "Manizha—Russian woman—Russia—Official video—Eurovision 2021," Eurovision Song Contest YouTube channel, March 10, 2021, https://www.youtube.com/watch?v=ajfaz1CKZq0.

Of course, not all Russian feminists are happy with Manizha's claim to Russian belonging and Russianness. Some activists and researchers reject the all-inclusive idea of a multinational Russianness as a colonial construct that erases non-Russian ethnicities or positions them as inferior. Some nonwhite Russian citizens have appropriated the identity marker of the "non-Russian" (нерусская, *nerusskaya*), a label frequently used as a derogatory term or slur, to avoid the Western terminology of white vs. Black and people of color, which does not do justice to the complexity of the racial and ethnic dynamics across the Eurasian space. Researcher and activist Anna Dashieva argues that the term *nerusskaya* signifies ethnicized and cultural otherness in the Russian-language space, where race, in terms of phenotype, has never been the most important category for segregation, which was structured instead by the line between Russian and non-Russian.[162] The Western, and particularly US-American, dichotomy between a white colonizer and colonized, racialized BIPOC cannot be applied in the Russian context, according to Dashieva, due to the country's long and violent

---

162 К. Дашиева, "Самоцензура, или почему мы стесняемся говорить о расизме," in *Квирь Сибирь*, p. 27, accessed December 12, 2024, https://www.academia.edu/44546783/Квирь_Сибирь_без_опасность_и_забота_о_себе.

history of oppressing many different ethnicities identified as non-Russian, including Ukrainians, Poles, Chechens and Indigenous Siberians.[163] Russian settler colonialism introduced the social and cultural segregation between (white) Russians and (racialized/ethnicized) non-Russians in the context of the country's imperial expansion in the seventeenth century,[164] which the Soviets continued under the banner of modernization far into the twentieth century.[165] The displacement of ethnic minorities was equally part of settler colonial imperialism, as was the expansion of Russian culture through "Russianization," which extinguished minority and Indigenous languages and replaced them with the Russian language and Cyrillic alphabet.[166]

Manizha's feminism does not address these factors through her claim to Russianness from a minoritarian perspective. Yet neither does Tolokonnikova or the Jewish Gessen. By focusing on the white Russian feminists and overlooking Manizha, the Anglophone media perpetuates the imaginary whiteness of Russianness within Western discourses. It thereby misses a chance to make visible the growing resistance against structural racism and racist violence in Russia, with BIPOC becoming more visible, and challenging white hegemony and white nationalism from a queer feminist perspective.

163 Dashieva, "Samotsenzura ili pochemu my stesniaemsia govorit' o rasizme," 26. For a thorough discussion of different feminist viewpoints, see also: Dinara Yangeldina, "The Politics of Racial Translation: Negotiating Foreignness and Authenticity in Russophone Intersectional Feminism and Timati's Hip-Hop (2012–2018)" (PhD diss., University of Bergen, 2023).

164 Willard Sunderland, *Taming the wild field: Colonization and empire on the Russian steppe* (Ithaca, CT: Cornell University Press, 2004), https://doi.org/10.7591/9781501703256.

165 Alexander Etkind, *Internal Colonization: Russia's Imperial Experience* (Cambridge: Polity Press, 2011).

166 Дашиева, "Самоцензура, или почему мы стесняемся говорить о расизме," 26–27.

CHAPTER 5

Shameless: The Racialized Whiteness of Russian Women in American TV

Over the last two decades, many female Russian characters have populated North American TV shows. Their increased presence, which, not accidentally, coincides with the recent popularity of superhero comic adaptations (Marvel and DC), can be read as the emergence of New Cold War cultural[167] discourses across TV genres. While such discourses evidently build on past Cold War cultures, they do not simply adopt the conservatism, misogyny, and homophobia of the 1950s so definitive of its mindset, but rather rewrite them in interesting ways to align with neoliberalism. Most series introduce female Russian characters alongside multiple other female protagonists, both racialized and white, including lesbians and transgender women, such as the characters in *Orange Is the New Black*,[168] the Canadian *Lost Girl*,[169] *Orphan Black*,[170] *Killing Eve*,[171] *Nine Perfect Strangers*,[172] and *The Americans*.[173] In many of these shows, the Russian characters are clearly marked as distinct from white Americans and from other racialized Black, Indigenous, and women of color through their ethnicity,

---

167 Stephen Whitfield, *The Culture of the Cold War*, 2nd ed. (Baltimore, MD: Johns Hopkins University Press, 1996); Sakwa, "New Cold War."

168 *Orange Is the New Black*, created by Jenji Kohan, aired 2013–2019, Netflix, TV show.

169 *Lost Girl*, created by Michelle Lovretta, developed by Jay Firestone, aired 2010–2015, Showcase, TV show.

170 *Orphan Black*, created by Graeme Manson, directed by John Fawcett, aired 2013–2017, BBC America/Bell Media, TV show.

171 *Killing Eve*, produced by Sid Gentle Films, aired 2018–2022, BBC America, TV show.

172 *Nine Perfect Strangers*, based on the 2018 novel of the same name by Liane Moriarty. created by David E. Kelley, developed by David E. Kelley and John-Henry Butterworth, aired 2021, Hulu, TV show.

173 *The Americans*, created by Joe Weisberg, aired 2013–2018, FX, TV show.

gender expression, and sexual fluidity. Moreover, in quite a few of these shows, Russian women are pathologized.

In this chapter, I will investigate the visual, bodily, and cultural representations of Russian women in North American TV, focusing on the character Svetlana/Lana in the show *Shameless US*.[174] I will analyze the construction of this figure as the Russian "Other" at the juncture of American race and class relations in light of the tension between white American progressiveness and upward mobility and Black women's class-stagnant racialization.

Contemporary North American TV employs two parallel cultural discourses on Russian women. The first is a recent phenomenon and is represented by the character Red in *Orange Is the New Black*. Red, as I argue elsewhere,[175] is clearly marked as a heterosexual working-class woman in distinct contrast to the homosexual or hetero-flexible US women and transgenders. The second, older discourse that conflicts or contrasts with the first draws on an exoticized and hyper-sexualized 'savage' fluidity. The *Shameless* character of Svetlana embodies this stereotype. Despite her sexual fluidity, which could be termed queer, Svetlana stands in stark contrast to the white Irish American Ian and the white trans* Travor. This representation arguably mirrors a common interpretation of Russian homosexualities in Western queer theory, as I will show.

Both mentioned discourses racialize Russian women as white Other, at the intersection of sexuality, gender, and class. Their cultural stratification, ethnicization, racialization, and class are visualized through the contrast to other ethnic groups, particularly white American and Black woman. As I will show, these comparative representations rely heavily on American race history, such as the history of slavery,[176] and liken the precarious status of white Russian women to aspects of this history.

I read the character of Svetlana against the background of contemporary New Cold War discourses, in their homonationalism[177] and construction of whiteness. Recent literature on the exoticizing and Othering of Russian women falls short in analyzing the specific racialization of subjects and groups within North/Western popular culture discourses. Most feminist scholars, such as

---

174 *Shameless*, produced by Paul Abbott, developed by John Wells, aired 2011–2021, Showtime, TV show.

175 Katharina Wiedlack, "Seeing 'Red' (Orange Is the New Black)—Russian Women, US Homonationalism and New Cold War Cultures," *Gender, Rovné Příležitosti, Výzkum* 17, no. 1 (2016): 29–40, https://doi.org/10.13060/12130028.2016.17.1.253.

176 *Shameless*, season 7, episode 4, "I Am a Storm," directed by Emmy Rossum, written by Sheila Callaghan, aired October 23, 2016, Showtime, TV show.

177 Puar, "Rethinking Homonationalism."

Kimberly Williams,[178] Agnieszka Tuszynska,[179] Valentina Glajar, and Domnica Radulescu,[180] interpret the Othering of Russian women on TV as sexualization, ignoring the ways in which racialization, sexualization, and gendering manifest on the characters' bodies. While Anca Parvulescu focuses on aspects of racialization, she equates Russian and Ukrainian female representations with a variety of female Eastern European immigrant representations in the Western European media,[181] without adequately differentiating between their racialized significations. While her analyses of individual cases—for example, of Romanian women (who are often wrongly identified as Romani) and her readings of representations of immigrants from the Balkan regions—very aptly identify the specific processes of Othering and racialization through the classification of "not quite white," her reading of Russian and Ukrainian immigrant women through the same framework is sometimes lacking. It ignores the hegemonic privilege of whiteness, on the one hand, and again makes non-Western bodily differences invisible, on the other. In contrast to Parvulescu, Claudia Sadowski-Smith has identified the signification of post-Soviet immigrant otherness as "new immigrant whiteness."[182] I build on Sadowski-Smith's groundbreaking work in close conjunction with the existing works on sexualized female Russian bodies to develop a more nuanced understanding of the construction of bodily difference, taking into consideration factors like whiteness, style, body language, and bodily affect, as well as representations of class.

Indifference, Whiteness, and the Discovery That Ukrainians Are Not Russians

Since the dissolution of the Soviet Union, Post-Soviet Russians and Ukrainians have migrated to the US through "virtually all forms of human movement

---

178 Kimberly A. Williams, *Imagining Russia: Making Feminist Sense of American Nationalism in U.S.-Russian Relations* (Albany: State University of New York Press, 2012).

179 Agnieszka Tuszynska, "Eastern Girls, Western Boys: The Image of Eastern European Women in the Birthday Girl," in *Vampirettes, Wretches and Amazons: Western Representations of East European Women*, ed. Valentina Glajar and Domnica Radulescu (New York: Columbia University Press, 2004), 203–214.

180 Valentina Glajar, and Domnica Radulescu, "Introduction," in Glajar and Radulescu, *Vampirettes, Wretches and Amazones*, 1–11.

181 Anca Parvulescu, *The Traffic in Women's Work: East European Migration and the Making of Europe* (Chicago, IL: University of Chicago Press, 2014).

182 Claudia Sadowski-Smith, *The New Immigrant Whiteness: Race, Neoliberalism, and Post-Soviet Migration to the United States* (New York: NYU Press, 2018).

available under current migration law."[183] They have arrived as highly skilled workers and temporary laborers, as political and religious refugees, and through marriage and adoption. Not surprisingly, many visitors have overstayed their visas and remained in the US illegally.

The 2021 census counted 425,429 Russians and 398,040 Ukrainians living in the US.[184] In the same year, 2,407,434 people were self-reported to be of Russian ancestry and 980,819 were self-reported to be of Ukrainian ancestry. A further 2,728 said their ancestral roots were in the Soviet Union.[185] As a result of the Russian full-scale invasion of Ukraine, an additional 270,000 Ukrainians, mostly children and women, entered the US by April, 2023 to seek asylum.[186] The flow of Russian citizens to the US has been growing due to the increasing persecution of politically dissenting voices and the increasingly homo- and transphobic, and more generally xenophobic, illiberal climate. The numbers of Russian citizens that have fled Russia since February 2022 is unclear; as of June, 2023, the estimates vary between 600,000 and more than a million.[187] What is evident is that men who fear to be drafted into military service have joined the streams of Russian migrants in masses; how many of those fleeing Russia go to the US is unclear. In September, 2022, the US government announced that these Russian men would be ineligible for asylum.[188] By the end of November, 2022, newspapers reported that "[t]housands of Russians are crossing the U.S. southern border to claim asylum."[189] Academic institutions, including those in the US, but also "law firms and groups that arrange placements abroad for scholars seeking

---

183 Sadowski-Smith, *The New Immigrant*, 3.
184 "B05006: Place of Birth for the Foreign-Born Population in the United States—2021 American Community Survey 5-Year Estimates," United States Census Bureau, https://data.census.gov/table?tid=ACSDT1Y2021.B05006.
185 "B04006: People Reporting Ancestry—2021 American Community Survey 5-Year Estimates," United States Census Bureau, December 6, 2024, https://data.census.gov/table?tid=ACSDT1Y2021.B04006.
186 Katherine Fung, "The Complicated Future of Ukrainian Refugees in the U.S.," *Newsweek*, April 4, 2023, https://www.newsweek.com/2023/04/14/complicated-future-ukrainian-refugees-us-1792294.html.
187 Maria Kiseleva and Victoria Safronova, "Why are people leaving Russia, who are they, and where are they going?" BBC News Russian, June 4, 2023, https://www.bbc.com/news/world-europe-65790759.
188 Steve Holland and Nandita Bose, "White House: U.S. welcomes Russians seeking asylum," *Reuters*, September 27, 2022, December 6, 2024, https://www.reuters.com/world/us/white-house-us-welcomes-russians-seeking-asylum-2022-09-27/.
189 Miriam Jordan, "Antiwar Activists Who Flee Russia Find Detention, Not Freedom, in the U.S.," *New York Times*, November 28, 2022, December 6, 2024, https://www.nytimes.com/2022/11/28/us/russian-activists-asylum.html?searchResultPosition=1.

refuge indicate a dramatic increase in the number of researchers trying to leave Russia since the invasion [. . .]."[190]

Before the recent military escalation by Russia, the US public paid relatively little attention to ethnic and cultural differences among post-Soviet migrants. During the Cold War, the Soviet Union was frequently referred to with the short-hand term "Russia." While a similar tendency could be observed in the Soviet Union, where it reflected increasing Russian chauvinism, most Americans, unlike Russians, were unaware that the Soviet Union included many different peoples (Azerbaijanis, Belarusians, Georgians, Kazakhs, Latvians, Lithuanians, Moldavians, Ukrainians, Uzbeks, Romani and Sinti, Chechens, and Indigenous peoples such as Aleuts, Chukchis, Siberian Yupik, Evens, Kets, Nanais, Tatars, and Buryats, etc.). Only now, and very slowly, journalists, media producers, cultural commentators, academics, and public figures are starting to rethink what it meant to ignore the diversity concealed behind the word "Russian." Slowly it is beginning to dawn on people that this Western ignorance intersects in specific ways with Russian imperialist ideology. This ideology bore ramifications, some of them contradictory, for Soviet hierarchies. On the one hand, these hierarchies made claims to ethnic plurality, or, in Soviet parlance, a multiplicity of "nations" under a single Soviet citizenship. At the same time, they prioritized not only Slavic heritage, which included Ukrainians and Belarusians, but also "Russianness."

The racialized hierarchization of ethnic belonging survives today in the signification of people from the Caucasus as "black,"[191] as well as in frequent incidents and expressions of racism against people from Central Asia and Asia, and a growing white "Slavic pride" movement throughout Russia. The Russian imperialist categorization, as well as the self-identification of many non-Russian, post-Soviet immigrants, does not necessarily, or easily, overlap with US-American patterns of ethnic and racial categorization. Many holders of Russian passports, for example, identify with their ethnic or "national" identity, rather than with their citizenship.[192] Seen through the lens of US categories, however, these same people appear to be white, despite the fact that they are perceived as "black" or racialized in Russia and the post-Soviet space in general, due to the effects and influence of Russian imperialism. "Despite their internal ethnic diversity,

190 Andrew Silver, "Is Russia facing an academic exodus over Ukraine?" Research Professional News, September 26, 2022, https://www.researchprofessionalnews.com/rr-news-world-2022-9-is-russia-facing-an-academic-exodus-over-ukraine/.
191 Sadowski-Smith, *The New Immigrant*, 5.
192 Ibid.

members of the [post-Soviet] diaspora are [...] collectively racialized as white in the United States."[193] Moreover, they are seen as a monolithically white, intolerant Other[194] and associated "with notions of a pan-European whiteness that is supposedly shared by all those of European descent in the United States and that consolidated after World War II."[195]

After February 24, 2022, when the Russian military began marching towards the Ukrainian capital Kyiv, the US media started differentiating between Russian and Ukrainian heritage when referring to people of post-Soviet heritage, especially figures in popular culture. One of the most prominent figures to succeed in creating awareness of the issue was the actor Mila Kunis. Kunis, who was born in the Ukrainian city of Chernivtsi and migrated to the US as a child, previously referred to her origin as Russian when she was asked. She said that she reverted to calling herself Russian when she realized that her fellow residents of LA would react with confusion when she told them she was from Ukraine. They would ask: "Where is Ukraine? [...] And then I'd have to explain Ukraine and where it is on the map and [...] that's exhausting."[196] Everyone in her American environment seemed to be familiar with Russia, on the other hand. But since the full-scale invasion, Kunis has taken a new pride in her Ukrainian heritage; she openly and often expresses her sense of belonging to Ukraine.[197]

Although on a much smaller scale, the media reporting on the massacres in the Ukrainian city of Bucha, which laid sole responsibility for the atrocities on ethnic Buryats and the subsequent protests of the Free Buryatia Foundation,[198] have created some awareness of the ethnic diversity of Russia and the plight of Indigenous Russian minorities.[199] While news discourses can no longer afford to be completely oblivious to the diversity of peoples within the

193 Ibid., 6.

194 Neda Atanasoski, *Humanitarian Violence: The U.S. Deployment of Diversity* (Minneapolis: University of Minnesota Press, 2013).

195 Sadowski-Smith, *The New Immigrant*, 6.

196 Kunis qtd. in Elyse Wanshel, "Mila Kunis, Who Is Ukrainian, Reveals Why She Used to Say She Was Russian," *Huffington Post*, March 11, 2022, https://www.huffpost.com/entry/mila-kunis-who-is-ukrainian-reveals-why-she-used-to-say-she-was-russian_n_622b9e67e4b0e01d97ab01cf.

197 Ibid.

198 "Buryats in Bucha: The Biggest Myth of the War," Buryats against War, April 28, 2022, https://freeburyatia.org/en/buryats-against-war/.

199 Mariya Petkova, "'Putin is using ethnic minorities to fight in Ukraine': Activist," Aljazeera, October 25, 2022, https://www.aljazeera.com/features/2022/10/25/russia-putin-is-using-ethnic-minorities-to-fight-in-ukraine; Amy Mackinnon, "Russia Is Sending Its Ethnic Minorities to the Meat Grinder," *Foreign Policy*, September 23, 2022, https://foreignpolicy.com/2022/09/23/russia-partial-military-mobilization-ethnic-minorities/; Dan Storyev, "The

post-Soviet sphere, and can certainly no longer subsume all of the post-Soviet space under the label "Russia," popular culture still represents post-Soviet heritage as white and features predominantly Russian characters. And although the actually existing post-Soviet diaspora consists of people of all classes and legal and illegal immigrants, US-American popular culture, and particularly TV, features predominantly lower working-class or underclass Russians, criminals, and sex workers.

Between Heightened Heteronormative Femininity and Promiscuous Sexual Fluidity

Sexuality, often heightened to promiscuity, plays a significant role in the construction of Russian, and more generally post-Soviet, women on US TV. The particular sexual quality of figures marked as Eastern European and Russian goes back to the European, particularly German, Enlightenment. Within this orientalist scheme, the "Slavic Race" was constructed as a paradox of similarity and difference; neither Western-enlightened, nor fully barbaric. German philosophers such as Johann Gottfried Herder and Johann Gottlieb Fichte developed a notion of Slavic people as economically, ethnographically, and racially distinct, a notion in many ways echoing their antisemitic views.[200] Fichte, in particular, created the myth that Slavic women had "a stronger sex drive than German females."[201]

Almost all the current literature that fosters the othering of Russian women in the US media and focuses on the construction of female gender mentions their strong sexualization.[202] Roumiana Deltcheva, a media studies scholar, identifies sexuality as one of the dominant features of post-1991 film depictions of Slavic women, which she categorizes as "the scrupulous slut, the conniving trickster, and the helpless victim."[203] Each of these three stereotypes "carr[ies] distinct negative connotations that, in their totality, reinforce the idea of Otherness as negation: negation of voice, negation of space, negation

War in Ukraine Is Decimating Russia's Asian Minorities," *Diplomat*, October 10, 2022, https://thediplomat.com/2022/10/the-war-in-ukraine-is-decimating-russias-asian-minorities/.

200 Wolff, *Inventing Eastern Europe*, 333.
201 Ibid., 334
202 E.g. in Glajar and Radulescu, *Vampirettes, Wretches and Amazones*.
203 Deltcheva, "Eastern Women in Western Chronotypes: Representation of East European Women in Western Film after 1989," in ibid., 164.

of experience."[204] The negative connotation of hypersexuality has an effect on the construction and perception of whiteness in Russian women. In her book *Imagining Russia: Making Feminist Sense of American Nationalism in U.S.-Russian Relations*, Kimberly Williams addresses the specific quality of this whiteness, arguing that "gendered Russian imaginaries [. . .] are inherently racialized and heterosexualized."[205] Although Russian women are viewed as ethnically Slavic, and therefore as white Europeans, they are structured through a "complex cold-war-era version of orientalism,"[206] which signifies them as particularly feminine, sensual, and sexual. Analyzing a wide range of cultural products from cinema, TV, and literature, as well as government documents, Williams claims that "[w]omen in post-Soviet Russia are [. . .] always already positioned within Russian nationalist discourse as heterosexed and gendered subjects"[207] and that this cultural myth significantly influences US-American imaginaries. Partly in reaction to Russian self-representations during the 1990s, and partly based on Russia myths that date back to the age of European Enlightenment, US viewers imagined Russia as a land populated by beautiful, feminine women, and riddled "with crime, corruption and chaos, [and] prostitution."[208]

Williams's analysis builds heavily on Eliot Borenstein's analysis of Russian popular culture in the 1990s and early 2000s, which identifies sex and violence as the most prevailing and hypervisible themes.[209] Borenstein proposes that in "the 1990s, the Russian prostitute [sic] was routinely deployed in the symbolic battle for Russia's soul. The collapse of the Russian state, the decline of patriotism, and the absence of a workable national idea shared center stage in the Russian media and culture industry with tales and images of sexually uninhibited young women offering their bodies and their services for pay."[210] These sensationalist Russian discourses intersected with reports on the widespread trafficking of Russian and Ukrainian women into the United States for work in the sex industry in the 1990s. Together, these discourses significantly shaped public views on Russian women, creating the myth of beautiful, overtly sexual, Russian immigrant women.[211] While I fully agree with Williams's thesis that

---

204 Deltcheva, "Eastern Women in Western Chronotypes," 181.
205 Williams, *Imagining Russia*, 4.
206 Ibid.
207 Ibid.
208 Ibid., 104
209 Eliot Borenstein, *Overkill: Sex Violence, and Russian Popular Culture after 1991* (Ithaca, NY: Cornell University Press, 2008).
210 Borenstein, *Overkill*, 78.
211 Williams, *Imagining Russia*, 37.

Russian women are perceived to be highly feminine and highly sexual, I suggest that the allocation of heterosexuality is frequently extended to a promiscuity that is depicted as sexual fluidity.

Williams mentions the racialization and Orientalization of Russian women and emphasizes the connection between this racialization and (hetero)sexualization.[212] Yet her work concentrates on gender as cultural representation and does not go into the specifics of the sexualized and racialized stratifications of its embodiment. In her book *The Traffic in Eastern European Women*, Anca Parvulescu addresses the specific exoticizing and sexualization of white Slavic migrant women as bodily difference. I draw on Parvulescu's important work in my close reading of the character Svetlana in *Shameless*. At the same time, and based on Sadowski-Smith's findings that Slavic immigrants are perceived through the prism of whiteness within the US, I challenge Parvulescu's claim that the othering of the white Slavic body, together with other Eastern European female bodies, is based on their racialization as "not quite white." I appreciate Parvulescu's focus on the dimension of class in the process of othering Eastern European women, which includes Slavic women. Parvulescu demonstrates wonderfully how the bodies of women from the postsocialist and post-Soviet sphere are always already relegated to a working-class or underclass position, and that their sexuality and femininity are intrinsically connected to this class dimension. Although I agree with her thesis that women from the Balkans, Romani, and Sinti are perceived to be "not quite white," I disagree that this is true for all Eastern European (working-class) migrant women. On the contrary, I argue that Slavic women within Western, and particularly within US-American contexts are perceived through an especially classed and sexualized form of whiteness. While Russian and Ukrainian women are viewed as white, they are constructed through forms of bodily difference, such as style, body language, and bodily affect, which are all connected to class markers.

Imagining the Russian in *Shameless*

While this class-based, sexualized, and gendered classification of an "other" whiteness is visible in virtually all contemporary examples of North American TV shows, Svetlana in *Shameless* represents the most unvarnished stereotype

---

212 Ibid., 3, 10, 37–38.

of the Russian woman.[213] *Shameless* is a comedy drama that works through all kinds of stereotypes and does not shy away from content that could be perceived as derogatory or hurtful. It is a remake of the British series[214] and is set in Chicago's poor South Side. The show aired from January 2011 to 2021 on the American channel *Showtime*. It revolves around the dysfunctional family of Frank Gallagher, a stereotypical Irish American alcoholic, and his six children. While Frank sets out on ever new adventures, dealing with US homelessness, lack of healthcare, disability, and so on, the eldest daughter, high school dropout Fiona, raises her five younger siblings: super-intelligent and gifted, but alcoholic, Phillip; Ian, who has schizophrenia and is gay; Debbie, a teenage mother; the violent and hyperactive Carl; and the Black genius, Liam. The diversity of the show's main characters, which is even more diversified through the introduction of recurring characters, has inspired critics to rave about the show. Its multiple strong female characters with complex personalities and elaborate storylines, through which the show addresses sexualized and gendered inequality, and the multiple characters that live their queer sexuality, has prompted commentators to call it "one of the queerest and most progressive television shows on right now."[215]

Sexuality is generally a strong theme in the show. The members of the Gallagher family and their neighbor and best friend Veronica "V" Fisher are sexually active from a young age and enjoy sex without much shame or restraint. This dimension of their behavior might be seen as progressive, but it also marks their affiliation as working-class poor, a class that has been historically understood as generally more sexually active or promiscuous.[216]

---

213 Other TV characters embodying this stereotype mail order bride are Svetlana from the TV show *Svetlana* (HDNet, 2010), Paulina, the Russian waitress in the first episode of *2 Broke Girls* (CBS, 2011), or Russian American Marina in the reality TV show *Russian Dolls* (Lifetime, 2011).

214 *Shameless*, produced by Paul Abbott, developed by John Wells, aired 2004–2013, Showtime and Channel 4, TV show.

215 Trish Bendix, "'Shameless' delves into polyamory with Svetlana becoming V and Kevin's third," AfterEllen, March 29, 2016, https://afterellen.com/shameless-delves-polyamory-svetlana-becoming-v-kevins-third/#wKjEUkiKxMuMvuBa.99.

216 Pamela Fox, "Who Is Shameless This Election Season? One TV Show's Challenging Depiction of the Working Poor," Working-Class Perspectives, September 26, 2016, https://workingclassstudies.wordpress.com/2016/09/26/who-is-shameless-this-election-season-one-TV shows-challenging-depiction-of-the-working-poor/; John Hendel, "Showtime's 'Shameless' New Show About Poverty," *Atlantic*, January 8, 2011, https://www.theatlantic.com/entertainment/archive/2011/01/showtimes-shameless-new-show-about-poverty/69108/.

The theme of homosexuality is introduced through the character of teenager Ian Gallagher and his various lovers. In the first season, Ian has a secret affair with the closeted Kash, a married Muslim and his employer. Ian is regularly beaten up by his homophobic classmate, Mickey Milkovich. However, it turns out that the Polish American Mickey is in love with Ian and the two develop a romantic relationship that runs for several seasons, until Mickey is sent to prison in season six.

Ian goes through various phases that are strongly oriented towards the development of US LGBTIQ+ history: he comes out, must fight against prejudices towards gay identity; he becomes a sex worker, meets a sexually fluid African American who confronts Ian with the possibilities of fluid identities; and, finally, he meets Travor, a transgender man who confuses Ians categories and self-identification anew.

While Ian's family responds well to his homosexuality, Mickey is put under a lot of pressure. His father, an alcoholic who abuses Mickey's sister while intoxicated, forces Mickey to sleep with Russian sex worker Svetlana when he discovers that Mickey and Ian are a couple. Ian's development parallels and overlaps with Svetlana's story through the character of Mickey. Beyond this intersection of their story lines, it is interesting to juxtapose the two characters because they are both represented as queer. Yet while Ian signifies American liberated queer sexuality, Svetlana's sexuality signifies first of all her class-based and gendered Russianness.

Svetlana Milkovich, later Svetlana Fisher, is played by Isidora Goreshter, a second-generation Russian American. Mickey is forced by his family to marry her because she claims to be pregnant by him. Already at that point it is suggested that Svetlana is the victim of human trafficking and that she resides illegally in the US—Kevin Ball, the neighbor and Veronica Fisher's boyfriend, calls her a sex slave. After Mickey frees her from the prostitution ring run by a Russian woman, she works in Kevin's bar, first as a sex worker, then as a breast milk sweatshop operator, and later, with Veronica, as a stripper. At first, Svetlana is not happy with Mickey and Ian's increasingly close relationship. She changes her mind, however, and lives for a time with the two of them and another Russian-speaking female sex worker, with whom a same-sex relationship is also hinted at. When Mickey is sent to prison, Svetlana becomes Veronica's and Kevin's roommate and babysitter and marries Veronica to keep her residency permit. Svetlana sees it as her job as roommate and caretaker of the Fischer-Ball family to sexually satisfy both Kevin and Veronica. In the process, Veronica discovers her affection and sexual attraction for Svetlana, whom she affectionately calls Lana. In seasons six and seven, the three develop a loving polyamorous relationship.

Svetlana represents the 'Slavic Femme,' an incarnation of the so-called New Russian woman who is deeply invested in her feminine appearance, likes to show off her physical attributes, and aspires to acquire material wealth. At the same time, she also represents the Soviet worker and mother: practical, smart, corrupt, and who would kill for her family. Moreover, she is portrayed as an emotional and temperamental woman, a common attribute of Slavic women in TV shows.

Svetlana's violent temperament is frequently on display in the show; but it becomes particularly apparent when her alleged father, Yvon, appears in episode three of season seven titled "Home Sweet Homeless Shelter."[217] The two of them get into physical fights, and when Kevin and Veronica surprise the two of them while they are having sex, they confess that Yvon is not Svetlana's father, but her Russian husband. Throughout season seven, Yvon's violent, and often inappropriate, ("Russian") behavior is increasingly irritating to Kevin and Veronica, and they pressure Svetlana to make him leave. In Spisode Seven, titled "You'll Never Ever Get a Chicken in Your Whole Entire Life," she grants their wish quite literally, returning home in blood-splattered clothes and proclaiming that Yvon is officially gone. Whether she hurt him, killed him, or just beat him up to make him go is not clear.

Svetlana's working-class habits and manner, her mafia-style actions, and her Russianness are tightly intertwined. Her violence, criminal activities, and specific gender and sexuality markers all combine to contribute to the signification of her Russianness. Svetlana's storyline draws heavily on the cultural stereotype of strong, family oriented Russian women and providers. But while these Russian traits are portrayed as admirable in seasons five and six, allowing viewers to sympathize with her, these traits turn increasingly negative as the story progresses. By the end of season seven, Svetlana's caring personality becomes paternalistic and overbearing when she tricks Kevin and Veronica into signing their bar, the Alibi, over to her. This act is motivated by her savvy business sense and her estimation that neither V nor Kevin are good business owners; and under her reign the bar does indeed make a profit for the first time. Her methods are morally wrong, though, and this leads to a breakup of the polyamorous relationship.

---

217 *Shameless*, season 7, episode 3, "Home Sweet Homeless Shelter," directed by Iain B. MacDonald, written by Krista Vernoff, aired October 16, 2016, Showtime and Channel 4, TV show.

Svetlana's ruthless entrepreneurialism and murky character is part of her class-based, sexualized, and racialized stratification. American TV has a long history of using depictions of organized crime, from which Svetlana's character arguably arrives in the Gallaghers' lives, to focus on ethnicized social communities and individuals. Matthew Jacobson has demonstrated how TV characters connected to organized crime, such as Tony Soprano from *The Sopranos*,[218] offer "ethnicity" as a reference point for seemingly lost "values such as loyalty, rootedness, and interdependence," values "America [...] is hostile to."[219] At the same time, paradoxically, America mourns the loss of those values. Whereas the Italian figures who represent organized crime revert to "antimodernist"[220] values through their masculinity, Svetlana's affiliation to crime highlights her ethnic, in fact racialized, belonging (despite her whiteness) and her female gender. Svetlana's criminal activity signifies the above-mentioned antimodernist and seemingly un-American values, such as strong family bonds, rootedness, independence, and her threat to the US system. However, her Russianness highlights her female gender and hypersexuality, and vice versa. Williams argues that Russian women in US-American TV series often represent a threat to the US system at the intersection of their sexuality and gender.[221] Thus, Svetlana not only breaks the law through her sex work, but also forges passports and steals.[222] Although some types of formerly "deviant" sexuality are now included in the notion of "Americanness," particularly gay and lesbian sexuality,[223] Svetlana's ambiguous, fluid hypersexuality is still identifiable as part of this racialized, culturalized, and gendered construction of a foreign enemy.

As I have already suggested, the character of Svetlana is heavily sexualized, conforming fully to the stereotype of the female Russian illegal migrant. In the scene from which this screenshot is taken, she successfully lures an old wealthy white man into her spider's web, with the ambition to marry him and inherit his fortune, once he is gone.

---

218 *The Sopranos*, created by David Chase, aired 1999–2007, HBO, TV show.
219 Matthew Jacobson, *Roots Too: White Ethnic Revival in Post-Civil Rights America* (Cambridge, MA: Harvard University Press, 2006), 26.
220 Ibid.
221 Williams, *Imagining Russia*, 123–132.
222 *Shameless*, season 7, episode 8, "You Sold Me the Laundromat, Remember?" directed by Allison Liddi-Brown, written by Krista Vernoff, aired November 20, 2016, Showtime and Channel 4, TV show.
223 Puar, *Terrorist Assemblages*.

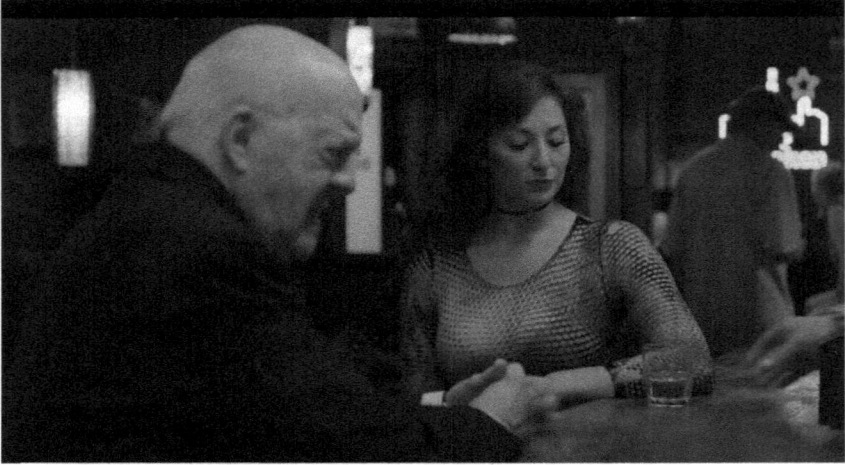

Figure 18. Screenshot of Isidora Goreshter, *Shameless*, season eight, episode ten, "Church of Gay Jesus," directed by Anna Mastro and written by Sheila Callaghan, aired January 14, 2018, on HBO.

The representation of Svetlana, here and in basically every scene in which she appears, conforms to ideas that emerged in the 1990s, which identified trafficked Slavic women as "alluring, slightly Oriental or exotic temptresses with an edge of vampirism,"[224] as described by Glajar and Radulescu. Williams and Radulescu argue that such representations easily and logically objectified actual migrants, and were both a reflection of the increased incidence of Russian and Ukrainian trafficking to the US, and an explanation for the increase in demand for trafficked women.[225]

Williams, in particular, emphasizes that the construction of US national identity during the 1990s and early 2000 was closely tied to the end of the Cold War, the emergence or exposure of the trafficking of Russian and Ukrainian women for sex work, and so-called development assistance to Russia. She describes in detail how US anti-trafficking legislation was formulated on the basis of trafficking cases of post-Soviet women. The focus on Russian and Ukrainian victims of trafficking and sex work under duress lent credence to the idea that the US had won the Cold War and was confirmed in its role as a moral model for

---

224 Glajar and Radulescu, *Vampirettes, Wretches and Amazones*, 6.
225 Williams, *Imagining Russia*, 37; Domnica Radulescu, "Amazones, Wretches and Vampirettes: Essentialism and Beyond in the Representation of East European Women," in Glajar and Radulescu *Vampirettes, Wretches and Amazons*, 45–46.

the entire world. US national identity was thus identified as masculine, and the entire Russian nation conceived as a female victim.[226] Only slowly did this view change, when Vladimir Putin began to emerge more prominently in the media and on the political stage as a male role model, macho hunter, and so on.

In *Shameless*, the character of Svetlana reverts back to this idea of a desolate and weak Russia, with its poor and criminal populace. She corresponds in every detail to the cliché of the young woman from a poor background who was forced into sex work in early puberty and later sold to the US for a few hundred dollars to work as a coerced sex worker. She is oversexualized and uses that sexuality to survive and rise socially and economically—something that Radulescu highlights in her analyses of media images of the 1990s. Svetlana's pronounced sexualization is significant in relation to her racialization. In addition, her role as a mother and her business as a breast milk producer and seller are also significant. In her analysis of Western media representations of Slavic women, Parvulescu points out that they often embody the reproduction of Western societies. These women are predominantly represented in the media as sex workers, surrogate mothers, care workers, and organ donors.[227] Taking Parvulescu further, one can argue that sex work and motherhood are two opposite ends of the same continuum which signifies Slavic women, through notions of reproductive labor and sex work or trafficking, which occupy a social position other than white, nonimmigrant American women. Moreover, these labels mark their difference to the latter as "racial Otherness." As such, the Russian body of Svetlana is frequently shown to mark or negotiate an opposition to Fiona, the superior, enlightened US subject, who is the only one who will eventually emancipate herself from her lower working-class status and, more importantly, in contrast to the African American V. In her last appearance on the show, she is additionally juxtaposed to a white, heterosexual, affluent (geriatric) man. Tuszynska identifies the oppositionality between white, heterosexual, affluent (older) men, and beautiful, younger, white Eastern-European women as one of common, dichotomous co-constructions. The more interesting juxtaposition to the Russian oriental Svetlana is embodied in the African American Veronica, which I will discuss a bit later.

The racialization of Russian women as white, in combination with their hegemonically inferior social position, makes them well suited to provide Western society with children, wives, organ donators, and care. Parvulescu's argument that the racialization and trafficking of Eastern European bodies serves as a

---

226 Williams, *Imagining Russia*, 38.
227 Parvulescu, *The Traffic in Women's Work*, 11, 86–87, 93, 107.

means of reproductive exploitation for rejuvenating the West is very insightful. However, designating the status of such bodies as "not quite white" is not fully convincing. On the one hand, such a designation renders invisible the specific racialization of women marked as "Slavic" by equating it with the racialization of persons of color. On the other hand, such a designation diminishes or negates the white privilege that accrues to women marked as Slavic, thereby downplaying the social significance of nonwhite skin color.

More problematically, Parvulescu draws on the vocabulary of slavery to refer to trafficking and forced sex work and exploitation in care work, reproduction, and organ donation in relation to white women racialized as Slavic. Particularly in the US context, with its legacies of chattel slavery and its role in the transatlantic slave trade, I find the appropriateness of such an application questionable, since it seems unable to address the specific aspects of anti-Black racism on which the institution of US slavery was based. This equation of the enslavement of Africans with the trafficking of Russian women and the forced sex work of Svetlana also occurs in *Shameless*. In addition, slavery is also equated with the reproductive activity of Irish American Fiona and the exploitation of Fiona's brother Phillip as an unpaid intern.

Although the show portrays Svetlana's initial activity as a sex worker quite negatively, not all sex-related ways of earning money are depicted as amoral, exploitative, and harmful. In fact, even in the case of Svetlana's coerced sex work, sex itself is not necessarily portrayed negatively; rather, it is the fact that she was coerced into dependency on her madam that is criticized. Later, a history of domestic violence and abuse by a sexual partner is also revealed. Although somewhat stereotypical, Svetlana's entrepreneurial take on sex work is depicted as quite productive. As her relationship to Kevin and V progresses in seasons seven and eight, she even initiates a topless maid service with Kevin and Veronica.[228] This creates the opportunity for applying some dark sexual humor; but it comes at the cost of white, middle- and upper-class hegemonic men, rather than at the expense of the women's dignity. On the contrary, Svetlana and V are shown as clever workers, who have full command of their bodies and agency.

---

228 *Shameless*, season 7, episode 2, "Swipe, Fuck, Leave," directed by Rob Hardy, written by Nancy M. Pimental, aired October 9, 2016, Showtime and Channel 4, TV show.

Figure 19. Screenshot of Isidora Goreshter (left) and Shanola Hampton (right) in *Shameless* season eight, episode five, "The (Mis)Education of Liam Fergus Beircheart Gallagher," directed by Iain B. MacDonald, written by Sheila Callaghan, aired December 3, 2017, on HBO.

Svetlana embodies the Western perspective on Russia, inhabiting a liminal space between the democratic, developed, white world, and the barbaric (and terrorist) racialized territories or majority world. She is the sly Russian trickster, the women with many faces, which is indicated in this screenshot from season eight, episode five. It is evident not only in her sexy, but tacky animal print outfit, and her crimson or communist-red lips, but through the double representation of the nesting dolls—one a traditional female doll, and one with Putin's portrait painted on it. In this screenshot, as in the one before, Svetlana is easily identifiable as the very popular stereotype, delineated by Deltcheva, of "the Slavic slut, ready to sell her body and soul for greenbacks."[229] Interestingly, in this picture her body embraces as much of the bar table as possible, which indicates that she is in the process of a hostile, but cunningly sly, takeover of the Alibi.

Svetlana's occupation as sex worker, in combination with her entrepreneurism, her physical appearance, clothing, makeup style, and (body) language identify her as Russian or 'Slavic.' In this combination, her whiteness, feminine curves, glowing eyes, arrogantly upward tilting chin, and her constantly unsmiling lips read as signs of Russianness. This construct of signs and features must, in turn, be read as racialization. Deploying the notion of race and racialization in reference to white post-Soviet bodies is not without risk, as it appears to essentialize

---

229 Deltcheva, "Eastern Women in Western Chronotypes," 162.

and naturalize cultural significations. However, the decision to emphasize racialization rather than culturalization represents a choice to highlight the bodily architecture of her signification as Russian in Svetlana's case.

Stuart Hall understands the essentializations and naturalizations of culture and heritage or nationality as race as "a sliding signifier."[230] Race is a "badge, a token, a sign, [. . .] a signifier, and [. . .] racialized behavior and difference needs to be understood as a discursive, not necessarily as a genetic or biological fact."[231] Thus, signifiers like race need to be understood as unstable and always in flux. Yet their meaning is not arbitrary or random. The "stratification insignia"[232] that racially determine Slavic women are subtle, and there are no analytical tools yet to "recognize and read [. . .] racialized physical characteristics like hair, teeth, body type, and clothing styles as well as education, religion, and 'values.'"[233] However, these insignia are perceived visibly and can be identified in contrast to the surroundings against which they appear, particularly in the frequent juxtaposition of white Slavic women to other racialized and classed characters. Parvulescu and Bridget Anderson[234] argue that Eastern European and Slavic women are hierarchically arranged on a scale that includes differently racialized immigrant women. The determining factors of their social position within this racialized hierarchy among migrants from the Global South and Eastern Europe in North/Western countries are of a class-based and economic nature. Arguably, economic factors not only determine this racialized hierarchy, but rather significantly shape who becomes racialized in the first place. While skin color plays a significant role in arranging female migrants in this hierarchy, occupation, gender attributes, and sexualization contribute significantly to the respective social position.

Considering the class- and occupation-based racialization of Eastern European and Slavic women within North/Western contexts, Parvulescu acknowledges that skin color is not the determining factor. However, she nevertheless argues that these women are hierarchically positioned or labeled as "not quite white,"[235] as I have already mentioned. She builds her argument on Rosi Braidotti's observation that "[p]eople from the Balkans, or the South-Western regions of Europe,

230 Hall, "Race, The Floating Signifier. A lecture given at Goldsmiths College in London, 1997," transcript by Sut Jhalley, Media Education Foundation, 2015, http//:www.mediaed.org.
231 Ibid.
232 Hall qtd. in Parvulescu, *The Traffic in Women's Work*, 14.
233 Ibid.
234 Bridget Anderson, *Doing the Dirty Work? The Global Politics of Domestic Labor* (London: Zed, 2000).
235 Parvulescu, *The Traffic in Women's Work*, 14.

in so far as they are not yet 'good Europeans,' they are also not quite as 'white' as others."[236] Although Braidotti's observation that the racialization of women from the Balkans and South-Western Europe is based on their class-affiliated occupational stratification, and so are "not-quite-white," is comprehensible, her decision to subsume of all Central-Eastern, South-Eastern, Eastern-European, and Slavic Women under one umbrella gives rise to questions. I agree with Parvulescu's argument that class-based and occupational signification racializes white Eastern-European and Slavic women, but I disagree that this signification is marked as "not quite white." Rather, by strongly building on Sadowski-Smith's work, I argue that very specific forms of racialization mark Russian, Ukrainian, Belarussian, Serbian, or Polish women, despite, or in correspondence with, their evaluation as white. At the same time very different tropes of Southernness mark the bodies of women from the Balkans, particularly Muslim women.

I find support for my argument in critical whiteness studies scholars such as Nancy Foner,[237] David Roediger,[238] Matthew Jacobson,[239] and Robert Zecker,[240] whose historical work has demonstrated how the late nineteenth and early twentieth-century Jewish, Polish, Lithuanian, Italian, Greek, and Russian immigrant populations in the US, while initially racialized as nonwhite, became white as their social status changed during the process of their Americanization. Economic necessities, such as the need for loyal laborers, the "'war against racism' in Europe,"[241] and the emerging Cold War supported a shift from racial difference to universalism and American unity. The melting pot ideology gave a "progressive spin to the idea of a particularly freedom-loving American race,"[242] and 'whitened' the new immigrants, including many Russian Jews and other 'Slavic' people. This melting pot Americanism ended with the growing civil rights movement of the late 1950s and 1960s.

Confronted with an increasingly confident Black Power movement, as well as a growing Chicana/o and Indigenous movement, "descendants of earlier

---

236 Rosi Braidotti, "On Becoming European," in *Women Migrants from East to West: Gender, Mobility and Belonging in Contemporary Europe*, ed. Luisa Passerini et al. (New York: Berghahn, 2007), 32–44, 34.

237 Nancy Foner, *From Ellis Island to JFK: New York's Two Great Waves of Immigration* (New Haven, CT: Yale University Press, 2000).

238 David Roediger, *Colored White: Transcending the Racial Past* (Berkeley: University of California Press, 2002).

239 Jacobson, *Roots Too*.

240 Robert Zecker, *Race and America's Immigrant Press: How the Slovaks Were Taught to Think like White People* (New York: Continuum, 2011).

241 Jacobson, *Roots Too*, 30.

242 Roediger, *Colored White*, 167.

European immigrants quit the melting pot"[243] and 'ethnicity' emerged to differentiate white Americans from each other. A desire for 'authenticity,' supported by antimodernist thinking, promoted the new labels of Italianness, Jewishness, Greekness, and Irishness as "a badge of pride."[244] As a reaction to Black consciousness, Black Pride, and demands for affirmative action by anti-racist movements, many white groups sought to distance themselves from white privilege by claiming ethnic belonging, rather than whiteness.[245] This (self-)discovery of ethnicity did not, however, challenge white privilege, but rather confirmed the whiteness of these ethnic markers.[246] While the category of race primarily signified biology, ethnicity emphasized culture, "a cultural affiliation rather than a bloodline; a set of sensibilities and associational habits that, however tenacious, were subject to the forces of assimilation and change."[247] Jacobson argues that while race was meant to differentiate, "the concept of ethnicity accomplished less as a term of distinction than it did as a partial erasure of 'difference'—a universalizing appeal to the underlying sameness of humanity and to the assimilative powers of American culture."[248] That it did not completely lose its connection to race can be seen, however, in the racial residues of ethnicity in various examples of ethnically marked figures on American TV; for example, in *The Nanny*,[249] *The Sopranos, Will & Grace*,[250] *Everybody Loves Raymond*,[251] and *Rizzoli & Isles*.[252] The racial stratification of the main characters of these shows does not take away from their whiteness. On the contrary, the ethnic revival in American culture further naturalized the "whiteness of the white republic."[253] With the public

---

243 Jacobson, *Roots Too*, 2.
244 Ibid.
245 Ibid., 20–22.
246 Ibid. 7.
247 Ibid., 32.
248 Ibid., 33.
249 *The Nanny*, created by Fran Drescher and Peter Marc Jacobson, CBS, 1993–1999, TV show.
250 *Will & Grace*, created by Max Mutchnick and David Kohan, NBC, 1998–2006, 2017–2020, TV show.
251 *Everybody Loves Raymond*, created by Philip Rosenthal, CBS, 1996–2005, TV show.
252 *Rizzoli & Isles*, developed by Janet Tamaro, TNT, 2010–2016, TV show. Some other white ethnic exemplars include shows like: *Chicken Soup*, created by Saul Turteltaub and Bernie Orenstein, ABC 1989, TV show; *thirtysomething*, created by Edward Zwick and Marshall Herskovitz, ABC, 1987–1991, TV show; *Brooklyn Bridge*, created by Gary David Goldberg, CBS, 1991–1993, TV show; *To Have and to Hold*, created by Joanne T. Waters, CBS, 1998, TV show; *Seinfeld*, created by Larry David and Jerry Seinfeld, NBC, 1989–1998, TV show; *The Education of Max Bickford*, created by Dawn Prestwich and Nicole Yorkin, CBS, 2001–2002, TV show; or *Costello*, created by Sue Costello and Cheryl Holliday, Fox, 1998, TV show.
253 Jacobson, *Roots Too*, 316.

embrace of 'ethnic roots' of American whiteness emerged a new focus on the potential 'foreign' threat.[254] The hysteria about a possible foreign threat focused frequently on the topic of migration, and the seeming potential for assimilation became the demarcation line. While nonwhite migrants are seen as foreign by definition, and therefore unfit for assimilation, migrants of "the new immigrant whiteness" as Sadowski-Smith calls it, are granted greater opportunities to become American. Although white immigrants have the potential to assimilate, this assimilation depends on upward mobility into at least the middle class and white-collar occupations. For Slavic women, this road is full of pitfalls, though, since upward mobility might inauspiciously intersect with the stereotype of the hypersexualized hyper-materialistic New Russian, which blocks upward mobility regardless of rising wealth. In this case, the class-occupational stratification as lower class continues to signify the female Slavic body as other, despite of its economic potential.

Moreover, and very importantly, the whiteness of the new Eastern European, Slavic, and particularly Russian immigrants, most especially women, has the potential to allow them to pass as 'civilized,' trustworthy Americanized people, when in reality they are 'savage tricksters.' The most iconic stereotype of the deceitful Russian woman is the Russian femme fatale. Eastern European and Slavic women have often been portrayed as cunning femmes fatales (tricksters), who instrumentalize their "deceptive sexuality"[255] or "sluttiness"[256] to lure American men into their web, that is, to steal their money or power. Analyzing popular media from the 1990s and 2000s, Williams finds many female Russian characters that represent this American fear,[257] often in the form of highly sexualized figures, who are willing to use sex as a weapon and means to an end. She traces this figuration back to "the Cold War-era assumptions about Orientalist stereotypes of female KGB officers engaging in sexpionage as a means of accomplishing Soviet intelligence goals."[258] This is precisely what Svetlana does over the last three episodes of season eight, finally marrying her "old senile sugar daddy" in episode twelve, "Sleepwalking."[259]

---

254 Ibid., 316.

255 Williams, *Imagining Russia*, 36.

256 Deltcheva, "Eastern Women in Western Chronotypes," 181.

257 Williams, *Imagining Russia*, 123.

258 Ibid.

259 *Shameless*, season 8, episode 12, "Sleepwalking," created and written by John Wells, aired January 28, 2018, Showtime and Channel 4, TV show.

Following Sadowski-Smith and Parvulescu, I read Svetlana's Russian body as constructed through her sexualized working-class occupation. While her whiteness gives Svetlana the potential to Americanize, her otherness rests on her working-class status, occupation as a sex worker, and her (other) criminal activities. These occupational habits correspond to her strong position in and devoted care for her family—which partially or temporarily includes Kevin, Veronika, and their twin girls—as well as her powerful sexual desire and willingness to use sex to reach her goals. This mixture of personality traits and physical characteristics corresponds to Svetlana's style: her reddish hair, often red lipstick and nails, her wickedly glowing eyes, her always straight back, and, of course, and her provocative clothes. Together with her thick accent, curvy body, and large breasts, her sex work, criminality, strength, melancholia, struggles, and style construct Svetlana as post-Soviet Russian woman. However, her otherness would not be visible if it weren't displayed next to the Black V, the Irish American Fiona, and the multiple white American men she lures into her net.

The co-construction of Svetlana and Veronica becomes particularly apparent in the context of their love affair. While Ian's sexuality corresponds to his identity and seems to come from his inner desire, the Russian Svetlana's and Black Veronica's desires are more due to circumstances. They are both extremely sexual, willing to sell their bodies for money. Veronica and Kevin previously sold pornographic, sado-masochistic streaming content, in which she played Kevin's sex slave, in addition to the abovementioned nude maid service, where Veronika and Svetlana performed sexual acts on each other. Their desire for each other, however, is not pegged to any particular sexual identity, but, rather, seems to stem more from their generally exuberant sexual appetite. Svetlana's impressive sexual skills, in particular, which Veronika, even as she tries, is unable to resist, deserve mention here. This view of Russian women's (homo)sexuality corresponds to a long-standing stereotype that originated during the Enlightenment. This exoticization of Russian women's ebullient sexuality survived into the Cold War, when the West, and particularly North America, was refashioning its attitude toward sex, from a conservative, heteronormative position to a liberal and sexually progressive one. During this same period, the Soviet sphere was increasingly constructed as hostile towards sexual liberation. Yet Russian women were seen as sexually emancipated and very active. Brian Baer[260] and others have pointed out that this contradictory view persists in much Western queer theory. The hegemonic view about that period is that actively same-sex

---

260 Baer, "Russian Gays/Western Gaze."

people were denied a homosexual identity due to a lack of such terms as "gay" or "lesbian." It was argued that emancipated sexual identities did not form until the 1990s and that the struggle against the resistance of a backward society continues up till today.

In the 1990s, alongside this interpretation of backwardness and unfreedom, and arguably based on the notion of Russian women's sexual appetite, Laurie Essig and others developed a critique that viewed Russian same-sex practices as a queer alternative to Western modernity, which seeks to pin homosexuality on identities. Russian subjects were again perceived as not yet civilized, not yet modern; however, this evaluation was signified as a queer, hence positive, counter-model to Western identity discourses. The parameters remain the same, even if the valences have been reversed. The co-appearance of Svetlana and Veronika, however, reveal that the racialized demarcation of not yet civilized sexuality is colored white. This whiteness corresponds to Svetlana's control over Veronika's Black body and the fact that Veronika is unable to resist Svetlana's appeal. V embodies a version of what Karla D. Scott calls "The Myth of the Strong Black Woman."[261] Yet although she is seemingly invincible in her dedication to others and is equipped with powerful "street smarts," the cunning Svetlana easily has her way with her. Svetlana cannot be said to submit to her own desires because sex for her is a means to an end and not necessarily a bodily desire that she is unable to control. As I have already mentioned, this fact also sets her apart from other white, sexually nonnormative characters, such as Iain and Travor, who represent gay, trans*, and queer identities, and are, accordingly, seen to be more Western, more American, and more progressive. Iain's struggle with his identity is a class struggle that marks him as upward mobile, and later as a queer critique on identities, which needs to be seen as progressive and enlightened.

In contrast, while Veronika's and Svetlana's sexuality is represented as naturally fluid, their fluidity does not come from an identitarian consciousness or critique. Nevertheless, although Veronika is portrayed as an emancipated American woman, and plays the dominant role in her relationship with her boyfriend Kevin, she is unable to fully control her bodily desires when it comes to Svetlana. Svetlana, in contrast is always in control of her sexuality. Through Veronika, the show succeeds in critically reflecting on the stereotypical roles available to Black women in American society. She is depicted as the sole responsible, fully capable person in her family, for example, due to her training as an assistant nurse. She

---

261 Karla D. Scott, *The Language of Strong Black Womanhood: Myths, Models, Messages, and a New Mandate for Self-Care* (New York: Lexington Books, 2017).

patches up the bruised and bleeding Gallagher men after they have gotten into drunken brawls or injured themselves doing risky things to prove their white masculinity. The show devotes much less attention to her problematic sexual responses to Svetlana, however. And although Veronika is, at the same time, the caring supporter or sidekick to her best friend Fiona Gallagher, who is the only person who manages to leave the family and lower working-class milieu behind in the end, Veronika's subordination to Svetlana is far more pronounced than the subservient role she plays in her relationship to Fiona.

Conclusion

Shameless exaggerates the sexualization, ethnicization, racialization, and class stereotyping of its characters, thus pointing out societal stereotypes and offering the possibility of a critical reading. At the same time, however, the series also repeats and perpetuates these very structural significations, thus ensuring its popularity. Svetlana embodies the specific forms of othering and racialization of Slavic women in North/Western and US-American media discourses. Racialized, but white, she embodies "Russianness" as a distinct notion that emerges at the intersection of gender, class, age, origin, language, and sexuality. Importantly, these distinctive markers of otherness become discernable in Svetlana's co-appearance with the Black American Veronika and several white characters, such as the progressive feminist and upwardly mobile Fiona, the gay Iain, and several heterosexual men who fall victim to her.

Svetlana's racial significations of white Slavic "Russianness" are an amalgam of facial expressions, language particularities (accents), hairstyles, body postures, values, morals, sexual abilities, and so forth. As cunning femme fatal and trafficked sex worker, Svetlana perfectly fits the mold of earlier imaginations of Russian women deeply rooted in German Enlightenment thought and Cold War ideologies. The character of Svetlana also embodies the hypersexualization of Russian women during the years of the dissolution of the Soviet Union. Interestingly, her figure is located on a racially marked occupational and class-based spectrum, which allows American liberal and national values to emerge. At one end of the spectrum is the white emancipated feminist Fiona, who manages to struggle herself out of 'the ghetto' into a better future, and her equally progressive homosexual brother Iain, who becomes a queer rights activist and social worker. They are both model citizens with high moral standards, which they sometimes deviate from, but always return to, in contrast to Svetlana, who seems to have no morals whatsoever. On the other side of the spectrum is the racialized Veronika, a "strong Black woman" who is rarely allowed to break down or receive help, but always ready to give her last ounce of strength for the benefit of others. Veronika stagnates amid her poverty, under the burden of responsibility for her family and her community. Significantly, she is unable to resist the cunning Svetlana, and just barely manages to get her bar back after Svetlana steals it. The Russian Svetlana inhabits a fluid and opaque position between these poles: half-civilized, half-enlightened; but never to be trusted.

CHAPTER 6

Concluding Remarks

From Russian Anti-Gay Propaganda to Brittney Griner

While writing, revising, and rewriting these chapters, I followed closely the case of Brittney Griner, the American Phoenix Mercury basketball player, member of the Women's National Basketball Association (WNBA), and two-time Olympic gold medalist, who was detained and arrested on smuggling charges by Russian customs officials in February 2022, for carrying less than a gram of hash oil in her luggage. Griner was in Russia to play for the Russian Premier League during the WNBA off-season. The hash oil she carried for her vape was medically prescribed and part of her pain treatment. It is unclear how Russian border control detected this minimal amount of oil for her vape, and it is not entirely unthinkable that the close search was either motivated by racism or that they had been tipped off. However, marijuana is illegal in Russia and possession of it is punishable by up to ten years in prison. The trial against Griner was concluded with an astonishingly harsh sentence for the small amount of oil she carried. She was sentenced to nine years in prison in early August, 2022. From November to December 2022, Griner served in a Russian penal colony.

The American liberal media was sympathetic towards Griner, emphasizing that marijuana is frequently used by American athletes to treat pain.[1] They further amplified the US officials' position, which was that she was wrongfully detained. But where was the huge public outcry? Where were the thousands of

---

1   Jonathan Abrams and Tania Ganguli, "Why Pros like Brittney Griner Choose Cannabis for Their Pain," *New York Times*, August 1, 2022, https://www.nytimes.com/2022/08/01/sports/basketball/brittney-griner-athletes-cannabis-marijuana.html.

actors,[2] musicians,[3] political leaders, activists,[4] institutions, and athletes[5] that had expressed solidarity with Pussy Riot[6] and Russian gays[7]? Why did they not protest in front of the Russian consulate and other places throughout the US in support of Griner? Of course, some efforts were made, such as the black-and-white, building-sized mural in Washington, DC featuring Griner and other political prisoners detained globally.[8] Pictures of the mural circulated in social media, for example on X, formerly known as Twitter, and the mainstream media.[9]

---

2   Jase Peeples, "PHOTOS: Go Inside Star-Studded L.A. Benefit for Pussy Riot," *OUT Traveler*, April 9, 2014, http://www.outtraveler.com/destination-guide/los-angeles/2014/04/09/photos-go-inside-star-studded-la-benefit-pussy-riot.

3   Marina Koreneva, "Madonna's Pink Ribbon Concert Draws Russia's Wrath," *Agence France-Presse*, August 9, 2012, A1.

4   Cari Romm, "NYC group running to support Russia's LGBT's community," *amNY*, February 17, 2014, http://www.amny.com/news/nyc-group-running-to-support-russia-s-lgbt-s-community-1.7110229; Queer Voices, "'Uprising of Love Hangouts on Air' Will Tackle Russian LGBT Issues Ahead of Sochi Olympics," *Huffington Post*, January 21, 2014, http://www.huffingtonpost.com/2014/01/21/uprising-of-love-hangouts-on-air-_n_4637286.html; Mark Gevisser, "Life Under Russia's 'Gay Propaganda' Ban," *New York Times*, December 27, 2013, https://www.nytimes.com/2013/12/28/opinion/life-under-russias-gay-propaganda-ban.html?searchResultPosition=5; Sally McGrane, "A Terrible Time to Be Gay in Russia," *New Yorker*, August 1, 2013, http://www.newyorker.com/culture/culture-desk/a-terrible-time-to-be-gay-in-russia; Betsy Isaacson, "Read the Heartbreaking Online Letters of Young, LGBT Russians," *Huffington Post*, February 24, 2014, http://www.huffingtonpost.com/2014/02/25/lgbt-russians_n_4823323.html; Carina Kolodny, "Here Are 9 Ways You Can Help Support LGBT Equality in Russia during the Sochi Olympics," *Huffington Post*, February 12, 2014, http://www.huffingtonpost.com/2014/02/12/sochi-olympics-lgbt_n_4762697.html.

5   Alison Wade, "Runners Show Support for LGBT Community in Russia," *Newswire*, February 20, 2014, http://www.runnersworld.com/newswire/runners-show-support-for-lgbt-community-in-russia; Owen Gibson and Shaun Walker, "Olympians urge Russia to reconsider 'gay propaganda' laws," *Guardian*, January 30, 2014, https://www.theguardian.com/sport/2014/jan/30/olympic-athletes-russia-repeal-anti-gay-laws; Justin Palmer, "Russia Must Explain Its Anti-Gay Law, Says International Olympics Committee," *Huffington Post*, August 9, 2013, updated February 2, 2016, https://www.huffpost.com/entry/russia-gay-olympics-committee_n_3730925.

6   Wiedlack, "Pussy Riot and the Western Gaze"; Nichols, "Front Runners New York Launches 'To Russia with Love'"; Mills, "Jailed Pussy Riot member ends hunger strike"; Harvey Morris, "We're All Pussy Riot Now."

7   Andy Greene, "Elton John Blasts Russia: 'Vicious Homophobia Has Been Legitimized'" *Rolling Stone*, January 22, 2014, http://www.rollingstone.com/music/news/elton-john-blasts-russia-vicious-homophobia-has-been-legitimized-20140122.

8   P. J. Morales, "Mural of Brittney Griner, other detained Americans unveiled in Georgetown," *Washington Post*, July 20, 2022, https://www.washingtonpost.com/sports/2022/07/20/brittney-griner-mural-washington/.

9   Ibid.

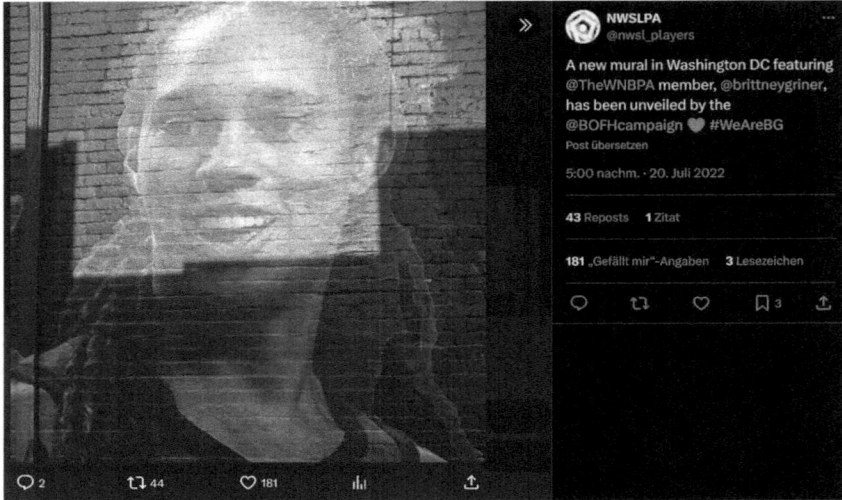

Figure 20. Screenshot of a post by WSLPA @nwsl_playersA, "A new mural in Washington DC featuring @TheWNBPA member, @brittneygriner, has been unveiled by the @BOFHcampaign 💜#WeAreBG," accessed December 12, 2024, https://x.com/nwsl_players/status/1549771181305106438/photo/4.

Even this kind of support paled in comparison with the outcry about Pussy Riot and Russian gays, however. Why did no one write a song about Griner[10] or dedicate an art exhibition to her? Eventually, Griner was released in a prisoner exchange, traded for a Russian prisoner in American custody in December 2022.[11] The deal that freed her was controversial because she was exchanged with a high-profile Russian arms dealer Viktor Bout.[12] Griner returned to the WNBA in June 2023.[13]

---

10   Several songs have been written about Pussy Riot, for example by the queer feminist band MEN: MEN, "Let Them Out or Let Me In," August 17, 2012, video, http://www.menmakemusic.com/.

11   Andres Triay et al., "Brittney Griner released by Russia in 1-for-1 prisoner swap for arms dealer Viktor Bout," CBS News, December 9, 2022, https://www.cbsnews.com/live-updates/brittney-griner-back-us-release-russia-prisoner-swap-viktor-bout/?linkId=192874405.

12   Michael D. Shear and Peter Baker, "Inside the Prisoner Swap That Freed Brittney Griner," *New York Times*, December 9, 2022, https://www.nytimes.com/2022/12/09/us/politics/brittney-griner-prisoner-swap.html.

13   Oren Weisfeld, "'She brings light': Brittney Griner's triumphant return to the WNBA," *Guardian*, June 28, 2023, https://www.theguardian.com/sport/2023/jun/28/she-brings-light-brittney-griners-triumphant-return-to-the-wnba.

I can only speculate about why Griner did not become the kind of queer feminist martyr that the feminist Tolokonnikova, the queer activist Gessen, and even Fedorov have become. Is it because she is Black? Because she is Queer? Was it because she pleaded guilty to having less than one gram of hashish oil? Within the contemporary political climate, it seems clear that the racist, particularly anti-Black, sexist, and homophobic Right would not support Griner. She embodies all the identities that are at stake in the current American culture wars.[14] Right-wing commentators responded to Griner's sentencing with "messages that praised Russia and Vladimir Putin for having these 'tough-on-drugs' laws (as if Griner's nine-year imprisonment doesn't have far more to do with hostage diplomacy and Russia's war on Ukraine than with a vape cartridge)."[15] Sports journalist Dave Zirin recounted that "the barrage of racism, sexism, and homophobia" in response to his call for solidarity with Griner "was more than [he had] received for any article in years of doing this work."[16] He believes that the American Left has seriously underestimated support for Russian politics on the political Right and that the celebration of Putin's "perceived masculinity, his anti-gay laws, and his control" are the loci of this support. Zirin thereby implicitly supports my argument that liberal media significantly contributed to creating "a cult of Putin"—a cult that is arguably not only attractive to the right wing, but, increasingly, to conservatives and liberals. Co-constructing Russian masculinity and queer inferiority, American and Russian media both support white patriarchy and heteronormativity at the juncture of national identity politics.

To return to the case of Brittney Griner, another reason why Americans did not support her in the way they supported Pussy Riot is that while the latter could be read as confirmation of Western, particularly American, superiority—because during the Obama presidency, pro-queer and pro-feminist stances became increasingly signified as American—Griner complicated the celebration of Americanness. Griner, along with other Black American athletes, had participated in awareness-raising of anti-Black racism by taking a knee during the national anthem, played at the beginning of every basketball game. Right-wing and conservative voices who opposed this form of protest argued that "she

---

14 Kiara Alfonseca, "Culture wars: How identity became the center of politics in America," ABC News, July 7, 2023, December 6, 2024, https://abcnews.go.com/US/culture-wars-identity-center-politics-america/story?id=100768380.

15 Dave Zirin, "The Response to Brittney Griner's Capture Is an Indictment of the Right and the 'Left,'" Nation, November 29, 2022, https://www.thenation.com/article/world/brittney-griner-russia-putin-right-left/.

16 Ibid.

hates 'America,' so she shouldn't count on 'America' to fight for her freedom."[17] While support for Tolokonnikova and the other Pussy Riot members allowed the US to appear to spearhead liberal progress, Griner challenged this self-image. Moreover, while Tolokonnikova and Co. can be seen as heroic damsels in distress who do not challenge the stereotypes of white beauty, the African American Griner's 6' 9" stature is hyper-visible, disrupting gender and sexual norms and expectations of whiteness.

According to the Zirin, the American Left was afraid to support Griner because it feared that doing so would mean they supported "US imperial and NATO imperial aims."[18] Others thought that by focusing on the cruelty of the Russian judicial and prison system, they would divert criticism away from the American prison-industrial complex, "giving prison conditions in the United States a pass."[19] I am not quite sure that I follow these arguments; criticizing Russian injustice neither automatically translates into support of US imperialism or NATO, nor does it legitimize the US justice and prison systems. These arguments seem to point, however, to widespread racist homophobia that does not deem Black nonnormative people worthy of solidarity actions or discourses. The contrast is all the more evident if we recall that the US media, groups, and individuals were happy to support Pussy Riot members Nadya Tolokonnikova and Masha Alyokhina, and their independent news platform Media Zona, which was, at least in the beginning, focused "on courts, law enforcement, and the prison system in Russia."[20] Political figures such as Mayor de Blasio, Chirlane McCray, and others were happy to discuss prison reform with Pussy Riot on a transnational basis.[21] One wonders why such transnational conversations were not forthcoming in regard to Griner's case.

---

17 Zirin, "The Response."
18 Ibid.
19 Ibid.
20 Molly Beauchemin, "Pussy Riot Launches MediaZona, an Independent News Service in Russia," *Pitchfork*, September 4, 2014, https://pitchfork.com/news/56568-pussy-riot-launches-mediazona-an-independent-news-service-in-russia/.
21 Jennifer Fermino and Corinne Lestch, "Pussy Riot meets with Mayor de Blasio, Chirlane McCray at City Hall to discuss prison reform," *New York Daily News*, February 8, 2014, http://www.nydailynews.com/news/politics/pussy-riot-meets-bill-de-blasio-chirlane-mccray-article-1.1606655.

Bibliography

Abrams, Jonathan, and Tania Ganguli. "Why Pros like Brittney Griner Choose Cannabis for Their Pain." *New York Times*, August 1, 2022. https://www.nytimes.com/2022/08/01/sports/basketball/brittney-griner-athletes-cannabis-marijuana.html.

Adams, Joanna. "Pussy Riot: Nadezhda Tolokonnikova's Husband Pyotr Verzilov Says Canadian Connection Puts Band at Risk." *Huffington Post*, 18 August 2012. http://www.huffingtonpost.ca/2012/08/18/pussy-riot-pyotr-verzilov-canada_n_1803475.html.

Adelman, Gary. *Retelling Dostoyevsky*. Lewisburg, PA: Bucknell University Press, 2001.

"Africans in Ukraine: Jessica's story—BBC Africa." March 1, 2022. Video. https://www.youtube.com/watch?v=ldBKmPsST6A&t=101s.

Agard, Chancellor. "Laverne Cox reacts to Trump lifting transgender student bathroom protections." *Entertainment Weekly*, February 23, 2017. http://ew.com/tv/2017/02/23/laverne-cox-gavin-grimm-transgender-student-bathroom-protections/.

Agerholm, Harriet. "Theresa May condemns Chechen persecution of gay men as 'utterly barbaric.'" *Independent*, May 10, 2017. www.independent.co.uk/news/world/europe/theresa-may-chechnya-gay-men-chechen-torture-detain-camps-barbaric-russia-region-a7728641.html.

Alekseev, Veniamin. "The Russian Idea: From Messianism to Pragmatism." *Russian Social Science Review* 56, no. 3 (2015): 2–17.

Alexander, Amy. "Today's Feminism: Too Much Marketing, Not Enough Reality." NPR, February 21, 2017. http://www.npr.org/sections/codeswitch/2017/02/21/515799019/today-s-feminism-too-much-marketing-not-enough-reality.

Alexander, Michelle. *The New Jim Crow: Mass Incarceration in the Age of Colorblindness*. New York: The New Press, 2010.

Alfonseca, Kiara. "Culture wars: How identity became the center of politics in America." ABC News, July 7, 2023. https://abcnews.go.com/US/culture-wars-identity-center-politics-america/story?id=100768380.

Allman, Tim. "Blind girl criticises Kremlin over US adoption laws." BBC, January 15, 2013. https://www.bbc.com/news/av/world-europe-21022222.

Anderson, Benedict. *Imagined Communities: Reflections on the Origins and Spread of Nationalism*, rev. ed. London: Verso, 1991.

Anderson, Bridget. *Doing the Dirty Work? The Global Politics of Domestic Labor*. London: Zed, 2000.

Anderson, John. "Rocks, Art, and Sex: The 'Culture Wars' Come to Russia?" *Journal of Church and State* 55, no. 2 (2013): 307–334. Https://doi:10.1093/jcs/css085.

"*Angry* Black HoeMo? I absolutely am." Angry Black HoeM, February 24, 2016. https://angryblackhoemo.com/2016/02/24/angry-black-hoeme-i-absolutely-am.

Anonymous members of Pussy Riot. "We wish Nadia and Masha well—but they're no longer part of Pussy Riot." *Guardian*, February 6, 2014. https://www.theguardian.com/commentisfree/2014/feb/06/nadia-masha-pussy-riot-collective-no-longer.

Antonopoulos, Georgios A. "Book Review: Russian Criminal Tattoo: Encyclopaedia Volume III: Danzig Baldaev, Sergei Vasiliev and Alexander Sidorov." *Crime, Media, Culture* 5, no. 2 (2009): 232–234.

Arayasirikul, Sean, Caitlin Turner, Dillon Trujillo, Sofia L. Sicro, Susan Scheer, Willi McFarland, and Erin C. Wilson. "A global cautionary tale: discrimination and violence against trans women worsen despite investments in public resources and improvements in health insurance access and utilization of health care." *International journal for equity in health* 21, no. 1 (2022), 32. https://doi:10.1186/s12939-022-01632-5.

Arianna. "Donald Trump Gives Speech about 'Survival' of Western Civilization during Poland Visit." The Organization for World Peace, July 15, 2017. https://theowp.org/donald-trump-gives-speech-about-survival-of-Western-civilization-during-poland-visit/.

Armitage, Susie. "Russian Women Unfurled a Feminist Banner on the Kremlin like It Was NBD." *BuzzFeed News*, March 8, 2017. https://www.buzzfeednews.com/article/susiearmitage/feminists-arrested-for-demonstrating-in-moscow-and-st-peters.

Arnold, Richard. "Systematic Racist Violence in Russia between 'Hate Crime' and 'Ethnic Conflict.'" *Theoretical Criminology* 19, no. 2 (2015): 239–56. https://doi:10.1177/1362480615581102.

Ashenden, Robin. "Putin's feminist crackdown won't crush the spirit of Russia's women." *Spectator*, April 9, 2023. https://www.spectator.co.uk/article/putins-feminist-crackdown-wont-crush-the-spirit-of-russias-women/.

"Vladimir Putin signs law banning gender changes in Russia." *Guardian*, July 24, 2023. https://www.theguardian.com/world/2023/jul/24/vladimir-putin-signs-law-banning-gender-changes-in-russia.

Atanasoski, Neda. *Humanitarian Violence: The U.S. Deployment of Diversity*. Minneapolis: University of Minnesota Press, 2013.

Bacardi, Francesca. "Jay Leno Compares Russian Olympics to Nazi Germany." *Variety*, December 17, 2013. http://variety.com/2013/tv/news/jay-leno-nazi-olympics-1200969781/.

Background to "Assessing Russian Activities and Intentions in Recent US Elections": The Analytic Process and Cyber Incident Attribution. Office of the Director of National Intelligence, January 6, 2017. Baer, Brian James. "Now You See It: Gay (In)Visibility and the Performance of Post-Soviet Identity." In *Queer Visibility in Post-Socialist Cultures*, edited by Narcisz Fejes and Andrea P. Balogh, 35–55. Bristol: Intellect 2013.

Baer, Brian James. "Russian Gays/Western Gaze: Mapping (Homo)Sexual Desire in Post-Soviet Russia." *GLQ: A Journal of Lesbian and Gay Studies* 8, no. 4 (2002): 499–521.

Baer, Brian James. *Other Russias: Homosexuality and the Crisis of Post-Soviet Identity*. New York: Palgrave Macmillan, 2009.

Bal, Mieke. *Reading "Rembrandt": Beyond the Word-Image Opposition*. Cambridge: Cambridge University Press, 1991.

Baldwin, Kate A. *Beyond the Color Line and the Iron Curtain: Reading Encounters between Black and Red, 1922–1963*. Durham, NC: Duke University Press, 2002.

Barragán, Paco. "Voina: A Russian Revolution." *Art Plus*, 2012. http://artpulsemagazine.com/voina-a-russian-revolution.

Barros, Aline. "Comparing Immigration Raids under Trump, Obama." Voice of America, February 16, 2017. https://www.voanews.com/a/comparing-immigration-raids-under-trump-and-obama/3727706.html.

Barsotti, Natasha. "Amnesty International calls for arrests in St Petersburg." *Daily XTra*, November 5, 2013. Page now unavailable. http://www.dailyxtra.com/world/news-and-ideas/news/amnesty-international-calls-arrests-in-st-petersburg-73038.

Barton, Laura. "Pussy Riot's Kremlin protest owes much to riot grrrl." *Guardian*, February 3, 2012. https://www.theguardian.com/commentisfree/2012/feb/03/pussy-riot-kremlin-protest-riot-grrrl.

Basulto, Dominic. "What the Media Gets Dangerously Wrong about the Trump-Putin Narrative." *Medium*, December 18, 2016. https://medium.com/@dominicbasulto/what-the-media-gets-dangerously-wrong-about-the-trump-putin-narrative-45771aa5f9e4#.s2ciclp8b.

Beauchamp, Zack. "Russia has weaponized the American press." *Vox*, October 17, 2016. http://www.vox.com/world/2016/10/17/13245200/russia-wikileaks-american-press-democracy.

Beauchemin, Molly. "Pussy Riot Launches MediaZona, an Independent News Service in Russia." *Pitchfork*, September 4, 2014. https://pitchfork.com/news/56568-pussy-riot-launches-mediazona-an-independent-news-service-in-russia.

Beck, Koa. *White Feminism: From the Suffragettes to Influencers and Who They Leave Behind*. New York: Atria Books, 2021.

Beckerman, Gal. "Masha Gessen Resigns in Protest from PEN America Board." *Atlantic*, May 16, 2023. https://www.theatlantic.com/books/archive/2023/05/what-happens-when-the-free-speech-absolutists-flinch/674069.

Bendix, Trish. "'Shameless' delves into polyamory with Svetlana becoming V and Kevin's third." AfterEllen, March 29, 2016. https://afterellen.com/shameless-delves-polyamory-svetlana-becoming-v-kevins-third/#wKjEUkiKxMuMvuBa.99.

Berezkin, Aleksander. "Breaking the ice: the intersex movement in Russia." Intersex Day Project, November 7, 2016. http://intersexday.org/en/breaking-ice-intersex-berezkin.

Berger, Stefan and Alexei Miller. *Nationalizing Empires*. Budapest: Central European University Press, 2015.

Berman, Russell. "A Trump-Inspired Hate Crime in Boston." *Atlantic*, August 20, 2015. https://www.theatlantic.com/politics/archive/2015/08/a-trump-inspired-hate-crime-in-boston/401906.

Bernstein, Anya. "An Inadvertent Sacrifice: Body Politics and Sovereign Power in the Pussy Riot Affair." *Critical Inquiry* 40, no. 1 (2013): 220–41. https://doi:10.1086/673233.

Bernstein, Basil. *The structure of pedagogic discourse. Class, codes and control*. London: Routledge, 1990.

Bessonov, Ania. "Russian ethnic minorities bearing brunt of Russia's war mobilization in Ukraine." CBC News, October 5, 2022. https://www.cbc.ca/news/world/russia-mobilization-ethnic-minorities-buryat-1.6605501.

Binnie, John. *The Globalization of Sexuality*. London: Sage, 2004.

Binnie, John, and Christian Klesse. "The Politics of Age, Temporality and Intergenerationality in Transnational Lesbian, Gay, Bisexual, Transgender and Queer Activist Networks." *Sociology* 47, no. 3 (2013): 580–595.

Boatcă, Manuela. *Global Inequalities Beyond Occidentalism*. London: Routledge, 2016.

Boot, Max. "Donald Trump: A Modern Manchurian Candidate?" *New York Times*, January 11, 2017.

Borenstein, Eliot. *Overkill: Sex Violence, and Russian Popular Culture after 1991*. Ithaca, NY: Cornell University Press, 2008.

Borenstein, Eliot. *Pussy Riot: Speaking Punk to Power*. London: Bloomsbury, 2020.

Boutsko, Anastassia. "Eurovision: Tajik singer polarizes Russia." *DW*, May 19, 2021. https://www.dw.com/en/eurovision-manizha-from-tajikistan-polarizes-russia/a-57577536.

Brady, Diane. "Pussy Riot's Nadya on Putin and Being on Russia's Most Wanted List." *Forbes*, May 19, 2023. https://www.forbes.com/sites/dianebrady/2023/05/19/pussy-riots-nadya-tolokonnikova-on-punk-putin-and-being-on-russias-most-wanted-list/?sh=4f21bdbf1109.

Braidotti, Rosi. "On Becoming European." In *Women Migrants from East to West: Gender, Mobility and Belonging in Contemporary Europe*, edited by Luisa Passerini, Enrica Capusotti, Dawn Lyon, and Ioanna Laliotou, 32–44. New York: Berghahn, 2007.

Bramham, Daphne. "Toothless International Olympic Committee ensures that Russia can get away with anti-gay law." *Windsor Star*, August 2, 2013. http://www.windsorstar.com/opinion/columnists/Toothless%2BInternational%2BOlympic%2BCommittee%2Bensures%2Bthat/8744020/story.html. Page now unavailable.

Braun, Lundy. *Breathing Race into the Machine: The Surprising Career of the Spirometer from Plantation to Genetics*. Minneapolis: University of Minnesota Press, 2014.

"British government calls abuse of gay men in Chechnya 'utterly barbaric.'" *Pink News*, April 20, 2017. www.pinknews.co.uk/2017/04/20/british-government-calls-abuse-of-gay-men-chechnya-utterly-barbaric.

Bronnikov, Arkady. "Decoding Russian criminal tattoos—in pictures." *Guardian*, September 18, 2014. https://www.theguardian.com/artanddesign/gallery/2014/sep/18/decoding-russian-criminal-tattoos-in-pictures.

Brook, Tom. "Hollywood stereotypes: Why are Russians the bad guys?" BBC, November 5, 2014. http://www.bbc.com/culture/story/20141106-why-are-russians-always-bad-guys.

Bruner, Raisa. "Exclusive: How Pussy Riot's Nadya Tolokonnikova Is Using Crypto to Fight for Equality." *Time*, March 3, 2022. https://time.com/6154118/pussy-riot-unicorn-dao-nadya.

Brzezinski, Zbigniew. *Strategic Vision: America and the Crisis of Global Power*. New York: Basic Books, 2012.

Bubola, Emma. "Putin Signs Law Banning Expressions of L.G.B.T.Q. Identity in Russia." *New York Times*, December 5, 2022. https://www.nytimes.com/2022/12/05/

world/europe/russia-ban-lgbtq-propaganda.html?smid=nytcore-ios-share&referr ingSource=articleShare.

Buck-Morss, Susan. "Aesthetics and Anaesthetics: Walter Benjamin's Artwork Essay Reconsidered." *October* 62 (1992): 3–41.

Burke, Dave. "Chechnya 'is attempting to eliminate its gay community by the start of the Muslim holy month of Ramadan.'" *Daily Mail*, April 25, 2017. www.dailymail. co.uk/news/article-4443890/Chechnya-attempting-eliminate-gay-community. html#ixzz4fkdAsMaP.

"Buryats in Bucha: The Biggest Myth of the War." Buryats against War, April 28, 2022. https://www.freeburyatia.org/project/buryaty-v-butche/?lang=en.

Buryat Democratic Movement Erkheten. "The Pope Blames Our People for Russia's Crimes." *Wallstreet Journal*, December 10, 2022. https://www.wsj.com/articles/ pope-francis-russia-putin-ukraine-war-crimes-buryat-11670535297.

Butler, Judith. *Precarious Life: The Powers of Mourning and Violence.* London: Verso, 2006.

Caldwell, Alicia A. "Trump wants to build 30-foot-high wall at Mexican border." *Associated Press*, March 18, 2017. https://apnews.com/article/4453616f041f4ebaa4912 8bd6f390f1c.

Carpenter, Zoë. "What's Killing America's Black Infants?" *Nation*, March 6, 2017. https://www.thenation.com/article/archive/whats-killing-americas-black-infants/.

Carré, John le. *Our Kind of Traitor.* New York: Viking Press, 2010.

Carrey, Jim. "Jim Carrey meets the Pussy Riot." Jim Carrey Online, April 9, 2014. http:// jimcarreyonline.com/forum/viewtopic.php?f=6&t=12284.

Carrigan, Tim, Bob Connell, and John Lee. "Toward a new sociology of masculinity." In *The Making of Masculinities: the New Men's Studies*, edited by Harry Brod, 63–100. Winchester, VA: Allen and Unwin, 1987.

Cathey, Boyd D. "Russia-West Divide Boils Down to the Gay Issue: Conservative Russia, Post-Modern West." Russia Insider, January 5, 2015. https://russia-insider. com/en/2015/01/05/2226. Page now unavailable.

Caute, David. *The Dancer Defects: The struggle for cultural supremacy during the Cold War.* Oxford: Oxford University Press, 2003.

Chan, Julia B. "Capturing the rage and resilience of Russian homophobia" *Reveal*, September 30, 2016. https://revealnews.org/article/capturing-the-rage-and-resil-ience-of-russian-homophobia.

Charles, Cody. "Reclaim Anger: I am the Rage Baldwin Speaks of." *Medium*, February 28, 2017. https://medium.com/reclaiming-anger/black-joy-we-deserve-it-1ab8dc7569b1#.rj81nx7ud.

Chatterjee, Choi. "The Russian Romance in American Popular Culture, 1890–1939." In *Americans Experience Russia: Encountering the Enigma, 1917 to the Present*, edited by Choi Chatterjee and Beth Holmgren, 87–104. New York: Routledge, 2013.

Chatterjee, Choi, and Beth Holmgren, eds. *Americans Experience Russia: Encountering the Enigma, 1917 to the Present.* New York: Routledge. 2013.

"Chechnya anti-gay violence: Newspaper fears 'retribution' for reports." BBC News, April 14, 2017. www.bbc.com/news/world-europe-39600124.

Child, Ben. "Moscow may ban anti-Russian films from cinemas in new censorship threat." *Guardian*, August 27, 2014. https://www.theguardian.com/film/2014/aug/27/russia-ban-anti-russian-movies.

Chotiner, Isaac. "Donald and Vlad: Compare and Contrast." *Slate*, February 27, 2017. https://slate.com/news-and-politics/2017/02/how-trump-and-putin-are-similar-and-different-according-to-masha-gessen-and-what-it-means-for-americans.html.

Chotiner, Isaac. "Why Masha Gessen resigned from the PEN America board." *New Yorker*, May 24, 2023. https://www.newyorker.com/news/q-and-a/why-masha-gessen-resigned-from-the-pen-america-board.

Chumakov, Egor M., Yulia V. Ashenbrenner, Nataliia N. Petrova, Michael S. Zastrozhin, Larisa A. Azarova, and Oleg V. Limankin. "Anxiety and Depression among Transgender People: Findings from a Cross-Sectional Online Survey in Russia." *LGBT health* 8, no. 6 (2021): 412–419. https://doi:10.1089/lgbt.2020.0464.

Cohen, Rebecca, and Natalie Musumeci. "Putin says Russia must undergo a 'self-cleansing of society' to purge 'bastards and traitors' as thousands flee the country." *Business Insider*, March 16, 2022. https://www.businessinsider.com/putin-says-russia-must-undergo-self-cleansing-society-2022-3.

Connell, Raewyn W. *Gender and Power: Society, the Person and Sexual Politics*. Cambridge: Polity Press, 1987.

Connell, Raewyn W. *Masculinities*. St. Leonards, MD: Allen and Unwin, 1995.

Connell, Raewyn W. *The Men and the Boys*. St. Leonards, MD: Allen and Unwin, 2000.

Corbett, Sara. "Enemies of the State." *Vogue*, June 30, 2014. http://www.vogue.com/magazine/article/pussy-riot-members-start-new-organization-zona-prava/#1. Page now unavailable.

Corredor, Elizabeth S. "Unpacking 'Gender Ideology' and the Global Right's Antigender Countermovement." *Signs* 44, no. 3 (2019): 613–38. https://doi:10.1086/701171.

Courtois, Stéphane, Nicolas Werth, Jean-Louis Panné, Andrzej Paczkowksi, Karel Bartosek, and Jean-Louis Margolin. *The black book of communism: crimes, terror, repression*. Cambridge, MA: Harvard University Press, 1999.

Craven, Julia. "More Than 250 Black People Were Killed by Police in 2016." *Huffington Post*, July 7, 2016. https://www.huffpost.com/entry/black-people-killed-by-police-america_n_577da633e4b0c590f7e7fb17.

Crawford, Tiffany, and Brian Morton. "Vancouver bars boycott Russian vodka after anti-gay law passed." *Vancouver Sun*, June 27, 2013. http://www.vancouversun.com/life/Anti%2BRussia%2Bprompts%2BVancouver%2Bbars%2Bstop%2Bserving%2BRussian%2Bvodka/8713709/story.html. Page now unavailable.

Crenshaw, Kimberley. "Demarginalizing the Intersection of Race and Sex: A Black Feminist Critique of Antidiscrimination Doctrine, Feminist Theory and Antiracist Politics." University of Chicago Legal Forum (1989): 138–167.

Crispin, Jessa. "The Failures of Mainstream Feminism." *New Republic*, February 13, 2017. https://newrepublic.com/article/140248/failures-mainstream-feminismmisogyny-doom-hillary-clinton.

Cruz, Ronald Allan Lopez. "Mutations and Metamorphoses: Body Horror Is Biological Horror." *Journal of Popular Film & Television* 40, no. 4 (2012): 160–168.

"The Cult of Putin." CNN, December 25, 2015. http://www.cnn.com/2012/03/02/europe/gallery/cult-of-vladimir-putin/.

Dartford, Katy. "Russian Eurovision star fights back after tour cancelled over opposition to Ukraine war." *EuroNews*, March 7, 2023. https://www.euronews.com/culture/2023/03/07/russian-eurovision-star-fights-back-after-tour-cancelled-over-opposition-to-ukraine-war.

Dashieva, Anna. "Samotsenzura ili pochemu my stesniaemsia govorit' o rasizme" [Self-censorship or why we shy away from talking about racism]. In *Kvir' Sibir': bez_opasnost' i zabota o sebe* [Queer Siberia: un_safety and self-care], 22–27. Novosibirsk, 2020. https://www.academia.edu/44546783/Квирь_Сибирь_без_опасность_и_забота_о_себе.

Davenne, Julien. "Homophobia in Russia." January 21, 2016. Video. https://vimeo.com/152622170.

Davydova, Darja. "Between Heteropatriarchy and Homonationalism: Codes of Gender, Sexuality, and Race/Ethnicity in Putin's Russia." PhD diss., York University, 2019.

Day, Michael. "As Putin mulls a Ukraine attack, experts paint scary psychological picture of what makes Russia's tyrant tick." *i-News*, January 26, 2022. https://inews.co.uk/news/world/russia-ukraine-vladimir-putin-attack-psychological-picture-what-make-tick-1424732.

Deakin, Pete. *White Masculinity in Crisis in Hollywood's fin de Millennium Cinema.* London: Lexington Books, 2019.

Dean, Robert D. *Imperial Brotherhood: Gender and the Making of Cold War Foreign Policy.* Amherst, MA: University of Massachusetts Press, 2001.

Deltcheva, Roumiana "Eastern Women in Western Chronotypes: Representation of East European Women in Western Film after 1989." In *Vampirettes, Wretches and Amazons: Western Representations of East European Women*, edited by Valentina Glajar and Domnica Radulescu, 161–185. New York: Columbia University Press, 2004.

Demillo, Andrew. "Here are the restrictions on transgender people that are moving forward in US statehouses." *Associated Press*, May 19, 2023. https://apnews.com/article/restrictions-targeting-transgender-people-legislative-updates-df66b5a86be47b03dd5a50449d239275.

Diamond, Jeremy. "Timeline: Donald Trump's praise for Vladimir Putin." CNN. July 29, 2016. http://www.cnn.com/2016/07/28/politics/donald-trump-vladimir-putin-quotes.

Die 12 Opossums. "Gekommen, um zu bleiben! Und das Lied/Leid der Solidarität." *Migrazine: online Magazin von Migrantinnen für alle* 1 (2016). http://migrazine.at/artikel/gekommen-um-zu-bleiben-und-das-liedleid-der-solidarit-t.

Diehl, Jessica. "Caitlyn Jenner: The Full Story." *Vanity Fair*, June 25, 2015. https://www.vanityfair.com/hollywood/2015/06/caitlyn-jenner-bruce-cover-annie-leibovitz.

"Dmitry Chizhevsky: 'I Feel Really Sorry for the Stupid Guys Who Did This to Me.'" *The Russian Reader*, November 9, 2013. https://therussianreader.com/2013/11/09/dmitry-chizhevsky.

Donaldson, Mike. "What is hegemonic masculinity?" *Theory and Society* 22 (1993): 643–657.

Dovere, Edward-Isaac. "Obama: 'No patience' for Russia's anti-gay laws." *Politico*, August 6, 2013. http://www.politico.com/story/2013/08/barack-obama-russia-anti-gay-laws-095266.

Dunlap, Aron, and Joshua Delpech-Ramey. "Grotesque Normals: Cronenberg's Recent Men and Women." *Discourse* 32, no. 3 (2010): 321–337.

Dutkiewicz, Piotr. "Missing in Translation: Re-Conceptualizing Russia's Developmental State." In *Russia: Challenges of Transformation*, edited by Piotr Dutkiewicz and Dmitri Trenin, 9–40. New York: NYU Press, 2011.

"Eastern Promises." Box Office Mojo, November 4, 2007. http://www.boxofficemojo.com/movies/?id=easternpromises.htm.

Edelman, Lee. *No Future: Queer Theory and the Death Drive*. Durham, NC: Duke University Press, 2004.

Edelstein, David. "Post-Traumatic Mystery." *New York Times*, September 17, 2007.

Edenborg, Emil. "Homophobia as Geopolitics: 'Traditional Values' and the Negotiation of Russia's Place in the World." In *Gendering Nationalism: Intersections of Nation, Gender and Sexuality*, edited by Jon Mulholland, Erin Sanders-McDonagh, and Nicola Montagna, 67–87. Cham: Palgrave Macmillan, 2018. https://doi.org/10.1007/978-3-319-76699-7.

Edenborg, Emil. "Putin's Anti-Gay War on Ukraine." *Boston Review*, March 14, 2022. https://www.bostonreview.net/articles/putins-anti-gay-war-on-ukraine/.

"Exclusive: Pope Francis discusses Ukraine, U.S. bishops and more." *America: The Jesuit Review*, November 28, 2022. https://www.americamagazine.org/faith/2022/11/28/pope-francis-interview-america-244225.

"Exile or repression: Russian opposition members face tough choice." *Malaymail*, May 7, 2015. https://www.malaymail.com/news/life/2015/05/07/exile-or-repression-russian-opposition-members-face-tough-choice/891951.

Ehrman, John. "Intelligence in Public Literature." Review of *Mr. Putin: Operative in the Kremlin*, by Fiona Hill and Clifford Gaddy. *Studies in Intelligence* 57, no. 4 (2013). https://www.cia.gov/resources/csi/static/Mr-Putin.pdf.

Elder, Miriam. "Pussy Riot Trial: Closing Statement Denounces Putin's Totalitarian System." *Guardian*, August 8, 2012, http://www.theguardian.com/music/2012/aug/08/pussy-riot-trial-closing-statement.

Elgot, Jessica. "Pussy Riot's Nadezhda Tolokonnikova Describes Depravity of 'Stalinist' Work Camp." *Huffington Post*, September 23, 2013. https://www.huffingtonpost.co.uk/2013/09/23/pussy-riot-work-camp_n_3975953.html.

Essig, Laurie. *Queer in Russia: A Story of Sex, Self, and the Other*. Durham, NC: Duke University Press, 1999.

Etkind, Alexander. *Internal Colonization: Russia's Imperial Experience*. Cambridge: Polity Press, 2011.

Falk, Richard. "The Confused Russian Hacking Debate, Trump Victory, and U.S. Global State." *Foreign Policy Journal*, December 20, 2016. http://www.foreignpolicyjournal.com/2016/12/20/the-confused-russian-hacking-debate-trump-victory-and-u-s-global-state.

Farbar, Kateryna. "Trans people are caught in the war in Ukraine." Open Democracy, February 8, 2023. https://www.opendemocracy.net/en/odr/ukraine-trans-people-war-lgbt-gender-identity-documents-hormones-zelenskyy-eu.

Fateman, Joanna. "Pussy Riot Realness." *Art in America*, February 27, 2015. https://www.artnews.com/art-in-america/features/pussy-riot-realness-63065/. Page now unavailable.

Feder, J. Lester. "How Russia's War against Ukraine Is Advancing LGBTQ Rights." *Politico*, July 3, 2023. https://www.politico.com/news/magazine/2023/03/07/russias-war-ukraine-advancing-lgbtq-rights-00085841.

"Feminism in Russia: From Soviet Samizdat to Online Activism." Wilson Center, November 2, 2020. https://www.wilsoncenter.org/event/feminism-russia-soviet-samizdat-online-activism.

Ferguson, Roderick, and Grace Hong. *Strange Affinities: The Gender and Sexual Politics of Comparative Racialization*. Durham, NC: Duke University Press, 2011.

Fermino, Jennifer, and Corinne Lestch. "Pussy Riot meets with Mayor de Blasio, Chirlane McCray at City Hall to discuss prison reform." *New York Daily News*, February 8, 2014. http://www.nydailynews.com/news/politics/pussy-riot-meets-bill-de-blasio-chirlane-mccray-article-1.1606655. Page now unavailable.

Ferris-Rotman, Amie. "Putin's War on Women: Why #MeToo skipped Russia." *Foreign Policy*, April 9, 2018. https://foreignpolicy.com/2018/04/09/putins-war-on-women/.

Field, Douglas. "Passing as a Cold War Novel: Anxiety and Assimilation in James Baldwin's Giovanni's Room." In *American Cold War Culture*, edited by Douglas Field, 88–108. Edinburgh: Edinburgh University Press, 2005.

Fikenauer, James O., and Elin J. Waring. *Russian Mafia in America: Immigration Culture and Crime*. Boston, MA: Northeastern University Press, 1998.

Fineman, Martha Albertson. "The vulnerable subject: Anchoring equality in the human condition." *Yale Journal of Law and Feminism* 1, no. 20 (2008): 1–23.

Fisher, Max. "Putin's Case for War, Annotated." *New York Times*, February 24, 2022. https://www.nytimes.com/2022/02/24/world/europe/putin-ukraine-speech.html.

Fitzgerald, Nora, and Vladimir Ruvinsky. "The Fear of Being Gay in Russia: Putin's state has allowed violence against the Russian LGBT community to spike." *Politico*, March 22, 2015. http://www.politico.com/magazine/story/2015/03/russia-putin-lgbt-violence-116202#ixzz3phdIzSE7.

Flurry, Gerald. "How can leaderless Europe survive in a world of strong men?" *Philadelphia Trumpet*. May–June 2015.

Foer, Franklin. "Vladimir Putin Has a Plan for Destroying the West, and It Looks a Lot like Donald Trump." *Slate*, July 4, 2016. http://www.slate.com/articles/news_and_politics/cover_story/2016/07/vladimir_putin_has_a_plan_for_destroying_the_west_and_it_looks_a_lot_like.html.

Foner, Nancy. *From Ellis Island to JFK: New York's Two Great Waves of Immigration*. New Haven, CT: Yale University Press, 2000.

Foran, Clare. "Donald Trump and the Rise of Anti-Muslim Violence: Research suggests that extreme political rhetoric can contribute to a spike in hate crimes." *Atlantic*, September 22, 2016. https://www.theatlantic.com/politics/archive/2016/09/trump-muslims-islamophobia-hate-crime/500840/.

Fousek, John. *To Lead the Free World: American Nationalism and the Cultural Roots of the Cold War*. Chapel Hill: University of North Carolina Press, 2000.

Fox, Pamela. "Who Is Shameless This Election Season? One TV show's Challenging Depiction of the Working Poor." Working-Class Perspectives, September 26, 2016.. https://workingclassstudies.wordpress.com/2016/09/26/who-is-shameless-this-election-season-one-TV shows-challenging-depiction-of-the-working-poor/. Page now unavailable.

Foxall, Andrew. "Photographing Vladimir Putin: Masculinity, Nationalism and Visuality in Russian Political Culture." *Geopolitics* 18, no. 1 (2013): 132–156.

Frank, A. "The Autumn of Western Civilization." Today in Politics. February 21, 2017. https://tipolitics.com/the-autumn-of-Western-civilization-5c695fc980f1. Page now unavailable.

Freeland, Cynthia. "Tragedy and Terrible Beauty in a History of Violence and Eastern Promises." In *The Philosophy of David Cronenberg*, edited by Simon Riches, 24–35. Lexington: University Press of Kentucky, 2012.

French, Jasmine. "Pussy Power: Feminism, Protest and the Remasculinisation of Putin's Russia." *Canadian-American Slavic Studies* 56, no. 2 (May 10, 2022): 127–51. https://doi:10.30965/22102396-05602005.

Friedman, Thomas L. "Pussy Riot, Tupac and Putin." *New York Times*, December 19, 2012.

Fung, Katherine. "The Complicated Future of Ukrainian Refugees in the U.S." *Newsweek*, April 4, 2023. https://www.newsweek.com/2023/04/14/complicated-future-ukrainian-refugees-us-1792294.html.

Gajanan, Mahita. "Pussy Riot's Nadya Tolokonnikova on Resisting President Trump: 'We Have a Ton of Work to Do.'" *Time*, February 21, 2017.https://time.com/4671189/pussy-riot-nadya-tolokonnikova-donald-trump-resistance.

Gapova, Elena. "Becoming Visible in the Digital Age." *Feminist Media Studies* 15, no. 1 (2014): 18–35. https://doi:10.1080/14680777.2015.988390.

Garcia, Michelle. "At least 100 gay men in Chechnya have been abducted by police." *Vox*, April 18, 2017. www.vox.com/identities/2017/4/18/15326500/gay-men-chechnya-violence-homophobia-antigay-torture.

Geiling, Natasha. "The Myth of Liberal Ivanka Trump." Think Progress, May 22, 2017. https://archive.thinkprogress.org/liberal-myth-of-ivanka-trump-68195b8039cc/.

Gentleman, Amelia. "Nadya Tolokonnikova: 'I suppose we have nothing more to lose.'" *Guardian*, September 19, 2014. https://www.theguardian.com/theguardian/2014/sep/19/nadya-tolokonnikova-pussy-riot-interview-nothing-to-lose.

Gerbner, George. "The Image of Russians in American Media and the 'New Epoch.'" In *Beyond the Cold War: Soviet and American Media Images*, edited by Everette E. Dennis, George Gerbner, and Yassen N. Zassoursky, 31–35. London: Sage Publications, 1991.

Gessen, Masha. "Dead Soul." *Vanity Fair*, October 1, 2008.

Gessen, Masha. "The Gay Men Who Fled Chechnya's Purge." *New Yorker*, July 3, 2017. www.newyorker.com/magazine/2017/07/03/the-gay-men-who-fled-chechnyas-purge.

Gessen, Masha. "Time to Panic: It's like the Early Days of AIDS All over Again." *Out Magazine*, December 14, 2016. https://www.out.com/news-opinion/2016/12/14/time-panic-its-early-days-aids-all-over-again.

Gessen, Masha. "When Putin Declared War on Gay Families, It Was Time for Mine to Leave Russia." *Slate*, August 26, 2013. https://slate.com/human-interest/2013/08/when-putin-declared-war-on-gay-families-it-was-time-for-mine-to-leave-russia.html.

Gessen, Masha. *The Man without a Face: The Unlikely Rise of Vladimir Putin*. New York: Riverhead Books, 2012.

Gessen, Masha. *Words will break cement: the passion of Pussy Riot*. London: Granta. 2014.

Gettys, Travis. "Keith Olbermann: Trump wants to mimic Putin and turn White House press briefings into chaotic circus." *Rawstory*, January 19, 2017. http://www.rawstory.com/2017/01/keith-olbermann-trump-wants-to-mimic-putin-and-turn-white-house-press-briefings-into-chaotic-circus.

Gevisser, Mark. "Life under Russia's 'Gay Propaganda' Ban." *New York Times*, December 27, 2013. https://www.nytimes.com/2013/12/28/opinion/life-under-russias-gay-propaganda-ban.html?searchResultPosition=5.

Ghosh, Bobby. "An Unarmed Putin Wants a Culture War with the West." Bloomberg, September 14, 2022. https://www.bloomberg.com/opinion/articles/2022-09-14/an-unarmed-putin-wants-to-fight-a-culture-war-with-the-west#xj4y7vzkg.

Gibson, Owen, and Shaun Walker. "Olympians urge Russia to reconsider 'gay propaganda' laws." *Guardian*, January 30, 2014. https://www.theguardian.com/sport/2014/jan/30/olympic-athletes-russia-repeal-anti-gay-laws.

Gladkov, Fedor. *Cement*. Translated by A. S. Arthur and C. Ashleigh. Evanston, IL: Northwestern University Press, 1980. Originally published as *Tsement* (Leningrad: Zemlia i fabrika, 1926).

Gladstone, Rick. "Pussy Riot Members Take Tour to New York." *New York Times*, February 6, 2014. https://www.nytimes.com/2014/02/06/world/europe/pussy-riot-members-say-prison-emboldened-them.html.

Glajar, Valentina, and Domnica Radulescu. Introduction to *Vampirettes, Wretches and Amazones: Western Representations of East European Women*, edited by Valentina Glajar, and Domnica Radulescu, 1–11. New York: Columbia University Press, 2004.

Glissant, Édouard. *Caribbean Discourse: Selected Essays*. Charlottesville: University Press of Virginia, 1989.

Gold, Michael. "Russian paratroopers attack gay rights activist during one-man protest." *Baltimore Sun*, August 2, 2013. Page now unavailable. http://darkroom.baltimoresun.com/2013/08/russian-paratroopers-attack-gay-rights-activist/#2.

Goldberg, Jeffrey. "It's Official: Hillary Clinton Is Running against Vladimir Putin." *Atlantic*, July 21, 2016. https://www.theatlantic.com/international/archive/2016/07/clinton-trump-putin-nato/492332/.

Golgowski, Nina. "Pussy Riot Founder Says More Russians Are against Putin's War Than We've Seen." *Huffington Post*, March 6, 2022. https://www.huffpost.com/entry/pussy-riot-nadya-tolokonnikova-russians-oppose-putin-war_n_622513d6e4b012a2628c4b47.

"Ikona: Chetyre LGBT Rossiiane." [Icon: Four LGBT Russians.] *Goluboi Ikonostas Eastern Orthodox Style Iconography*, March 20, 2014. http://goluboy-ikonostas.tumblr.com/post/80220089822/icon-four-lgbt-russians-икона-четыре-лгбт.

Goluboi Ikonostas [The Blue Iconostasis]. "Kirill Fёdorov—One of the Pride Marchers of St. Petersburg." Goluboi Ikonostas Modern Eastern Orthodox Style Iconography, July 6, 2014. http://goluboy-ikonostas.tumblr.com/post/91003436038/kirill-f%C3%ABdorov-one-of-the-pride-marchers-of-st.

Gorodnichenko, Yuriy, and Ilona Sologoub. "The Ukraine-Russia Culture War." Project Syndicate, June 7, 2023. https://www.project-syndicate.org/commentary/ukraine-russia-culture-war-gessen-pen-resignation-by-yuriy-gorodnichenko-and-ilona-sologoub-2023-06.

Goscilo, Helena. "Russia's Ultimate Celebrity: VVP as VIP Objet d'Art." In *Putin as Celebrity and Cultural Icon*, edited by Helena Goscilo, 6–36. London: Routledge, 2013.

Gould, Deborah B. *Moving Politics: Emotion and ACT UP's Fight against AIDS*. Chicago, IL: University of Chicago Press, 2009.

Graham, Thomas. "Was the Collapse of US-Russia Relations Inevitable?" *Nation*, August 22, 2023. https://www.thenation.com/article/archive/us-russia-putin-relations-nato.

Gray, Carmen. "Film news. Cut and Wrapped this week: the Pussy Riot doc, new Michael Douglas and a Herzog classic." *Dazed*, June 7, 2013. https://www.dazeddigital.com/artsandculture/article/16272/1/film-news.

Greatrick, Aydan, Tyler Valiquette, and Yvonne Su. "Other frontlines: How the war in Ukraine is transforming the LGBTQ+ rights landscape in Europe." *Conversation*, May 10, 2022. https://theconversation.com/other-frontlines-how-the-war-in-ukraine-is-transforming-the-lgbtq-rights-landscape-in-europe-182209.

Greenberg, Jon. "Fact Check: Putin Says Russians Face 'genocide' in Ukraine." *WRAL*, February 28, 2022. https://www.wral.com/fact-check-putin-says-russians-face-genocide-in-ukraine/20163715.

Greene, Andy. "Elton John Blasts Russia: 'Vicious Homophobia Has Been Legitimized.'" *Rolling Stone*, January 22, 2014. http://www.rollingstone.com/music/news/elton-john-blasts-russia-vicious-homophobia-has-been-legitimized-20140122.

Greenfield, Liah. *Nationalism: Five Roads to Modernity*. Cambridge, MA: Harvard University Press, 1992.

Greenfield, Rebecca. "Patrisse Cullors, Alicia Garza, and Opal Tometi, Activists against Racial Injustice." Bloomberg, December 3, 2020. https://www.bloomberg.com/news/features/2020-12-03/blm-activists-patrisse-cullors-alicia-garza-and-opal-tometi-bloomberg-50-2020#xj4y7vzkg.

Greenwood, Shannon. "Uganda on Their Anti-Gay Legislation: It Was All for the Children." Think Progress, July 7, 2014. https://thinkprogress.org/uganda-on-their-anti-gay-legislation-it-was-all-for-the-children-ec5a27313daa.

Griffin, Elizabeth. "Here's Donald Trump and Vladimir Putin Kissing." *Esquire*. May 15, 2016. http://www.esquire.com/news-politics/news/a44886/political-street-art/.

Grow, Kory. "Pussy Riot's Nadya Tolokonnikova Added to Russia's Most Wanted Criminals List." *Rolling Stone*, March 29, 2023. https://www.rollingstone.com/music/music-news/pussy-riot-nadya-tolokonnikova-russia-most-wanted-criminals-1234705647.

Gržinić, Marina, Tjaša Kancler, and Piro Rexhepi. "Decolonial Encounters and the Geopolitics of Racial Capitalism." *Feminist Critique: East European Journal of Feminist and Queer Studies* 3 (2020): 13–38.

"Madonna Shows Support for Pussy Riot at Moscow Concert—Video." Video. *Guardian*, August 8, 2012. https://www.theguardian.com/music/video/2012/aug/08/madonna-pussy-riot-moscow-video.

Gurovich, Michal Mika. 'World Press Photo-Winner—Mika Photography at the Culture Magazine at I24news.' i24NEWS, February 24, 2015. Video. https://www.youtube.com/watch?v=kZ1gnewaacw.

Haas, Astrid. "'To Russia and myself': Claude McKay, Langston Hughes, and the Soviet Union." In *Transatlantic Negotiations*, edited by Christa Buschendorf and Astrid Franke, 111–131. Heidelberg: Winter Verlag, 2007.

Hall, Stuart. "Race, The Floating Signifier. A lecture given at Goldsmiths College in London, 1997." Transcript by Sut Jhalley. Media Education Foundation, 2015. https://cadmoremediastorage.blob.core.windows.net/4eeb24da-b65f-4889-a106-30eb1695d4dd/Stuart-Hall-Race-the-Floating-Signifier-Transcript.pdf?sv=2018-03-28&sr=c&sig=jEjj%2BlsedJMkDhfVDri9LIA7a4KizHBgkyC4RcZNm9k%3D&st=2024-12-04T13%3A41%3A35Z&se=2024-12-04T17%3A46%3A35Z&sp=r.

Hall, Stuart. *Representation: Cultural Representations and Signifying Practices.* London: Sage Publications and Open University, 1997.

Hall, Stuart. "The West and the Rest: Discourse and Power." In *The Formations of Modernity*, edited by Stuart Hall and Bram Gieben, 275–331. Cambridge: Polity, 1993.

Haritaworn, Jin, Tamsila Tauqir, and Esra Erdem. "Queer-Imperialismus: Eine Intervention in die Debatte über 'muslimische Homophobie." In *Re/Visionen: postkoloniale Perspektiven von People of Color auf Rassismus, Kulturpolitik und Widerstand in Deutschland*, edited by Kien Nghi Ha, Nicola Lauré al-Samarai, and Sheila Mysorekar, 409–454. Münster: Unrast, 2007.

Hartley, Eve. "LGBT Rights: Uganda, Russia and Saudi Arabia Show Why the Fight for Equality Continues." *Huffington Post*, December 26, 2015. http://www.huffingtonpost.co.uk/2015/12/26/reasons-why-this-wasnt-the-year-for-lgbt-rights_n_8812534.html.

Hassett, Maurice. "Martyr." *The Catholic Encyclopedia*, vol. 9. New York: Robert Appleton Company, 1910. http://www.newadvent.org/cathen/09736b.htm.

Healey, Dan. "Active, passive, and Russian: The national idea in gay men's pornography." *Russian Review* 6, no. 2 (2010): 210–230.

Healey, Dan. "Violence Shows Risks of Being Gay in Chechnya." *Huffington Post*, April 27, 2017. www.huffingtonpost.co.uk/professor-dan-healey/violence-shows-risks-of-b_b_16260984.html.

Healey, Dan. *Homosexual Desire in Revolutionary Russia: The Regulation of Sexual and Gender Dissent.* Chicago, IL: University of Chicago Press, 2001.

Heller, Steven, and Michael Barson. *Red Scared! The Commie Menace in Propaganda and Popular Culture.* San Francisco, CA: Chronicle Books, 2001.

Hendel, John. "Showtime's 'Shameless' New Show about Poverty." *Atlantic*, January 8, 2011. https://www.theatlantic.com/entertainment/archive/2011/01/showtimes-shameless-new-show-about-poverty/69108.

Herridge, Catherine, Matthew Dean, and the Associated Press. "Intel report says Putin ordered campaign to influence US election." Fox News, January 6, 2017. http://www.foxnews.com/politics/2017/01/06/trump-to-be-briefed-on-russia-hacking-report-as-unclassified-version-set-for-release.html.

Herzinger, Blake. "U.S. Right-Wingers Keep Confusing Culture War with Actual War." *Foreign Policy*, April 19, 2023. https://foreignpolicy.com/2023/04/19/us-military-culture-war-right-wing-russia-china-propaganda.

Holland, Steve, and Nandita Bose. "White House: U.S. welcomes Russians seeking asylum." *Reuters*, September 27, 2022. https://www.reuters.com/world/us/white-house-us-welcomes-russians-seeking-asylum-2022-09-27.

hooks, bell. *Black Looks: Race and Representation*. Boston, MA: South End Press, 1992.

Horne, Sharon G., and Lindsey White. "The return of repression: Mental health concerns of lesbian, gay, bisexual, and transgender people in Russia." In *LGBTQ mental health: International perspectives and experiences*, edited by Nadine Nakamura and Carmen H. Logie, 75–88. American Psychological Association, 2020. https://doi:10.1037/0000159-006.

Howson, Richard. *Challenging Hegemonic Masculinity*. London: Routledge, 2006.

Hylton, Emily, Andrea L. Wirtz, Carla E. Zelaya, Carl Latkin, Alena Peryshkina, Vladimir Mogilnyi, Petr Dzhigun, Irina Kostetskaya , Noya Galai, and Chris Beyrer. "Sexual Identity, Stigma, and Depression: The Role of the 'Anti-gay Propaganda Law' in Mental Health among Men Who Have Sex with Men in Moscow, Russia." *Journal of Urban Health*, (February 2017): 1–11.

Imara, Nia. "The Commodification of Black Death." *Progressive*, July 27, 2020. https://progressive.org/latest/commodification-of-black-death-imara-200727.

Impose Automaton. "JD Samson working with Pussy Riot's Nadya Tolokonnikova and Masha Alyokhina." *Impose*, December 9, 2014. https://www.imposemagazine.com/bytes/news/jd-samson-working-with-pussy-riots-nadya-tolokonnikova-and-masha-alyokhina.

Ioffe, Julia. "'Tomorrow, They'll Shoot Us.'" *New Yorker*, December 9, 2011. http://www.newyorker.com/news/news-desk/tomorrow-theyll-shoot-us.

Isaacson, Betsy. "Read the Heartbreaking Online Letters of Young, LGBT Russians." *Huffington Post*, February 24, 2014. http://www.huffingtonpost.com/2014/02/25/lgbt-russians_n_4823323.html.

Jackson, David. "Obama sanctions Russian officials over election hacking." *USA Today*, December 29, 2016. http://www.usatoday.com/story/news/politics/2016/12/29/barack-obama-russia-sanctions-vladimir-putin/95958472.

Jacobson, Matthew. *Roots Too: White Ethnic Revival in Post-Civil Rights America*. Cambridge, MA: Harvard University Press, 2006.

Janes, Dominic. *Visions of Queer Martyrdom from John Henry Newman to Derek Jarman*. Chicago, IL: University of Chicago Press, 2015.

Jay, Martin. *Downcast Eyes: The Denigration of Vision in Twentieth-Century French Thought*. Berkeley: California University Press, 1993.

Jeffords, Susan. *The Remasculinization of America: Gender and the Vietnam War*. Bloomington, IN: Indiana University Press, 1989.

Jordan, Miriam. "Antiwar Activists Who Flee Russia Find Detention, Not Freedom, in the U.S." *New York Times*, November 28, 2022. https://www.nytimes.com/2022/11/28/us/russian-activists-asylum.html?searchResultPosition=1.

Kancler, Tjaša. "Speaking against the Void: Decolonial Transfeminist Relations and Radical Potentialities." In *Postcolonial and Postsocialist Dialogues: Intersections, Opacities,*

Challenges in Feminist Theorizing and Practice, edited by Redi Koobak, Madina Tlostanova, and Suruchi Thapar-Björkert, 155–170. New York: Routledge, 2021.

Karaganov, Sergei. "A new epoch of confrontation." *Russia in Global Affairs* 5, no. 4
(2007): 23–36. Originally published as "Nastupaet novaya epokha," *Rossiiskaya
gazeta,* July 6, 2007.

Karaganov, Sergei. "We Are Shaking off the Western Yoke . . ." Russian International
Affairs Council, June 20, 2023. https://russiancouncil.ru/en/analytics-and-
comments/comments/we-are-shaking-off-the-Western-yoke.

Kargaltsev, Alexander. *Asylum.* Engels: Studio Van Stralen, 2013.

Kasich, John. "Kasich Ad: Trump/Putin 2016, 'Make Tyranny Great Again.'" Real Clear
Politics, December 19, 2015. http://www.realclearpolitics.com/video/2015/12/
19/kasich_ad_trumpputin_2016_make_tyranny_great_again.html.

Kaul, Kate. "Vulnerability, for Example: Disability Theory as Extraordinary Demand."
Canadian Journal of Women and the Law/Revue Femmes et Droit 25, no. 1 (2013):
81–110.

Kedmey, Dan. "Pussy Riot Member Detained in Russia for Protest over 'Sadistic' Prison
Law." *Time,* June 12, 2015. https://time.com/3919412/pussy-riot-nadya-prison-
camp-police-protest.

Kelleher, Patrick. "Trans Ukrainians being forced back into closet as cruel despot Putin's
bloodthirsty war rages on." *Pink News,* May 6, 2022. https://www.thepinknews.
com/2022/05/06/gay-alliance-ukraine-russia-war-trans.

Kellner, Douglas. *Media Spectacle.* New York: Routledge, 2003.

Kesslen, Ben. "Does Putin have 'roid rage'? Sources believe health could explain
despot's behavior: report." *New York Post,* March 13, 2022. https://nypost.
com/2022/03/13/does-putin-have-roid-rage-sources-believe-health-could-
explain-despots-behavior-report.

Khrushcheva, Nina. "Hollywood Made Him Do It?" NinaKhrushcheva (blog),
September 8, 2014. https://ninakhrushcheva.wordpress.com/2014/09/08/
hollywood-made-him-do-it. Page now unavailable.

King, Laura. "Ill? 'Unhinged'? Or calculating? Russia's Putin keeps everyone guessing."
Los Angeles Times, February 28, 2022. https://www.latimes.com/world-nation/
story/2022-02-28/russia-putin-behavior-mental-health.

Kinkead, Mic. "Leaving Trans Women out of the Women and Criminal Justice System
Convening." Silvia Rivera Law Project, April 9, 2016. http://srlp.org/speaking-
about-us-without-us-leaving-trans-women-out-of-the-women-and-criminal-
justice-system-convening.

Kirey-Sitnikova, Yana. "Psychiatric abuse of transgender people: a case from Russia."
Transadvocate, November 14, 2016. http://transadvocate.com/psychiatric-abuse-
of-transgender-people-a-case-of-russia_n_15245.htm.

Kiseleva, Maria, and Victoria Safronova. "Why are people leaving Russia, who are they,
and where are they going?" BBC News Russian, June 4, 2023. https://www.bbc.
com/news/world-europe-65790759.

Kishi, Katayoun. "Anti-Muslim assaults reach 9/11-era levels, FBI data show."
Pew Research Center, November 21, 2016. http://www.pewresearch.org/fact-
tank/2016/11/21/anti-muslim-assaults-reach-911-era-levels-fbi-data-show.

Klein, Naomi. *The Shock Doctrine: The Rise of Disaster Capitalism*. New York: Metropolitan Books, 2007.

Klumbytė, Neringa. "Russian imperialism shapes public support for the war against Ukraine." Atlantic Council, October 9, 2023. https://www.atlanticcouncil.org/blogs/ukrainealert/russian-imperialism-shapes-public-support-for-the-war-against-ukraine.

Kohn, Hans. *American Nationalism: An Interpretive Essay*. New York: The Macmillan Company, 1957.

Kolodny, Carina. "Here Are 9 Ways You Can Help Support LGBT Equality in Russia during the Sochi Olympics." *Huffington Post*, February 12, 2014. http://www.huffingtonpost.com/2014/02/12/sochi-olympics-lgbt_n_4762697.html.

Kolstø, Pal, and Helge Blakkisrud. *The New Russian Nationalism: Imperialism, Ethnicity and Authoritarianism 2000–15*. Edinburgh: Edinburgh University Press, 2016.

Kolthoff, Daan. "Telnyashka's." *I Sea Stripes* (blog), April 5, 2010. http://iseastripes.blogspot.com/2010/03/telnyashkas.html.

Kordunsky, Anna. "Russia Not Only Country with Anti-Gay Laws: Many other countries, from Iran to Cameroon, have harsh anti-gay laws." *National Geographic*, August 15, 2013. https://www.nationalgeographic.com/history/article/130814-russia-anti-gay-propaganda-law-world-olympics-africa-gay-rights.

Koreneva, Marina. "Madonna's Pink Ribbon Concert Draws Russia's Wrath." *Agence France-Presse*, August 9, 2012.

Korte, Gregory. "Obama: Gay marriage ruling is 'a victory for America.'" *USA Today*, June 26, 2015. https://eu.usatoday.com/story/news/politics/2015/06/26/obama-gay-marriage-ruling/29328755.

Kozlov, Vladimir. "Pussy Riot: Anonymous Members Distance Themselves from Two Former Bandmates." *Hollywood Reporter*, February 6, 2014. http://www.hollywoodreporter.com/news/pussy-riot-anonymous-members-distance-677713.

Kozlov, Vladimir. "Russian Officials Push for a Ban on Films That 'Demonize' Their Country." *Hollywood Reporter*, August 26, 2014. http://www.hollywoodreporter.com/news/russian-officials-push-a-ban-728056.

Krafft, Erin Katherine. "Punk Prayers Versus Neoliberalism: Pussy Riot and the Fractured Feminist Family Tree." *Canadian-American Slavic Studies* 56, no. 2 (May 10, 2022): 152–77. https://doi:10.30965/22102396-05602006.

Kramer, Andrew E. "'They Starve You. They Shock You': Inside the Anti-Gay Pogrom in Chechnya." *New York Times*, April 21, 2017. https://www.nytimes.com/2017/04/21/world/europe/chechnya-russia-attacks-gays.html.

Kramer, Andrew E. "Gay Men in Chechnya Are Killed, Paper Says." *New York Times*, April 2, 2017.

Krivotulova, Kseniia. "Solov'ev raskritikoval Manizha i nashel v ee pesne 'gendernye hreni'" [Solovyev criticized Manizha and found "gender crap" in her songs"]. Lenta.ru, March 25, 2021. https://lenta.ru/news/2021/05/25/soloviev/?utm_source=yxnews&utm_medium=desktop&utm_referrer=https%3A%2F%2Fyandex.com%2Fnews%2Fsearch%3Ftext%3D.

Krugman, Paul. "Donald Trump, the Siberian Candidate." *New York Times*, July 22, 2016. https://www.nytimes.com/2016/07/22/opinion/donald-trump-the-siberian-candidate.html.

Krzyżanowska, Kasia, and Ewa Thompson. "Imperialism in Russian Literature." *Review of Democracy*, June 7, 2022. https://revdem.ceu.edu/2022/06/07/imperialism-in-russian-literature/.

Kulpa, Robert, and Joanna Mizielińska. "Guest editors' Introduction: Central and Eastern European Sexualities 'in transition.'" *Lambda Nordica: Journal of LGBTQ Studies* (2012): 19–29.

Kulpa, Robert, Joanna Mizielińska, and Agatha Stasinska. "(Un)translatable Queer?, or What Is Lost and Can Be Found in Translation." In *Import—Export—Transport: Queer Theory, Queer Critique and Activism in Motion*, edited by Sushila Mesquita, Maria Katharina Wiedlack, and Katrin Lasthofer, 115–146. Vienna: Zaglossus, 2012.

Kushnir, Ostap. *Russian Neo-Imperialism: The Divergent Break*. London: Rowman & Littlefield, 2018.

Langston, Henry. "Meeting Pussy Riot." *Vice*, March 12, 2012. https://www.vice.com/en/article/a-russian-pussy-riot.

Laruelle, Marlene. "Making Sense of Russia's Illiberalism." *Journal of Democracy* 31, no. 3 (2020): 115–29.

Lavietes, Matt. "Here's what Florida's 'Don't Say Gay' bill would do and what it wouldn't do." NBC News, March 16, 2022. https://www.nbcnews.com/nbc-out/out-politics-and-policy/floridas-dont-say-gay-bill-actually-says-rcna19929.

Law, Ian. *Red Racisms: Racism in Communist and Post-Communist Contexts*. Basingstoke: Palgrave Macmillan, 2012.

LeBlanc, Fred Joseph. "Between a Rock and a Hard Place: Why the Ukrainian Crisis is a Queer Issue." Paper presented at International Norms and East European Nations, Victoria University of Wellington February 5, 2015. https://www.academia.edu/10356627/Between_a_Rock_and_a_Hard_Place_Why_the_Ukrainian_Crisis_is_a_Queer_Issue.

LeBlanc, Fred Joseph. "Sporting Homonationalism: Russian Homophobia, Imaginative Geographies and the 2014 Sochi Olympic Games." Paper presented at Sociology Association of Aotearoa New Zealand Annual Conference, December 2013. https://www.academia.edu/5318682/Sporting_Homonationalism_Russian_Homophobia_Imaginative_Geographies_and_the_2014_Sochi_Olympic_Games.

Lee, Julia. "'Danger everywhere': War and transphobia create perfect storm for trans Ukrainians." NBC News, April 8, 2022. https://www.nbcnews.com/nbc-out/out-news/danger-everywhere-war-transphobia-create-perfect-storm-trans-ukrainian-rcna23567.

Lee, Traci. "Pussy Riot gets prison for Putin protest." MSNBC, August 17, 2012. https://www.msnbc.com/melissa-harris-perry/pussy-riot-gets-prison-putin-protest-msna35545.

Lehourites, Chris. "Russia's world champion Yelena Isinbayeva condemns homosexuality, rips Swedes for 'rainbow' nails." *Vancouver Sun*, August 14, 2013. https://vancouversun.com/sports/russias-world-champion-yelena-isinbayeva-condemns-homosexuality-rips-swedes-for-rainbow-nails.

Leight, Elias. "Pussy Riot Slam Trump in 'Make America Great Again' Video." *Rolling Stone*, October 27, 2016. https://www.rollingstone.com/music/music-news/pussy-riot-slam-donald-trump-in-make-america-great-again-video-126889.

Lemon, Alaina. "'What Are They Writing about Us Blacks?'—Roma and 'Race' in Russia." *Anthropology of East Europe Review* 13, no. 2 (1995): 34–40.

Lenskyj, Helen Jefferson. *Sexual Diversity and the Sochi 2014 Olympics: No More Rainbows*. New York: Palgrave MacMillan, 2014.

Lenti, Erica. "Gay Russian teen desperate to come to Canada to escape homophobic laws." Postmedia Network, October 9, 2013. http://o.canada.com/news/gay-russian-teen-desperate-to-come-to-canada-to-escape-homophobic-laws. Page now unavailable.

Levine, Sam. "Bill Clinton Says 'Make America Great Again' Is Just a Racist Dog Whistle." *Huffington Post*, September 8, 2016. http://www.huffingtonpost.com/entry/bill-clinton-make-america-great-again_us_57d06ccfe4b0a48094a749fc.

Levintova, Hannah. "From Russia with Love: Photos of Brave Gay Activists Fighting Homophobia." *Mother Jones*, January/February 2014. https://www.motherjones.com/media/2014/02/russia-love-gay-propaganda-photos-wedding.

License to Harm—Violence and Harassment against LGBT People and Activists in Russia. December 15, 2014. https://www.hrw.org/report/2014/12/15/license-harm/violence-and-harassment-against-lgbt-people-and-activists-russia.

Lichtblau, Eric. "Attacks against Muslim Americans Fueled Rise in Hate Crime, F.B.I. Says." *New York Times*, November 15, 2016.

Lieven, Anatol. *America Right or Wrong: An Anatomy of American Nationalism*. New York: Oxford University Press, 2004.

Lipman, Masha. "The Pussy Riot Verdict." *New Yorker*, August 17, 2012. http://www.newyorker.com/online/blogs/newsdesk/2012/08/the-pussy-riot-verdict.html.

Lister, Tim, Maria Ilyushina, and Darya Tarasova. "UN experts condemn reports of violence against gay men in Chechnya." CNN, April 14, 2017. www.cnn.com/2017/04/14/europe/un-chechnya-gay-men.

Litvinova, Daria. "Russian feminist runs for Duma to take on domestic violence." *Associated Press*, September 15, 2021. https://apnews.com/article/europe-religion-russia-elections-violence-83c6446d2d7813c4f2900c852e4bf08b.

Lowenstein, Adam. "Promises of Violence: David Cronenberg on Globalized Geopolitics." *Boundary 2* 36, no. 2 (2009): 199–208.

Luhn, Alec. "Gay Pride Versus 'Gay Propaganda:' In Russia, activists struggle against rising homophobia and a government crack down on LGBT rights." *Nation*, June 28, 2013. https://www.thenation.com/article/archive/gay-pride-versus-gay-propaganda.

MacFarquhar, Neil, and Georgy Birger. "Putin's Crackdown Leaves Transgender Russians Bracing for Worse." *New York Times*, August 1, 2023. https://www.nytimes.com/2023/08/01/world/europe/russia-transgender-ban.html.

MacFarquhar, Neil. "Putin signs a harsh new law targeting transgender people in Russia." *New York Times*, July 24, 2023. https://www.nytimes.com/2023/07/24/world/europe/putin-transgender-transition-surgery-russia.html.

Macgillis, Alec. "The Original Underclass: Poor white Americans' current crisis shouldn't have caught the rest of the country as off guard as it has." *Atlantic*, September 2016. https://www.theatlantic.com/magazine/archive/2016/09/the-original-underclass/492731.

Mackey, Robert, and Glenn Kates. "Russian Riot Grrrls Jailed for 'Punk Prayer.'" *New York Times*, March 7, 2012. https://archive.nytimes.com/thelede.blogs. nytimes.com/2012/03/07/russian-riot-grrrls-jailed-for-punk-prayer/?search ResultPosition=1.

Mackinnon, Amy. "Russia Is Sending Its Ethnic Minorities to the Meat Grinder." *Foreign Policy*, September 23, 2022. https://foreignpolicy.com/2022/09/23/russia-partial-military-mobilization-ethnic-minorities.

MacKinnon, Kenneth. *Representing Men: Maleness and Masculinity in the Media*. London: Arnold, 2003.

Mailer, Norman. "The White Negro." In *White Riot: Punk Rock and the Politics of Race*, edited by Stephen Duncombe and Maxwell Tremblay, 19–22. London: Verso, 2011.

Manizha. "Mama." Manizha, February 28, 2019. Video. https://www.youtube.com/ watch?v=iCwuW3yClO4.

Manizha. "Manizha—Russian woman—Russia—Official video—Eurovision 2021." Eurovision Song Contest, March 10, 2021. Video. https://www.youtube.com/ watch?v=l01wa2ChX64.

Manizha. "Mozhet li eto… predstavliat' Rossiiu na Evrovidenii?" [Can it . . . represent Russia at Eurovision?], Manizha, March 17, 2021. Video. https://www.youtube. com/watch?v=g7J4lAGeFKo.

Margolis, Eleanor. "When it comes to Russia's draconian anti-gay laws, Nazi comparisons are apt." *New Statesman*, August 8, 2013. http://www.newstatesman.com/lez-miser-able/2013/08/when-it-comes-russias-draconian-anti-gay-laws-nazi-comparisons-are-apt.

Marrs, David. "Donald Trump and Vladimir Putin enjoy riding bareback together." *Daily Squat*, August 2, 2016.://www.dailysquat.com/donald-trump-vladimir-putin-en-joyriding-bareback-together. Page now unavailable.

Marshall, Josh. "You Can't Understand American Politics without Reading This Study." *TalkingPointsMemo*, December 1, 2015. http://talkingpointsmemo.com/edblog/ you-can-t-understand-american-politics-without-reading-this-study.

Martin, Daniel. "Pussy Riot members nominated for 'Time' magazine's Person of the Year award." *NME*, November 28, 2012. https://www.nme.com/news/music/ pussy-riot-71-1257775.

Martinez, Michael. "3 issues that have chilled U.S.-Russia ties." CNN, September 5, 2013. https://edition.cnn.com/2013/09/05/world/us-russia-key-issues/index. html.

Martinez, Michael. "Flint, Michigan: Did race and poverty factor into water crisis?" *New York Amsterdam News*, January 27, 2016. https://amsterdamnews.com/ news/2016/01/27/flint-michigan-did-race-and-poverty-factor-water-c.

Massad, Joseph A. *Desiring Arabs*. Chicago, IL: The University of Chicago Press, 2007.

Mathijs, Ernst. *The Cinema of David Cronenberg: From Baron of Blood to Cultural Hero*. London: Wallflower Press, 2008.

McClintock, Anne. "Family Feuds: Gender, Nationalism and the Family." *Feminist Review*, no. 44 (1993), 61–80.

McDuffie, Erik S. *Sojourning for Freedom: Black Women, American Communism, and the Making of Black Left Feminism*. Durham, NC: Duke University Press, 2011.

McEwan, Ian. "We are haunted by ghosts—and Vladimir Putin's sickly dreams." *Guardian*, March 5, 2022. https://www.theguardian.com/commentisfree/2022/mar/05/vladimir-putin-ukraine.

McGrane, Sally. "A Terrible Time to Be Gay in Russia." *New Yorker*, August 1, 2013. http://www.newyorker.com/culture/culture-desk/a-terrible-time-to-be-gay-in-russia.

Messerschmidt, James. *Hegemonic Masculinities and Camouflaged Politics: Unmasking the Bush Dynasty and Its War against Iraq*. Boulder, CO: Paradigm Publishers, 2010.

Messerschmidt, James. *Masculinities in the Making: From the Local to the Global*. Lanham, MD: Rowman & Littlefield, 2016.

Messner, Michael. *Politics of Masculinities: Men in Movements*. Thousand Oaks, CA: Sage Publications, 1997.

Miller, Ryen W. "Black Lives Matter: A primer on what it is and what it stands for." *USA Today*, July 11, 2016 http://www.usatoday.com/story/news/nation/2016/07/11/black-lives-matter-what-what-stands/86963292/.

Mills, Laura. "Jailed Pussy Riot member ends hunger strike." *USA Today* and *Associated Press*, October 1, 2013. http://www.usatoday.com/story/news/world/2013/10/01/pussy-riot-russia-hunger/2902631.

Milne, Seumas. "The demonisation of Russia risks paving the way for war." *Guardian*. March 4, 2015. https://www.theguardian.com/commentisfree/2015/mar/04/demonisation-russia-risks-paving-way-for-war.

Milton, Josh. "Russia's Eurovision act is a fearless feminist and LGBT+ rights campaigner and—shock—Russian bigots are mad." *PinkNews*, March 15, 2021. https://www.thepinknews.com/2021/03/15/russia-eurovision-2021-manizha-sangin-2021-lgbt.

Morales, P. J. "Mural of Brittney Griner, other detained Americans unveiled in Georgetown." *Washington Post*, July 20, 2022. https://www.washingtonpost.com/sports/2022/07/20/brittney-griner-mural-washington.

Morgan, Joe. "Russian man blinded by anti-gay shooting speaks out." *Gay Star News*, November 5, 2013. http://www.gaystarnews.com/article/russian-man-blinded-anti-gay-shooting-speaks-out051113/#gs.2oEfvCo. Page now unavailable.

Morris, Harvey. "We're All Pussy Riot Now." *New York Times*, August 17, 2012. http://rendezvous.blogs.nytimes.com/2012/08/17/were-all-pussy-riot-now.

Morrison, Sarah. "Vladimir Putin's attack on homosexuality is shattering the lives of Russians." *Independent*, January 13, 2014. http://www.independent.co.uk/news/world/europe/vladimir-putin-s-attack-on-homosexuality-is-shattering-the-lives-of-russians-9054660.html.

Moss, Kevin. "Why are these pages blue?" Russian Gay Culture, October 17, 2016. http://community.middlebury.edu/~moss/goluboy.html.

"Mounting Reports of Crimes against Women, Children in Ukraine Raising 'Red Flags' over Potential Protection Crisis, Executive Director Tells Security Council." UNHCR Meeting Coverage and Press Releases, April 11, 2022. Murphy, Matt. "Russian parliament bans gender reassignment surgery for trans people." BBC, July 14, 2023. https://www.bbc.com/news/world-europe-66200194.

Murray, Charles. *Coming Apart: The State of White America, 1960–2010*. New York: Crown Forum, 2012.

"MUST WATCH: Highlight Reel of Vladimir Putin Doing Macho Things." Fox News, March 6, 2014. http://nation.foxnews.com/2014/03/06/must-watch-highlight-reel-vladimir-putin-doing-macho-things.

"'My freedom defends yours:' Propaganda and truth about homophobia in Russia." Amnesty International, October 11, 2014. https://www.amnesty.org/en/latest/news/2014/10/my-freedom-defends-yours-propaganda-and-truth-about-homophobia-russia/.

Myers, Steven Lee. "Putin's Olympic Fever Dream." *New York Times*, January 22, 2014.

Nadel, Alan. *Containment Culture: American Narratives, Postmodernism, and the Atomic Age.* Durham, NC: Duke University Press, 1995.

Nakashima, Ellen, Karoun Demirjian, and Philip Rucker. "Top U.S. intelligence official: Russia meddled in election by hacking, spreading of propaganda." *Washington Post*, January 5, 2017. https://www.washingtonpost.com/world/national-security/top-us-cyber-officials-russia-poses-a-major-threat-to-the-countrys-infrastructure-and-networks/2017/01/05/36a60b42-d34c-11e6-9cb0-54ab630851e8_story.html?utm_term=.b61fb3369487&wpisrc=nl_most-draw10&wpmm=1.

Nashrulla, Tasneem, "Trump and Putin Kiss Passionately on a Wall. Not that kind of wall." *BuzzFeed*, May 14, 2016. https://www.buzzfeed.com/tasneemnashrulla/putin-out?utm_term=.hfAOnJANL#.booldDYex.

Nelson, Louis. "Obama pushes back against Trump's suggestion on Russia sanctions." *Politico*, January 18, 2017. http://www.politico.com/story/2017/01/obama-last-press-conference-trump-russia-sanctions-233784.

Nemtsova, Anna. "Pussy Riot Witch Hunt by Kremlin-Backed 'Youth Movement.'" *Daily Beast*, September 30, 2012. https://www.thedailybeast.com/pussy-riot-witch-hunt-by-kremlin-backed-youth-movement.

Nemtsova, Anna. "Russia Slides Back to the Middle Ages." *Daily Beast*, June 8, 2015. https://www.thedailybeast.com/russia-slides-back-to-the-middle-ages.

Nes, Solrunn. *The Mystical Language of Icons.* Cambridge: Wm. B. Eerdmans Publishing, 2005.

Neufeld, Masha, and Maria Katharina Wiedlack. "Visibility, Violence, and Vulnerability: Lesbians Stuck Between the Post-Soviet Closet and the Western Media Space." In *LGBTQ+ Activism in Central and Eastern Europe*, edited by Radzhana Buyantueva, and Maryna Shevtsova, 51–76. Basingstoke: Palgrave Macmillan, 2019.

Neuman, Scott. "Obama: Supreme Court Same-Sex Marriage Ruling 'A Victory For America.'" *NPR*, June 26, 2015. https://www.npr.org/sections/thetwo-way/2015/06/26/417731614/obama-supreme-court-ruling-on-gay-marriage-a-victory-for-america.

Neumann, Iver B. *Russia and the Idea of Europe: A Study in Identity and International Relations.* London: Routledge, 1995.

Neumann, Iver B. *Uses of the Other: "The East" in European Identity Formation.* Manchester: Manchester University Press, 1999.

Newman, Dina. "The 'Savage Warriors' of Siberia: How an Ethnic Minority in Russia Came to Be Unfairly Blamed for the Worst War Crimes in Ukraine." Media Diversity Institute, August 12, 2022. https://www.media-diversity.org/the-savage-warriors-of-siberia-how-an-ethnic-minority-in-russia-came-to-be-unfairly-blamed-for-the-worst-war-crimes-in-ukraine.

"Narusheniia prav I diskriminatsiia v otnoshenii LGBT v Rossii s sentiabria 2012 g. po avgust 2013 g." [Human rights violations and discrimination against LGBT people in Russia from September 2012 to August 2013]. Russian LGBT Network, 2014. http://lgbtnet.ru/sites/default/files/monitoring_2013.pdf.

"Olympics Has Made Russia Totalitarian—Pussy Riot." Newshub, February 21, 2014. http://www.newshub.co.nz/world/olympics-has-made-russia-totalitarian--pussy-riot-2014022106#axzz44zPsZ2nL.

Nichols, James Michael. "Here's What Happens When Two Men Hold Hands While Walking The Streets of Russia." Huffington Post, July 14, 2015. http://www.huffingtonpost.com/entry/heres-what-happens-when-two-men-hold-hands-while-walking-the-streets-of-russia_us_55a5206ae4b0ecec71bcf80b.

Nichols, James. "'Art Speaks Louder Than Words' Showcases Support for LGBT Russians." Huffington Post, October 25, 2013. http://www.huffingtonpost.com/2013/10/25/art-speaks-louder-than-wor_n_4159546.html.

Nichols, James. "Front Runners New York Launches 'To Russia with Love.'" Huffington Post, January 28, 2014. https://www.huffpost.com/entry/front-runners-new-york_n_4680750.

Nissen, Mads. "Photo Essay: The Dangers of Being Gay in Russia." Newsweek, February 10, 2014. http://www.newsweek.com/being-gay-russia-just-got-harder-228592.

Nolan, Megan. "Nadya Tolokonnikova: 'I have nightmares about being in prison again.'" Guardian, April 20, 2019. https://www.theguardian.com/lifeandstyle/2019/apr/20/this-much-i-know-nadya-tolokonnikova-pussy-riot.

OCHA Service. "Protection of LGBTIQ+ people in the context of the response in Ukraine." Relief Web, May 17, 2022. https://reliefweb.int/report/ukraine/protection-lgbtiq-people-context-response-ukraine.

https://www.dni.gov/files/documents/ICA_2017_01.pdf.

Olsen, Jan M. "Lithuanian Artist Makes Massive Poster of Trump and Putin Smooching." Huffington Post, May 15, 2016. https://www.huffpost.com/archive/au/entry/lithuanian-artist-makes-massive-poster-of-trump-and-putin-smooch_au_5cd36c0de4b02317c3c9714c.

Ong, Aihwa. "Colonialism and Modernity: Feminist Re-presentations of Women in Non-Western Societies." Inscriptions 3–4 (1988): 79–93. https://www.researchgate.net/publication/287172314_Colonialism_and_modernity_Feminist_re-presentations_of_women_in_non-western_societies.

Osborn, Andrew. "A do-over for Russian history? Putin-backed manual spurs concern nation is whitewashing its past." Wall Street Journal, July 6, 2007. https://www.wsj.com/articles/SB118367568881058545.

Osborn, Andrew. "Bloggers who are changing the face of Russia as the Snow Revolution takes hold." Telegraph, December 10, 2011. https://www.telegraph.co.uk/news/worldnews/europe/russia/8948414/Bloggers-who-are-changing-the-face-of-Russia-as-the-Snow-Revolution-takes-hold.html.

Osnos, Evan, David Remnick, and Joshua Yaffa. "Trump, Putin, and the New Cold War: What lay behind Russia's interference in the 2016 election—and what lies ahead?" *New Yorker*, March 6, 2017. http://www.newyorker.com/magazine/2017/03/06/trump-putin-and-the-new-cold-war?mbid=synd_digg.

"Our Approach and Principles." Sylvia Rivera Law Project. http://srlp.org/about/principles.

"Our Kind of Traitor." Box Office Mojo, February 26, 2017. https://www.boxofficemojo.com/title/tt1995390.

Palmer, Justin. "Russia Must Explain Its Anti-Gay Law, Says International Olympics Committee." *Huffington Post*, August 9, 2013, updated February 2, 2016. https://www.huffpost.com/entry/russia-gay-olympics-committee_n_3730925.

Parker, Suzi. "What American women could learn from Pussy Riot, a Russian punk rock girl band." *Washington Post*, April 21, 2012. https://www.washingtonpost.com/blogs/she-the-people/post/what-american-women-could-learn-from-pussy-riot-a-russian-punk-rock-girl-band/2012/04/21/gIQAYr42XT_blog.html.

Parry, Robert. "The Politics behind 'Russia-gate.'" *Global Research*, March 6, 2017. http://www.globalresearch.ca/the-politics-behind-russia-gate/5578089.

Parvulescu, Anca. *The Traffic in Women's Work: East European Migration and the Making of Europe*. Chicago, IL: University of Chicago Press, 2014.

Paul, Heike. *The Myths That Made America: An Introduction to American Studies*. Bielefeld: Transcript, 2014.

Peake, Tony. *Derek Jarman: A Biography*. Woodstock, NY: Overlook Press, 1999.

Pechenkina, Ekaterina. "Are feminists next on Vladimir Putin's list?" *Politico*, April 14, 2023. https://www.politico.com/newsletters/women-rule/2023/04/14/are-feminists-next-on-vladimir-putins-list-00092070.

Peeples, Jase. "PHOTOS: Go Inside Star-Studded L.A. Benefit for Pussy Riot." *OUT Traveler*, April 9, 2014. http://www.outtraveler.com/destination-guide/los-angeles/2014/04/09/photos-go-inside-star-studded-la-benefit-pussy-riot.

"The persecution of a feminist Russian artist." *Economist*, October 14, 2020. https://www.economist.com/books-and-arts/2020/10/14/the-persecution-of-a-feminist-russian-artist.

"Persecution of LGBTI+ people in Russia: Increasing repressions 2021–2022." Anti-Discrimination Centre Memorial, May 18, 2022. https://adcmemorial.org/en/articles/persecution-of-lgbti-2021-22/.

Perez, Evan, and Daniella Diaz. "White House announces retaliation against Russia: Sanctions, ejecting diplomats." CNN, January 2, 2017. http://www.cnn.com/2016/12/29/politics/russia-sanctions-announced-by-white-house/.

Petersen, Freya. "Madonna joins celebrities backing Pussy Riot." *World*, August 19, 2012. https://www.pri.org/stories/2012-08-19/madonna-joins-celebrities-backing-pussy-riot.

Petkova, Mariya. "'Putin is using ethnic minorities to fight in Ukraine': Activist." *Aljazeera*, October 25, 2022. https://www.aljazeera.com/features/2022/10/25/russia-putin-is-using-ethnic-minorities-to-fight-in-ukraine.

Pinkham, Sophie. "Pussy Riot in Translation." *Dissent*, Summer 2014. https://www.dissentmagazine.org/article/pussy-riot-in-translation/.

Plakhotnik, Olga, and Maria Mayerchyk. "Pride Contested: Geopolitics of Liberation at the Buffer Periphery of Europe." *Lambda Nordica* 28 (June 15, 2023): 1–28. https://doi:10.34041/ln.v.874.

"The depiction of Russia at the Women's Marches [with photos]." PONARS Eurasia, January 30, 2017. http://www.ponarseurasia.org/article/ponars-eurasiadiscusses-depiction-russia-womens-marches-photos.

Potter, Claire. "Is Putin a Mad King?" Political Junkie Substack newsletter, February 28, 2022. https://clairepotter.substack.com/p/is-putin-a-mad-king.

Puar, Jasbir. "Rethinking Homonationalism." *Middle East Studies* 45, no. 2 (2013), 336–339.

Puar, Jasbir. *Terrorist Assemblages: Homonationalism in Queer Times*. Durham, NC: Duke University Press, 2007.

Putnam, Robert D. *Our Kids: The American Dream in Crisis that looked at issues of inequality of opportunity in the US*. New York: Simon & Schuster, 2015.

Queer Nation NY. "This Is Why We Fight." *Queer Nation New York*, November 14, 2013. http://queernationny.org/post/66984188441/this-is-why-we-fight-the-st-petersburg-times.

Queer Voices. "'Uprising of Love Hangouts on Air' Will Tackle Russian LGBT Issues Ahead of Sochi Olympics." *Huffington Post*, January 21, 2014. http://www.huffingtonpost.com/2014/01/21/uprising-of-love-hangouts-on-air-_n_4637286.html.

Radulescu, Domnica. "Amazones, Wretches and Vampirettes: Essentialism and Beyond in the Representation of East European Women." In *Vampirettes, Wretches and Amazons: Western Representations of East European Women*, edited by Glajar, Valentina and Domnica Radulescu, 45–46. New York: Columbia University Press, 2004.

Ramani, Samuel. *Putin's War on Ukraine: Russia's Campaign for Global Counter-Revolution*. London: Hurst, 2023.

Ray, Rashawn. "The Russian invasion of Ukraine shows racism has no boundaries." Brookings Institution, March 3, 2022. https://www.brookings.edu/articles/the-russian-invasion-of-ukraine-shows-racism-has-no-boundaries.

Razack, Sherene H. *Looking White People in the Eye: Gender, Race, and Culture in Courtrooms and Classrooms*. Toronto: University of Toronto Press, 1998.

Red iLyke. "Donald Trump Kisses Vladimir Putin on Wall of Lithuanian Restaurant." iLyke, May 16, 2016. http://ilyke.com/donald-trump-kisses-vladimir-putin-on-wall-of-lithuanian-restaurant/79893#ixzz4ZGnPNPdk.

"Trump responds to sanctions against Russia, says it's time to 'move on.'" Fox News, December 29, 2016. http://www.foxnews.com/politics/2016/12/29/obama-orders-sanctions-against-russia-expels-operatives-in-response-to-hacking.html.

Reddy, Chandan. *Freedom with Violence: Race, Sexuality, and the US State*. Durham, NC: Duke University Press, 2011.

Relates, Ashley. "Closer Look at the Butt: Appropriation and Exploitation of Black Female Sexuality." *Medium*, November 9, 2015. https://medium.com/@ashleyrelates/closer-look-at-the-butt-appropriation-of-black-female-sexuality-1153b1840c9c.

Reynolds, Daniel. "WATCH: Former Russian Paratroopers Attack Gay Activist." *Advocate*, August 2, 2013. http://www.advocate.com/politics/military/2013/08/02/watch-former-russian-paratroopers-attack-gay-activist.

Riabov, Oleg, and Tatiana Riabova. "The Decline of Gayropa?" *Eurozine*, February 5, 2014, 1–9. http://www.eurozine.com/the-decline-of-gayropa.

Ricoeur, Paul. *Reflections on the Just*. Translated by David Pellauer. Chicago, IL: University of Chicago Press, 2007.

Ritter, Martina. "Kulturelle Modernisierung und Identitätskonzeptionen im sowjetischen und postsowjetischen Rußland." *Feministische Studien* 1 (1999): 8–22.

Rivkin-Fish, Michele, and Cassandra Hartblay. "When Global LGBTQ Advocacy Became Entangled with New Cold War Sentiment: A Call for Examining Russian Queer Experience." *Brown Journal of World Affairs* 21, no. 1 (2014): 95–111.

Robertson, Dylan C. "Pride parade in St. Petersburg met with violence, hostility." *Toronto Star*, June 30, 2013. https://www.thestar.com/news/world/2013/06/30/pride_parade_in_st_petersburg_met_with_violence_hostility.html.

Robinson, Cedric J. *Black Marxism: The Making of the Black Radical Tradition*. Chapel Hill: The University of North Carolina Press, 2000.

Roediger, David. *Colored White: Transcending the Racial Past*. Berkeley: University of California Press, 2002.

Rogers, Wendy, Catronia Mackenzie, and Susan Dodds. "Introduction." *IJFAB: International Journal of Feminist Approaches to Bioethics* 5, no. 2 (2012): 1–10.

Roman, Meredith L. "Making Caucasians Black: Moscow since the fall of communism and the racialization of non-Russians." *Journal of Communist Studies and Transition Politics* 18, no. 2 (2002), 1–27. https://doi:10.1080/714003604.

Romanets, Maryna. "Virtual Warfare: Masculinity, Sexuality, and Propaganda in the Russo-Ukrainian War." *East/West: Journal of Ukrainian Studies* 4, no. 1 (2017): 159–177. https://doi:10.21226/t26880.

Romero, Dennis. "In the Era of Trump, Anti-Latino Hate Crimes Jumped 69% in L.A." *LA Weekly*, September 29, 2016. https://www.laweekly.com/in-the-era-of-trump-anti-latino-hate-crimes-jumped-69-in-l-a.

Romm, Cari. "NYC group running to support Russia's LGBT's community." *amNY*, February 17, 2014. http://www.amny.com/news/nyc-group-running-to-support-russia-s-lgbt-s-community-1.7110229.

Rosenthal, Andrew. "Is Trump Obsessed with Putin and Russia?" *New York Times*, July 20, 2016. https://www.nytimes.com/2016/07/20/opinion/campaign-stops/is-trump-obsessed-with-putin-and-russia.html.

Rothberg, Daniel. "Will gays be safe at Russia's Winter Olympics?" *Los Angeles Times*, July 26, 2013 https://www.latimes.com/opinion/opinion-la/la-ol-gay-law-russia-winter-olympics-boycott-20130726-story.html.

Rumer, Eugene. "Putin's War against Ukraine: The End of the Beginning." Carnegie, February 17, 2023. https://carnegieendowment.org/research/2023/02/putins-war-against-ukraine-the-end-of-the-beginning?lang=en.

"Russia: Artist detained amid clampdown on anti-war feminists." Amnesty International, April 13, 2022. https://www.amnesty.org/en/latest/news/2022/04/russia-artist-detained-amid-clampdown-on-anti-war-feminists/.

"Russian lawmakers propose extending 'gay propaganda' law to all adults." *Reuters*, July 11, 2022. https://www.reuters.com/world/europe/russian-lawmakers-propose-extending-gay-propaganda-law-all-adults-2022-07-11.

"Russian president signs legislation marking the final step outlawing gender-affirming procedures." *Associated Press*, July 24, 2023. https://apnews.com/article/russia-lgbtq-transgender-procedures-banned-21b88f53b9a74a646400d63ce93bde6f.

"Russia puts Pussy Riot member on wanted list for criminals." *Associated Press*, March 29, 2023. https://apnews.com/article/russia-pussy-riot-list-opposition-860d1f1288dca317e4b0783c68b49422.

"Russian sexologists to target homosexuality, other 'disorders' under new rules." *Reuters*, June 29, 2023. https://www.reuters.com/world/europe/russian-sexologists-target-homosexuality-other-disorders-under-new-rules-2023-06-29.

"Russia's Eurovision entry to be investigated for 'illegal' lyrics." *Guardian*, March 18, 2021. https://www.theguardian.com/world/2021/mar/18/russias-eurovision-entry-to-be-investigated-for-lyrcs.

"Russia's war on gays." *Washington Post*, August 8, 2013. https://www.washingtonpost.com/opinions/russias-war-on-gays/2013/08/08/41721722-0065-11e3-9711-3708310f6f4d_story.html?utm_term=.241f07f5e116.

Rutenberg, Jim. "A Warning for Americans from a Member of Pussy Riot." *New York Times*, December 4, 2016. https://www.nytimes.com/2016/12/04/business/rutenberg-lessons-in-free-speech-from-pussy-riot.html.

Ryzik, Melena. "Pussy Riot Was Carefully Calibrated for Protest." *New York Times*, August 22, 2012. https://www.nytimes.com/2012/08/26/arts/music/pussy-riot-was-carefully-calibrated-for-protest.html.

Sadowski-Smith, Claudia. *The New Immigrant Whiteness: Race, Neoliberalism, and Post-Soviet Migration to the United States*. New York: NYU Press, 2018.

Said, Edward. *Orientalism*. New York: Vintage Books, 1979.

Sakwa, Richard. "'New Cold War' or Twenty Years' Crisis? Russia and International Politics." *International Affairs* 84, no. 2 (2008): 241–267.

Sanders, Rachel. "The color of fat: racializing obesity, recuperating whiteness, and reproducing injustice" *Politics, Groups, and Identities* 7, no. 2 (2019): 287–304. https://doi:10.1080/21565503.2017.1354039.

Sanger, David E. "U.S. Punishes Russia over Election Hacking." *New York Times*, December 30, 2016.

Sanger, David E. "U.S. Reacting at Analog Pace to a Rising Digital Risk, Hacking Report Shows." *New York Times*, January 8, 2017.

Sarajeva, Katja. "Lesbian Lives: Sexuality, Space and Subculture in Moscow." PhD diss., University of Stockholm, 2011.

Satter, David 2016. "The Unsolved Mystery behind the Act of Terror That Brought Putin to Power." *National Review*, August 17, 2016. http://www.nationalreview.com/article/439060/vladimir-putin-1999-russian-apartment-house-bombings-was-putin-responsible.

Savage, Mark. "Manizha: Russian Eurovision star faces hate campaign over opposition to Ukraine war." BBC, August 25, 2022. https://www.bbc.com/news/entertainment-arts-62671940.

Savran, David. "The Sadomasochist in the Closet: White Masculinity and the Culture of Victimisation." *Differences: A Journal of Feminist Cultural Studies* 8, no. 2 (1996): 127–152.

Schrecker, Ellen. Introduction to *Cold War Triumphalism: The Misuse of History after the Fall of Communism*, edited by Ellen Schrecker, 1–24. New York: The New Press, 2006.

Schwirtz, Michael. "Vory v Zakone has hallowed place in Russian criminal lore." *New York Times*, July 29, 2008. http://www.nytimes.com/2008/07/29/world/europe/29iht-moscow.4.14865004.html?pagewanted=all&_r=0.

Scott, Karla D. *The Language of Strong Black Womanhood: Myths, Models, Messages, and a New Mandate for Self-Care.* New York: Lexington Books, 2017.

Seguino, Stephanie, and James Heintz. "Monetary Tightening and the Dynamics of Race and Gender Stratification in the US." *American Journal of Economics and Sociology* 71, no. 3 (2012): 603–638.

"Services under Siege: Violence against LGBT People Stymies HIV Prevention and Treatment." MSMGF, December 10, 2015. http://msmgf.org/high-levels-of-violence-against-lgbt-people-stymie-hiv-prevention-and-treatment-worldwide/.

Shaipov, Artem, and Yuliia Shaipova. "It's High Time to Decolonize Western Russia Studies." *Foreign Policy*, February 11, 2023. https://foreignpolicy.com/2023/02/11/russia-studies-war-ukraine-decolonize-imperialism-Western-academics-soviet-empire-eurasia-eastern-europe-university.

Sharlet, Jeff. "Inside the Iron Closet: What It's Like to Be Gay in Putin's Russia." *GQ*, February 4, 2014. http://www.gq.com/story/being-gay-in-russia.

Shear, Michael D., and Peter Baker. "Inside the Prisoner Swap That Freed Brittney Griner." *New York Times*, December 9, 2022. https://www.nytimes.com/2022/12/09/us/politics/brittney-griner-prisoner-swap.html.

Shekhovtsov, Anton. "Is Russia Insider Sponsored by a Russian Oligarch with Ties to the European Far Right?" *Interpreter*, November 23, 2015. http://www.interpretermag.com/is-russia-insider-sponsored-by-a-russian-oligarch-with-ties-to-the-european-far-right.

Shen, Yang. "Book Review: Masculinities in the Making: From the Local to the Global by James W. Messerschmidt." Review of *Masculinities in the Making: From the Local to the Global*, by James W. Messerschmidt. *Gender & Society* 31, no. 1 (2017): 138–40.

Shishkin, Mikhail. "Poets and Czars: From Pushkin to Putin: the sad tale of democracy in Russia." *New Republic*, July 1, 2013. https://newrepublic.com/article/113386/pushkin-putin-sad-tale-democracy-russia.

Shukla, Seb, and Jack Guy, "Pope Francis calls Chechens and Buryats 'the cruelest' Russian troops fighting in Ukraine." CNN, November 29, 2022. https://edition.cnn.com/2022/11/29/europe/pope-francis-chechens-buryats-intl/index.html.

Shuster, Simon. "Pussy Riot Unveils a Wildly NSFW Vision of America under Donald Trump." *Time*, October 27, 2016. https://time.com/4547274/pussy-riot-donald-trump-make-america-great-again.

Shuster, Simon. "The Blind Girl vs. Putin: A Plea for Russia's Handicapped Orphans." *Time*, January 14, 2013. https://world.time.com/2013/01/14/the-blind-girl-vs-putin-a-plea-for-russias-handicapped-orphans.

Signorile, Michelangelo. "Russian Gay Activist's Plea: 'Get Us the Hell Out of Here.'" *Huffington Post*, June 9, 2013. http://www.huffingtonpost.com/michelangelo-signorile/russian-gay-activists-plea-get-us-the-hell-out-of-here_b_3881059.html.

Silver, Andrew. "Is Russia facing an academic exodus over Ukraine?" Research Professional News, September 26, 2022. https://www.researchprofessionalnews.com/rr-news-world-2022-9-is-russia-facing-an-academic-exodus-over-ukraine.

Simonyi, András. "LGBT Rights—Modernity vs. Forces of Yesteryear." *Huffington Post*, May 11, 2015. http://www.huffingtonpost.com/andras-simonyi/lgbt-rights-modernity-vs-forces-of-yesteryear_b_7256178.html.

Smith-Peter, Susan. "What do Scholars of Russia owe Ukraine?" Jordan Center Blog, April 1, 2022. https://jordanrussiacenter.org/news/what-do-scholars-of-russia-owe-ukraine-today.

Smith, Patricia Juliana. *The Queer Sixties*. New York: Routledge, 1999.

Smyth, Regina, and Irina Soboleva. "Looking beyond the Economy: Pussy Riot and the Kremlin's Voting Coalition." *Post-Soviet Affairs* 30, no. 4 (2013): 257–275.

Snegovaya, Maria. "Russian Identity and War Support." PONARS Eurasia, June 14, 2024. https://www.ponarseurasia.org/russian-identity-and-war-support.

Socor, Vladimir. "Council of Europe condemns communism over Moscow's opposition." *Eurasia Daily Monitor* 3, no. 19, January 27, 2006. https://jamestown.org/program/council-of-europe-condemns-communism-over-moscows-opposition.

Solovey, Vanya Mark. "Feminism and Aggressive Imperialism: Russian Feminist Politics in Wartime." *Femina Politica—Zeitschrift Für Feministische Politikwissenschaft* 32, no. 1 (June 12, 2023): 95–101. https://doi:10.3224/feminapolitica.v32i1.08.

Sperling, Valerie. "A Case of Putin Envy: Behind the Obsession with Russia's Leader." *Foreign Affairs*, November 5, 2015. https://www.foreignaffairs.com/articles/russian-federation/2015-11-05/case-putin-envy.

Sperling, Valerie. *Sex, Politics, and Putin: Political Legitimacy in Russia*. New York: Oxford University Press, 2014.

St. Clair, André. "Stop Killing Us: Black Trans Lives Matter." *Huffington Post*, August 17, 2016. http://www.huffingtonpost.com/entry/stop-killing-us-black-trans-lives-matter_us_57b38d3ae4b03dd538089da9.

St. Julian-Varnon, Kimberly. "Black skin in the red land: African Americans and the Soviet experiment." *Russian File: A blog of the Kennan Institute*, February 28, 2020. https://www.wilsoncenter.org/blog-post/black-skin-red-land-african-americans-and-soviet-experiment.

Staff Reports. "Masked Thugs Invade Russian LGBT Activist Meeting, One Victim May Lose Eye." *LGBTQ Nation*, November 4, 2013. http://www.lgbtqnation.com/2013/11/masked-thugs-invade-russian-activist-meeting-one-victim-may-lose-an-eye.

Stanglin, Dough. "Freed Pussy Riot Members Call Russia Amnesty a PR Stunt." *USA Today*, December 23, 2013.

Starck, Kathleen. *Of Treason, God and Testicles: Political Masculinities in British and American Films of the Early Cold War*. Newcastle upon Tyne: Cambridge Scholars, 2016.

Steinholt, Yngvar B., and David-Emil Wickström. "The Pussy Riot Complex: Entering a New Stage of Academic Research into a Viral Russian Controversy." *Popular Music and Society* 39, no. 4 (2015): 393–395.

Steinmetz, Katy. "The Transgender Tipping Point." *Time*, May 29, 2014. https://time.com/135480/transgender-tipping-point/.

Stella, Francesca, and Nadya Nartova. "Sexual Nationalisms and the Boundaries of Sexual Citizenship." In *Sexuality, Citizenship and Belonging: Trans-National and Intersectional Perspectives*, edited by Francesca Stella, Yvette Taylor, Tracey Reynolds, and Antoine Rogers, 17–36. London: Routledge, 2016.

Stella, Francesca. "Queer Space, Pride, and Shame in Moscow." *Slavic Review* 72, no. 3 (2013): 458–480.

Stella, Francesca. *Lesbian Lives in Soviet and Post-Soviet Russia: Post/Socialism and Gendered Sexualities.* London: Palgrave Macmillan, 2015.

Stern, Marlow. "Ethan Hawke on Violence, Masculinity, and Donald Trump's 'Fascist Behavior.'" *Daily Beast*, October 24, 2016. https://www.thedailybeast.com/ethan-hawke-on-violence-masculinity-and-donald-trumps-fascist-behavior.

Stoeckl, Kristina, and Dmitry Uzlaner. *The Moralist International: Russia in the Global Culture Wars.* Bronx, NY: Fordham University Press, 2022.

Stoner, Kathryn. "The War in Ukraine: How Putin's War in Ukraine Has Ruined Russia." *Journal of Democracy* 33, no. 3 (2022): 38–44. https://doi:10.1353/jod.2022.0038.

Stopera, Matt. "36 Photos from Russia That Everyone Needs to See: It's a scary place for LGBT people in Russia right now." *BuzzFeed*, July 22, 2013. https://www.buzzfeed.com/mjs538/photos-from-russia-everyone-needs-to-see.

Storyev, Dan. "The War in Ukraine Is Decimating Russia's Asian Minorities." *Diplomat*, October 10, 2022. https://thediplomat.com/2022/10/the-war-in-ukraine-is-decimating-russias-asian-minorities.

Strasser, Max. "From Uganda to Russia, Homophobia Spreading Worldwide." *Newsweek*, February 27, 2014. http://www.newsweek.com/uganda-russia-homophobia-spreading-worldwide-230358.

Stuart, Tessa. "Pussy Riot's Nadya Tolokonnikova: Trump and Putin Both 'Dangerous Clowns.'" *Rolling Stone*, February 23, 2016. https://www.rollingstone.com/music/music-news/pussy-riots-nadya-tolokonnikova-trump-and-putin-both-dangerous-clowns-92754.

Suchland, Jennifer. "Contextualizing Pussy Riot in Russia and Beyond." E-International Relations, August 28, 2012. https://www.e-ir.info/2012/08/28/contextualizing-pussy-riot-in-russia-and-beyond.

Sunderland, Willard. *Taming the wild field: Colonization and empire on the Russian steppe.* Ithaca, NY: Cornell University Press, 2004.

"Supporting Vulnerable Black People." Global Black Coalition, February 2022. https://www.globalblackcoalition.org.

Tabahriti, Sam. "Financier Bill Browder: Vladimir Putin has been a 'psychopath' since childhood and lacks normal 'human emotions.'" *Business Insider*, June 26, 2022. https://www.businessinsider.com/bill-browder-vladimir-putin-psychopath-since-childhood-2022-6.

Tayler, Jeffrey. "What Pussy Riot's 'Punk Prayer' Really Said." *Atlantic*, November 8, 2012. https://www.theatlantic.com/international/archive/2012/11/whatpussy-riots-punk-prayer-really-said/264562.

Taylor, Adam. "The Putin-Trump Kiss Being Shared around the World." *Washington Post*, May 13, 2016. https://www.washingtonpost.com/news/worldviews/wp/2016/05/13/the-putin-trump-kiss-being-shared-around-the-world/?utm_term=.0f3d8c6433ef.

Taylor, Paul. "Inside Vladimir Putin's Head." *Politico*, February 27, 2022. https://www.politico.eu/article/vladimir-putin-russia-ukraine-nato-nuclear-inside-putins-head.

Telegraph. "Madonna Calls for Leniency in Pussy Riot Trial During Russian Leg of World Tour." *Telegraph*, August 7, 2012.

Telepneva, Natalia. "Saving Ghana's revolution: The demise of Kwame Nkrumah and the evolution of soviet policy in Africa 1966–1972." *Journal of Cold War Studies* 20, no. 4 (2018): 4–25.

"These Photos Show the Brutal Violence Inflicted on LGBT People in Russia." Newsflow24, August 3, 2015. http://www.newsflow24.com/these-photos-show-the-brutal-violence-inflicted-on-lgbt-people-in-russia-bitk. Page now unavailable.

The Late Show with Stephen Colbert. "Cartoon Trump and Cartoon Putin Make First Joint Public Appearance." November 17, 2016. https://www.youtube.com/watch?v=0aU3kX5V634.

Toesland, Finbarr. "Why tracking anti-LGBT war crimes in Ukraine is so difficult." Open Democracy, May 26, 2023. https://www.opendemocracy.net/en/5050/ukraine-russia-war-crimes-anti-lgbt-violence.

Tolokonnikova, Nadezhda. "Pussy Riot's Nadezhda Tolokonnikova: Why I have gone on hunger strike." *Guardian*, September 23, 2013. https://www.theguardian.com/music/2013/sep/23/pussy-riot-hunger-strike-nadezhda-tolokonnikova.

Tolokonnikova, Nadia. *Read & Riot: A Pussy Riot Guide to Activism*. New York: HarperOne, 2018.

Tolokonnikova, Nadya, and Slavoj Žižek. *Comradely Greetings: The Prison Letters of Nadya and Slavoj*. New York: Verso 2014.

Tolokonnikova, Nadya. "I'm an Activist in Russia. I Can't Believe What My Life Has Become." *New York Times*, August 28, 2020. https://www.nytimes.com/2020/08/26/opinion/navalny-russia.html.

Toronto Star Red. "Celebrities react on Twitter as Pussy Riot members sentenced." *Toronto Star*, August 17, 2012. https://storify.com/torontostar/celebritiesreact-on-twitter-as-pussy-riot-members.

Triay, Andres, Pat Milton, Margaret Brennan, Christina Ruffini, Steven Portnoy, Arden Farhi, and CBS News staff. "Brittney Griner released by Russia in 1-for-1 prisoner swap for arms dealer Viktor Bout." CBS News, December 9, 2022. https://www.cbsnews.com/live-updates/brittney-griner-back-us-release-russia-prisoner-swap-viktor-bout/?linkId=192874405.

Trudolyubov, Maxim. "Russia's Culture Wars." *International New York Times*, February 8, 2014. http://www.nytimes.com/2014/02/08/opinion/trudolyubov-russias-culture-wars.html.

Trudolyubov, Maxim. 2016. "American Politics Caught in a 'Russian Trap.'" IWM. http://www.iwm.at/transit/transit-online/american-politics-caught-in-a-russian-trap. Page no longer available.

Tudor, Alyosxa. "Ascriptions of Migration: Racism, Migratism and Brexit." *European Journal of Cultural Studies* 26, no. 2 (April 2023): 230–48. https://doi:10.1177/13675494221101642.

Turoma, Sanna, and Aitamurto, Kaarina. "Contesting cultural and religious identities in Russia: An introduction." In *Religion, expression, and patriotism in Russia*, edited by Sanna Turoma, Kaarina Aitamurto, and Slobodanka Vladiv-Glover, 7–24. Stuttgart: Ibidem, 2019.

Tuszynska, Agnieszka. "Eastern Girls, Western Boys: The Image of Eastern European Women in the Birthday Girl." In *Vampirettes, Wretches and Amazons: Western Representations of East European Women*, edited by Valentina Glajar and Domnica Radulescu, 203–214. New York: Columbia University Press, 2004.

"Ukraine: Women face grave risks as Russia's full-scale invasion enters its second year." *Amnesty International*, March 8, 2023. https://www.amnesty.org/en/latest/news/2023/03/ukraine-women-face-grave-risks-as-russias-full-scale-invasion-enters-its-second-year/.

Ulitskaya, Ludmila. *The Funeral Party*. Translated by Cathy Porter. London: Weidenfeld & Nicolson, 2015. https://press.un.org/en/2022/sc14857.doc.htm.

"Table B05006—Place of Birth for the Foreign-Born Population in the United States—2019 American Community Survey 5-Year Estimates." United States Census Bureau, 2019. https://data.census.gov/table?tid=ACSDT5Y2019.B05006.

Vakhitov, Volodymyr, and Natalia Zaika. "Beyond Putin: Russian imperialism is the no. 1 threat to global security." Atlantic Council, April 27, 2022. https://www.atlanticcouncil.org/blogs/ukrainealert/beyond-putin-russian-imperialism-is-the-no-1-threat-to-global-security.

Vasquez, Tina. "I've experienced a new level of racism since Donald Trump went after Latinos." *Guardian*, September 9, 2015. https://www.theguardian.com/commentisfree/2015/sep/09/donald-trump-racism-increase-latinos.

Verloo, Mieke, and David Paternotte. "The Feminist Project under Threat in Europe." *Politics and Governance* 6, no. 3 (2018): 1–5. https://doi:10.17645/pag.v6i3.1736.

"Video: Russian paratroopers violently attack lone gay rights activist in St Petersburg." *PinkNews*, August 5, 2013. http://www.pinknews.co.uk/2013/08/05/video-russian-paratroopers-violently-attack-lone-gay-rights-activist-in-st-petersburg/.

Vikhrest, Antonina. "Putin's tactical misogyny: A Kremlin-backed TV channel degrades Ukrainian women as part of Putin's wider culture wars." *Aljazeera America*, August 20, 2014. http://america.aljazeera.com/opinions/2014/8/putin-s-tacticalmisogyny.html.

Vlaeminc, Erik. "Masculinity Politics in Putin's Russia." *New Eastern Europe*, October 12, 2016. https://neweasterneurope.eu/2016/10/12/masculinity-politics-in-putin-s-russia.

Von Hagen, Mark. "Area Studies from Cold War to Civilizational Conflict: On Learning, Relearning, and Unlearning." *Harriman at 70* (Spring 2017): 29–41. http://www.columbia.edu/cu/creative/epub/harriman/2017/spring/from_cold_war_to_civilizational_conflict.pdf.

Vyushkova, Mariya, and Evgeny Sherkhonov. "Russia's Ethnic Minority Casualties of the 2022 Invasion of Ukraine." *Inner Asia* 25, no. 1 (2023): 126–136. https://doi:10.1163/22105018-02501011.

Wade, Alison. "Runners Show Support for LGBT Community in Russia." *Newswire*, February 20, 2014. http://www.runnersworld.com/newswire/runners-show-support-for-lgbt-community-in-russia.

Walker, Rachel. "Facing Race: Popular Science and Black Intellectual Thought in Antebellum America." *Early American Studies: An Interdisciplinary Journal* 19, no. 3 (2021): 601–40. https://doi:10.1353/eam.2021.0019.

Wanshel, Elyse. "Mila Kunis, Who Is Ukrainian, Reveals Why She Used to Say She Was Russian." *Huffington Post*, March 11, 2022. https://www.huffpost.com/entry/mila-kunis-who-is-ukrainian-reveals-why-she-used-to-say-she-was-russian_n_622b9e67e4b0e01d97ab01cf.

Weij, Frank, and Pauwke Berkers. "The Politics of Musical Activism: Western YouTube Reception of Pussy Riot's Punk Performances." *Convergence: The International Journal of Research into New Media Technologies* (2017): 1–20. https://doi:10.1177/1354856517706493.

Weingarten, Benjamin. "Do Not Be Fooled by Recent Struggles. Russia Poses a Direct Threat to America and Her Interests." *TheBlaze*, January 13, 2015. http://www.theblaze.com/contributions/do-not-be-fooled-by-recent-struggles-russia-poses-a-direct-threat-to-america-and-her-interests.

Weisfeld, Oren. "'She brings light': Brittney Griner's triumphant return to the WNBA." *Guardian*, June 28, 2023. https://www.theguardian.com/sport/2023/jun/28/she-brings-light-brittney-griners-triumphant-return-to-the-wnba.

Whitfield, Stephen. *The Culture of the Cold War.* 2nd ed. Baltimore: Johns Hopkins University Press, 1996.

Whitmore, Brian. "Russia: Nemtsov urges opposition to back single candidate." RFE/RL, Russia Report, June 11, 2007. https://www.rferl.org/a/1077074.html.

Wiedlack, Maria Katharina. "'both married, both moms, both determined to keep getting their message out'—The Russian Pussy Riot and US popular culture." In *Marlboro Men and California Gurls: Rethinking Gender in Popular Culture in the 21st Century*, edited by Astrid M. Fellner, Marta Fernández, and Martina Martausová, 131–159. Newcastle upon Tyne: Cambridge Scholars Publishing, 2017.

Wiedlack, Katharina. "A feminist becoming? Louise Thompson Patterson's and Dorothy West's sojourn in the Soviet Union." *Feminismo/s* 36 (2020): 103–128. https://doi:10.14198/fem.2020.36.05.

Wiedlack, M. Katharina. "Gays vs. Russia: Media Representations, Vulnerable Bodies and the Construction of a (Post)Modern West." *European Journal of English Studies* 21, no. 3 (September 2, 2017): 241–57. https://doi:10.1080/13825577.2017.1369271.

Wiedlack, Katharina. "Pussy Riot and the Western Gaze: Punk Music, Solidarity and the Production of Similarity and Difference." *Popular Music and Society* 23 (2015): 410–422. https://doi:10.1080/03007766.2015.1088281.

Wiedlack, Katharina. "Seeing 'Red' (Orange Is the New Black)—Russian Women, US Homonationalism and New Cold War Cultures." *Gender, Rovné Příležitosti, Výzkum* 17, no. 1 (2016): 29–40. https://doi:10.13060/12130028.2016.17.1.253.

Wiedlack, M. Katharina. "The Spectacle of Russian Feminism: Questioning Visibility and the Western Gaze." In *Subcultures, Bodies and Spaces: Essays on Alternativity and Maginalization*, edited by Samantha Holland, 131–49. Bingley: Emerald Publishing, 2018.

Wiedlack, Katharina, and Iain Zabolotny. "Race, Whiteness, Russianness and the Discourses on the 'Black Lives Matter' Movement and Manizha." In *The Routledge International Handbook of New Critical Race and Whiteness Studies*, edited by Rikke Andreassen, Catrin Lundström, Suvi Keskinen, and Shirley Anne Tate, 251–264. London: Routledge, 2023. https://doi:10.4324/9781003120612.Wiedlack, Maria Katharina. *Queer-Feminist Punk: An Anti-Social History*. Vienna: Zaglossus, 2015. https://doi:10.26530/OAPEN_574668.

Wiedlack, Katharina, and Masha Neufeld. "Lost in Translation? Pussy Riot Solidarity Activism and the Danger of Perpetuating North/Western Hegemonies." *Religion & Gender* 4, no. 2 (2014): 145–165.

Wiedlack, Katharina, and Masha Neufeld. "Lynchpin for Value Negotiations: Lesbians, Gays and Transgender between Russia and 'the West.'" In *Queering Paradigms VI: Interventions, Ethics and Glocalities*, edited by Bee Scherer, 173–194. New York: Peter Lang, 2016.

Wiedlack, Katharina, Olenka Dmytryk, and Syaivo. "Introduction to Fucking Solidarity: Queering Concepts on/from a Post-Soviet Perspective." *Feminist Critique* 5 (2022): 10–26. https://doi:10.52323/567892.

Williams, Jessie. "'This War Made Him a Monster.' Ukrainian Women Fear the Return of Their Partners." *Time*, March 13, 2023. https://time.com/6261977/ukraine-women-domestic-violence.

Williams, Kimberly A. *Imagining Russia: Making Feminist Sense of American Nationalism in U.S.-Russian Relations*. Albany: State University of New York Press, 2012.

Williams, Zoe. "Pussy Riot's Nadya Tolokonnikova: 'You cannot play nice with Putin. He is insane. He might open fire on his own people.'" *Guardian*, March 8, 2022. https://www.theguardian.com/artanddesign/2022/mar/08/pussy-riot-nadya-tolokonnikova-interview-putin-nfts-russian.

Wilson, Nancy. "To Russia with Love." *Huffington Post*, September 11, 2013. http://www.huffingtonpost.com/rev-dr-nancy-wilson/to-russia-with-love_1_b_3894300.html.

Wodak, Ruth. "Critical Discourse Analysis at the End of the 20th Century." *Research on Language and Social Interaction* 32, no. 1–2 (1999): 185–193.

Wojnicka, Katarzyna, Ulf Mellström, and Sam De Boise. "On War, Hegemony and (Political) Masculinities." *NORMA* 17, no. 2 (April 3, 2022): 83–87. https://doi:10.1080/18902138.2022.2069856.

Wolff, Larry. *Inventing Eastern Europe: the map of civilization on the mind of the Enlightenment*. Stanford, CA: Stanford University Press, 1994.

Woodward, Kathryn. *Identity and Difference. Culture, Media and Identities*. London: Sage, 2007.

Yangeldina, Dinara. "The Politics of Racial Translation: Negotiating Foreignness and Authenticity in Russophone Intersectional Feminism and Timati's Hip-Hop (2012–2018)." PhD diss., University of Bergen, 2023.

Yurchenko, Yuliya. "Ukraine and the (Dis)Integrating Empire of Capital." Lefteast, January 9, 2020. https://lefteast.org/ukraine-disintegrating-empire-of-capital.

Yuval-Davis, Nira, and Floya Anthias. *Racialised Boundaries. Race, Nation, Colour, Class and the Anti-racist Struggle*. London: Routledge, 1997.

Zakaria, Rafia. *Against White Feminism: Notes on Disruption*. New York: W. W. Norton & Co., 2021.

Zakharov, Nikolay. *Race and Racism in Russia*. New York: Palgrave Macmillan, 2015.

Zdravomyslova, Elena. "Die Konstruktion der 'arbeitenden Mutter' und die Krise der Männlichkeit." *Feministische Studien* 1 (1999): 23–34.

Zecker, Robert. *Race and America's Immigrant Press: How the Slovaks were Taught to Think like White People*. New York: Continuum, 2011.

Zirin, Dave. "The Response to Brittney Griner's Capture Is an Indictment of the Right and the 'Left.'" *Nation*, November 29, 2022. https://www.thenation.com/article/world/brittney-griner-russia-putin-right-left.

Žižek, Slavoj, and Nadezhda Tolokonnikova. "Nadezhda Tolokonnikova of Pussy Riot's prison letters to Slavoj Žižek." *Guardian*, November 15, 2013. https://www.theguardian.com/music/2013/nov/15/pussy-riot-nadezhda-tolokonnikova-slavoj-zizek.

Zychowicz, Jessica. "Performing Protest: Femen, Nation, and the Marketing of Resistance." *Journal of Ukrainian Politics and Society*, April 2015. https://jups.krytyka.com/articles/performing-protest-fe   men-nation-and-marketing-resistance?page=3

Zychowicz, Jessica. "The Global Controversy over Pussy Riot: An Anti-Putin Women's Protest Group in Moscow." *International Institute Journal* 2, no. 1 (2012): 13–15.

Zychowicz, Jessica. *Superfluous Women: Art, Feminism, and Revolution in Twenty-First-Century Ukraine*. Toronto: University of Toronto Press, 2020.

Index

www.ingramcontent.com/pod-product-compliance
Lightning Source LLC
Chambersburg PA
CBHW070843300326
41935CB00039B/1391